THE ART OF
PORTRAITURE

A practical guide to better drawing with **Stephen Bauman**

3dtotal Publishing

THE ART OF
PORTRAITURE

A practical guide to better drawing with **Stephen Bauman**

3dtotal Publishing

3dtotalPublishing

Correspondence: publishing@3dtotal.com
Website: store.3dtotal.com

First published in the United Kingdom, 2024, by 3dtotal Publishing.

Address: 3dtotal.com Ltd,
29 Foregate Street, Worcester,
WR1 1DS, United Kingdom.

Paperback ISBN: 978-1-912843-91-6
Hardback ISBN: 978-1-915992-09-3

Printed and bound in China
by C&C Offset Printing Co., Ltd
Visit store.3dtotal.com for a complete list of available book titles.

Reprinted in 2025 by 3dtotal Publishing.

Editor: Philippa Barker
Designer: Fiona Tarbet
Lead Editor: Samantha Rigby
Lead Designer: Joseph Cartwright
Studio Manager: Simon Morse
Managing Director: Tom Greenway

Front cover & back cover artwork
© Stephen Bauman

All artwork © Stephen Bauman, unless otherwise specified.

50% of net profits donated TO CHARITY

In 2022, 3dtotal Publishing became successful enough to make a pledge to donate **50% of its net profits to charity**. This continues to be possible due to the incredible support from all our customers, employees, and partners. At the time of printing, we have donated over $1.62 million (USD) to charity.

We focus our giving on three charitable areas: **environmental**, **humanitarian**, and **animal welfare**. We use organizations such as Effective Altruism and Founders Pledge to guide who we help within these causes. Some ways of doing good are over 100 times more effective than others, so donating this way hugely increases the impact of our contributions.

See **3dtotal.com/charity** for full details.

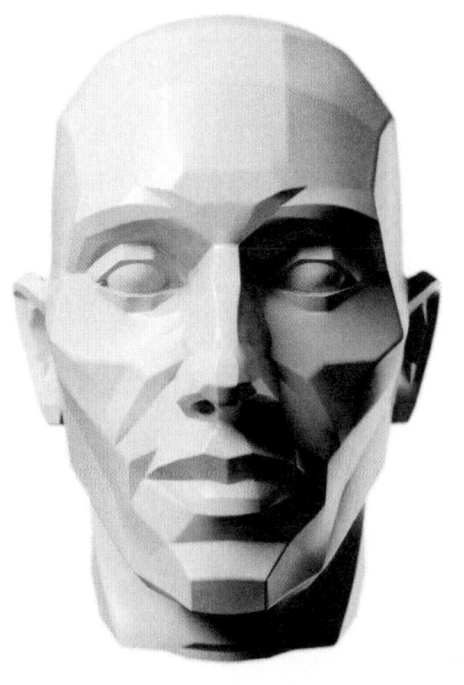
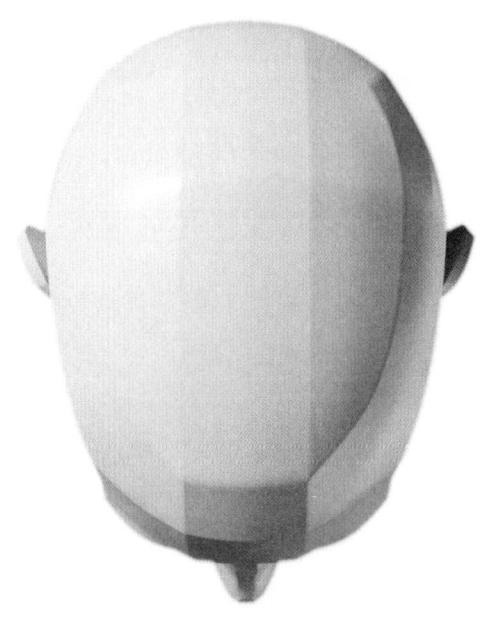
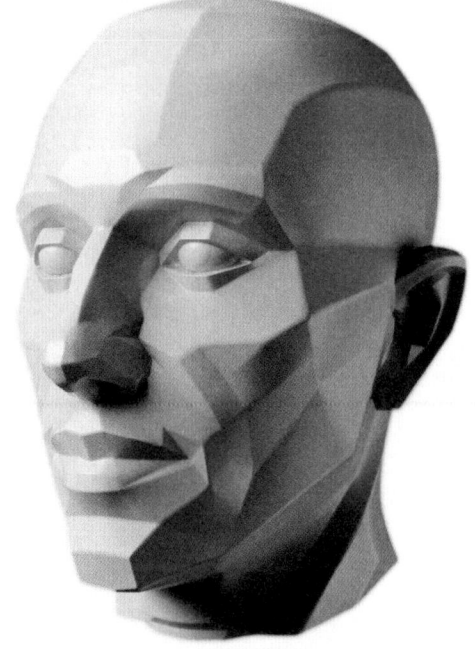
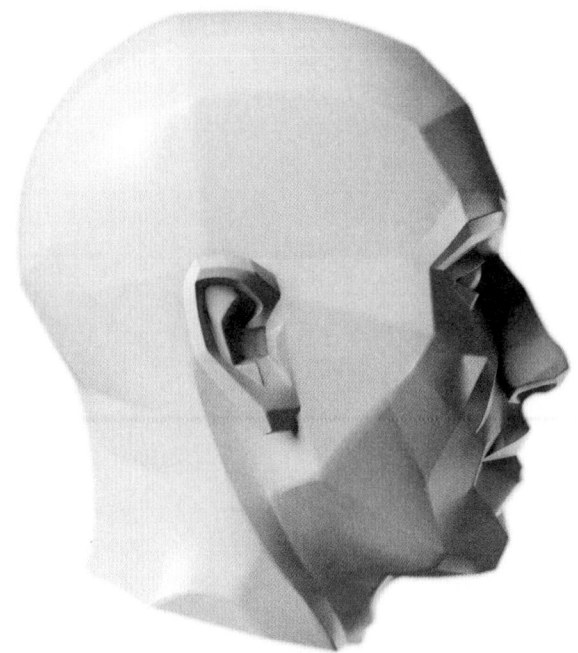

Contents

PRACTICE 142

PROCESS 200

GALLERY 219

GLOSSARY 226

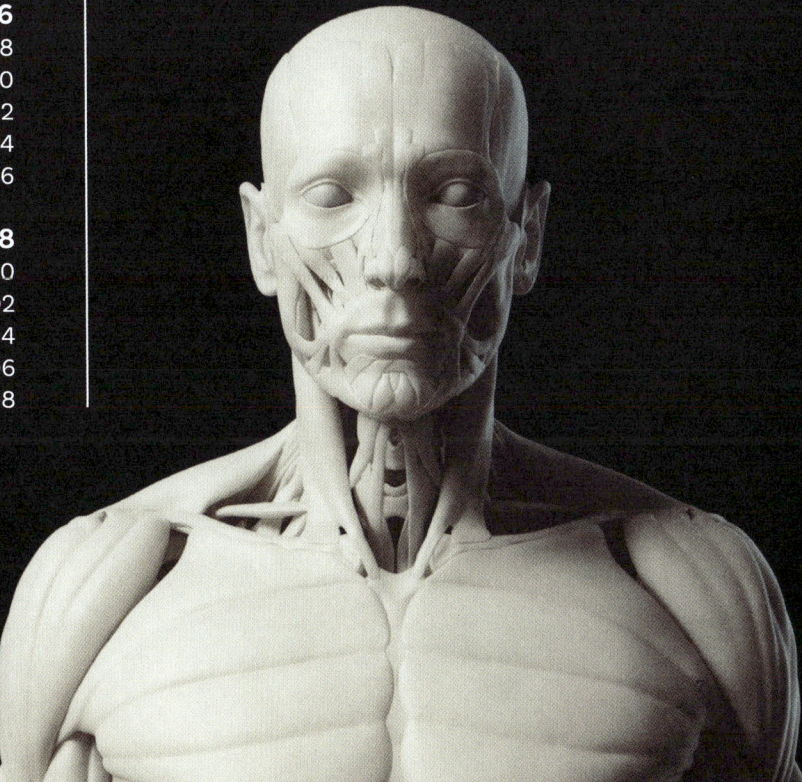

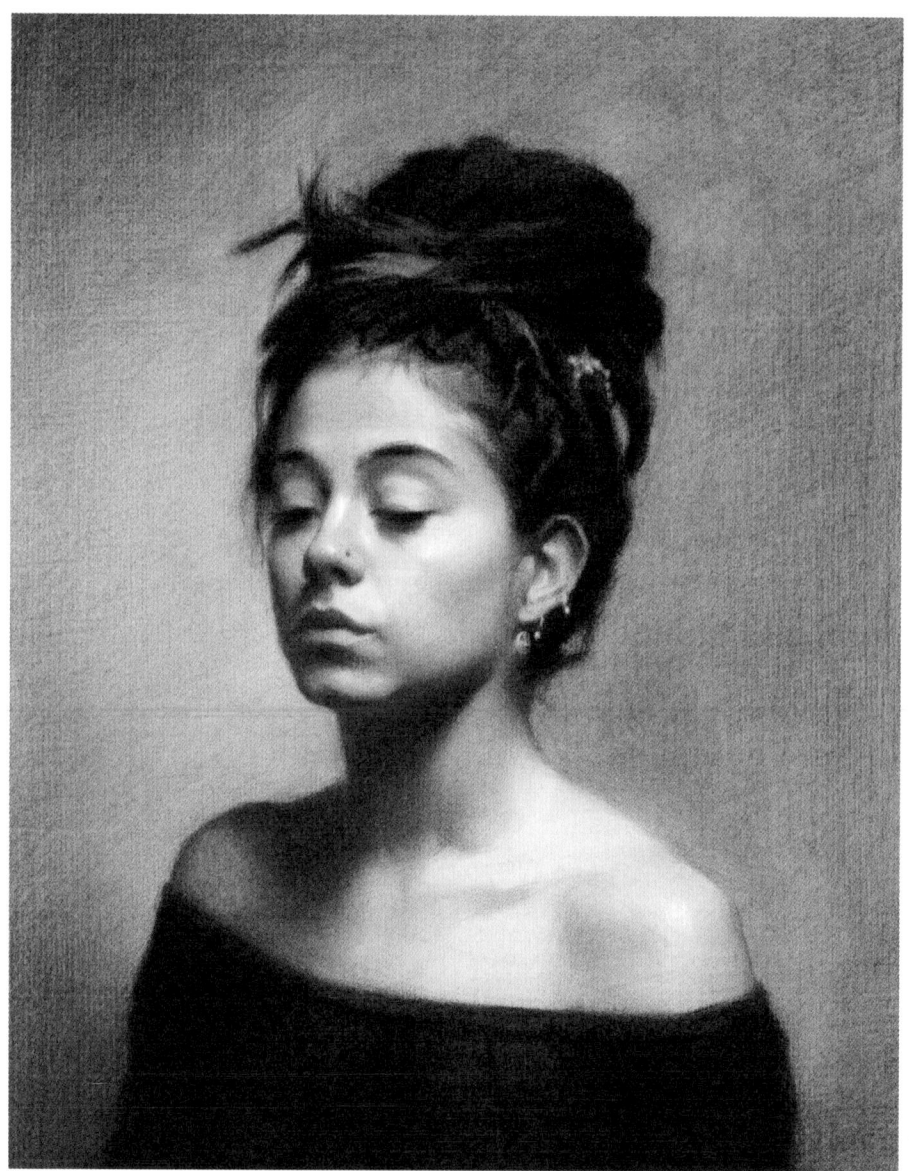

Image © Cornelia Hernes

Foreword

By Cornelia Hernes, **artist and instructor in classical drawing and painting**

As a student of drawing, you have placed yourself in the vulnerable position of learning. Along with expanding upon your knowledge through practice, you are likely to encounter some struggles along the way. Wisely you now hold *The Art of Portraiture* in your hands, which will be an invaluable reference and guide towards your artistic goals. This book is expertly organized according to the different building blocks of portraiture, with thorough explanations, diagrams, and drawings created by Stephen Bauman especially for this book. Viewed together, they represent a concise insight into his artistic methodology distilled throughout his career as an artist and instructor.

Nature presents us with an orchestration of phenomena that we have to decipher and organize when drawing. We must engage with anatomy, gesture, and proportion. We must closely observe the interaction between shadow and light upon the planes of the portrait. And there have to be defined shapes alongside fluid forms and transitions. Organizing this array of information with a coherent visual language can certainly be daunting for a beginner, and even overwhelming for an experienced artist. The allure of drawing lies in the deeply enriching experience of observing and capturing the nuances of nature. Depicting the portrait through hatch marks on paper can elevate our appreciation and connection to nature in all its forms. This is why we draw and why *The Art of Portraiture* is of timeless relevance.

Stephen received his academic training at the Florence Academy of Art, where he spent four formative years studying drawing, painting, anatomy, and ecorché. Subsequently, he devoted twelve years to imparting these disciplines as a teacher at the same academy. This cycle of learning and teaching has added a unique, holistic perspective to his artistic and educational practice. In his teaching method he draws upon a well-rounded spectrum that includes his academic training, art history, anatomy, and a wealth of personal insights.

In addition to the key concepts of drawing that can be implemented in your work, Stephen addresses the struggles that students of drawing often face and that he himself experienced. His years of grappling with the complexities of skill-building and artistic creation have led him to include these educational insights in this book. They offer not only tactical approaches to overcoming challenges, but also serve to encourage a resilience that will prove indispensable in your artistic journey. *The Art of Portraiture* celebrates the synergy between the academic and the artistic perspective, both of which play a part in a portrait that is structurally sound yet emotive and captivating.

Preface

It is impossible to speak at length about the art of portraiture without mentioning the crucial skills and concepts that all great representational drawing must rest upon. For example, the light we observe on our subject that we find so inspiring; it is the same light that falls across the form of a sphere or cylinder. To improve our ability to draw, we must seek to understand the light. In doing so, we will encounter a world of concepts and logic that will not only help us to draw one subject better, but to draw any and all subjects better. In order to draw better portraits, we must seek out the concepts and logic: the ideas that will support our vision.

It's equally important to recognize that the journey towards mastery is highly individualistic. There are a few truths that I have come to understand, which early in my education I did not. The first is that there is no right or wrong way to draw; there are just more or less useful ways to go about it, depending on your target. In addition, something that you find useless today may tomorrow become indispensable. When teaching, I have always encouraged a healthy scepticism in my students. Sure, trust that your teacher likely has some hard-won insights, but be equally aware that what works for one does not always work for all. I would therefore recommend to you, the reader, not to be the perfect student. Be both curious and stubborn. Test the ideas over and over to discover their value. Do not learn to draw as though you are simply assembling the skills that inevitably lead to a single outcome. Instead, learn to search.

On my first day at the academy, I arrived in Florence, Italy, armed with little more than an intuitive sense that I was in the right place to learn to draw. As I strolled down the art-adorned corridor towards the model room for the first time, I couldn't help but stand in awe of the drawings hanging on the walls; each line, each figure, excellent its own right. I appreciated them, admired their beauty, and yet, truth be told, I didn't quite 'get' them. Those half-finished studies contained secrets I was far from unravelling. In my youthful exuberance, I believed I could crack the code in just a few months. Three, maybe six at most. I was convinced I'd be a pro before long.

Fast forward two decades and I now have a more realistic perspective. The journey from clueless novice to seasoned veteran wasn't the swift ascent I once envisioned. Those 'few months' stretched into years, each filled with countless sketches, lessons learned, and an understanding that there's more to this than I ever could have imagined. Looking at my own drawings now, I see the evidence of my evolution. Sure, there were times when the proportions were horribly off and the shadows were way too flat. But they were the building blocks of progress – evidence of the challenges that pushed me forward. Through trial and error, countless examples of failing forward, and a few precious eureka moments when everything clicked, I've come to appreciate the depth of what it means to actually learn to draw.

'The only person who is educated is the one who has learned how to learn and change.'
Carl Rogers

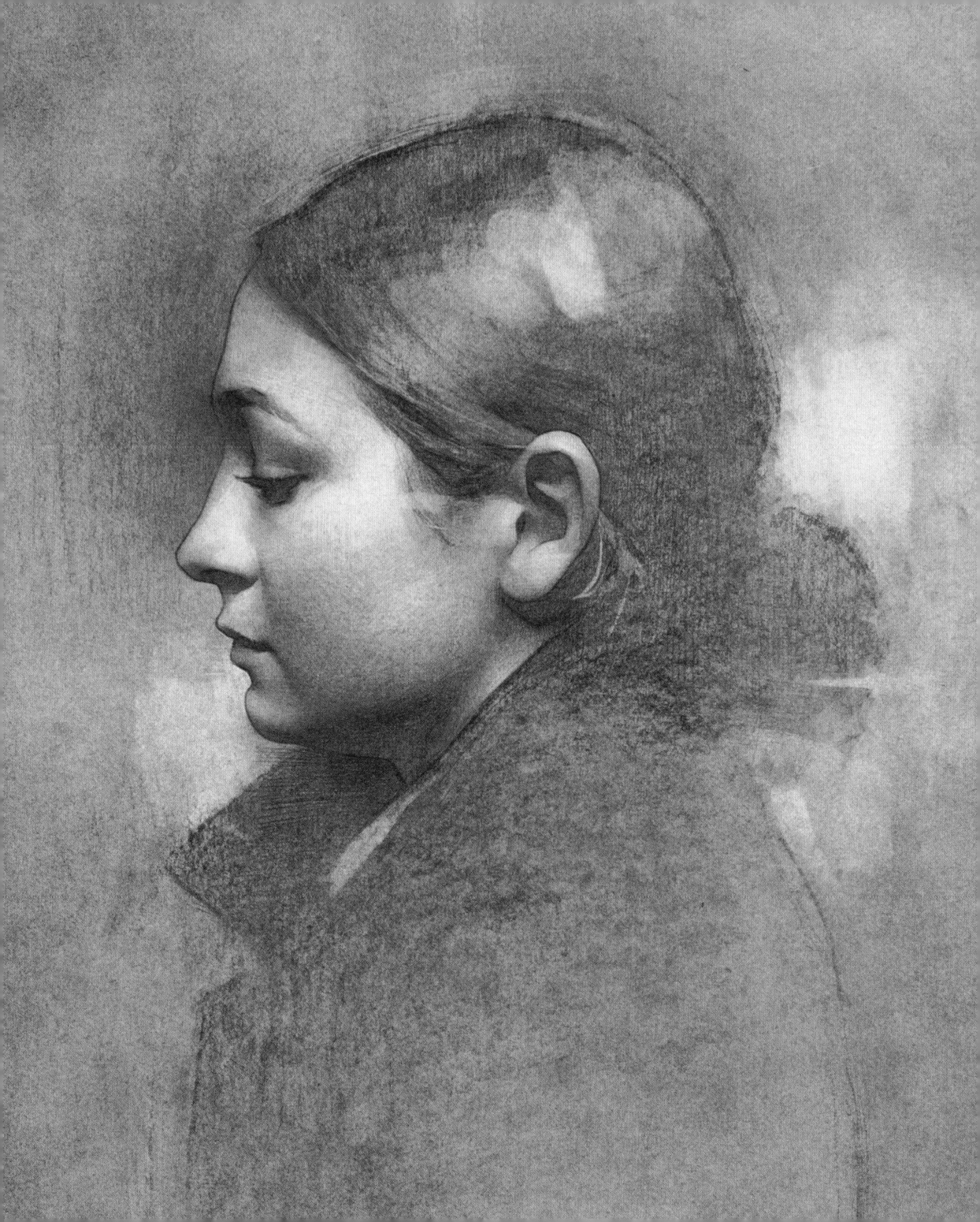

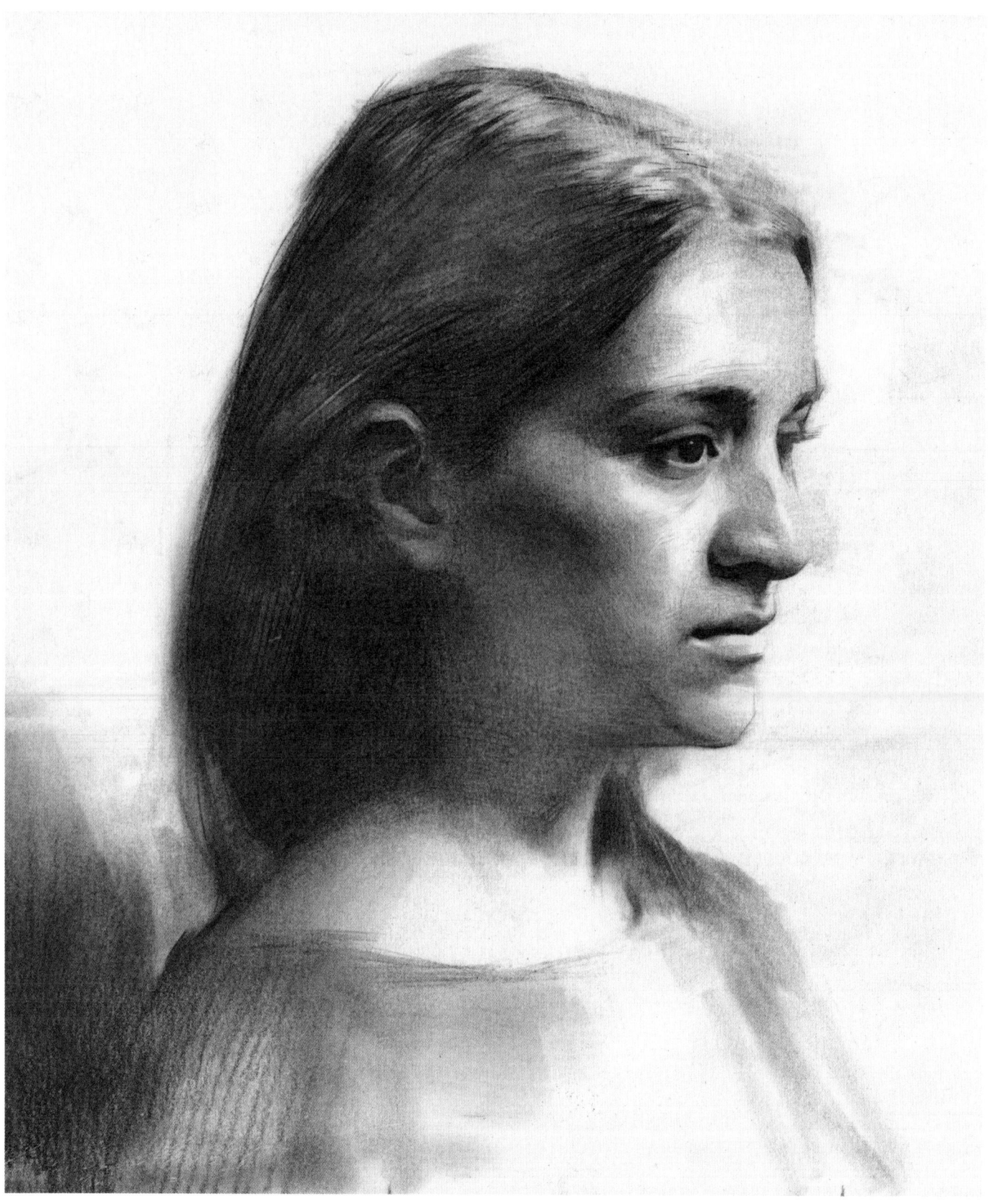

Practically speaking, my first lesson should have been that learning to draw is not a sprint, but a marathon. The focus should not be on speed and immediate gratification, but on endurance, tenacity, gradual progress, and the recognition that significant achievements take time. These are a set of associations that are far closer to the truth of the experience. Just as a marathon runner must pace themselves for the long haul, an artist must approach their craft with dedication, expect the inevitable hurdles, and understand that artistic excellence is achieved through a sustained effort over time.

It also follows that the race is run against the only possibly relevant party: yourself. A much more formidable opponent than you might think. There are all sorts of snares and obstacles waiting for you to put in your own way. An unfortunate truth for sure, but there is also good news: these obstacles are common to almost everyone who has undertaken this journey at any time in history, as are the solutions.

Access to knowledge is no longer a challenge for students of drawing. A wealth of resources are readily available online for anyone who wishes to search them out. The real barrier of entry lies in transforming that knowledge into practical skill through systematic and progressive exercises. It's about moving beyond information-gathering and focusing on deliberate hands-on engagement to internalize and apply what's learned. Just as a library's value is unlocked through reading, artistic progress emerges when theoretical insights are actively practised and refined. We're not simply 'learning to draw', but shaping ourselves into individuals who possess the skill of drawing – an evolution of identity that requires dedication, repetition, and an integration into your lifestyle. As you evolve into a person who draws, you will literally look at the world in a different way; you will start to see and think in the language of drawing.

Teaching drawing presents inherent challenges too, primarily stemming from the abstract nature of the topic itself: how to generate a realistic picture from a bunch of scratches and smears of graphite on a sheet of paper. At first glance, one might assume that teaching drawing simply involves demonstrating techniques and sharing knowledge of tools and materials. However, looking deeper into the art of drawing reveals its complexity.

Unlike subjects with concrete metrics and correct answers, drawing lacks definitive right or wrong outcomes. Assessing a drawing isn't as straightforward as grading a maths problem. In drawing you're using lines, shapes, and values to create something on a blank piece of paper. There's no single 'right' way to do it. In fact, there are countless ways to approach a drawing, and they can all be valid in their own way.

When a teacher assesses a portrait drawing, they're not simply looking for a right or wrong answer. It's not about whether the drawing is a perfect replica of what's in front of the artist. Instead, they consider a whole range of factors:

Composition: Is the arrangement of elements in the drawing visually pleasing? Does it guide the viewer's eye in an interesting way?

Technical skill: Are the lines, shapes, and values used effectively to convey the artist's intent? Does it show a mastery of the chosen techniques?

Expression: Is the portrait lifelike, full of subtlety and detail?

As there are many paths you can take to reach a correct solution to this visual problem, it is necessary to consider the process of drawing from all angles, rather than having a bias towards one type of solution.

In this book, I will show you the best concepts and exercises I have encountered in my time as a student, along with those I've found most effective as a teacher. But learning to draw isn't just about technique and exercises; it's also about understanding and overcoming the challenges that every student faces. Drawing is a creative and complex endeavour. Students are bound to encounter difficulties, whether that's struggling with proportions, maintaining motivation, or dealing with self-doubt. What's important to know is that these challenges are not unique to any one person. They are part of the journey, and every student encounters them in some form. What varies is the degree to which these challenges affect an individual and the time and effort required to overcome them.

I'll not only explore the solutions to these common hurdles, but also offer insights into why they occur in the first place. By shining a light on these shared experiences, you'll find reassurance in knowing you're not alone in facing them. Moreover, you'll have access to valuable strategies to help you navigate these obstacles with confidence. As with any book filled with recommendations, some will read as if written specifically with you in mind, while others won't resonate at all. If anything doesn't feel applicable to your experience, feel free to pass over it or save it for analysis at a later date.

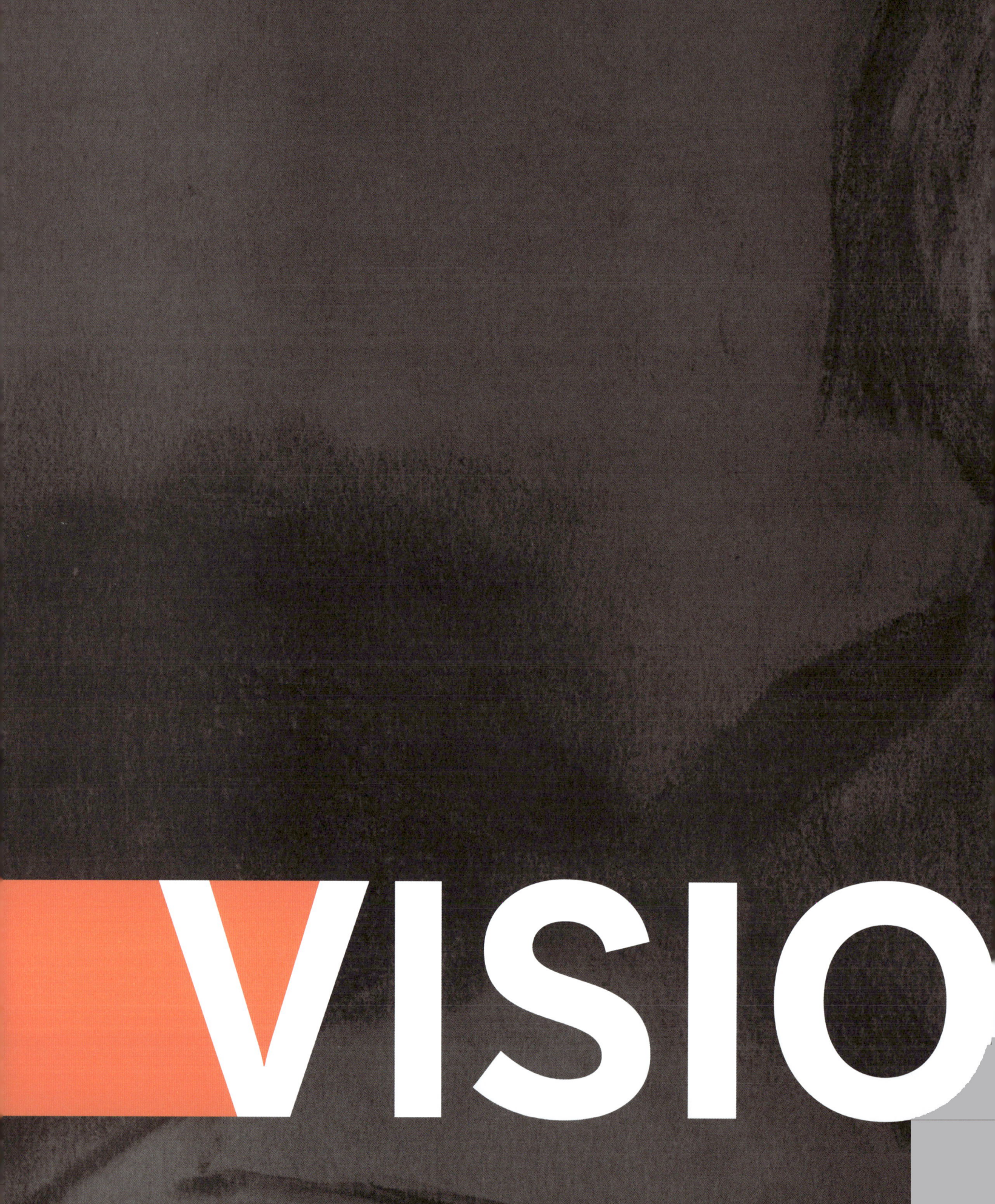

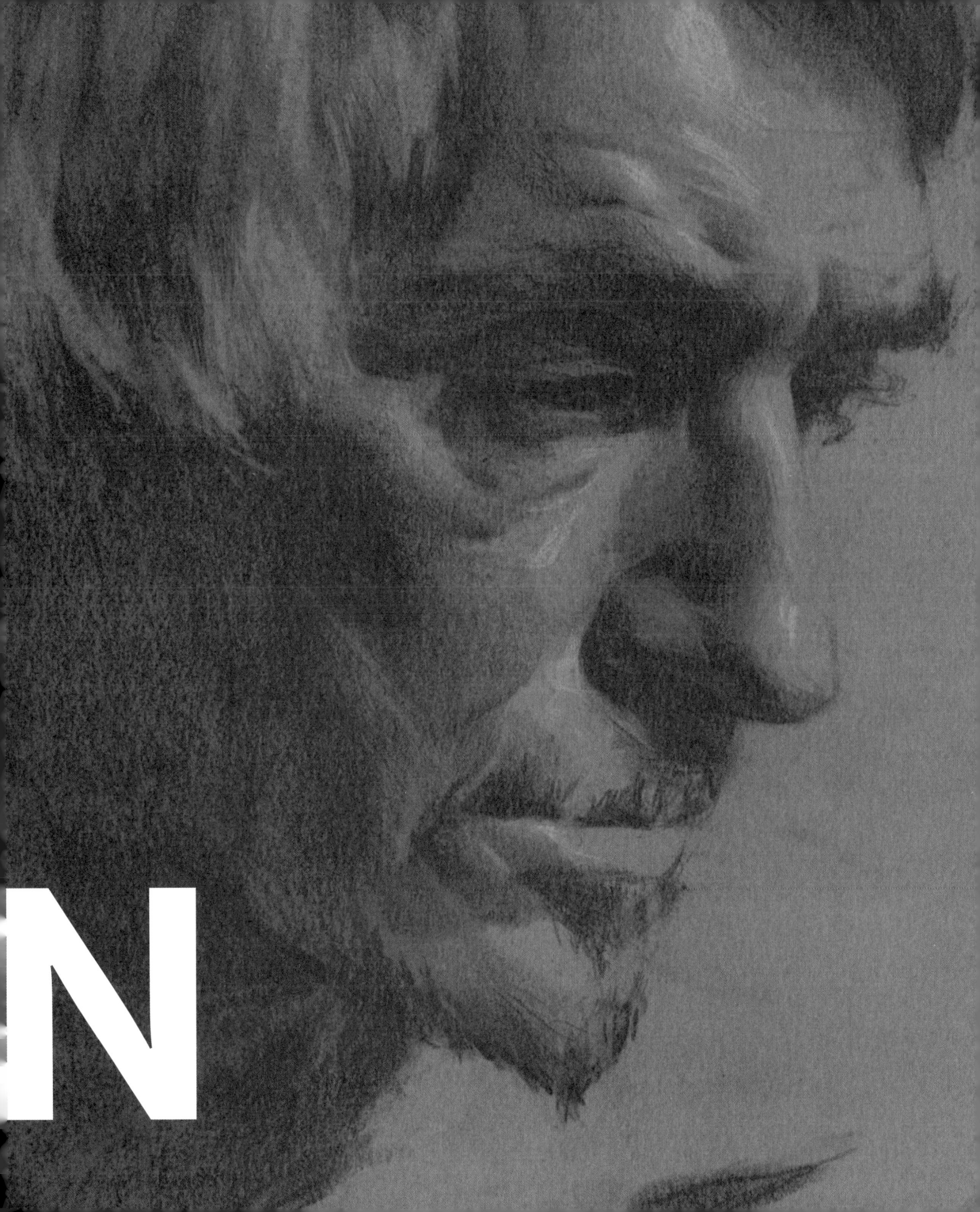

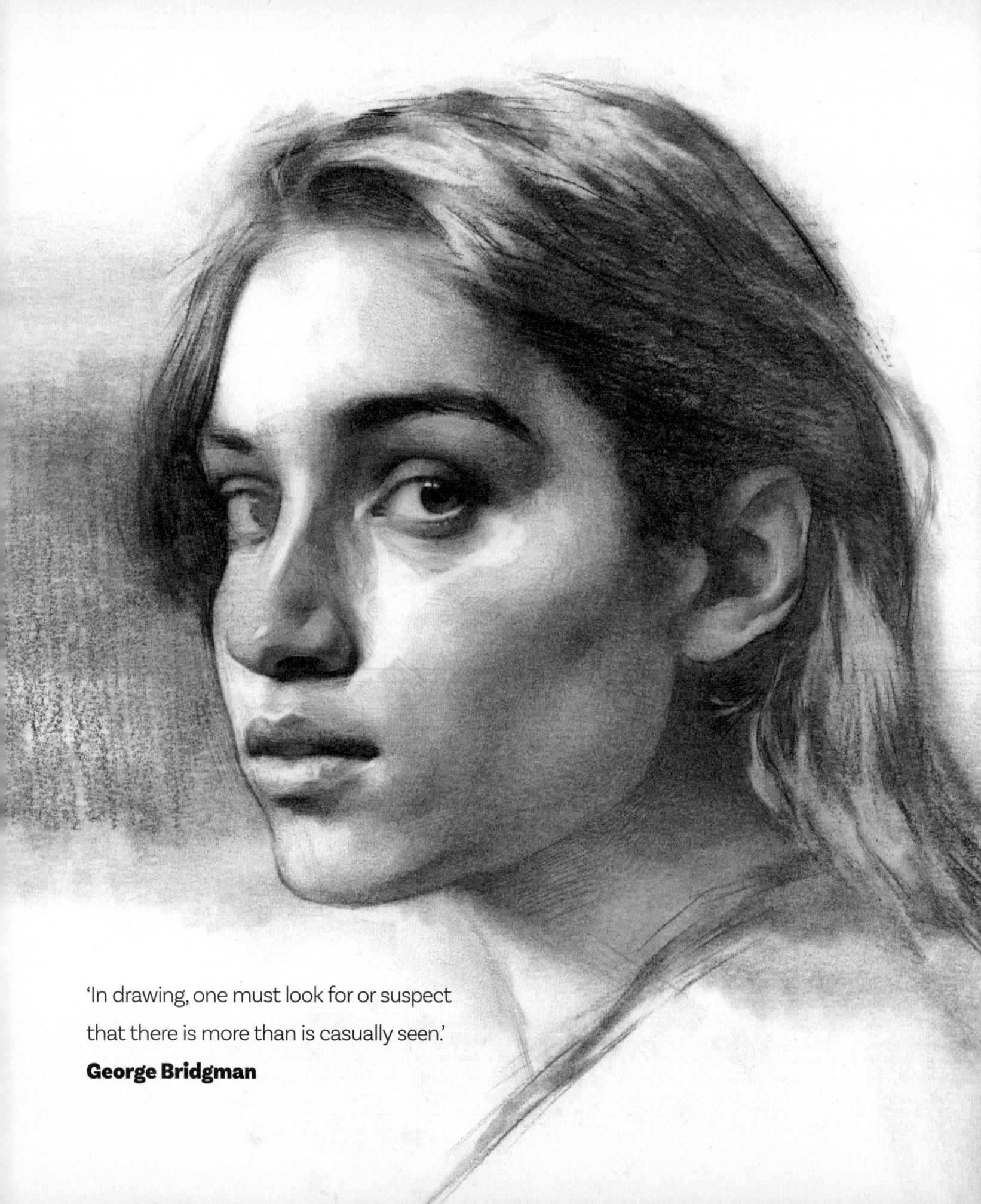

'In drawing, one must look for or suspect
that there is more than is casually seen.'
George Bridgman

Why do we draw?

TWO TYPES OF VISION

When we talk about 'vision' within the discipline of drawing, we're referring to more than just the physical act of seeing. Vision encompasses a holistic understanding and interpretation of the world around us, channelled through our artistic skill set. It's the unique lens through which each artist views, absorbs, and subsequently expresses their reality. Your vision is intrinsically tied to the core values that guide your artistic choices, as well as to the motivations that drive you to engage in the art-making process. Knowing what you stand for artistically equips you to make creative choices that are coherent and purposeful.

These values are like a compass, steering the decisions you make during the artistic process. Understanding your core values is akin to knowing the language you want to speak through your art. Once you're fluent in this 'language', your choices around technique, subject matter, and style become not just intuitive, but also deeply meaningful.

As a drawing student, there is also a vision required to advance your skills. It involves a mix of humility, tenacity, and foresight. It's a brave thing to be humble enough to accept you're at the beginning of a long journey and that you will make mistakes and face challenges. This acceptance is important because it opens you up to learning and prevents any premature self-judgement that might stifle your development. Tenacity because, if nothing else, the one single thing that success in this endeavour cannot do without is the act of showing up and trying again in spite of any setbacks. Foresight is perhaps the most subtle but important part of the vision needed to advance as a student. It's about planning and anticipating your growth trajectory. This foresight is partially intuitive, but becomes refined as you advance in your studies, receive feedback, and gain a broader understanding of the field.

It is the synthesis of these two types of vision that will guide your progress. One gives you the tools, while the other provides the narrative. One offers you the language, and the other supplies the poetry. Throughout the following chapters, exploring the bedrock principles and innovative techniques that define drawing, remember that your evolving vision is the thread that runs through all of these experiences and exercises.

WHAT IS THE GOAL OF DRAWING?

As far as I can tell, drawing has never been about being accurate or right all of the time. The ultimate goal is to reach a state where technical proficiency becomes second nature, operating seamlessly in the background. This state liberates our conscious mind, allowing it to concentrate fully on the forceful expression of our chosen theme. So, what is it about then?

At its heart, representational drawing is rooted in keen observation. We learn to see the world around us with a discerning eye, noticing details, shapes, and relationships that often escape casual observers. This core value teaches us to be present in the moment and deeply engaged with our subjects. The more you know, the more you can see. The more you can see, the more you have to choose from when selecting the useful features that best suit your vision.

When we talk about great drawing, we're not merely talking about the ability to capture the countenance of a person. Though an important skill, it has already been sufficiently accomplished by the camera. A truly remarkable drawing will transcend the surface appearance of its subject and delve into the realm of emotion, perception, and the human experience. In essence, great drawing is a form of storytelling. The story doesn't have to always be an epic one. In fact, sometimes the more intimate story carries a stronger effect to the viewer. It can be as simple as the shape of rim lighting grazing the edge of your model's face. Simple images like this can be evocative, subtly narrative, and contain more than enough material to satisfy this criteria. Understand that at the centre of this story is you, the artist, and your experience of the world. Many of the pages of this book will be filled with useful diagrams, specific technical advice, and recommended practices, none of which, on their own or taken together, could be mistaken for an artistic purpose. The story, the meaning, is not something that you find in the subject. It is something that you give to the subject through your thoughtful attention.

Influences and how they evolve may not immediately be obvious or intuitive, especially for someone new to the world of art. As a student you might find that the influence of a great artist or teacher may pronounce itself quite directly in your work. This initial phase of direct influence is a common experience shared by many students. As you grow and mature as an artist, you will continue to absorb these influences. You will travel to see museums and architecture, and experience different cultures. Books will be read, movies watched. Hundreds of artworks by artists you admire, each one with its own finely honed vision that took a lifetime to refine, become a part of your mental library; every one, an influence. Do this long enough and the edges of these influences will blend together, becoming a seamless tapestry that represents the taste you have cultivated through the art and experiences you have sought out.

Of course, it's a lot to ask for a student of any age to fully appreciate this process when they are within it. Even so, as with many causes of anxiety, knowing the outline of the ongoing process can be a relief in itself. Stick with your practice and your process. Over a long enough timeline, your style and perspective will emerge. In fact, it will most likely be impossible to repress.

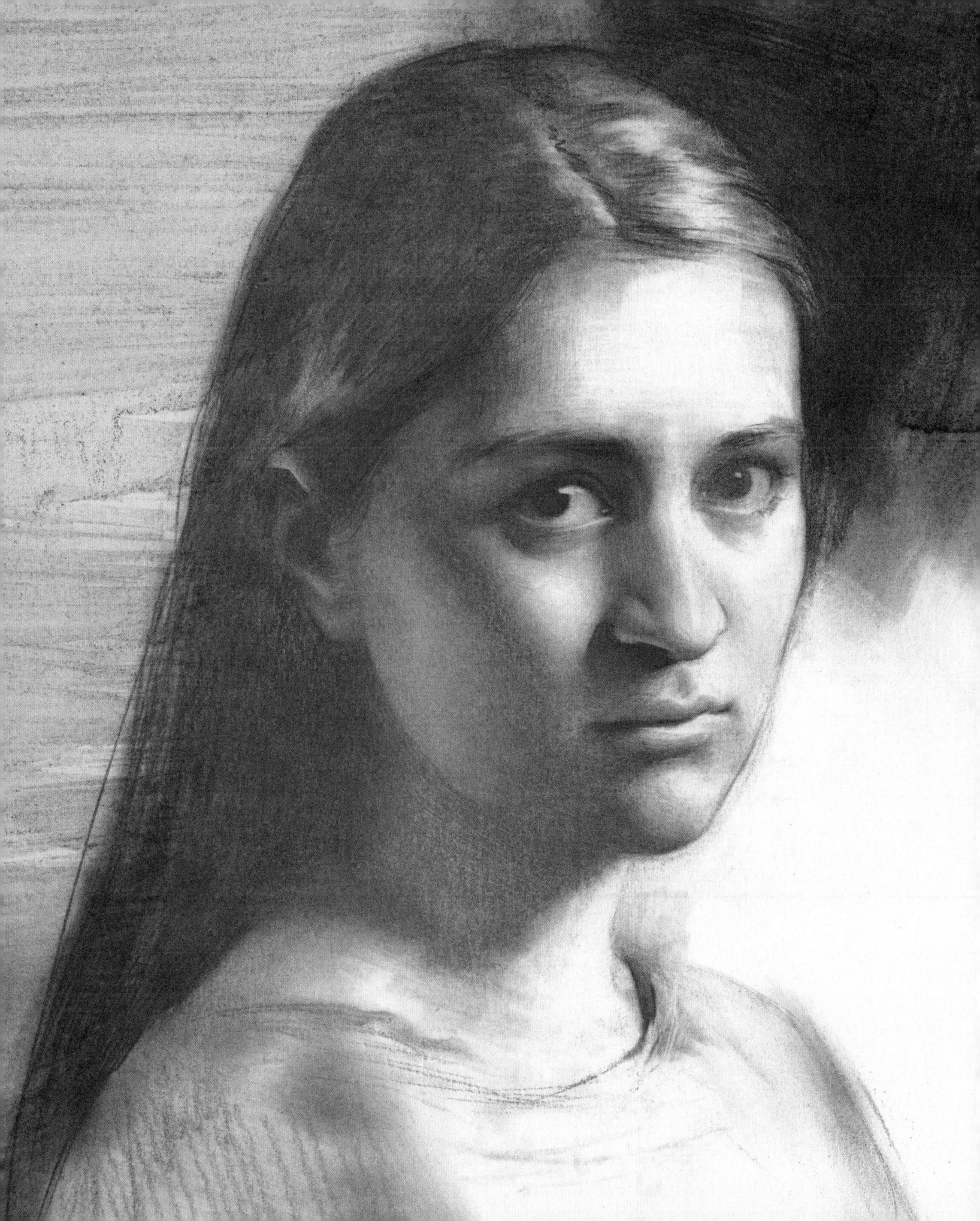

When considering the goal of drawing, my view is that there are two essential positions, each one important and each one informing a different part of our intent. I will explain these two theories below.

We draw to enrich our experience of the world

John Ruskin's philosophy about the role of drawing extends far beyond the boundaries of what most might consider 'artistic practice'. To Ruskin, the art of drawing was not merely the privilege of artists, but a skill that can enrich everyone's life, by honing observation and deepening our connection with the world around us.

Ruskin argued that drawing teaches you how to see differently. In our everyday lives, we often look at objects and scenes without really seeing them. Drawing takes this 'passive looking' and transforms it into 'active seeing'. This newfound perceptual awareness is not just an aesthetic asset, but a profound broadening of our interaction with our surroundings.

Drawing not only focuses the attention, but also deepens our connection with both nature and the man-made environment. For instance, sketching a plaster cast of a classical-era sculpture might reveal insights into cultural history, the logic behind the aesthetic, and the interplay of the artist's intent and representation. These layers of meaning and connection are often missed by the casual observer or the hurried photographer.

The implications of this kind of observational training are practical as well as philosophical. The skills honed by drawing - of observing closely, of appreciating subtlety - can have applications in everyday life. You might find yourself more attentive in a business meeting, more attuned to subtleties in your relationships, or simply more aware as you walk down the street or through a field.

Ruskin elevates the act of drawing from a specialized artistic skill to a vital tool for a richer, more attentive life. Through the lens of his philosophy, drawing emerges not as a niche activity, but as a universal human endeavour, essential for fostering a keen eye and a deep appreciation for the complexity and richness of our world.

'The times when a student accepted the style and traditions of their master

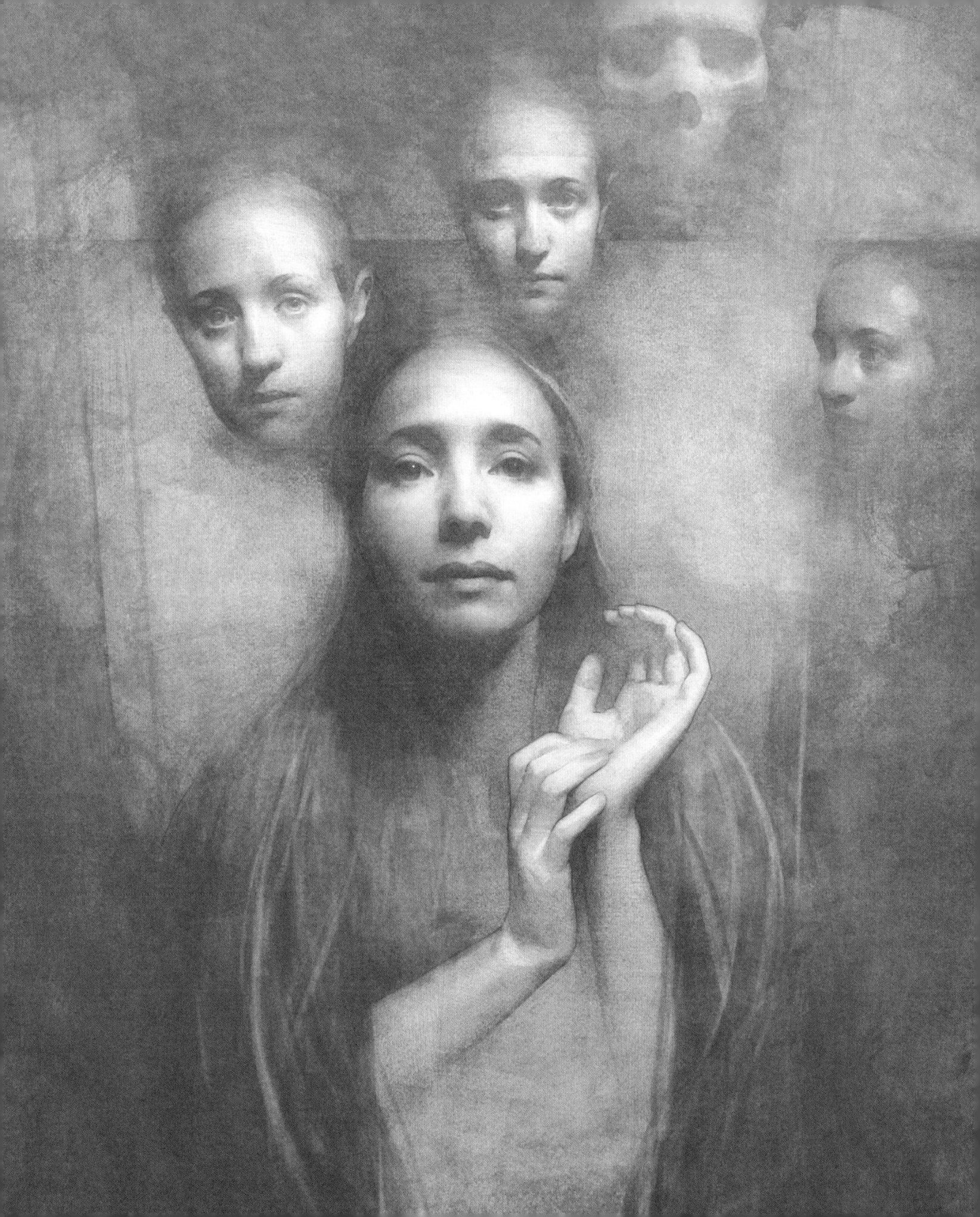

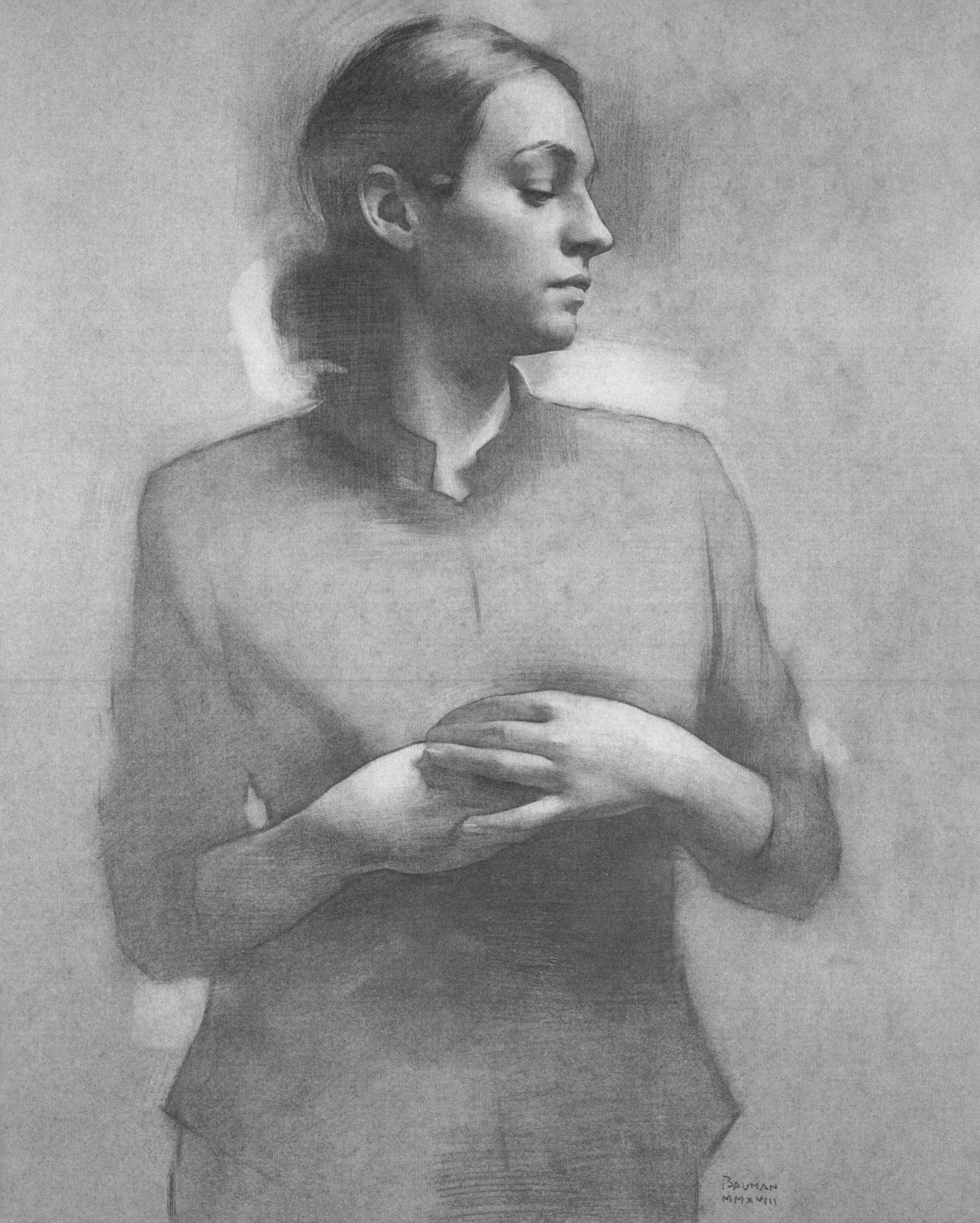

We draw to communicate

The Repin Institute offers a rich conceptual framework for understanding the role of drawing in artistic development, presenting it not merely as a skill, but as a foundational language for all visual arts. The practice transcends mere imitation of the visible world, becoming a structured language that allows for the clear and effective communication of complex ideas, emotions, and stories.

In this view, drawing is the lexicon and grammar of a visual language that every artist must master. It provides the basic syntax upon which other artistic disciplines – be it painting, sculpture, or even digital art – can be built. This is not merely about sketching a likeness, but about imbuing the work with nuance and depth, making it resonate with viewers on an emotional, intellectual, or even spiritual level.

There is a strong emphasis on the role of composition, elevating it from a technical requirement to an expressive tool. Composition becomes the framework within which the language of drawing operates. Students learn to manage elements like spatial balance, contrast, and enhancing focal points to guide the viewer's eye. It's akin to constructing a well-crafted sentence or paragraph in a book, where every element serves a role in conveying the overarching message or feeling.

In essence, drawing serves as a comprehensive language for visual communication, a tool for honing perceptive skills, and a foundational skill set.

In between these two ideas is where I have found my own perspective. Drawing is often seen as an intensely personal act. It trains your eye to see the world in a new light, picking up on tiny details and subtle changes that others might overlook. The curve of a model's cheek, the dappled light filtering through leaves and across the trunk of a tree – these become nuances you can understand and appreciate deeply. Drawing, in this sense, is a tool for seeing better and understanding more deeply what you see.

However, the act of creating art rarely occurs in isolation. Once your work is complete, there is an audience that will engage with it, which means you're not just drawing for yourself. The vocabulary of your visual language must be 'legible' to others. You're sharing your vision, so the terms you use to convey your message must be accessible enough to allow for that sharing.

This leads me to the concept of storytelling in art. The word 'story' often evokes ideas of a clear beginning, middle, and end, with plot twists and character arcs. But the stories told through drawing can be far simpler and yet profoundly impactful. Perhaps more so, at times. They don't need a traditional three-act structure. Instead, these stories can be told through the posture of a model's head and shoulders, or the smoothness or roughness of the shading used. Even their position on the paper alone can convey the artist's intent. These are narratives distilled down to their most basic elements, yet they can convey a world of emotion and meaning. Consider how light travels across a room, casting shadows and illuminating surfaces, until it finally settles on a subject's face. This too is a story – one that speaks volumes without uttering a single word.

My perspective on drawing synthesizes these ideas. It's about honing your personal vision and perception, while also ensuring that this vision is communicated in a way that resonates with others. We draw to better understand the world around us *and* to share that understanding, telling stories through the subtlest of details that capture the essence of a moment or your empathy with a subject.

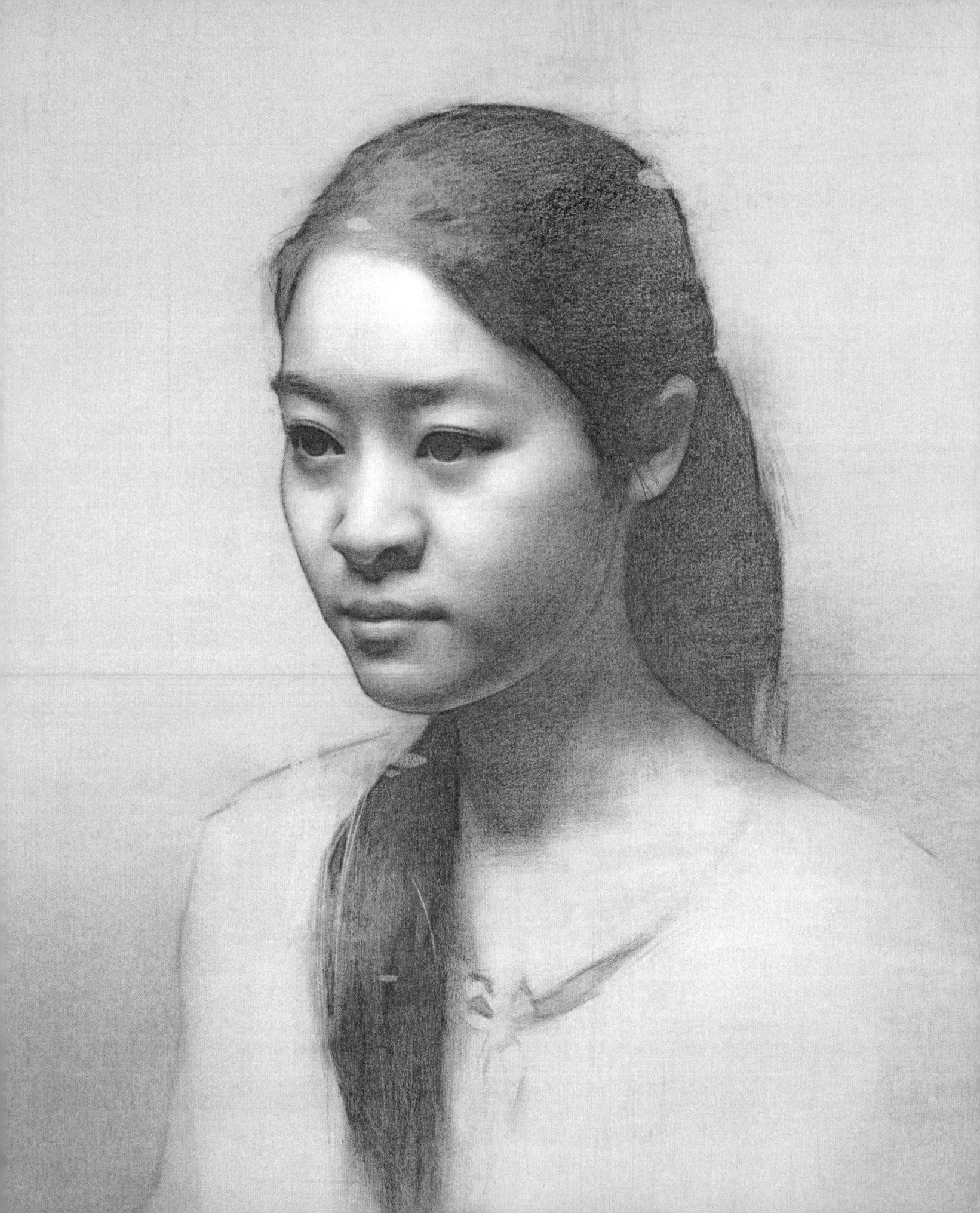

The learning journey

'You can't know about things you have yet to discover.'
Jonathan Raymond

The journey of a drawing student can be seen as a progression through four distinct stages, each marked by a transformation in their understanding and abilities.

In the first stage, which we can call 'unconscious incompetence', the student is unaware of their lack of skill. They do not understand or know how to draw proficiently and may even question the usefulness of acquiring such skills. There is a moment when they come to terms with their own incompetence and recognize the immense value of learning this new skill. In my view, this is the most difficult stage, as it represents the barrier of entry. Given the scarcity of returns on the investment of energy and time, it can be the stage where a student is most likely to simply give up due to a feeling of inertia.

As the student advances to the 'conscious incompetence' stage, they become acutely aware of their shortcomings in drawing. They acknowledge their deficits and understand the importance of acquiring skills to address those deficiencies. This is the phase where making 'bad' drawings is an integral part of the learning process. I kindly refer to this as 'failing forward' – a nickname that perhaps expresses better how it feels than what is actually occurring.

With dedication and practice, the student progresses to the 'conscious competence' stage. Here, they gain a deep understanding of drawing techniques. They can break down the process into deliberate steps and execute them with conscious effort. However, maintaining this skill still requires their full concentration, and lapses into incompetence can happen if focus is lost.

Finally, after continuous practice and refinement, the student reaches the 'unconscious competence' stage. At this point, drawing has become second nature to them. They can wield their skills with effort in many different conditions. This mastery allows them to not only create well-honed drawings, but also to share their knowledge and skills with others, becoming capable teachers in their own right.

In my experience, the transition that occurs is principally fuelled by tenacity, a trait that also grows with an application of effort over time.

WHAT IS THE MOST USEFUL WAY TO LEARN?

Much like mastering multiple spoken languages equips you with versatile communication skills and a deeper understanding of linguistic structures, learning diverse approaches to drawing offers you a richer visual vocabulary, greater adaptability to varied lighting conditions, and a more nuanced grasp of the artistic principles that underlie different styles.

Imagine learning languages as if it were like filling a toolbox. Each language you learn equips you with a different set of tools: words, phrases, and ways of structuring your thoughts. The more languages you learn, the more tools you have at your disposal. Interestingly, acquiring one language can make learning another easier. It's as if your toolbox now has compartments that can easily accommodate new tools, even if those tools are for tasks you've never done before. Children who grow up learning two languages usually find it easier to add more languages to their repertoire. They also often have a richer, deeper understanding of language in general because they can compare and contrast how different languages handle the same ideas.

Now, let's take this concept over to the world of visual art, specifically drawing. Just as there is more than one way to speak and write, there is more than one 'visual language' to depict the world around you. When you learn to draw, you are essentially learning a new language, but instead of words and sentences, you are using lines, shapes, and values.

Learning various approaches to drawing is akin to becoming multilingual. For example, if you learn to draw portraits using soft, diffuse lighting, that's like learning one 'dialect' of visual language. But suppose you also learn how to draw using harsh, dramatic lighting, capturing stark contrasts and strong shadows. In that case, you have added another dialect to your visual vocabulary.

Just like the bilingual child, an artist who practices drawing under various lighting conditions, or learns different styles and techniques, becomes more versatile. They not only become adept at adapting to new and diverse situations, but they can also understand the 'grammar' of visual language more deeply. They see how light behaves, how shadows form, how planes create form, and how all these elements can be manipulated to create a specific mood or effect. It's the difference between being able to ask for directions and being able to compose poetry in a new language.

SPECIFICALLY, HOW DO YOU LEARN TO DRAW BETTER?

In his book *The Story of Philosophy*, Will Durant wrote, 'We are what we repeatedly do. Excellence, then, is not an act, but a habit.' The variations of potentially successful paths to mastery are surely as diverse as the individuals that apply effort to this craft. That being said, many of them will share some characteristics – elements that represent a baseline for your approach to skill-building. These commonalities serve as the building blocks upon which individual styles and specialities can flourish.

Deliberate practice and consistency play pivotal roles in the journey from novice to expert, regardless of the discipline. For aspiring artists, the value of routine can't be overstated. Charles Duhigg, in his illuminating book *The Power of Habit*, delves into the mechanics of habit formation through what he calls 'the habit loop', which consists of a cue, a routine, and a reward. To integrate this into your art practice, you might set a specific time each day as your cue to begin drawing. The act of drawing itself becomes the routine, and a subsequent reward – be it a small treat, a walk, or even just the satisfaction of having practised – completes the loop. Over time, this structure not only becomes a self-sustaining habit but also serves as a scaffold on which you build and refine your skills. Having mastered the habit of drawing, you can now cycle through a linear series of exercises designed to help you progress.

Setting clear goals is another essential aspect of growing as an artist. James Clear's book *Atomic Habits* extols the virtues of well-defined, achievable objectives as the stepping stones towards mastery. In the context of drawing, this may mean singling out a specific area for improvement – be it the accurate depiction of proportions, mastering the nuances of shading, or capturing the subtlety of human expressions. These broad objectives can then be broken down into smaller, more manageable tasks, each contributing to the larger goal. The clarity offered by such segmentation not only makes the journey less daunting, but also offers waypoints at which to measure progress, reinforcing motivation and dedication.

The '10,000-hour rule' posited by Malcolm Gladwell suggests that to achieve mastery in any field, one must commit to approximately 10,000 hours of dedicated practice. Malcolm Gladwell, who popularized this concept in his book *Outliers*, drew upon research by psychologist K. Anders Ericsson. Although this rule has faced scrutiny and debate – for mastery isn't solely a function of hours spent – it serves as a useful guideline. It's worth mentioning that 'practice' doesn't mean mindlessly repeating the same task. Effective practice, often termed 'deliberate practice', involves mindful exercises, constructive feedback, and a focus on overcoming weaknesses. At its core, the '10,000-hour rule' serves as a reminder that mastery is rarely, if ever, the result of a sudden stroke of genius. It is the outcome of sustained, focused effort over time.

Together, these principles of deliberate practice, goal-setting, and sustaining that practice over time weave a fabric that not only cushions the inevitable falls that come with learning, but also serves as a ladder, helping you climb out of the initial phases of unconscious ignorance towards the peaks of conscious competence and, eventually, mastery. These aren't just abstract theories; they are actionable steps, grounded in behavioural psychology, which can provide a structured framework for your development. So, what is the best way to put them into action?

GOAL-SETTING AND THE 'SMART' APPROACH

The idea of setting SMART goals is essentially about making your aspirations concrete, actionable, and achievable. It's not enough to simply say you want to get better at drawing. To actually make progress, you'll need to make your goals 'SMART': Specific, Measurable, Achievable, Relevant, and Time-bound. Each of these aspects will help you to navigate your path more effectively.

'Specific' means your goal should be crystal clear. Rather than saying something vague, such as 'I want to improve my drawing skills', try to pinpoint what exactly you wish to improve. You might say, 'I want to get better at applying even tones when shading a drawing.' This focused target will help you to direct your efforts more effectively.

'Measurable' means you should be able to track your progress. For instance, you could decide to complete twenty foundational drawings, called 'block-ins', within a month. This quantifiable target not only lets you track how you're doing, but also gives you a motivational boost as you see the numbers add up.

An 'Achievable' goal is one that you can realistically accomplish given your current skill level and resources. It's tempting to aim high, but you don't want to discourage yourself with an overly ambitious target. If you are a beginner, completing two well-shaded portrait block-ins a week might be a more reasonable goal than striving for a masterpiece within the same timeframe.

A 'Relevant' goal aligns with your bigger career or life aspirations. If your dream is to be a portrait artist, then sketching simplified head forms from a variety of angles will be highly relevant. Relevance is about ensuring that your short-term efforts are feeding into your long-term dreams.

Lastly, a 'Time-bound' goal has a deadline. Instead of saying you'll complete those twenty block-ins 'someday', specify that you'll do it within the next thirty days. This adds a sense of urgency, helping you to prioritize and plan your time accordingly.

So, if you're a drawing student looking to improve, a SMART goal could look something like this: 'In the next two months, I want to complete ten block-in portraits, paying special attention to identifying and designing shadow shapes.' This goal ticks all the SMART boxes: it's specific in focusing on shadow shapes, measurable in aiming for ten block-ins, achievable based on your current skills, relevant to your desire to improve at portraiture, and time-bound with a two-month deadline.

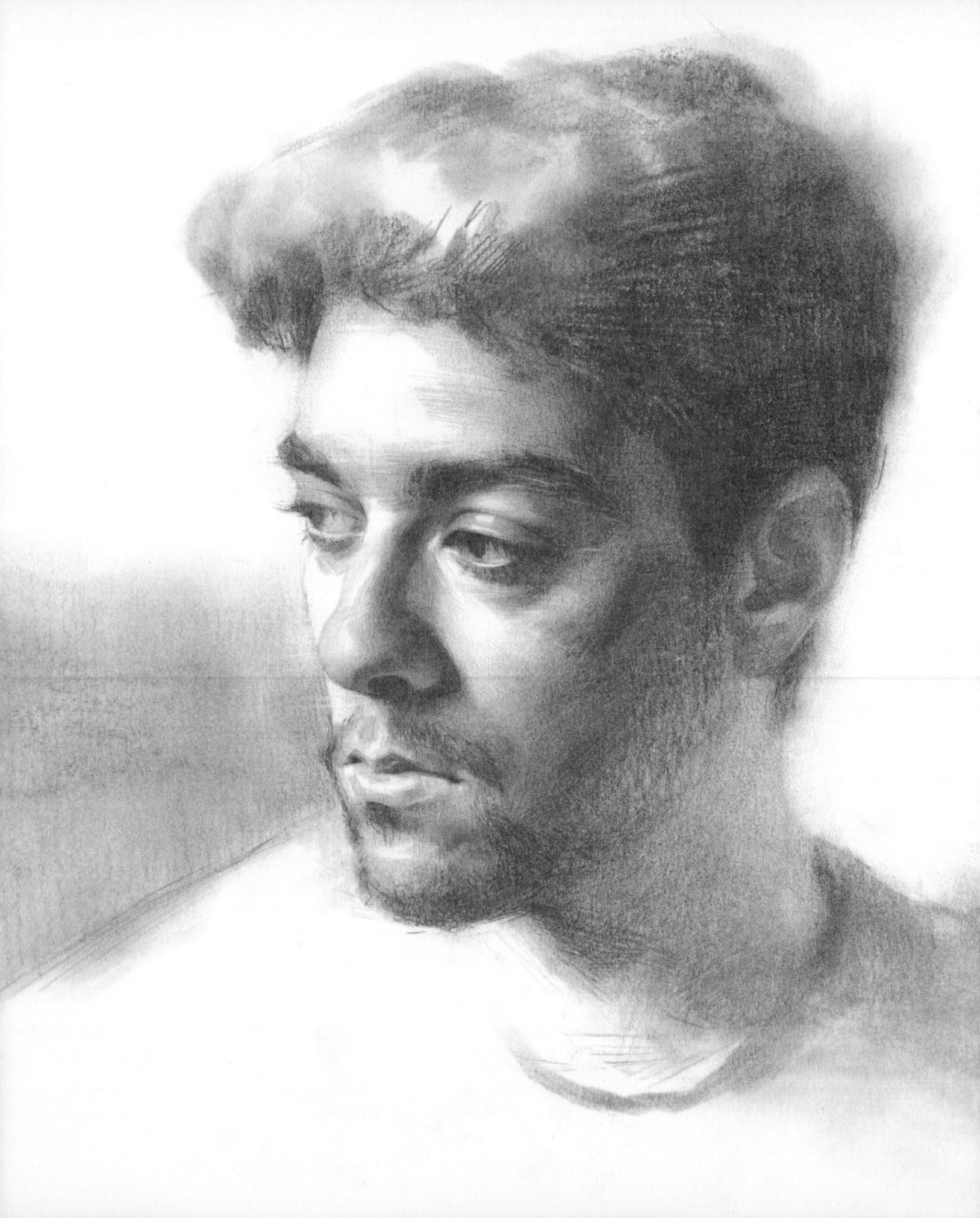

> 'If you are nervous,
> you limit your quality.'
>
> **Virgil Van Dijk**

PRACTICE

In case you're wondering, Virgil Van Dijk won't be found in any books on Northern Renaissance painting. As of 2024, he plays centre back for Liverpool Football Club. His quote frames precisely my feeling about the practice of drawing and how to be mentally strong when confronting its challenges.

What is it that athletes get out of practising? Out of performing simple actions over and over, hundreds of times each session? Repeating actions in this way helps to build what psychologists call 'automaticity', the ability to perform a task without conscious thought. This frees up mental bandwidth for other aspects of the game, such as strategy or adaptability to unexpected challenges. Through deliberate practice, athletes develop not just physical prowess, but also mental acuity, enabling them to make split-second decisions in high-pressure situations.

Practice also serves as a means of building confidence. James Clear, the author of *Atomic Habits*, posits that every action you take is a 'vote' for the person you wish to become. When athletes engage in deliberate practice, they are not only honing their craft, but also accumulating evidence of their abilities and dedication. Clear suggests that it's this evidence that leads to a fortified sense of self-belief and identity. Over time, these repeated actions build confidence and reduce performance anxiety, contributing to an athlete's overall effectiveness.

Every deliberate practice session that you engage in is a 'vote' for the artist you envision becoming. Every head study is not only a drawing, but an investment in becoming a person who understands portrait drawing. Every anatomical label in your sketchbook? A tangible example that you are an artist who understands applied artistic anatomy. How you practice is how you play, and you can prove it with every repetition.

Before we move on to the practical elements of the visual world and the grammar of drawing, it must be stated that our practice and interpretative skills are points along the same continuum. The time invested in study and practice crystalizes into the elements of your mature artwork. And although we operate within a universe of well-trodden ideas, defining and understanding your values has the power to transform the familiar into the singular. This is your vision. Understand it well and it will provide to you a point of truth in a career that can be filled with relativity.

FOUN

DATION

WHAT IS MEANT BY FOUNDATION?

Manifesting even a simple and believable study on paper has two basic components: concept and production. The 'concept' side of the endeavour refers to the rules, such as they are, that govern the light, form, organization, and motivations that guide every mark made during the production of the drawing. These 'rules' form the foundation of knowledge that every portraiture artist needs. 'Production', covered later in the Practice and Process chapters, is the technical means by which the artist's vision is manifested.

This dualism between concept and production can be traced back to some of the foundational texts and thinkers in art history. Leonardo da Vinci, for instance, placed equal importance on the science behind art and the skill needed to render it. He argued that a painter should know the 'anatomy of the natural world', emphasizing that the artist should be well-versed in the conceptual framework of the world they are trying to depict. From this perspective, the rules governing light and form are not just artistic conventions but natural laws to be studied and understood.

It's essential to recognize that every element in a representational drawing will be imbued with a certain logic. It's this innate logic that allows the viewer's eye to make sense of what's being depicted, lending credibility to the impression. Throughout this chapter, you will see these concepts illustrated through simplified forms, such as a sphere or cube. But why?

Going back to the time of the Renaissance, drawing education has used geometric shapes as starting points for understanding complex forms. These basic volumes serve as a controlled environment in which to study the consistent logic governing physical phenomena, such as the behaviour of light.

Light behaves according to predictable laws: light rays travel in straight lines and degrade in intensity at a consistent rate over a distance. When light rays hit a round form with a consistent surface, they bounce off at angles of consistent degree. There is an observable pattern to decipher. Once observed and internalized, this pattern can be applied in systems of almost any complexity.

In portraiture, this type of knowledge translates into a nuanced understanding of how to render the curve of a cheek, the subtle forms of the forehead, or the intricate dynamic of light and shadow that gives the planes of the face their sense of depth and three-dimensionality.

Moving forward, the versatility won through the study of these constants can be particularly empowering because it offers you both structure and freedom. *Structure* because these principles serve as guideposts that direct your hand and eye, and *freedom* because the more deeply you understand these tools, the more confidently you can improvise and adapt to the unique challenges each new drawing presents.

'The discipline of accurately rendering will form a foundation for whatever you wish to build upon it.'
Charles Bargue

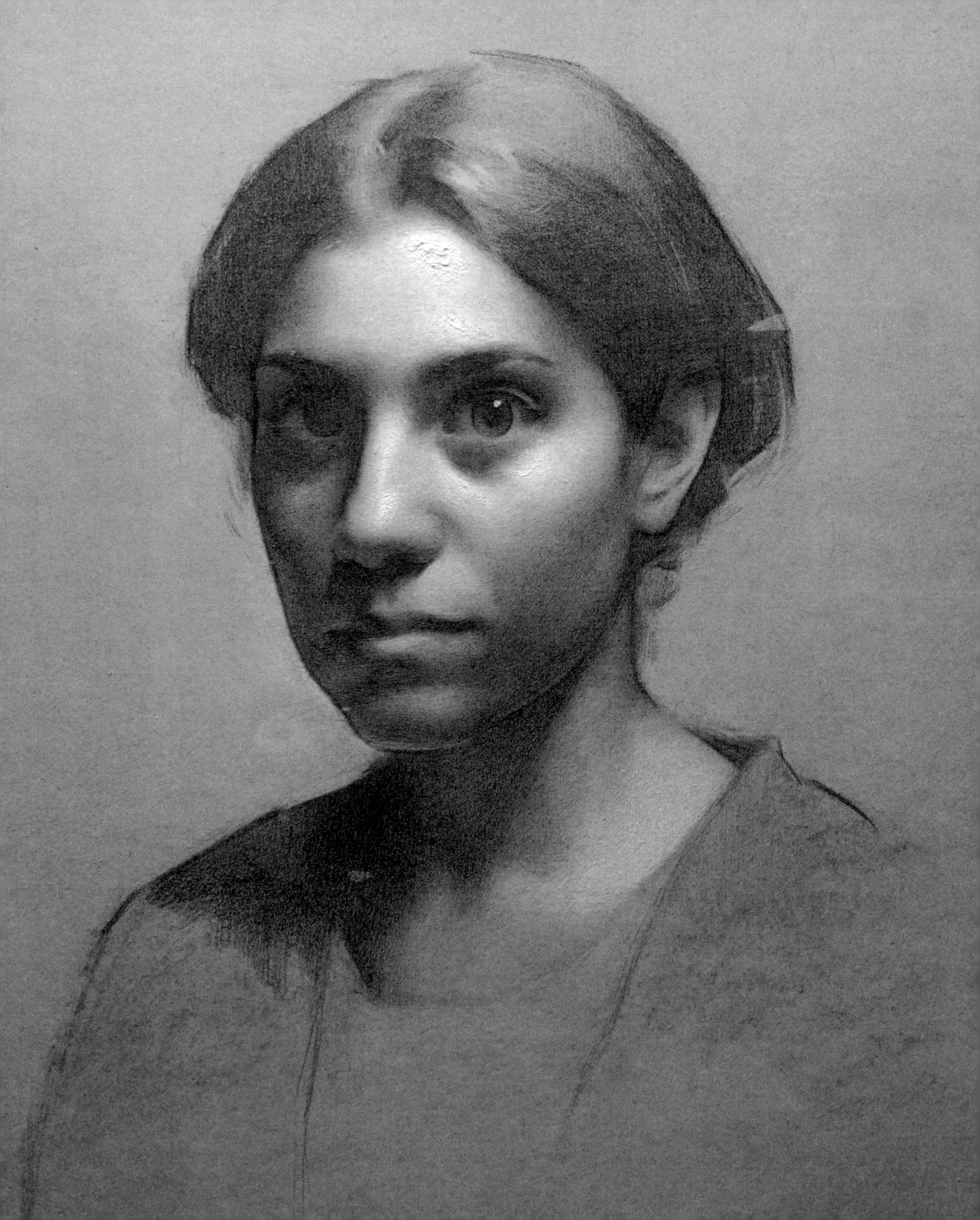

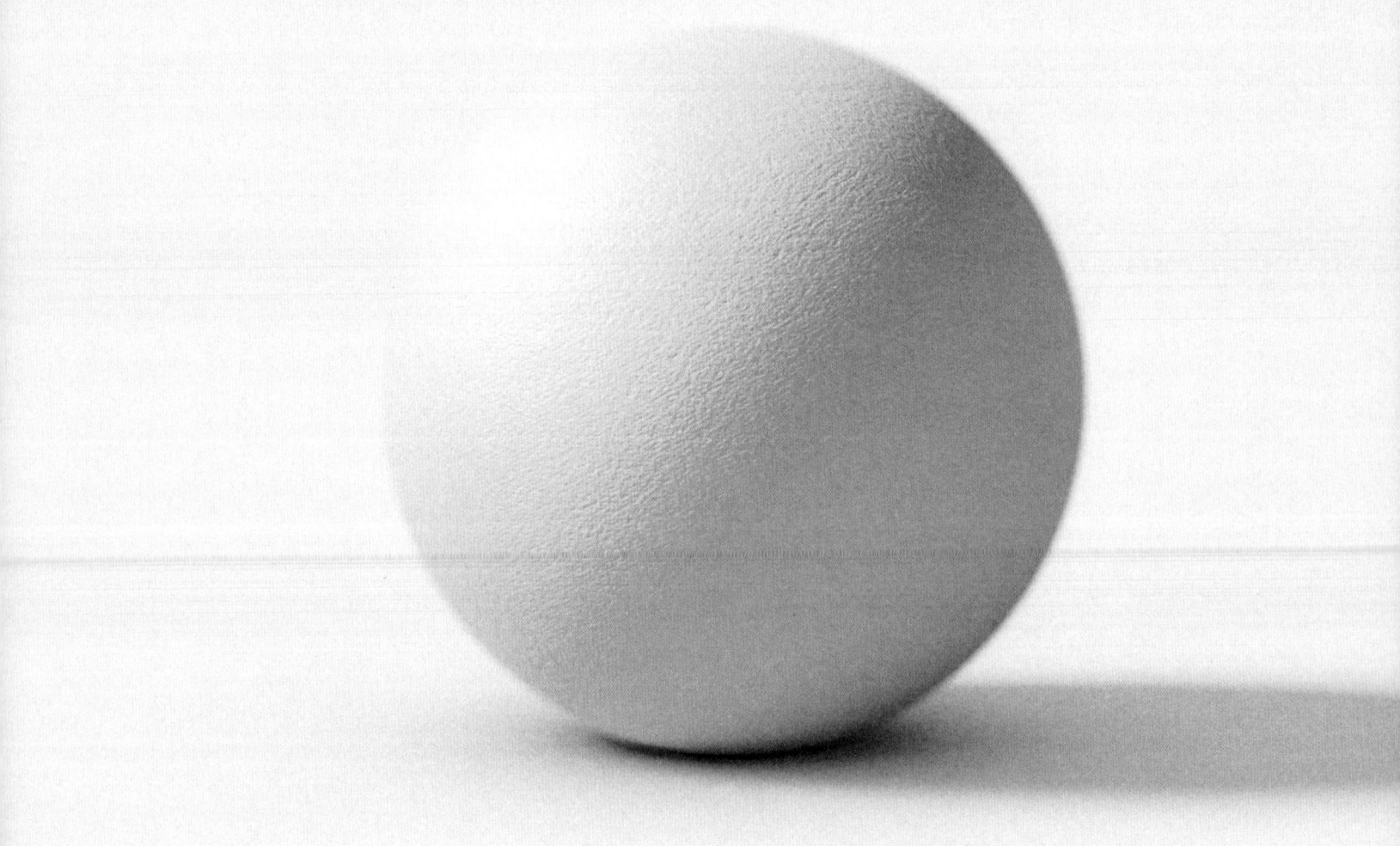

THE SIGNAL
AND THE NOISE

The signal is information that is of substance. It is useful and is most easily comparable to the truth. The noise, on the other hand, is the information that hides and distracts us from that truth. Take the idea of a shadow as an example. There are reams of mathematical equations and formulae that can be applied to the understanding and reproduction of how shadows function in the physical world. 3D rendering software is a product of this very fact. For artistic purposes, however, my experience tells me that only a precious few salient points need to be made clear for a student to grasp and apply the idea.

In this 'Foundation' chapter, we will be looking deeply into the elements of visual phenomena. As in the situation I just described, many of the subjects we encounter will have very complex and scientific principles available to explain them. In some instances, I will refer to those principles in great depth; other times, not as much. This is because drawing is a practical problem that is best suited to being solved by practical means. When a simple and effective solution is available, I want to direct you towards that. If a more complex definition is required to convey meaning, then I will offer that as well.

This perspective is by no means an airtight guarantee that everything that you will eventually find useful in your career as a portrait artist will be represented here. However, what I will offer are all of the things that I have found useful most often in my career, both as a professional artist and as a student.

We will progress through basic topics, such as value, shadow, and light, leading to organizational strategies, anatomy, and composition. As we do so, bear in mind that these are tools - the conceptual tools you will be using to manifest your vision, both in studies and final portraits.

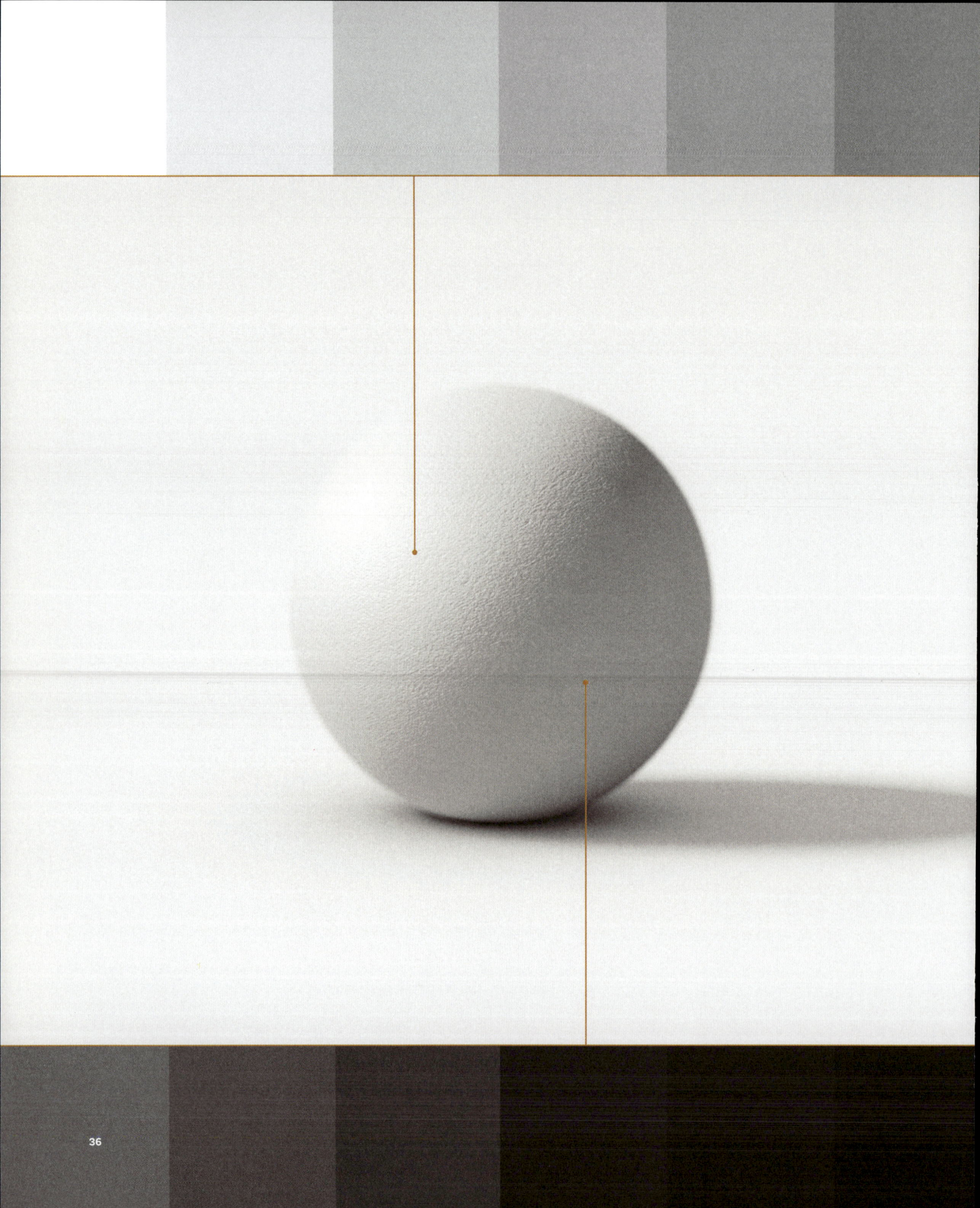

Value, light, and shadow

UNDERSTANDING VALUES

When you draw, 'values' are the different shades of grey you use. These shades help you to show the lightness and darkness in different parts of your drawing. It's like turning a colourful world into a black-and-white photograph.

To use values well, look closely at what you are drawing. Find the darkest area and the lightest area. In a simple example, such as a sphere on a table, the darkest part is usually the shadow right under the sphere. The lightest part is the bright spot where light hits the sphere directly. These are your two extremes.

Identifying the darkest and lightest areas in your drawing serves as a reference. You can think of them as bookends on a shelf. They help you place all the other shades of grey you will use in between them. Now, when you look at another part of your scene, such as the edge of a shadow, you can compare it to these two extremes. In this case, the shadow edge is a bit lighter than the value of the darkest dark, but is also far darker than the lightest light.

To observe value relationships better, you can use a deceptively simple technique: squinting. If you squint your eyes while looking at the subject you're drawing, you essentially simplify what you see. You reduce the amount of light entering your eyes, obscuring the smaller details and complexities, leaving only the larger shapes and most significant areas of light and dark.

Pause and look at the space around you. Wherever you are, it is likely filled with various objects – furniture, plants, people, and so on. When you squint, observe how a lot of those specific details fade away, leaving you with the big, essential value shapes. It's like turning down the 'volume' of visual information, allowing you to hear – or in this case, see – the fundamental 'tones'.

This simplification makes it much easier to identify and compare values. You will more readily notice which values tend to group together, and which ones remain distinct from one another. With this limited range of information, it becomes simpler to make decisions about how to represent what you see on paper.

Now I would like you to observe the sphere on the opposite page. With your eyes wide open, observe all of the varieties of value you are able to see in the shadows. Next, squint until you are looking through your eyelashes. How does your perception of the values in the shadow area change? What you likely observe is a more unified set of value relationships. This technique is an effective way to observe the large and simple relationships between value groups, which shadows to combine when blocking-in shadow shapes, and even the state of the 'big picture' impression of your entire drawing.

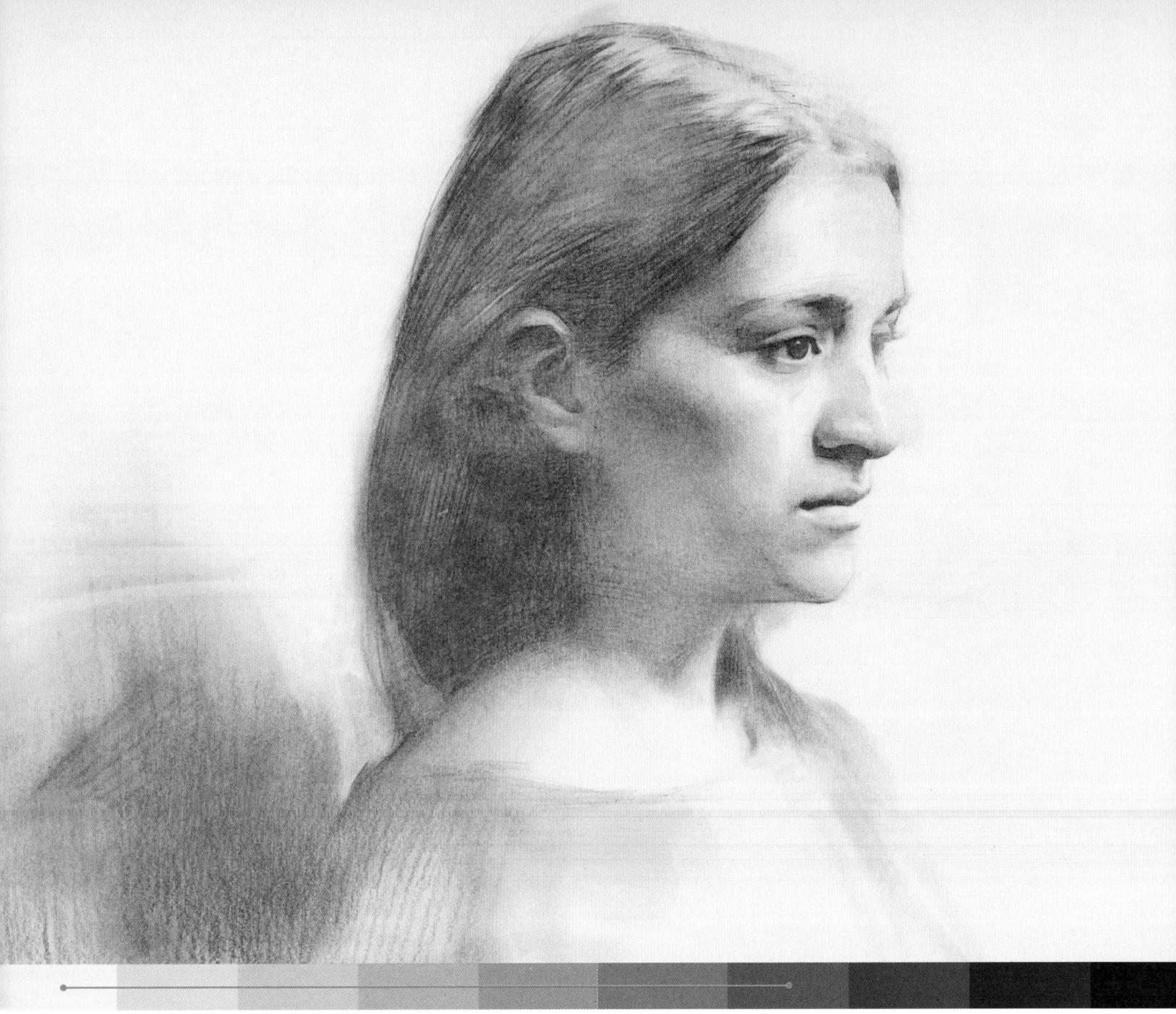

VALUE RELATIVITY

In the early stages of a drawing, you usually start with light values. This is mostly due to the production of values in graphite, which is most easily created in successive layers. That means your darkest areas won't yet be as dark as they will eventually become. While in this transitional state, it is still very useful to maintain a coherent resemblance to the subject. That is where the idea of 'value relativity' comes in. It's the notion that the relationship, on a value scale, of the darkest dark and the other values in the scene should remain relatively constant.

For example, you have started your drawing and have sketched in a light version of what will become your darkest area. Even if it's not as dark as it will be in the final drawing, it should still be the darkest part at this early stage. This sets the benchmark for everything else at that point. All other values should be lighter in comparison.

As you progress, you will start deepening the darks and refining the lights. As you have established your relativity

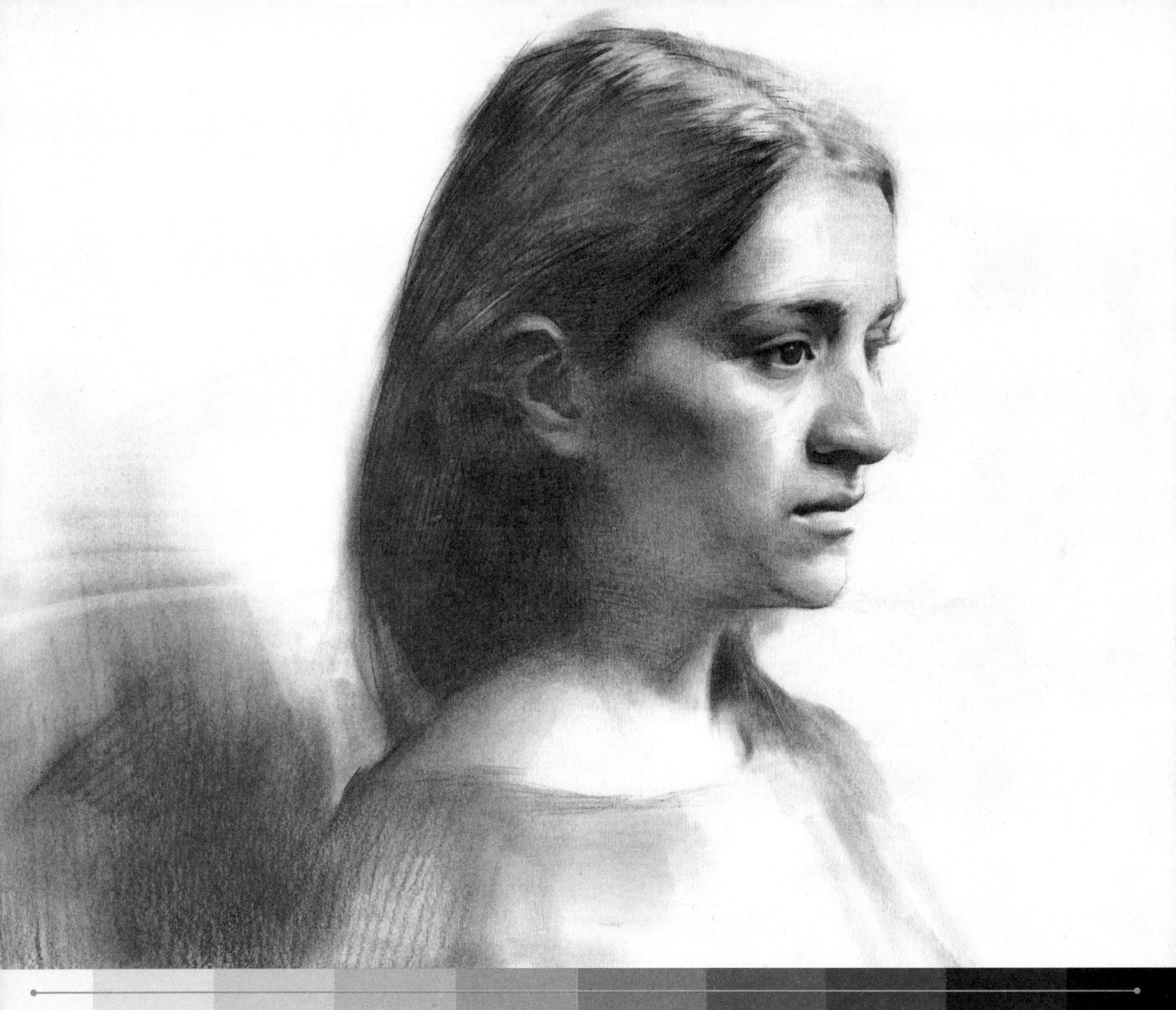

scale early on, you have a guide to help you maintain correct relationships between different areas of shading. Your darkest point will get darker, but so will other areas, all while keeping the same relative differences in value.

In essence, value relativity allows you to gradually build up the shading in your drawing while keeping everything looking realistic and harmonious, regardless of the stage you are at in the process. The analogue process of film development is a perfect analogy for this approach. When you place the exposed photo paper into the developer fluid, the first shapes to emerge are those that represent the darkest darks. Eventually, as the developer continues its work, the darkest spots grow darker still and begin to be accompanied by the darkest halftones. The expanding of the value scale continues until the photo paper is removed from the developing fluid and rinsed.

fig. **01**

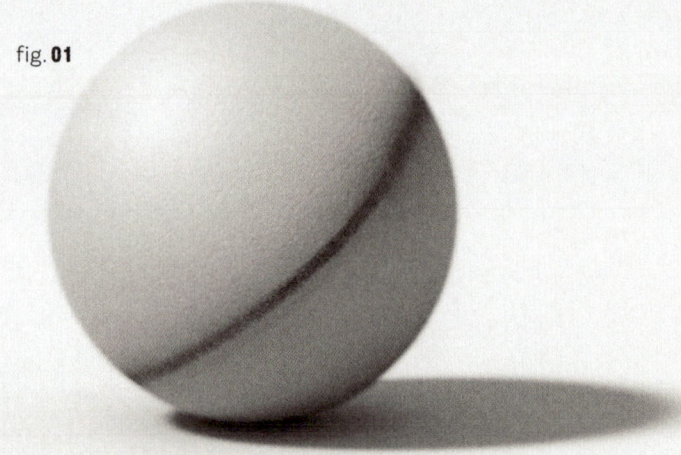

fig. **02**

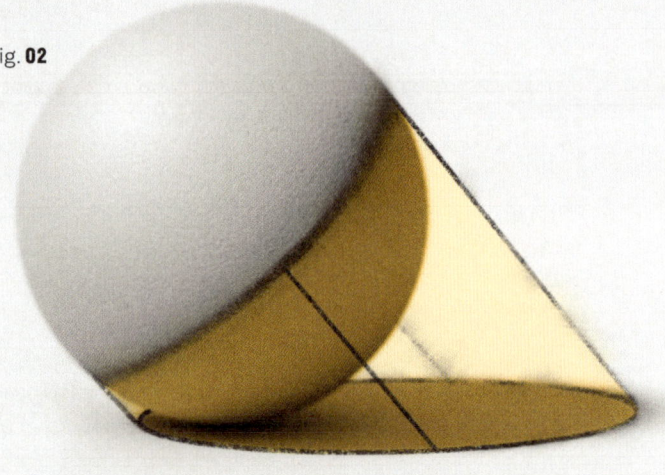

fig. **03**

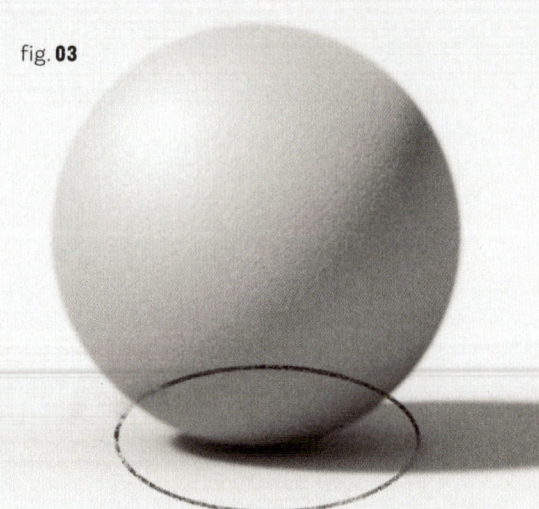

fig. **04**

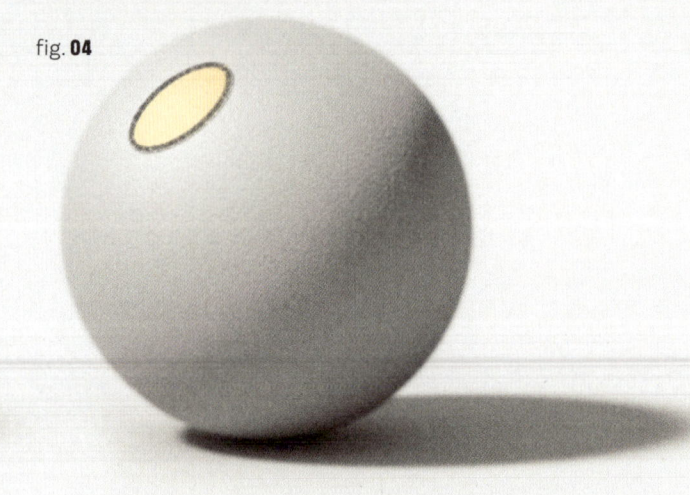

fig. **05**

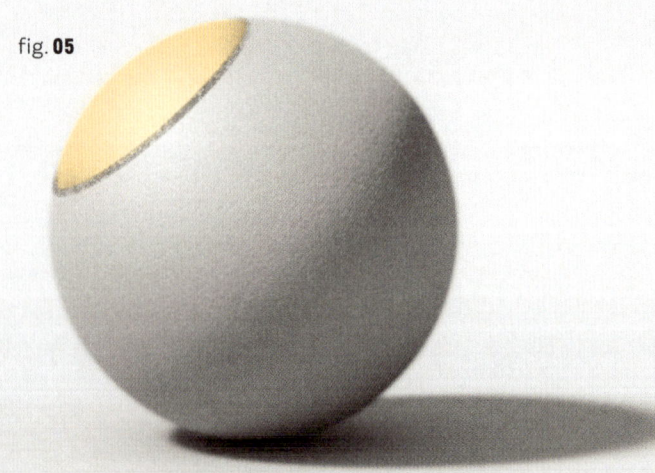

fig. **06**

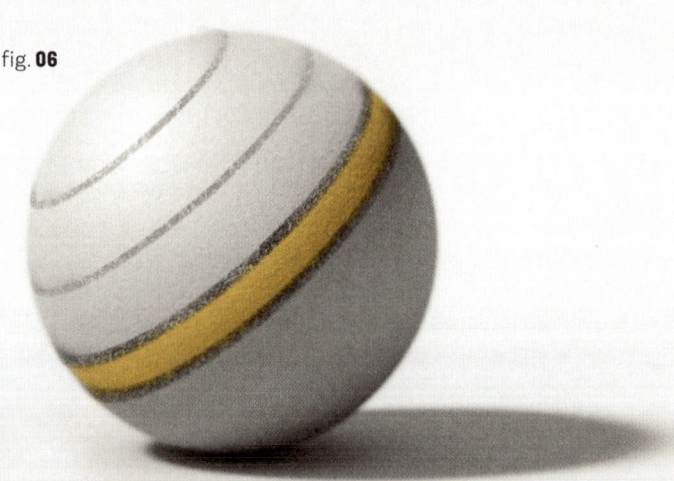

LIGHT AND SHADOW

It's important to consider how light interacts with your subject. Within this interplay, you encounter the shadow edge, which serves as the subtle boundary between light and shadow on an object. It's a delicate transition, not a harsh line, and understanding its nuances can add depth and realism to your work.

Close to the shadow edge is what we call the form shadow (**fig. 01**). Unlike a cast shadow, which will be discussed next, a form shadow is part of the object itself. It's the area turned away from the light source and contributes significantly to conveying the object's three-dimensional form.

Now let's consider the cast shadow (**fig. 02**). This is the shadow that extends from the object and falls onto the surface behind it. Cast shadows provide context; they tell us about the direction and intensity of the light source. When an object blocks light, it creates this shadow.

While we're in those darker areas, it's important to consider ambient occlusion (**fig. 03**). All shadows are a kind of 'occlusion', which simply means a blockage or closing of something. In this case, it is light that is being blocked, specifically the ambient light. Imagine placing this sphere on a flat surface, like a table. In the crevice where the sphere makes contact with the table, you'll notice a particularly dark area – this is where ambient occlusion makes itself evident.

In this contact area, light has difficulty penetrating. Even if your room is filled with light, that specific spot where the sphere meets the table is less exposed to both direct and reflected light. It's almost as if the sphere and the table are conspiring to create a little shadowy enclave, far removed from the bright world around them. This darker zone doesn't have as pronounced edges as a cast shadow, which extends outwards, but it's darker than the cast shadow and the general form shadow on the sphere.

When you're drawing, capturing this ambient occlusion requires a close observation of how light interacts with your subject. For the sphere, you would deepen the shade where it touches the table, making it slightly darker than the rest of the form shadow on the sphere. The gradient of this shading would be soft, not abrupt, gently transitioning into the surrounding shadows. The goal here is to subtly accentuate this area to add a sense of depth and weight to the sphere.

On the flip side, we have the specular highlight (**fig. 04**). This is the bright spot you see on a shiny or wet surface; the highlight often found on the surface of the eye is a good example. It's a point where the light source is directly reflected back at you. A well-placed specular highlight can bring life to your work, indicating the texture and material quality of the object. Bear in mind that the specular highlight and the centre light, as we'll see next, are two different things.

The centre light (**fig. 05**), along with all other values found in the light shape, is referred to as a 'diffuse reflection'. In the context of observational drawing, diffuse reflection refers to the way light scatters in many directions when it hits a rough or non-reflective surface, such as paper, fabric, or skin. Unlike specular reflection, where light reflects in a single direction and creates a distinct highlight, diffuse reflection softens and spreads the light, making it less directional and more evenly distributed.

Nestled between these worlds of light and shadow are the halftones. These are the diffuse reflections that serve as a transition, producing a gradual value shift from light areas to dark ones. Halftones are crucial for depicting rounded or complex forms and create a sense of volume. Among them, you will find the dark halftone (**fig. 06**), which is the darkest region within the halftones. It is closest to the form shadow and serves as an intermediate step that bonds together the shadow and the light shapes.

LAMBERT VS. LINEAR VALUE SCALE

We have already covered values and value scales, so let's talk about another variety of value scale that will be significant to the drawing process. The 'Lambert value scale' is a conceptual framework used in both computer graphics and traditional art to describe how light interacts with a matte or non-reflective surface. The Lambertian reflectance model, named after the eighteenth-century polymath Johann Heinrich Lambert, states that light falling on a surface is reflected uniformly in all directions. This means that, regardless of your viewing angle, the brightness of a Lambertian surface should appear consistent.

Understanding the Lambert value scale (**fig. 01**) can be very beneficial. It serves as a scientific counterpart to the linear value scale (**fig. 02**), which ranges from pure black to pure white with a uniform progression of shades of grey in between. The Lambert scale helps artists to understand how to render the values of an object accurately, based on the way it diffusely reflects light. Unlike the linear value scale, the steps in the gradation are not uniform. They appear much more unified in the lighter tones before accelerating in their progress towards darkness the closer they get to the form shadow edge.

Now, let's discuss how this connects to the phenomenon of the dark halftone, which, as you may recall from **fig. 06**, is the darkest area within the range of halftones, located closest to the form shadow. It serves as a transitional point between the lighter halftones and the darker form shadow. Essentially, if you were drawing an object under a consistent light source, the area where the dark halftone appears would align with a point on the Lambert value scale where the object begins to curve away from the light, receiving less direct illumination. The Lambert value scale allows you to understand that this isn't just an arbitrary area of darkness; it has a specific, scientifically explainable relationship to the way light interacts with your subject.

fig. **01**　　　　fig. **02**

fig. **01**

fig. **02**

fig. 01

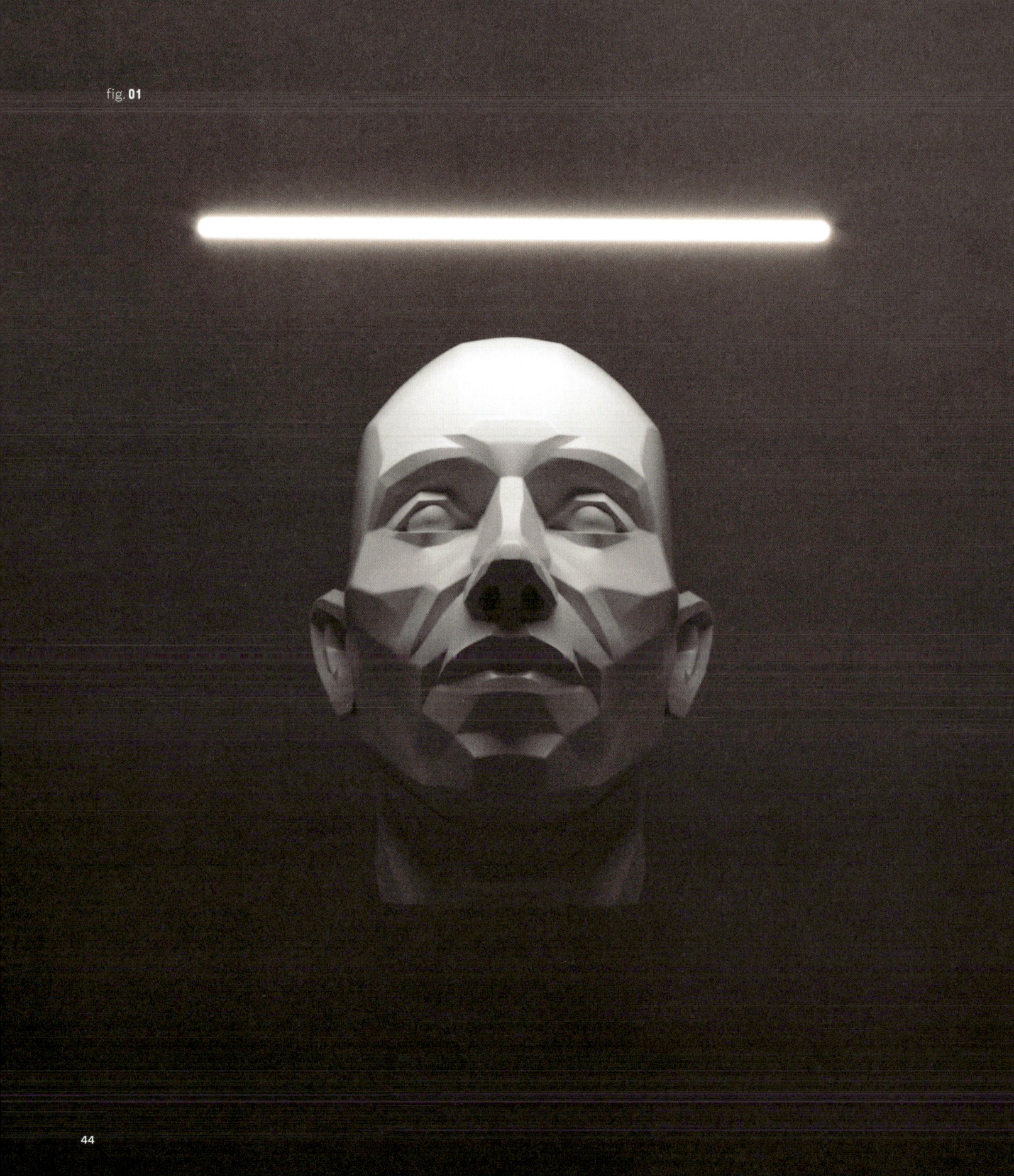

fig. **02**

THE FALL OF LIGHT

The concept of the 'fall of light' in drawing refers to the gradual transition of light to dark that occurs on a three-dimensional form as it recedes from a light source.

Imagine a long, flat plane that extends away from a single light source positioned at one end (**fig. 02**). Closest to the light, the surface of the plane will be brightly illuminated, showcasing the highest value or highlight. As the plane stretches away from the light source, you will notice that the light gradually fades, creating a gradation of values that become progressively darker the further they are from the light source.

The fall of light across a flat plane is typically more uniform than it is on a curved surface, making the transition from light to dark more linear and consistent. Unlike a curved form, where the fall of light rapidly changes due to the form turning away from the light, a flat plane presents a more even, gradual decrease in light intensity.

In portraiture, a light source positioned above the subject offers a more complex situation in which to observe this effect (**fig. 01**). In a portrait lit from above, the light cascades downward, casting its brightest values on the uppermost features. Imagine the forehead, nose, and chin as planes, all oriented at similar angles towards the overhead light source. Closest to the light, the forehead will display the highest value or brightest highlight. As we move down to the nose, even if it protrudes outward like the forehead, it is further from the light source and will therefore appear darker. The chin, even further away, will be darker still. All these planes share a similar angle relative to the light, but are at varying distances from it, so they exhibit a clear, gradual transition from light to dark values.

This phenomenon isn't just about aesthetic choices; it's rooted in the physics of light. Light follows the 'inverse square law', which means that the intensity of light diminishes with the square of the distance from the source. In simpler terms, if you move an object twice as far from the light source, it will only receive a quarter of the light intensity. That's why things appear darker the further they are from the light source.

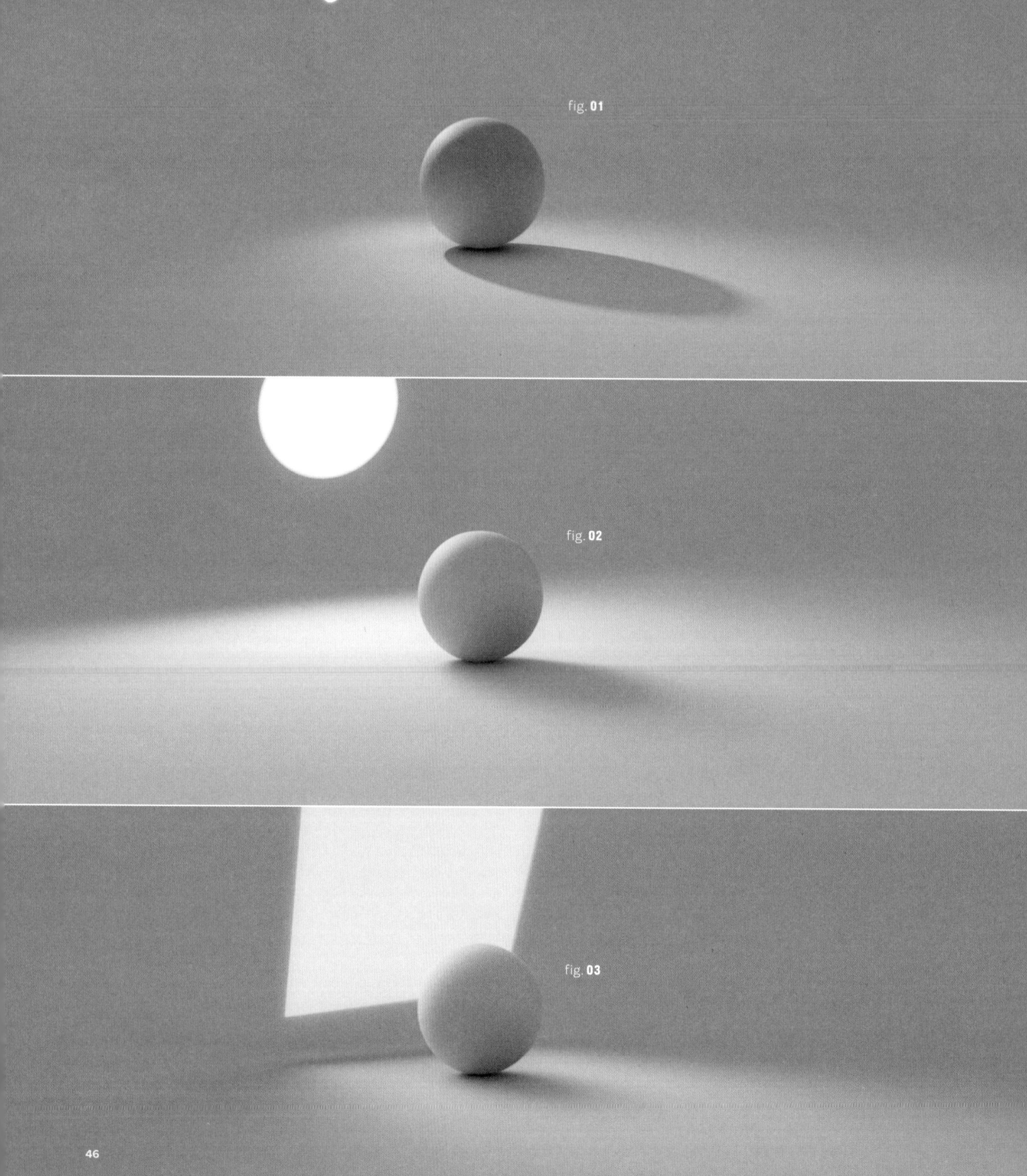

fig. 01

fig. 02

fig. 03

LIGHT FOR LEARNING

The paradigm of 'light for learning' refers to a studio set-up dominated by a single, primary light source. This type of controlled lighting environment is essential for learning purposes because it allows the artist to focus on understanding form, value, and shadow without the complications introduced by multiple light sources. A single dominant light source simplifies the value structure, making it easier to identify and replicate highlights, halftones, and shadows. This paradigm aids in mastering the basic principles of light and shadow, which can then be applied to more complex lighting situations.

Pin light

A pin light is a focused and concentrated source of light (**fig. 01**), often emitting a beam in a spotlight manner. Because of its narrow range, a pin light produces hard, clearly defined shadows with high contrast between light and dark. The transition from light to shadow is abrupt, leaving a stark terminator line, which can emphasize the form in a dramatic way. However, due to its concentrated nature, a pin light may not be ideal for capturing subtleties or nuances in the subject. Pin lights are often used to create a specific mood or to draw attention to a particular aspect of a composition.

Soft-box lighting

Soft-box lighting (**fig. 02**) offers a more diffused and evenly distributed light source. Due to its soft nature, the shadows it produces are less defined, with smoother, more gradual transitions from light to dark. This type of lighting can be ideal for capturing complex forms and subtle variations in texture. Soft-box lights are often used for portraiture, as they can flatter the subject by reducing the harshness of shadows and allowing for a more nuanced rendering of form.

Skylight

A skylight (**fig. 03**) provides natural, ambient light that is often soft and diffused, though its quality can vary depending on the time of day and weather conditions. Unlike artificial light sources, a skylight introduces a dynamic element to the studio, as the light quality changes throughout the day. Skylight generally produces soft, ambient shadows and often imbues the subject with a more naturalistic or organic feel. However, the variability of natural light can be both an advantage and a challenge, depending on the artist's intent and needs.

Each of these lighting permutations offers unique advantages and challenges, shaping the shadows and thus influencing how form is perceived and captured in a drawing.

I should also mention here that different challenges arise if you are working from daylight rather than artificial light alternatives. Neither is wholly better or worse; each one has more and less desirable qualities. Daylight, for example, is an ever-changing source. Morning, midday, and afternoon are all different expressions. This can be a great advantage as it reveals different aspects of your models and lighting situation, with a different overall hue as well. It can be frustrating for beginners, however, especially as it puts more responsibility on the artist to select the right moments for drawing. While artificial light is constant, even the best version will lack a little in its colour spectrum. Both options work, but remember that they have distinct personalities. Ideally, you should try both.

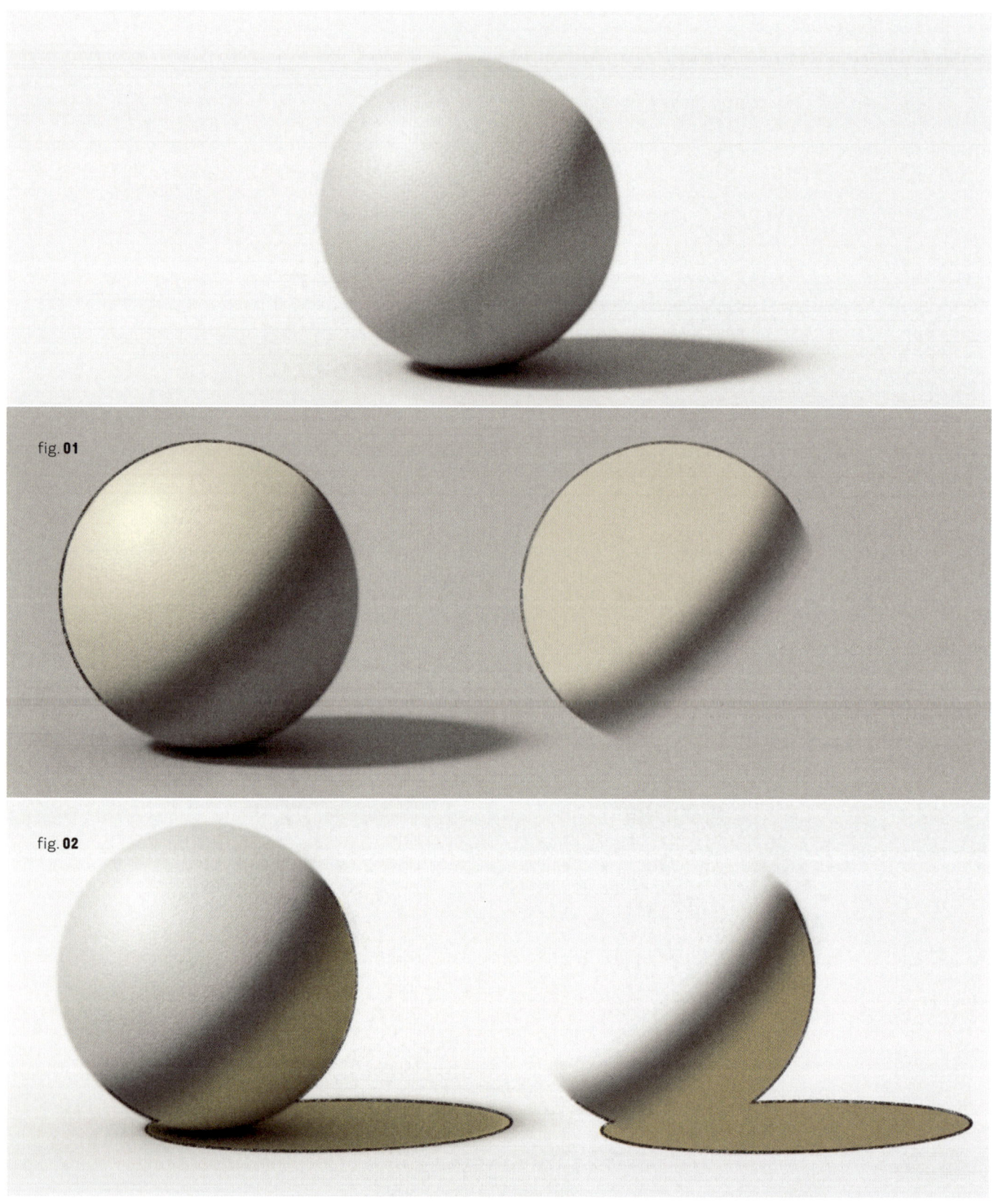

fig. 01

fig. 02

'The patches of light and dark can be considered as abstract shapes and judged as such.'

Harold Speed

SHADOW SHAPES, LIGHT SHAPES

The nuances of lighting conditions are incredibly important in the practice of drawing. Let's dig a little deeper into why different lighting scenarios make such a significant difference in your approach. The key to honing your observational skill is understanding how to break down complex visuals into simpler elements, often using light and shadow as your guide. In controlled indoor settings, especially where there is a primary dominant light source like a single lamp or spotlight, this task becomes easier. The strong light source creates distinct 'light shapes' (**fig. 01**) and 'shadow shapes' (**fig. 02**) on your subject.

These light and shadow shapes can be thought of as the building blocks for your drawing. Light shapes are the areas directly illuminated by your primary light source and often serve as the focus of your composition. Shadow shapes are areas obstructed from the light and help to define the form and contours of your subject. Once you understand how to observe and capture these shapes, the process becomes an efficient way to organize the visual information before you.

However, it's crucial to understand that this organizational system is highly dependent on having a single, dominant light source. Take that same skill outdoors on a cloudy day, and you'll find the model bathed in diffuse, soft light. The sun is still there, of course, but the clouds scatter its light in multiple directions, making it hard to determine a dominant light source. Consequently, the clear distinction between light shapes and shadow shapes starts to blur, complicating your ability to use this method for organizing what you see.

The indoor studio environment, with its controlled lighting, offers a simplified and consistent scenario that is conducive for learning the basics. The reason this setting is emphasized as 'light for learning' is because it minimizes variables. When you're just starting out, you don't want to be grappling with the complexities of natural light, or the unpredictable mix of light sources you might find in other settings. A controlled lighting situation allows you to focus on mastering the core skills of observation, shape recognition, and value organization, without distractions.

Organization and simplification

SHADOW IS ATMOSPHERE, LIGHT IS FORM

Understanding a visual phenomenon is just the beginning of the journey to being able to create a rendering of it. As we have to start out on a blank sheet of paper, a space of infinite possibility, it is useful to have a strategic plan for how we organize information at each stage. There are various schools of thought about what to do first and so on after that, each with a specific outcome in mind.

The set of rules you choose to guide your choices through this process should be aligned with the character of the light and the complexity of your subject. Your choices should be derived from that lighting situation. Endless frustration can be avoided by applying the appropriate drawing solution to the situation and subject with which you are working. It sets the tone for the entire piece, influencing how each subsequent layer of detail is added.

The strategy 'shadow is atmosphere, light is form' can be used as a technical guideline for organizing values within a drawing. And on the more artistic side, it can be a philosophical aesthetic jumping-off point.

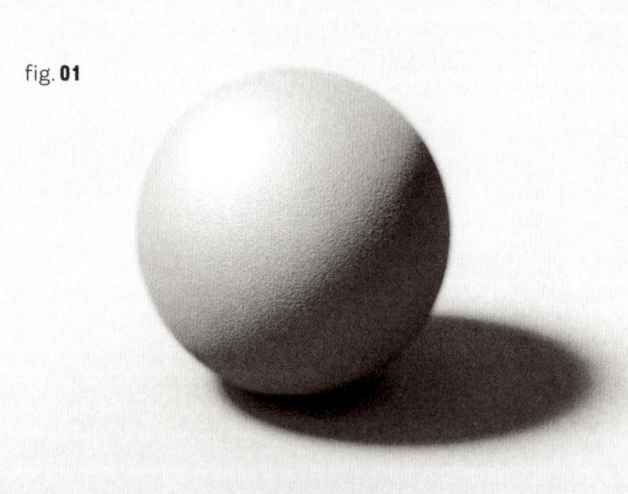

fig. **01**

Shadow is atmosphere
This first part implies a unified treatment of values in shadowed regions. The use of the word 'atmosphere' can refer to 'atmospheric perspective' – a term taken from landscape painting to describe the way objects appear lighter in colour, less distinct, and usually a cooler, bluer hue as they recede into the distance. This phenomenon occurs because particles in the air scatter light and cause distant objects to look faded and less saturated in colour compared to those close up.

Applied to drawing, this means that instead of a broad spectrum of values, shadows are to be rendered with less contrast and fewer transitions in value. This serves multiple purposes. First, it creates a kind of atmospheric unity or cohesion that can imbue the drawing with a particular mood or tone. Second, by limiting the range of values in the shadows, you avoid drawing undue attention to these areas, allowing them to serve as a backdrop against which the forms in the light can stand out (**fig. 01**).

fig. **02**

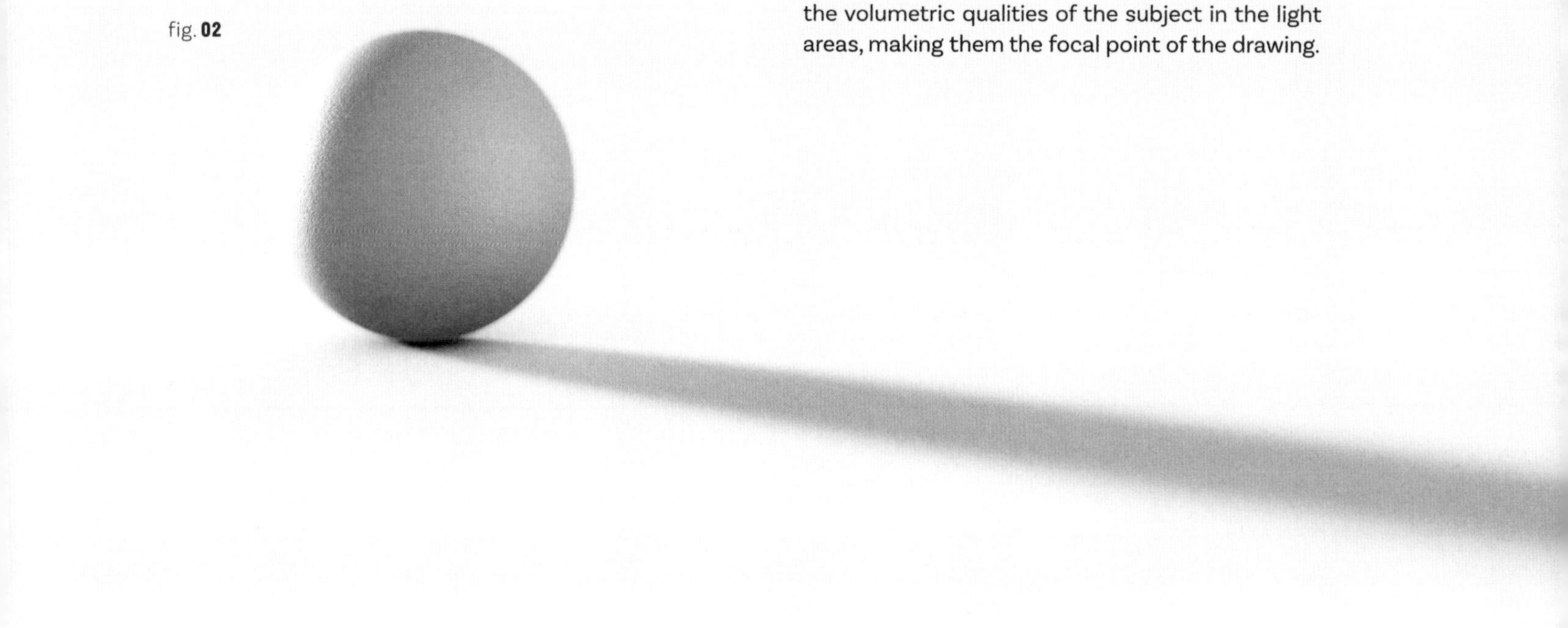

Light is form

This part of the concept advocates for a more varied application of values within the light shape (or illuminated portions) of your subject. The variety in value transitions serves to describe the topology and texture of the object. This organizational technique is particularly useful for emphasizing the volumetric qualities of the subject in the light areas, making them the focal point of the drawing.

'In a picture … one should be more conscious of the things that are unified than of the things that are disunited.'

John Singer Sargent

In this concept's practical application, shadows are rendered in a more uniform value to create flat shapes that appear three-dimensional, more or less. These unified shapes with clear boundaries enhance your ability to apply dynamic 2D design principles to them. In addition to that, they also serve as clear reference points for triangulation and comparative measurements (see page 71 on academic observations).

There are, however, some lighting situations that an artist can encounter that render this strategy somewhat ineffective – for instance, when the form of subject is primarily in shadow (**fig. 02**). In a case like this, I recommend simply flipping the strategy on its head, so shadow becomes form and light becomes atmosphere. This will mean that the value range is expressed with greater variety in the shadows and is more unified or washed-out in the lights.

ORGANIZING IN A CONTROLLED SETTING

fig. **01**

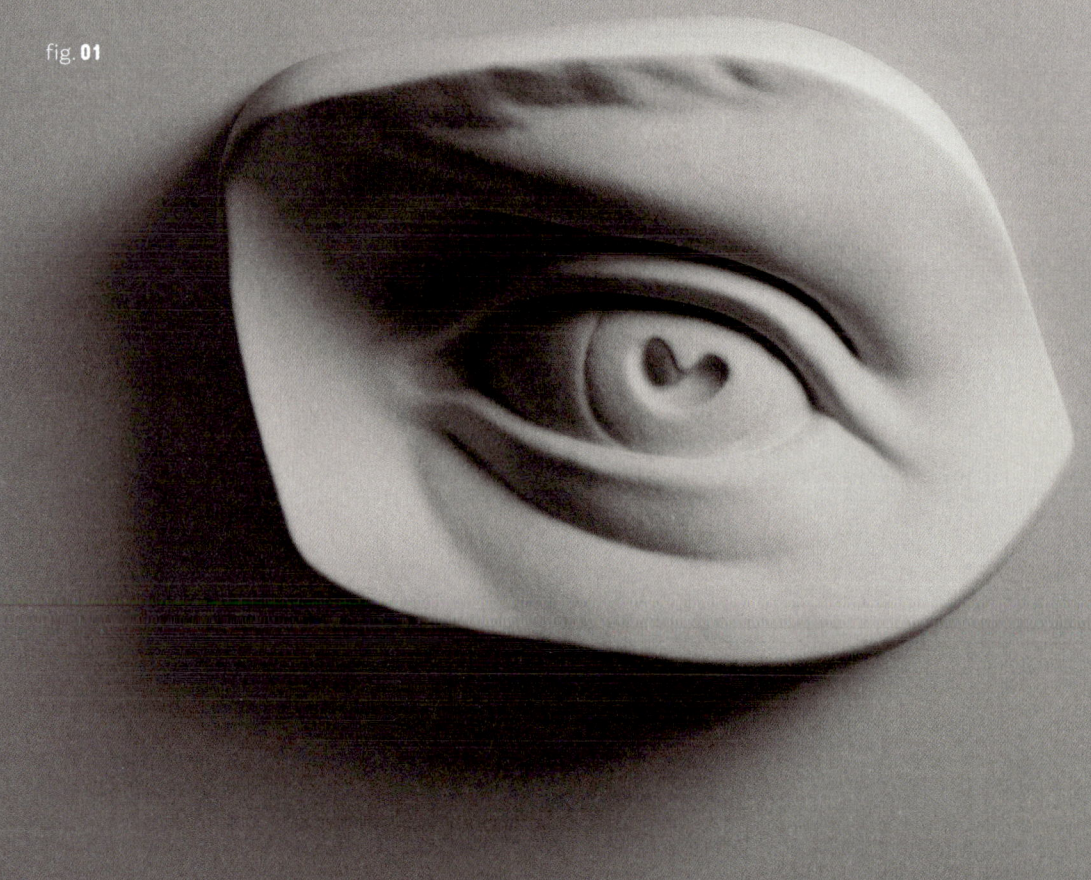

The concept of 'shadow is atmosphere, light is form' becomes particularly pertinent in the controlled setting of cast drawing, often acting as a revelatory moment for students. By focusing on the cast's inert white surface, students get to isolate and scrutinize how light behaves when it interacts with form. The lack of colour or texture variations removes additional variables, narrowing the focus solely to the behaviour of light and shadow.

This practice serves as an educational pivot, a shift from the conventional way of seeing to something entirely different. In a sense, the classroom becomes a laboratory for perceptual training. The plaster cast serves as a neutral test subject, allowing the subtleties of light and shadow to come forward unencumbered by the complexities of colour, emotion, or other elements. It's an exercise in deliberate limitation, which paradoxically expands the student's understanding and skills.

The drawings themselves are not the end goal; they are the means to an end. They act as both a record and a tool of the student's evolving understanding of light's role in defining

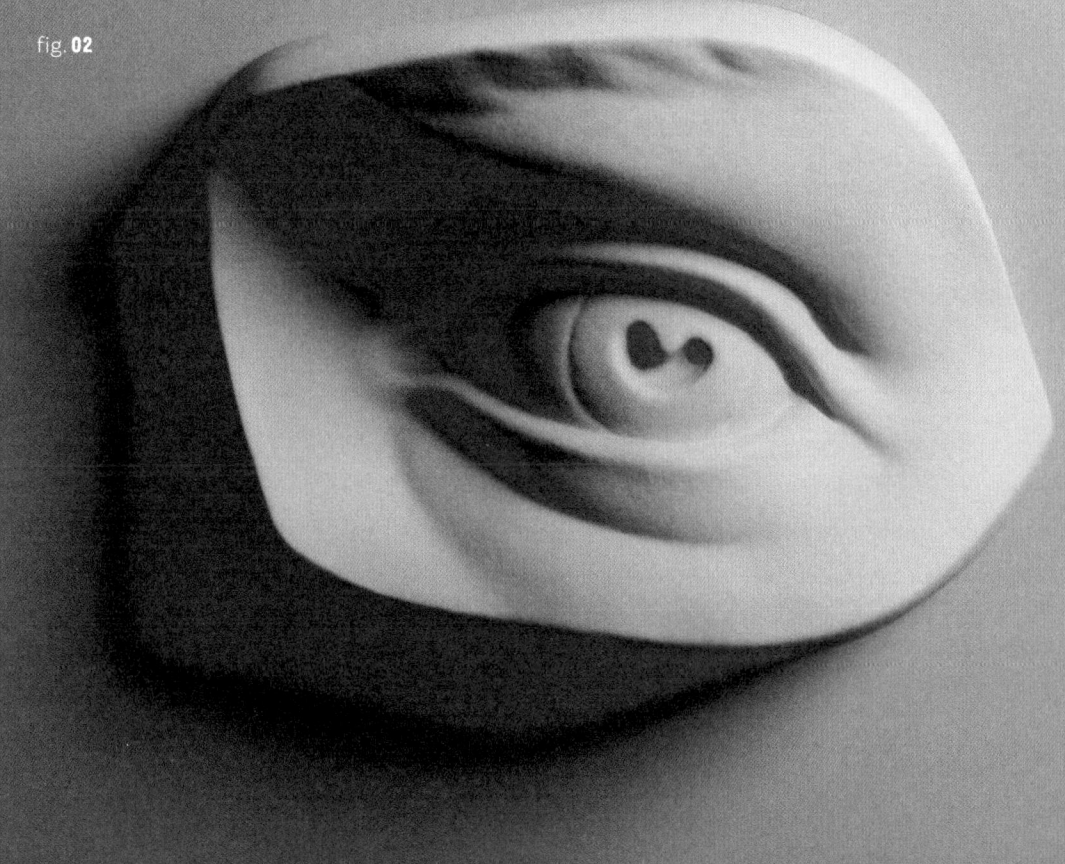

fig. **02**

form and shadow's role in creating atmosphere. Learning to be selective in what to include and what to leave out is one of the most crucial skills an artist can master.

The images above show the same plaster cast: the ubiquitous eye of Michelangelo's *David*. The treatment of shadow in **fig. 02** is what I would like to draw your attention to. Though the cast itself is just as 'real' as in **fig. 01**, the shadows here are given a unifying treatment. The shadow edge has also been emphasized through the addition of a slightly darker value than what is observed within the shadow shape. This

'atmosphere' directs the viewer's attention outwards, to the edge of the shadow and beyond, in particular into the 'light shape', to observe and appreciate the diversity of value and form to be found there.

Why then should we observe them side by side like this? To show explicitly that changes are being made to the subject – changes that are guided by a statement of purpose. To show that these kinds of changes, if taken under the influence of a coherent purpose, can be artfully executed and are well within the remit of the artist, and the art student.

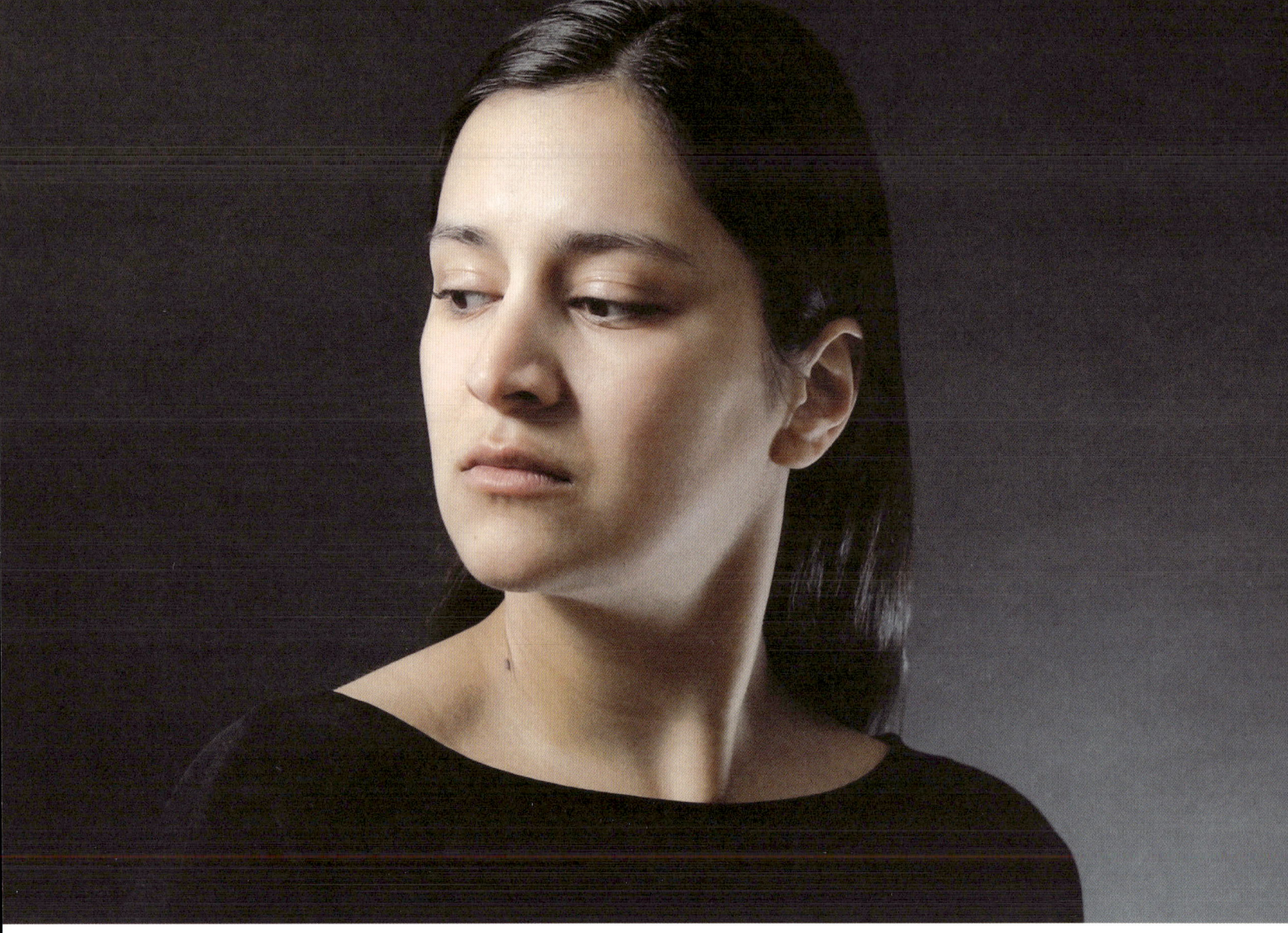

SELECTION AND CONTROL

Consider now a more complex subject, a portrait, in a lighting situation that is not exactly suited to the idea of 'shadow is atmosphere, light is form'. While the primary light source illuminates the model's face from the left side, casting her features into sharp relief, a secondary light source is subtly brightening the shadowed planes, particularly on the right side of her neck and below the jawline. This secondary illumination introduces additional layers of depth and dimensionality to the portrait, highlighting the nuances of the head structure.

It is easy to see how the principle of 'shadow is atmosphere, light is form' becomes more intricate here. While the primary light source clearly defines the form of the model's face, creating a luminous highlight on her forehead, cheekbone,

and nose, the secondary light source softly brightens areas that would otherwise remain in deep shadow. The challenge here lies in ensuring that this secondary illumination doesn't disrupt the atmospheric role of the shadow, which provides contrast and depth to the composition.

The skin tones in the shadowed areas, especially on the right side of the face and neck, need to be treated with clear intention. Instead of rendering each subtle variation in tone, consider the cumulative average of these values, aiming for a balanced representation that preserves the atmospheric quality of the shadow without making it too monolithic. By averaging out these shadow values, you can achieve a sense of unity and coherence.

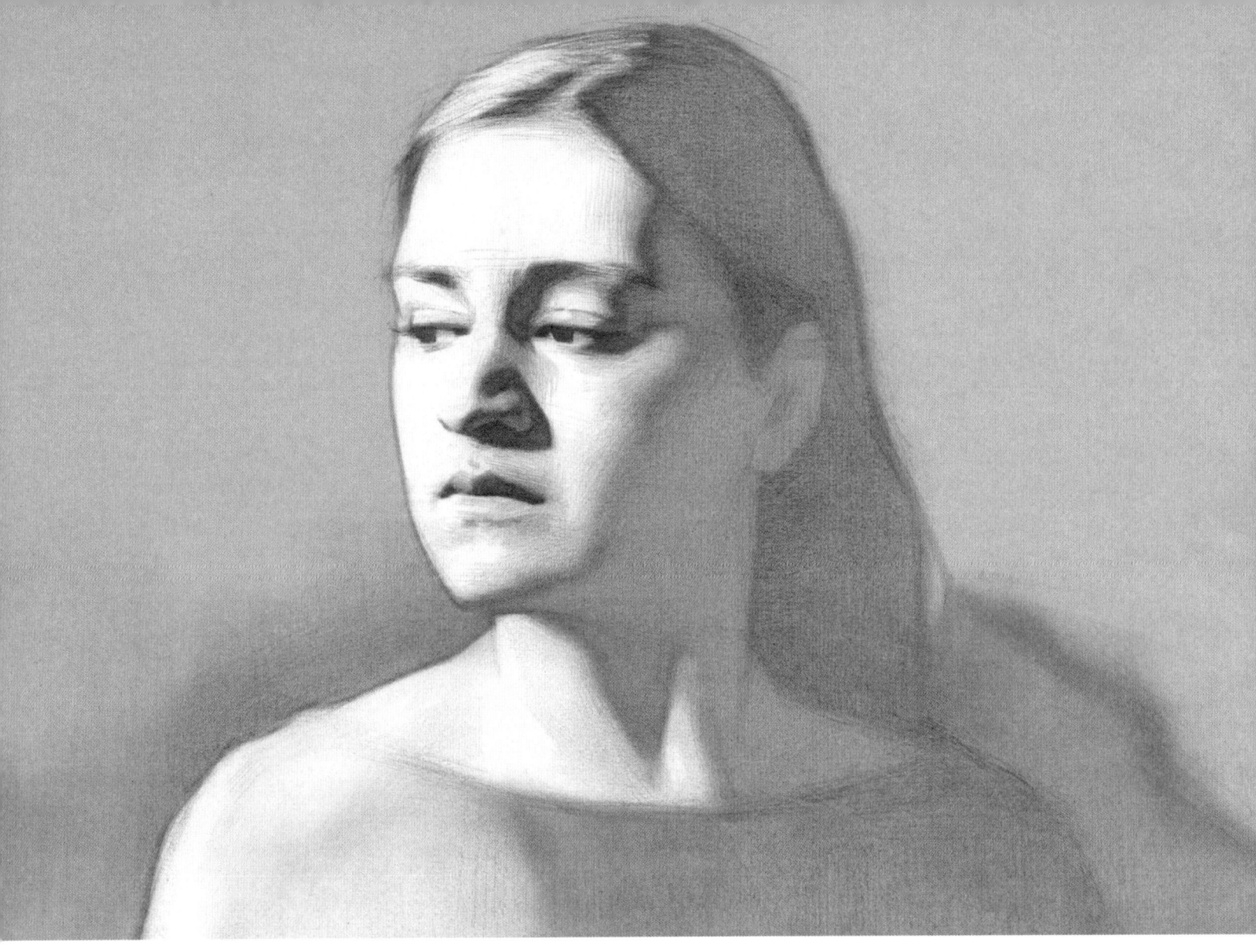

The dark hair of the model, slicked back and reflecting minimal light, offers a contrasting value (the darkest dark) that anchors the composition. The deep, almost ebony hue of the hair provides a stark juxtaposition to the averaged shadow values of the skin, creating a duo-tone effect. This not only maintains the relative value relationship between the two primary value groups, but also creates a dichotomy of shapes within the shadow that makes it easier to show the simplified structures contained therein.

Tackling a portrait with dual light sources offers a nuanced lesson in value management and intentionality. The tug-of-war between primary and secondary light sources is more than a technical challenge; it is a philosophical dilemma that must be resolved by the hand and mind of the artist. While multiple light sources introduce greater dimensionality, they also pose the risk of visual disunity. One might be tempted to depict every nuance, every subtle gradation of light and shadow, but caution is advised. A well-intended foray into such minutiae could lead to a cacophony of competing values, thereby detracting from the harmonious atmosphere one aims to achieve.

Thus, the student's role is not merely to observe and replicate but to select, to choose what must be emphasized and what must be subordinated or even omitted. The control of value is as much a product of decision-making as it is of observation. Fidelity to the subject is important, but it isn't an end in itself.

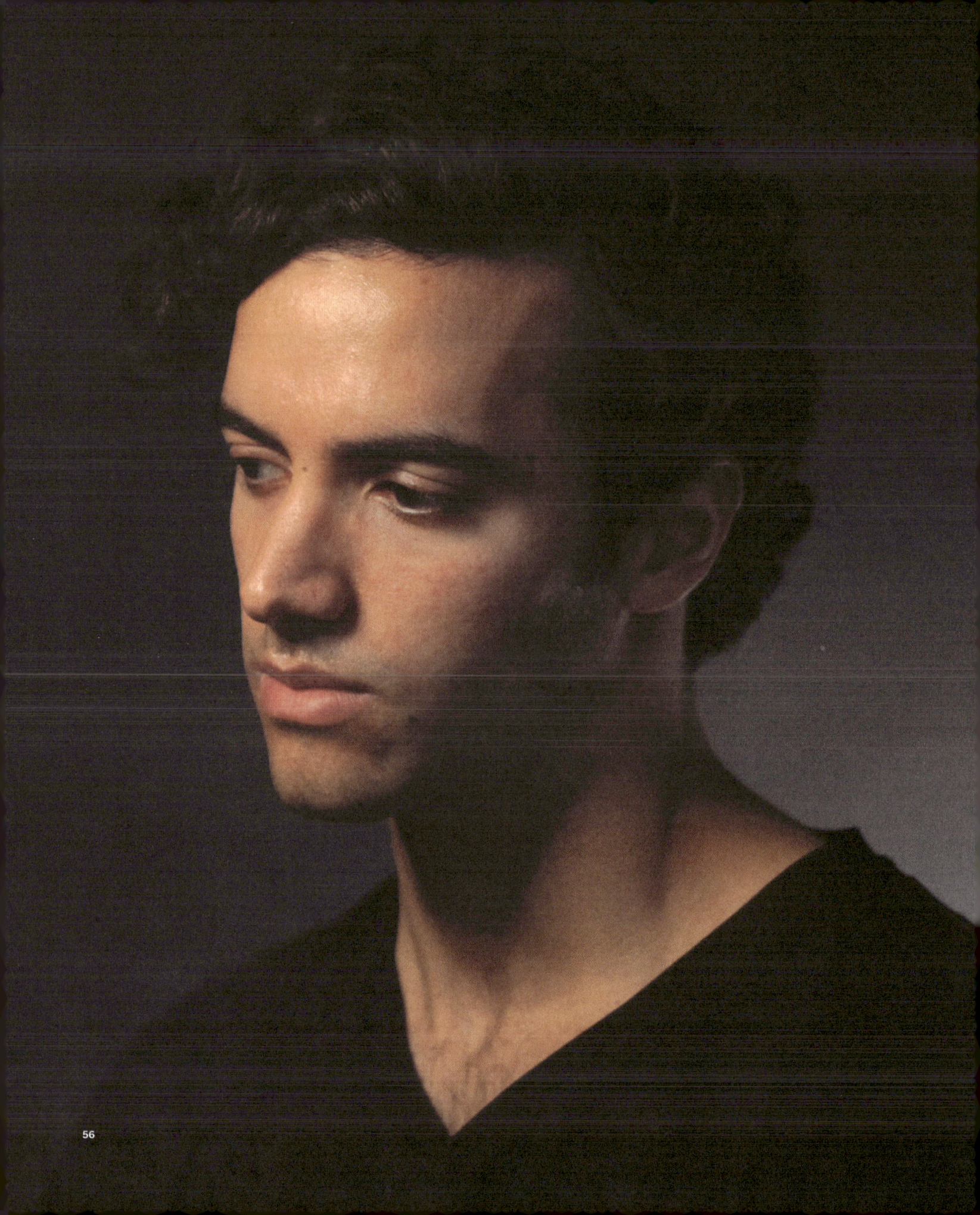

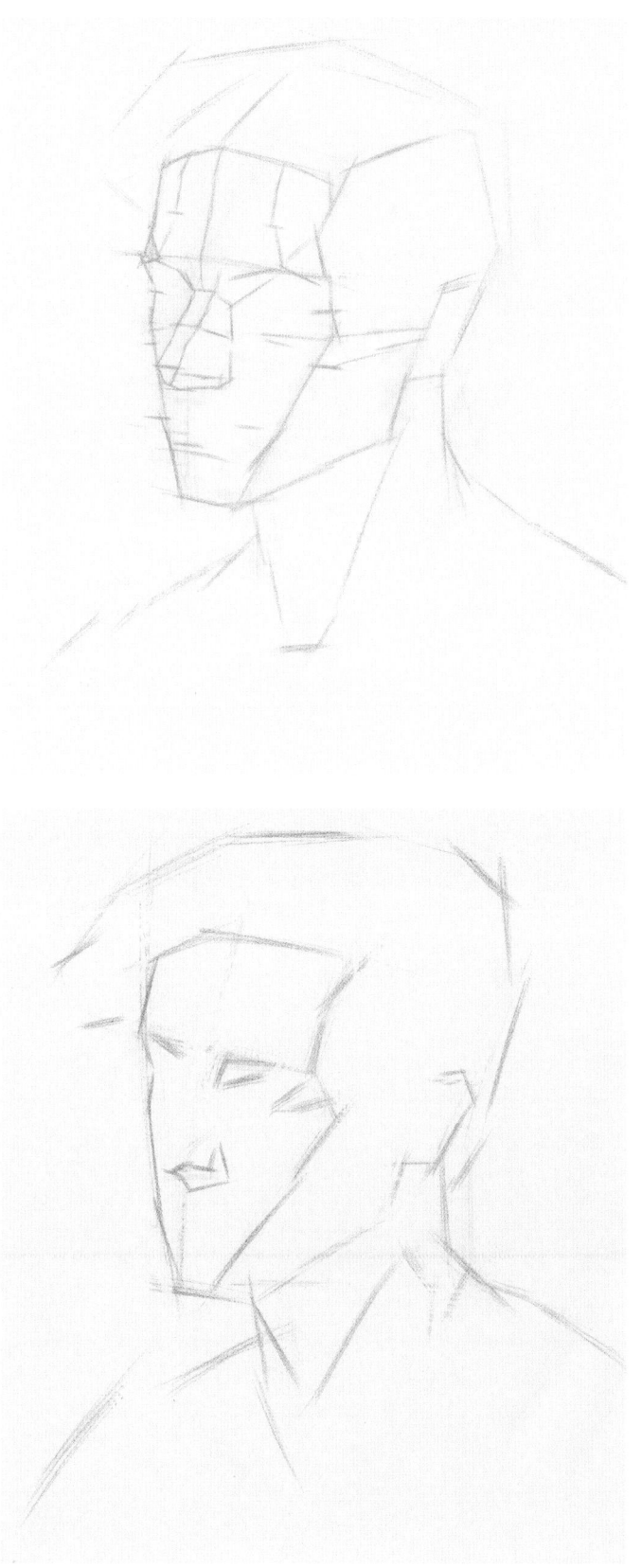

SIMPLIFICATION

At its heart, graphite drawing is a low-resolution exercise. It has more in common with early Nintendo graphics than it does with contemporary 8K ultra-HD images. Due, in part, to this fact, representational artists are forced to simplify their subjects in various ways. On the plus side, simplification can be a tool used to remove extraneous details from your work, helping you to cut straight to the heart of the picture you want to make.

When you begin a drawing, think of it as sketching out the broad strokes of a composition before adding the intricate shading and edge quality. Start with basic shapes and longest lines; they are your underdrawing, the scaffolding upon which the rest of your work will be built. This allows for easier adjustments, a blueprint that you have the latitude to change later. Jumping straight into the details is akin to adding fine gradations or intricate textures before the general form is correct. Corrections then become a laborious unravelling of tangled lines and misplaced values. By starting with a simplified framework, you have the latitude to move a line here or tweak an angle there, all without disturbing a complex constellation of details.

'Simple can be harder than complex. You have to work hard to get your thinking clean to make it simple.'
Steve Jobs

Simplification also helps you to establish accurate proportions in a more manageable way. If you're working with simple shapes and straight lines, it's easier to make the kinds of big measurements that will tell you if something is too big, too small, or out of place. Once you're confident that the basic proportions are correct, you can start to add more detail and complexity. You're breaking down a complex task into smaller, more manageable steps. Simplification at the start isn't about being less precise. It's a strategic approach that keeps your drawing flexible and helps you to build up to a more accurate and refined final drawing.

Simplification, at least the kind we are talking about here, makes its greatest impact on the first stage of the drawing: the block-in. It's important to remember that the extent of your creative and critical thinking about this stage is the only limit to how useful it can be. It is understandable but incorrect to think of your block-in, and the scarceness of likeness observable in it, as a perfunctory obligation. Rather it is a baseline you will set for the care you give to every thoughtful addition of information into your drawing. Give it great attention and it will reward you with a solid composition and proportions.

There are two basic types of simplification and they can be useful not only at the beginning of a drawing, but throughout the entire process. A complex or natural form (**fig. 01**) can be better understood through 2D shape-based simplification (**fig. 02**) and 3D form-based simplification (**fig. 03**). We are going to explore each of these independently, even though in practice there is almost always some overlap or simultaneous application.

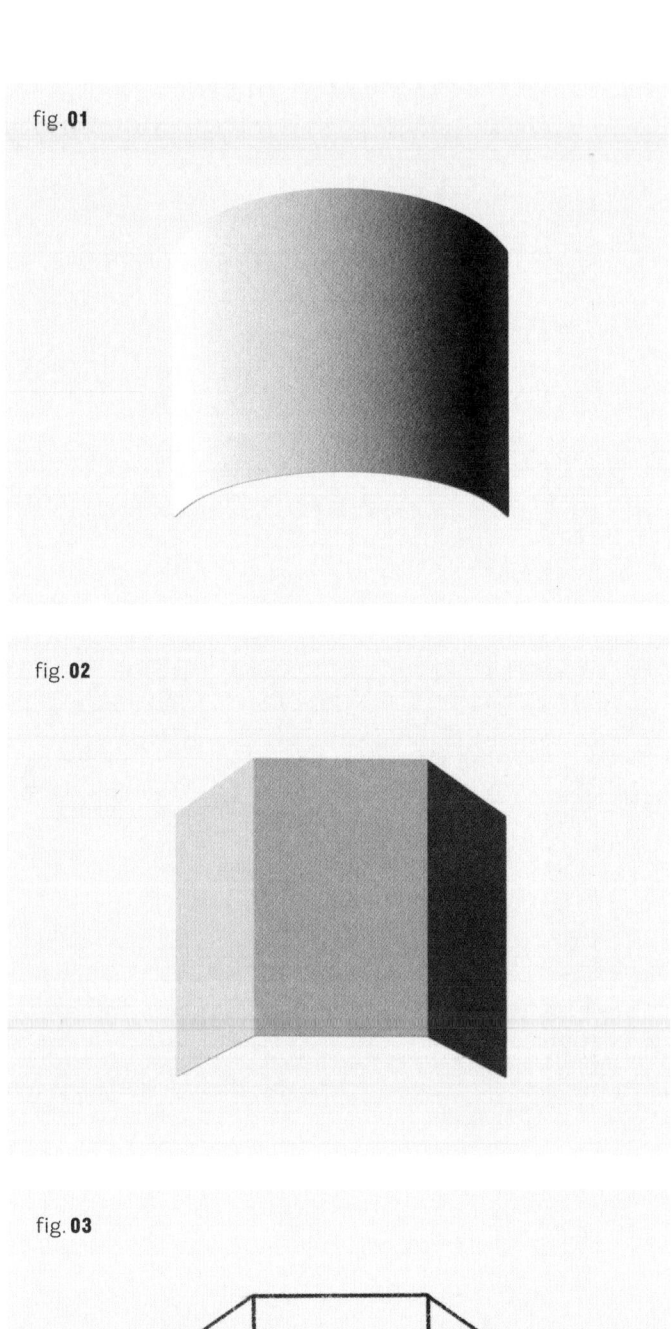

fig. **01**

fig. **02**

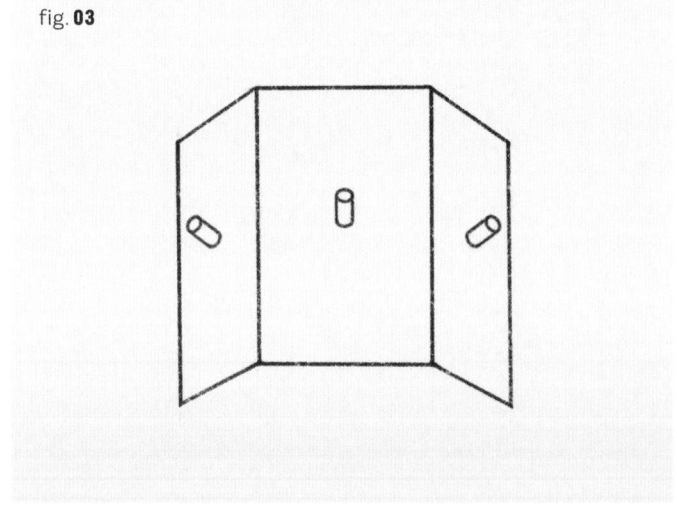

fig. **03**

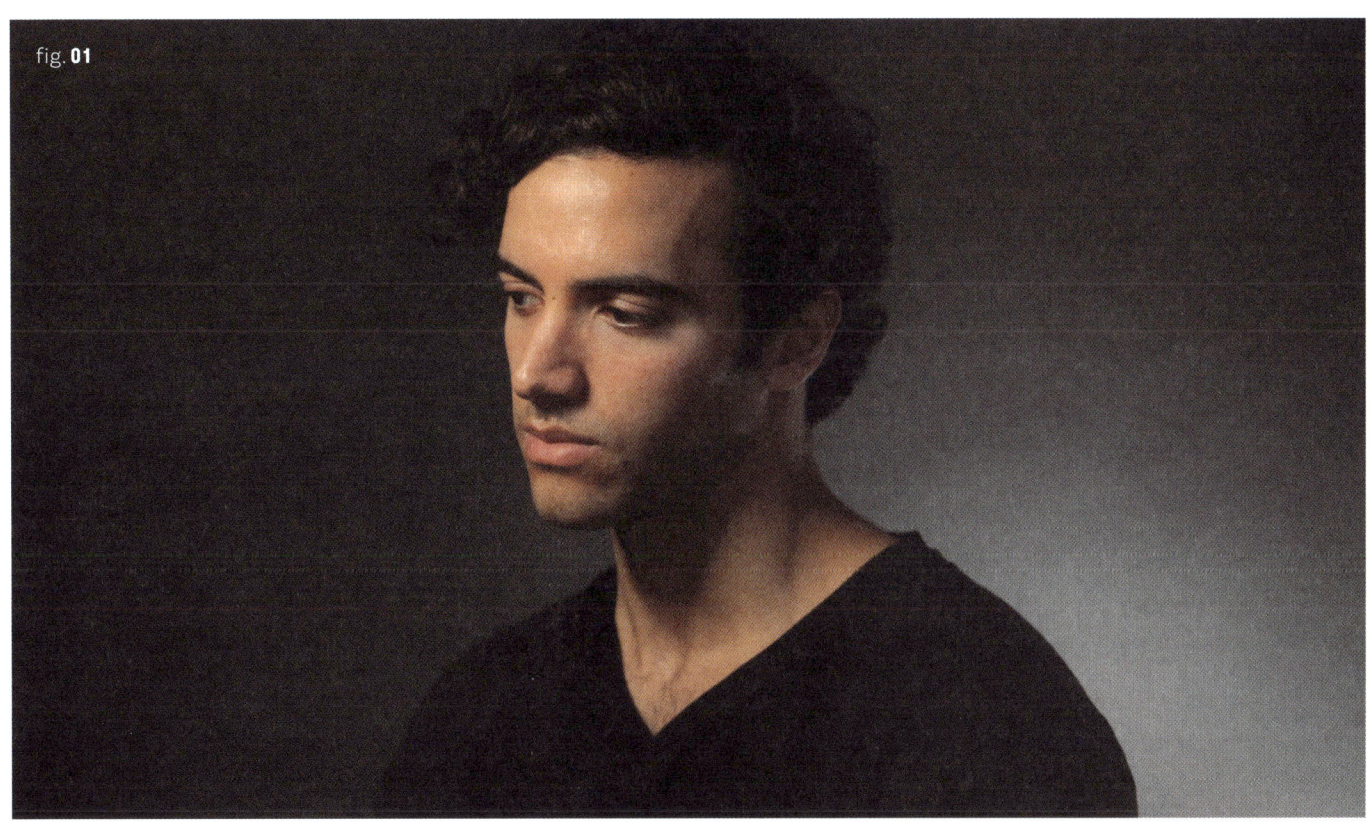

fig. 01

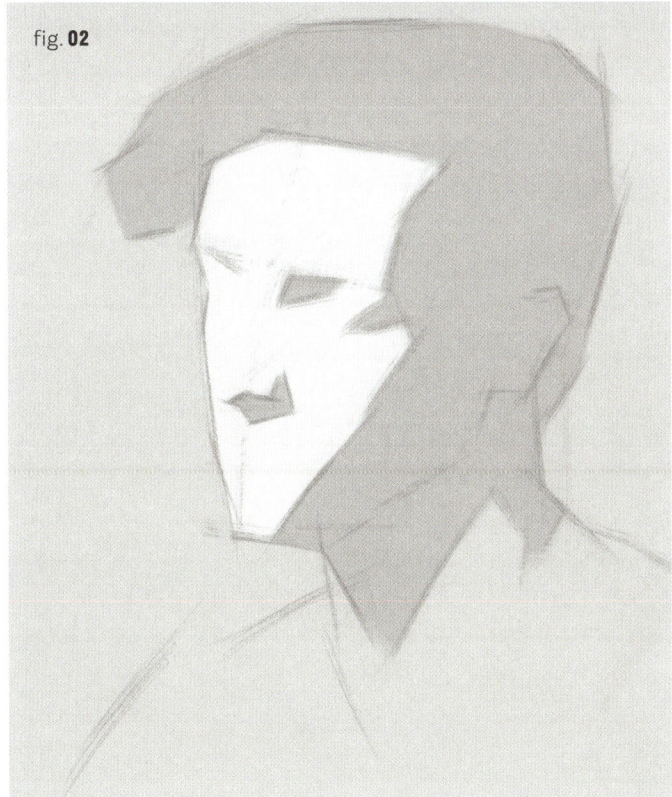

fig. 02

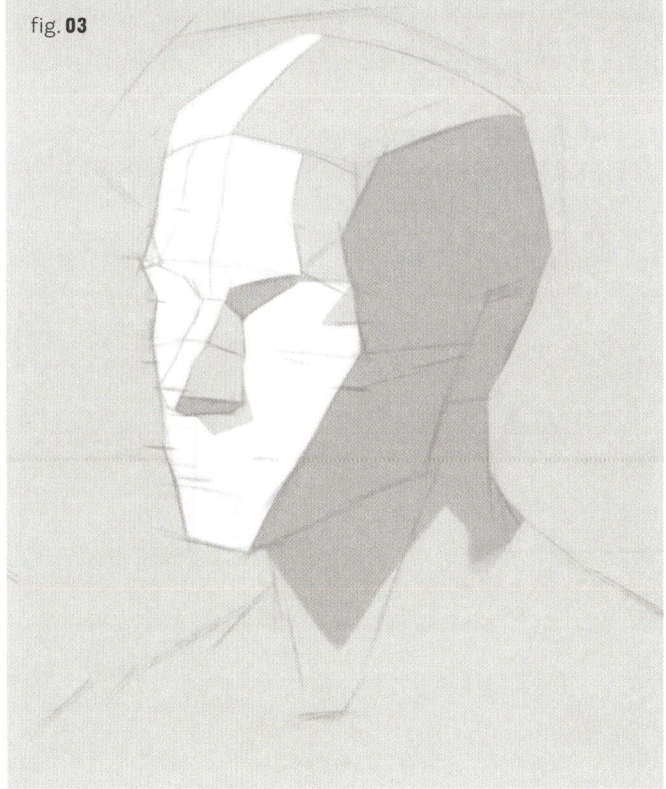

fig. 03

3D-FORM-BASED SIMPLIFICATION

By understanding your subject as a 3D form, you get a better grasp of how light will fall across it. We have already looked at a perfect geometrical sphere and visualized how light would create a bright spot, a transitional area, and a shadow. Now, let's apply this concept to a more complex subject – the human head. At first glance, the head is intricate and can be intimidating to draw. However, if you break it down into basic 3D forms, thinking of a face as a combination of flat planes, you can apply the same principles of lighting that you would to a single, simple sphere.

3D-form-based simplification is about looking at your subject as a set of simple three-dimensional forms instead of complex, organic structures. This approach enables you to think in terms of form and depth, setting the stage for a more volumetric representation.

In the first example (**fig. 01**) you can see a basic outline of a geometric shape; in this case, a hexagonal prism. It is a flat shape, and without context it would suggest nothing else. In the second stage (**fig. 02**) I have added three lines extending from the corners into the centre of the shape. These lines alone are enough to allow the pre-existing 2D shape to be read visually as a 3D form: a cube. This simple magic is at the heart of what structural drawing is all about; escaping the flatness of the paper. While it is not the only way, nor the only tool necessary, its immediate effect cannot be overstated.

In **fig. 02** I have also added 'vertex normals'. Normals, for short, are most commonly used by renderers to calculate the direction in which light reflects off a surface. For our purposes here, they are showing the direction the pieces of geometry are facing. That information, when combined with knowing the direction and quality of a light source, can be used to understand the values necessary to render a subject.

In the third example we have the cube itself (**fig. 03**). Well-lit and full of form, its visual properties serve to better illustrate the meaning of the first two examples. The value changes promised by the vertex normals are present along with a cast shadow extending outwards onto the otherwise unseen plane the cube rests upon. Taken as a group, these three designs represent the fundamentals of structural design.

When blocking-in a structural study of a head (**fig. 04**), understanding that the human form is structurally symmetrical can guide your simplification. You could start by envisioning the head as a sphere or rectangular cube with a vertical axis down the middle to represent the vertical centre line. Not only does this line help you to place the facial features in correct relation to one another, but it helps you to indicate the tilt and turn of the head as well.

Making any kind of study should involve some kind of evaluation of the observations made; some way to prove that the design arrived at bears a strong relationship to the subject. In the case of structural studies, this will involve the addition of some value. The ideal progression goes like this: design the form, observe the light direction and quality, and only then apply the values. By doing this, you're not just randomly adding dark and light areas to your drawing. You're applying a consistent logic of lighting based on a simplified 3D form. This makes the drawing feel more unified and believable, as each part is lit according to the same set of rules.

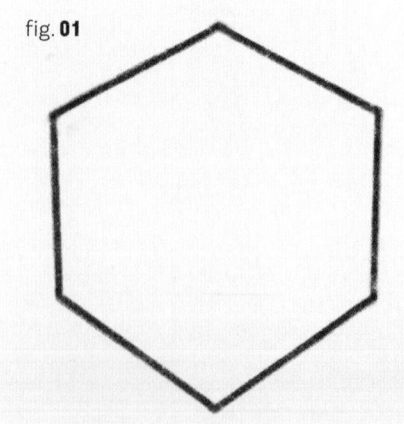

fig. **01**

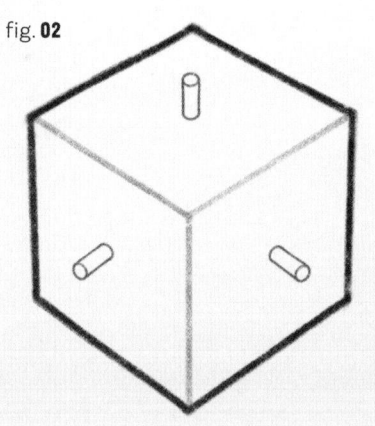

fig. **02**

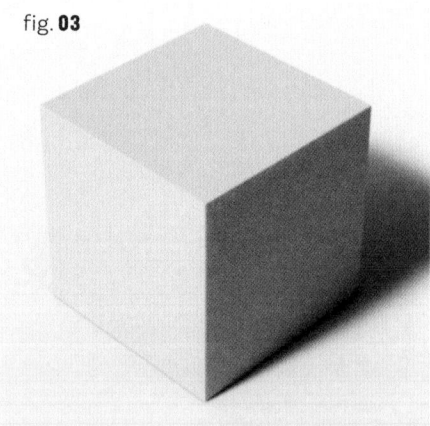

fig. **03**

fig. **04**

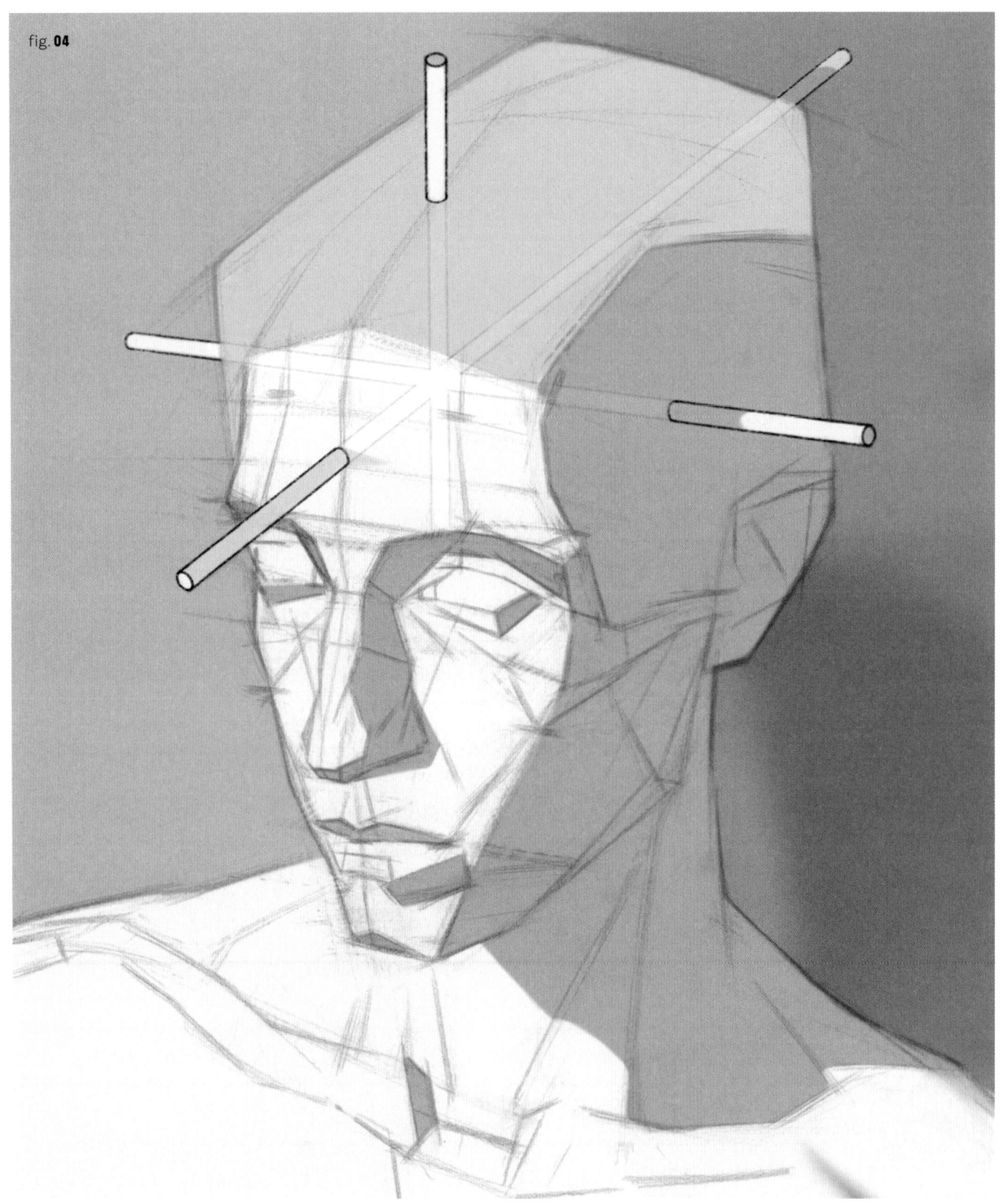

FLAT-SHAPE-BASED SIMPLIFICATION

Flat-shape-based design finds its most illustrative application in a drawing organized around the dichotomy of shadow shapes and light shapes. This method is akin to what Harold Speed refers to as 'mass drawing', where the emphasis lies in translating the complex visual information of your subject into unified, simplified value shapes. These simplified shapes serve as a foundational 'mosaic' upon which more nuanced details can later be superimposed.

How do we discern these shapes, you ask? In one way it is very simple: squint. It is, however, as much a mental exercise as a physical or visual one. One way or the other, remove the detail and reduce your subject to its simplest possible expression. Consider how you might simplify these everyday forms: a Christmas tree could be simplified into a triangle, a face into a basic oval with a squared-off jaw. Similarly, by focusing on patterns of light and shadow, individual facial features such as eyes, nose, and mouth cease to be intricate details and are reduced to basic value shapes, effectively contributing to the overall design and allowing for precise measurements.

The act of simplification helps us to identify key points and their spatial relationships, providing a form of visual shorthand that makes it easier to maintain proportionality. Flat shapes come into particular use in techniques like 'point-to-point measurement', where distances between specific points are compared to maintain proportional accuracy. The well-defined edges or 'angle breaks' in your flat shapes make this form of measurement more straightforward and accurate.

This approach, however, is not without its cautions. As Speed would argue, while it's important to unify the mass of your shapes, the process shouldn't compromise the visual coherence of your block-in. If you excessively simplify, pushing your flat shapes and angle breaks to an extreme, you risk losing the subtleties that bring life and depth to your work. The goal should be to maintain a harmonious balance between simplification and complexity, always considering the relationships between different values. This ensures that you are not merely filling in outlined shapes, but are building a unified, dynamic composition that adheres to the principles of good drawing.

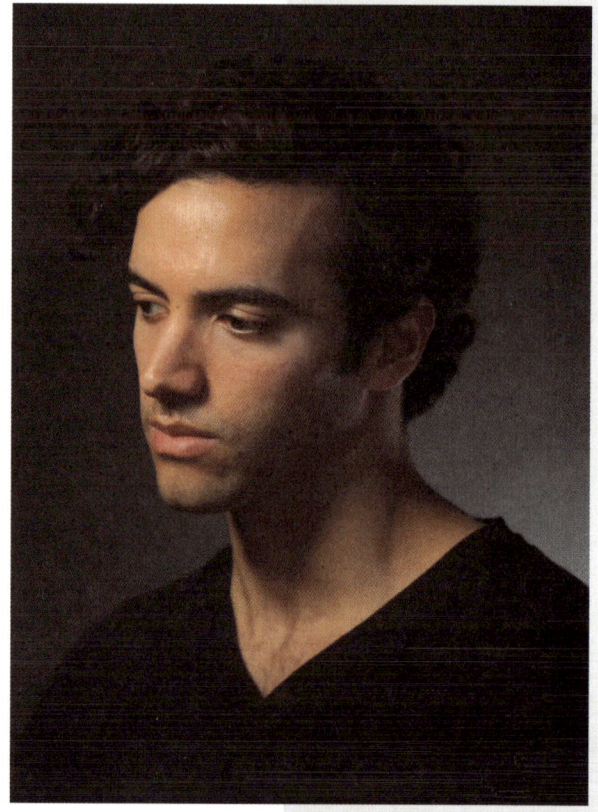

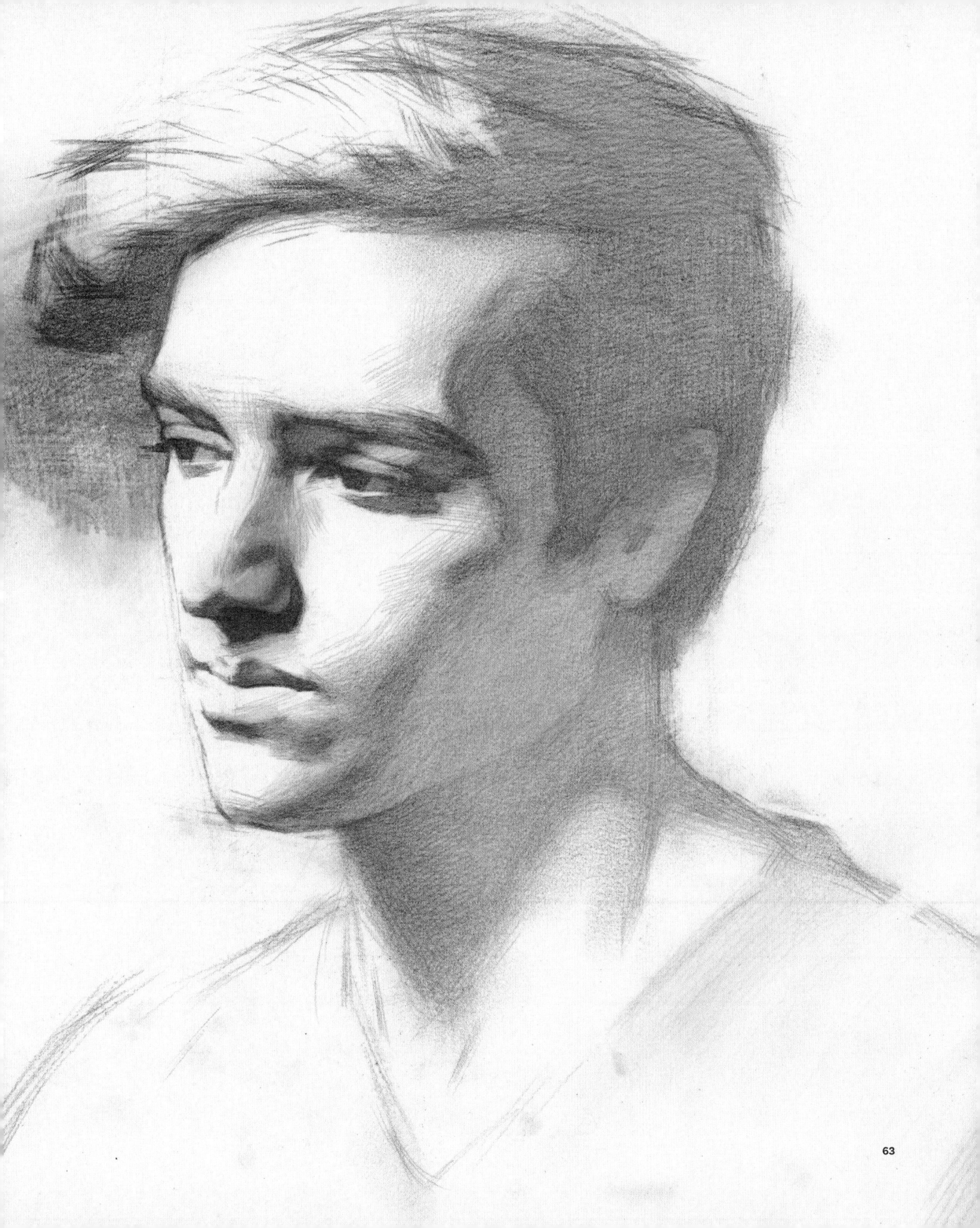

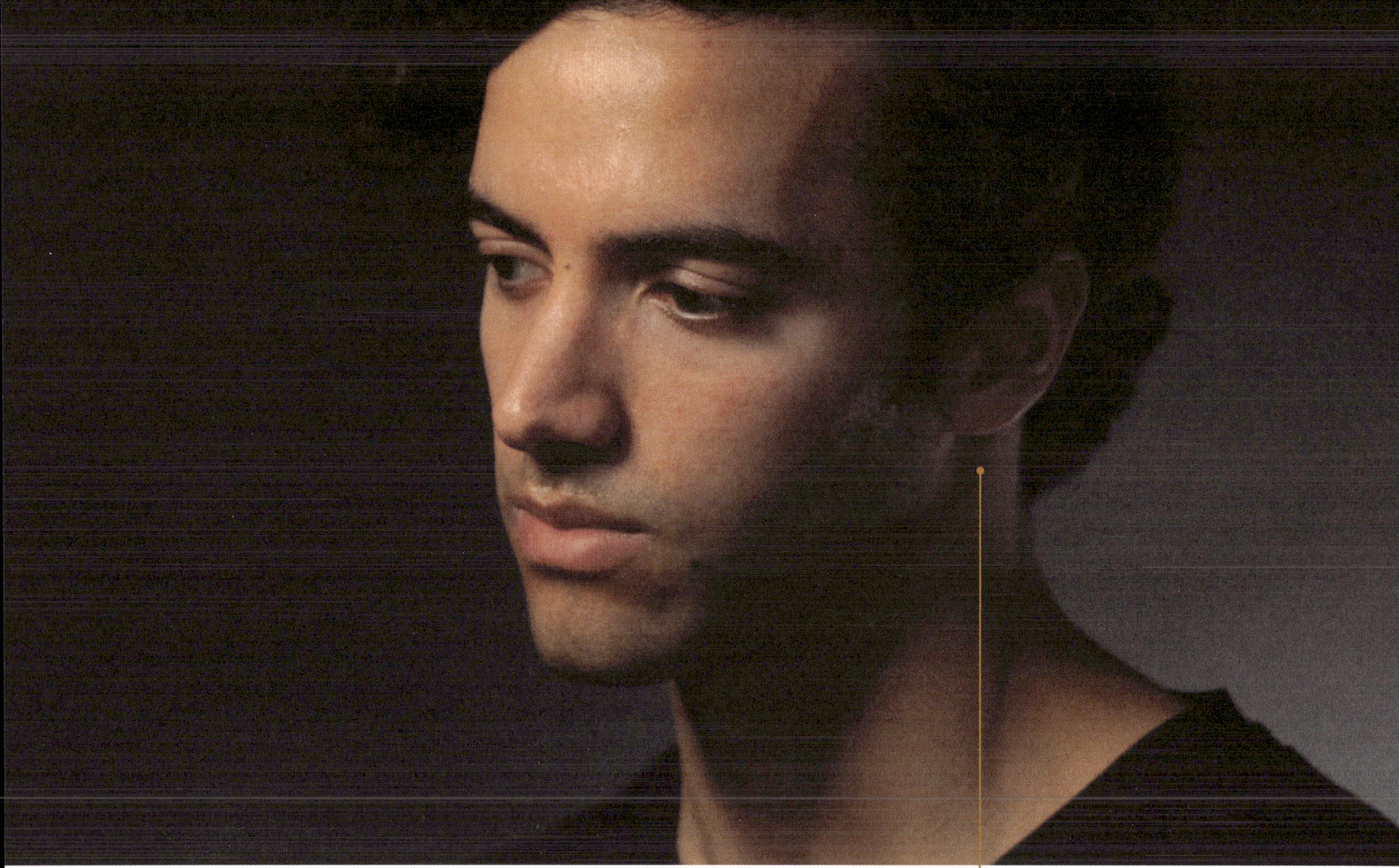

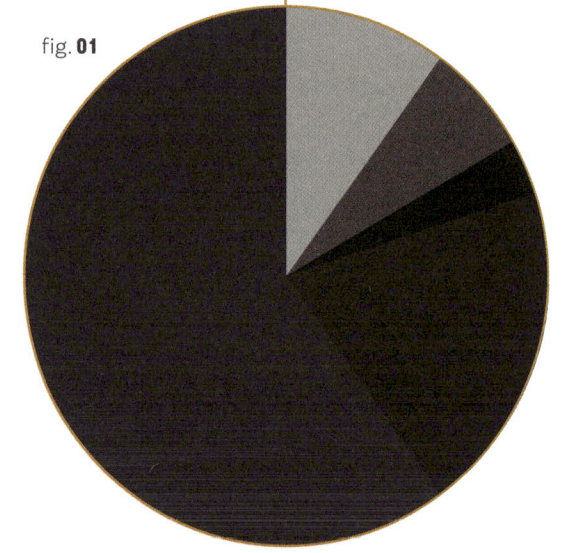

THE SIMPLIFICATION OF VALUES

fig. **01**

When beginning a drawing, starting with broad strokes and simplified values is crucial. This approach allows you to establish the primary shapes, overall proportion, and composition without getting bogged down in details. As seen in the examples provided (**figs. 01** and **02**), I have averaged out the values, particularly in shadowed areas.

The decision to unify values, especially in the shadow regions, ensures that you can distinguish the primary light source and the pattern of shadow and light it conveys upon the model. The darkest dark is quite light; in this case, his dark hair in shadow, showing that the value relationship between the drawing and the source image is a relative one. Because of this the light shape, primarily on the model's face, is almost totally unified.

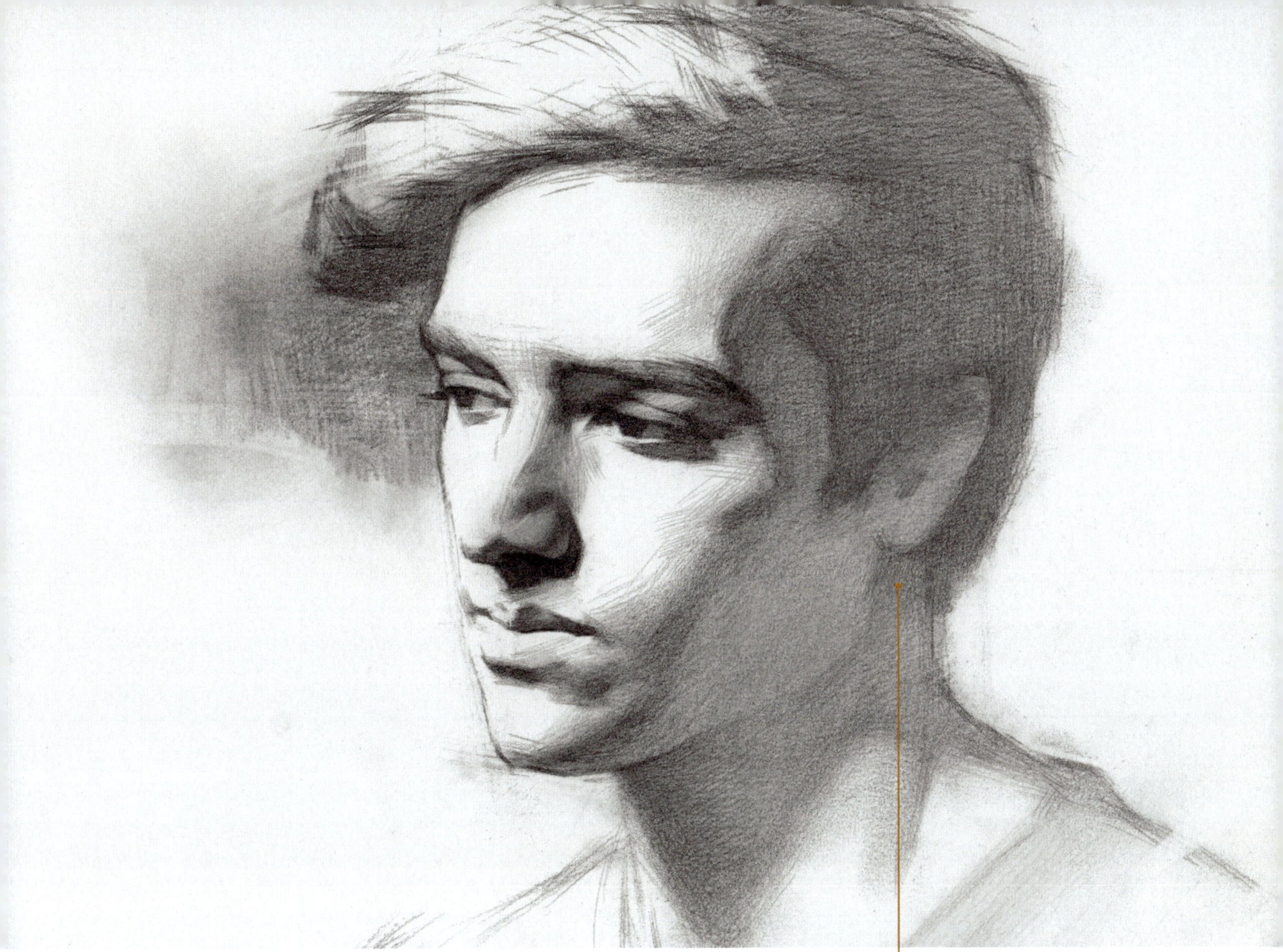

By breaking down the myriad tones seen in real life into three primary value groups – light, midtone, and dark – we more clearly see the essential components of the composition. This is the picture that will read from across the room, so to speak. These simplifications are what enable you to manifest the flat shapes needed to engage in the design process mentioned on the previous page.

Once the primary values are set and the composition is established, you can then decide where to introduce more nuanced values and details. This methodical layering ensures that the drawing retains its cohesiveness, while allowing for the introduction of intricate detail where necessary.

fig. **02**

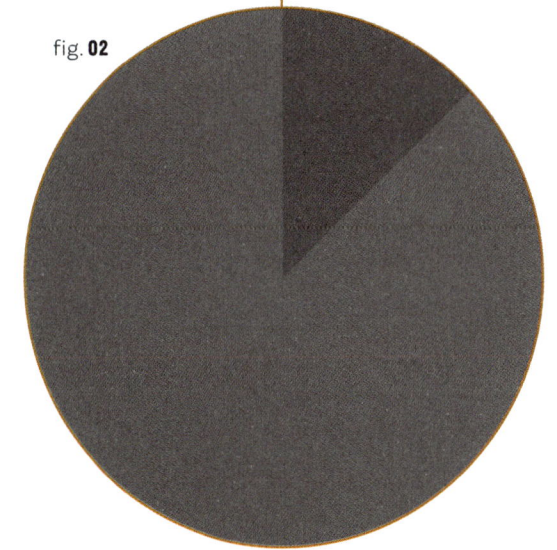

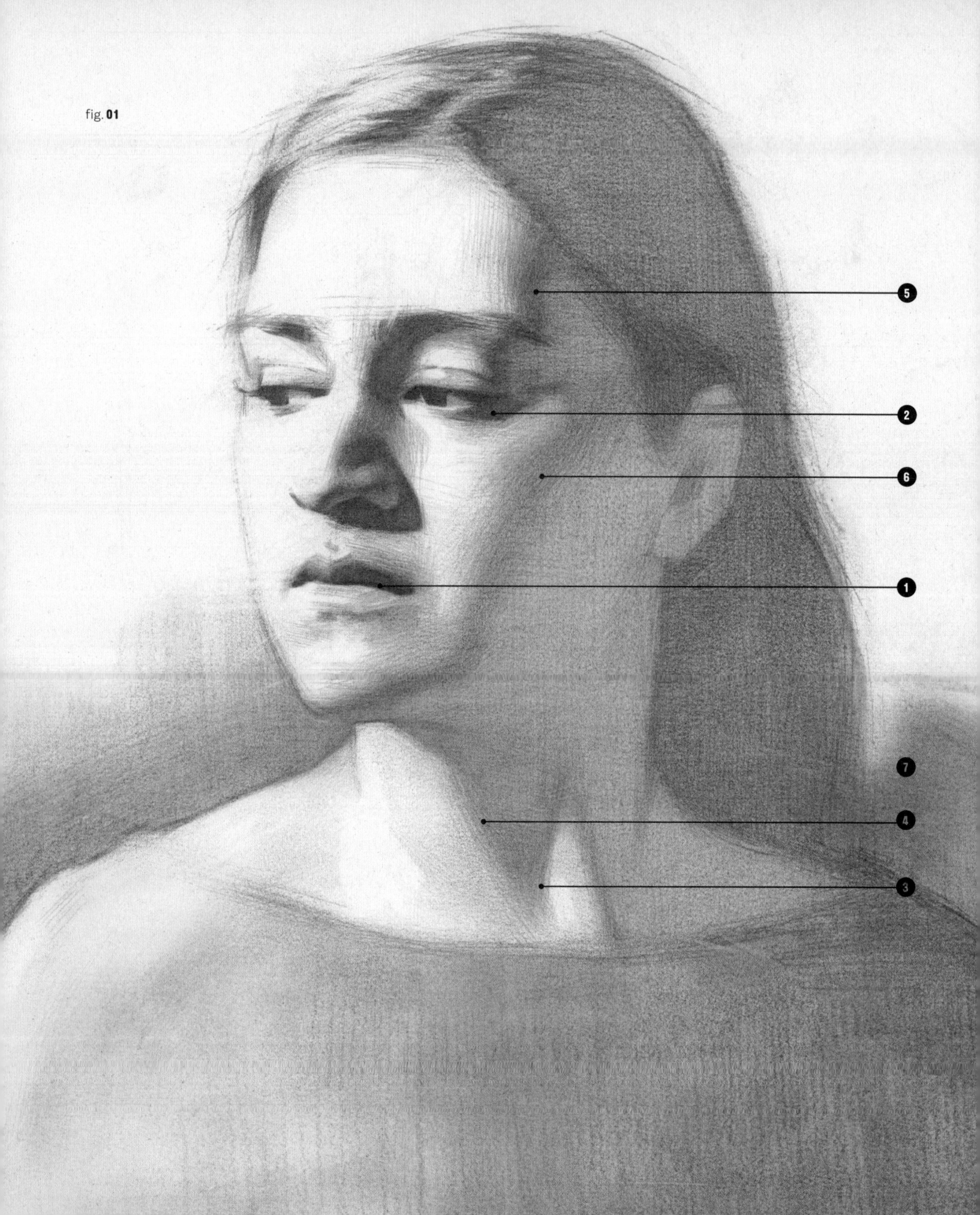

fig. **01**

fig. **02**

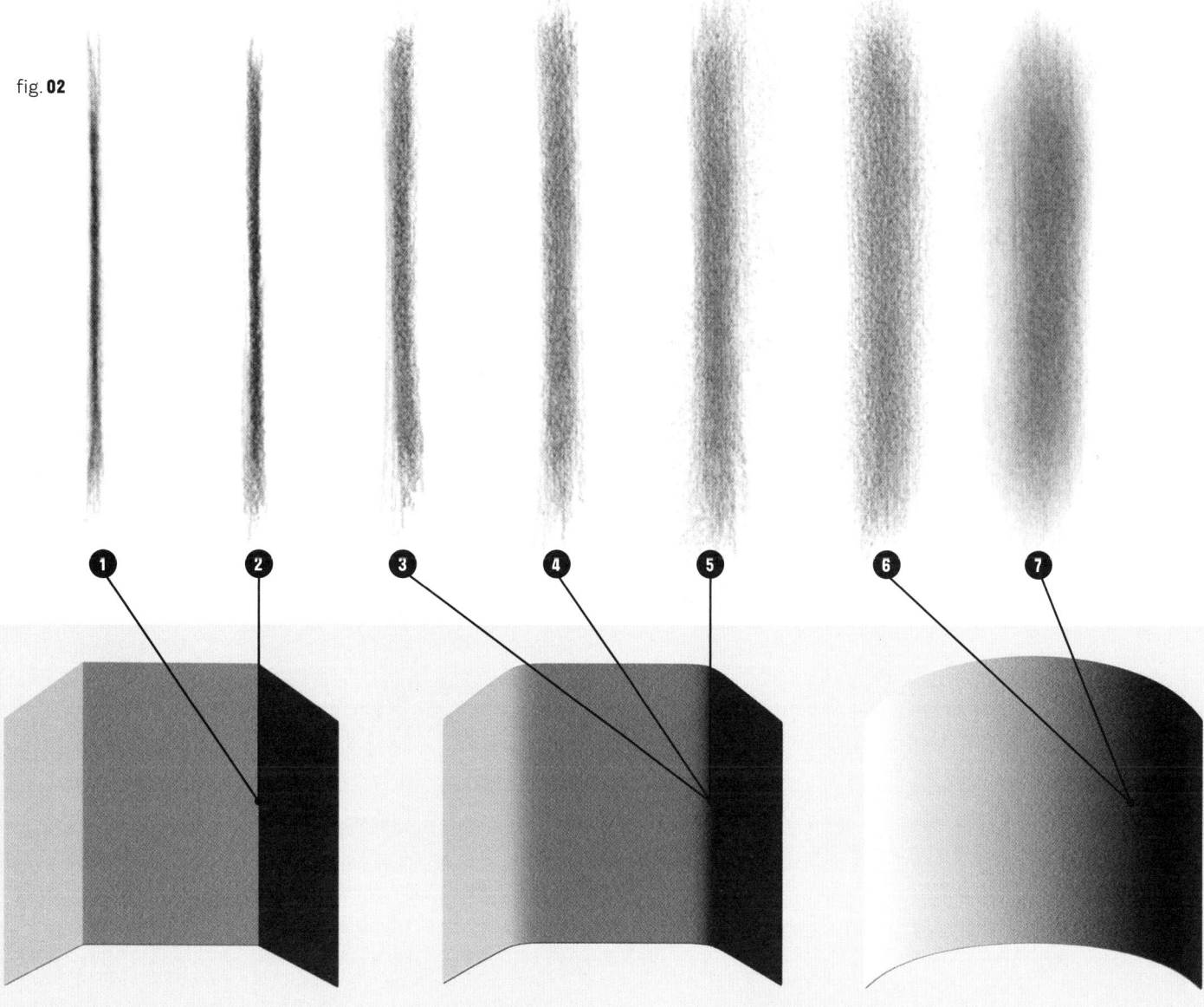

ORGANIZING AND KEYING EDGES

When we speak of organizing edges in portrait drawing, it refers to the thoughtful categorization of edges based on their varying degrees of softness or hardness. Edges are the boundaries that separate one shape or form from another. They can be rendered in line or as the boundaries of value shapes. They shouldn't be uniformly defined; some are sharp and crisp, while others are soft and diffused.

In these illustrations, you will find seven different edge designations. There can be many more or less depending on the needs of the project. **Fig. 01** shows the application of these edge types to an actual portrait drawing, while in **fig. 02**

we find a comparison between different edge types and the form types they can be used to represent.

In the context of a portrait, the edge around the outline of a nose, for example, may be sharp to indicate its prominence and solidity, while the transition between the light shape of the cheek and the ambient shadow could be softer to suggest roundness and subtlety of form. Rendering these edges accurately provides the opportunity to depict the anatomical structure, as well as indicate the 'speed' of a turning form. A hard edge may suggest certainty or boney-ness, while a soft edge might convey the volume of a thick muscle or fat pad.

Keying your edges takes the concept of edge organization a step further by prioritizing them in a hierarchy that serves your intent. This involves determining which edges are most critical for conveying an advancing form vs. a receding form, or drawing the viewer's attention and making those edges more defined, while allowing less important edges to be softer or even lost. This hierarchical arrangement lends a dynamic quality to the portrait, contributing to the overall sense of three-dimensional depth.

For example, in a portrait that aims to capture the essence of a person's character, rather than just their physical likeness, the eyes often hold the key. The artist might choose to 'key' the edges around the eyes with extra clarity and precision, thereby making them the focal point of the composition. Other edges, like those defining the hair or clothing, may be rendered more softly, providing a supportive role rather than stealing focus.

It's important to consider both organizing and keying edges as interrelated activities. Keying edges often requires a prior understanding of how edges are organized throughout the composition. The deliberate choice to soften or sharpen an edge should be dictated by the broader organizational logic that you have established.

John Singer Sargent was a master of edge control, particularly in his portraiture. He would often draw with broad, confident strokes, but would be meticulous in defining the edges that needed emphasis. For example, the eyes and lips in his portraits were often rendered with sharper edges, making them focal points, while the edges of clothing or backgrounds were softer. While Sargent was more of a practitioner than a teacher, his approach serves as posthumous advice on how to manage edges effectively.

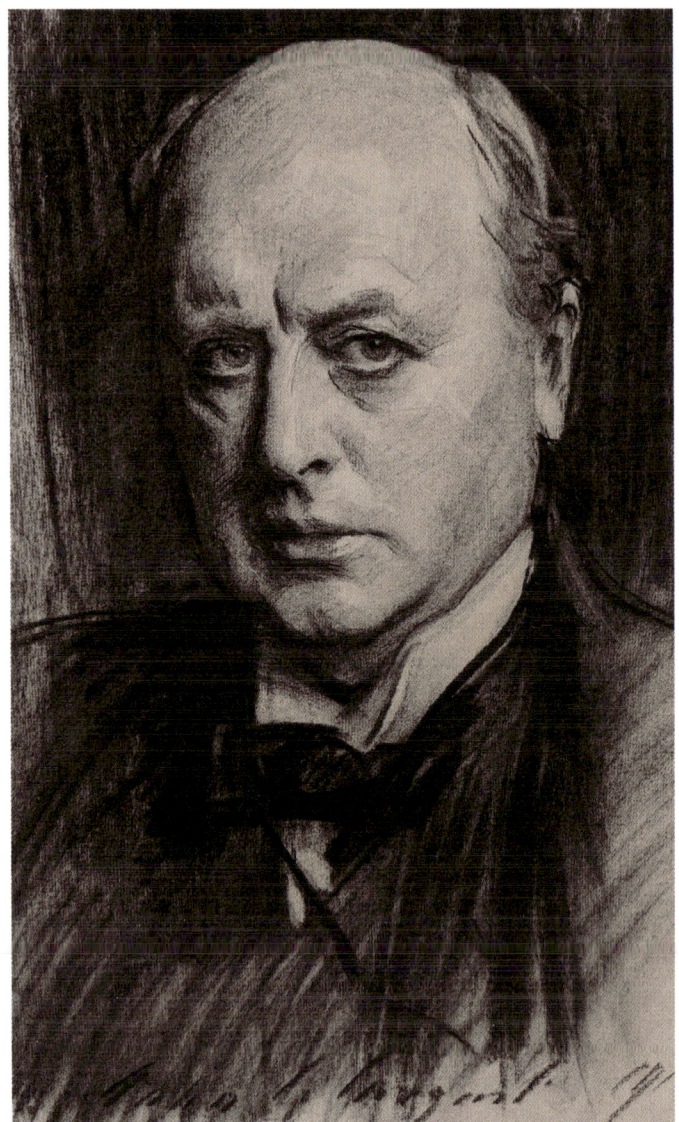

Henry James by John Singer Sargent

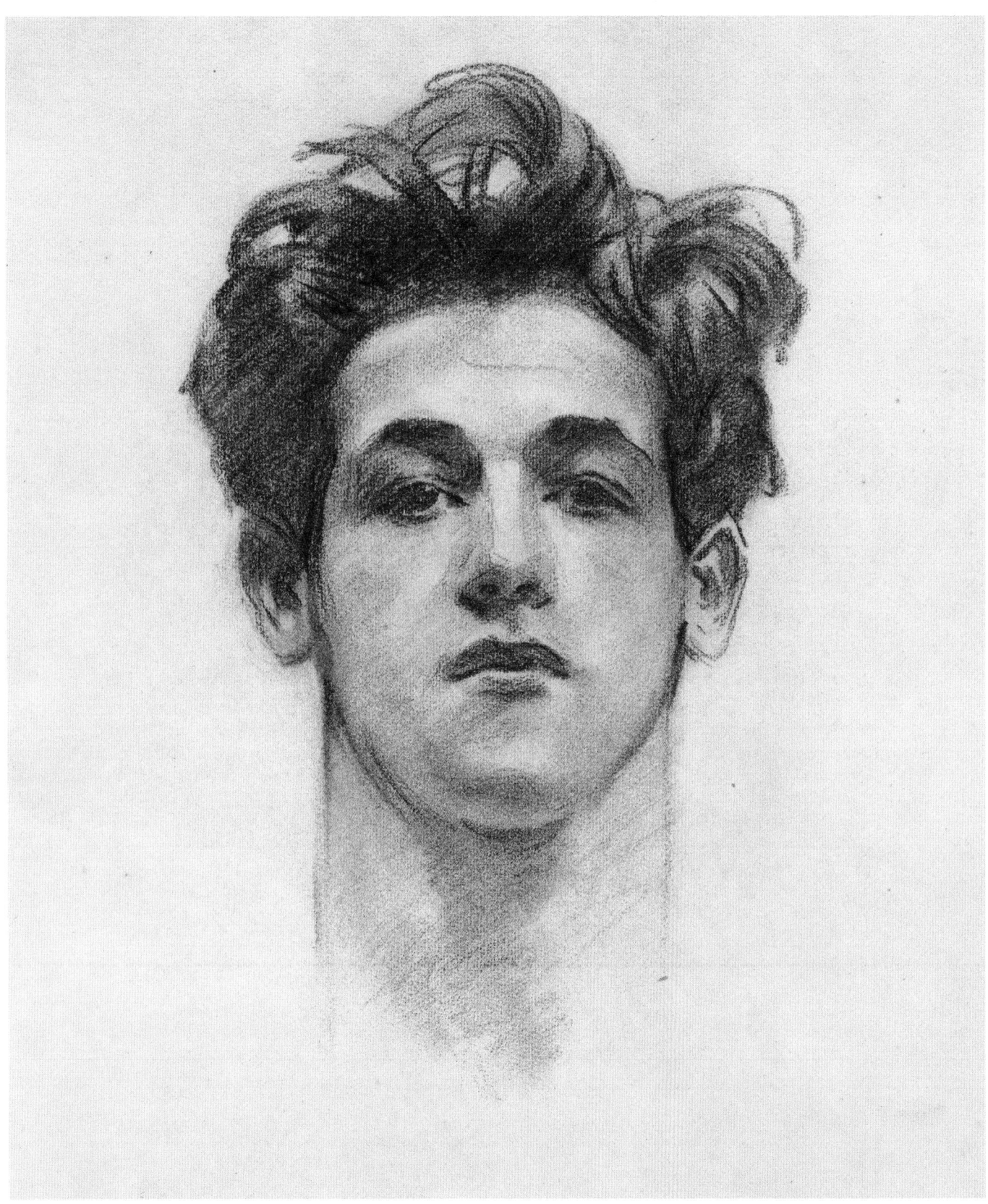

Olimpio Fusco by John Singer Sargent

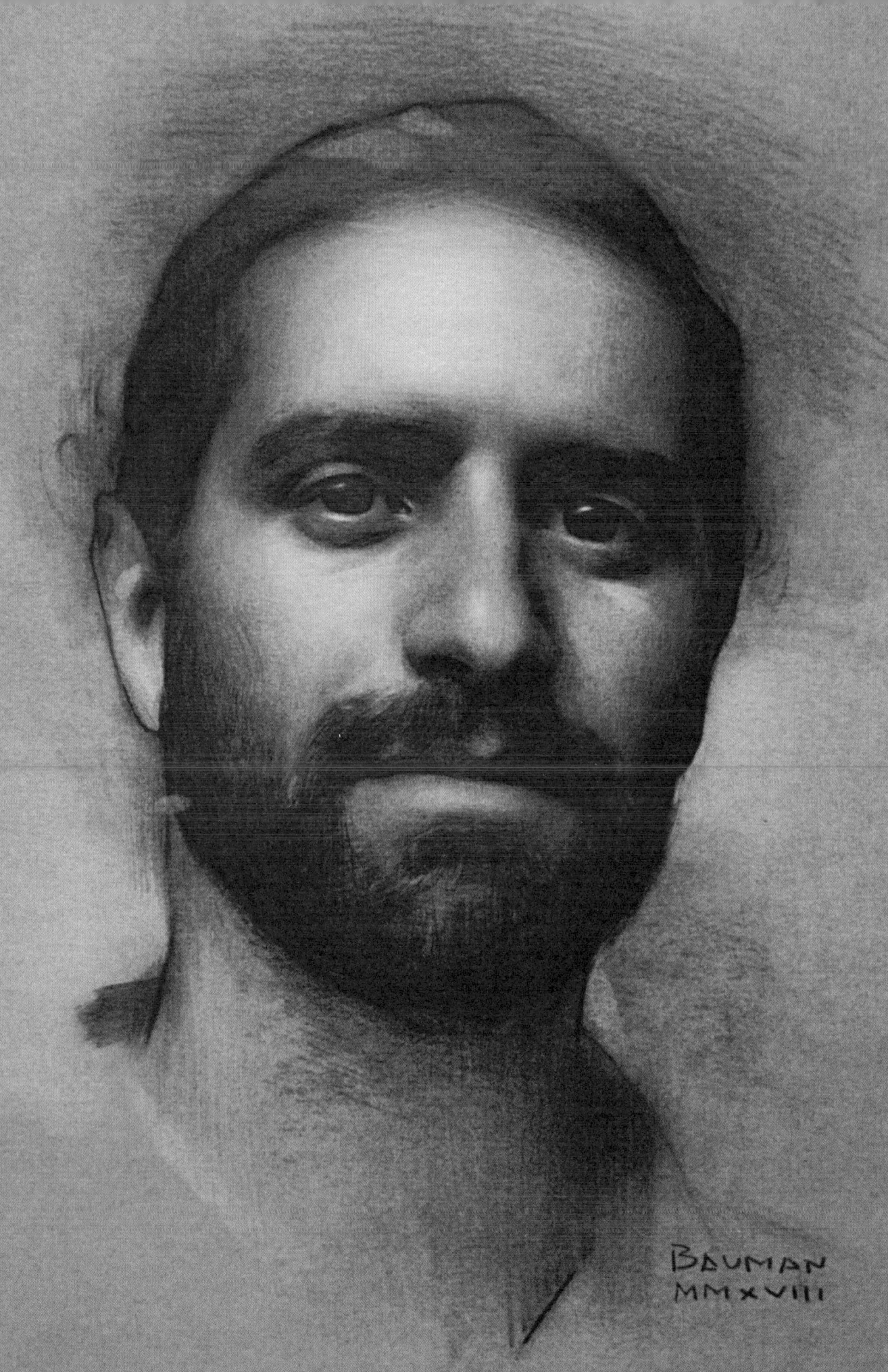

BAUMAN
MMXVIII

Visual memory

ALL DRAWING IS A VISUAL MEMORY EXERCISE, SO HOW DO WE REMEMBER?

Drawing, as an art form, is fundamentally the process of translating the three-dimensional world into a two-dimensional representation. This endeavour is as much a mental exercise as it is a physical one, requiring the artist to observe, recall, and interpret the myriad details of a visual reality. To enhance or supplement our visual memory in the service of drawing, three principal methods stand out: simplification, measurement, and memorization.

Simplification, which we explored in the previous chapter, helps the artist to see the world in terms of basic shapes and flat forms. Simplification is not a mere preliminary step but a strategy to distil complex visual information into its essence. By reducing a subject to its fundamental shapes and lines, the artist can better grasp and remember the core of what is seen, sidestepping the entanglement of superfluous detail. This process of abstraction aids in focusing on the overall composition and the interplay of value shapes.

Measurement is the second method. It involves the careful assessment of the distances and proportions that govern the subject. For the portrait artist, this could mean calculating the length of the nose in relationship to the width of the face from cheekbone to cheekbone. This quantitative approach offers a way to anchor one's observations in the objective metrics of the subject, providing a reliable foundation upon which to build.

The memorization of anatomical knowledge is the third method. Familiarity with the terms and structures of facial anatomy – the zygomatic arch, the nasolabial fold, the superciliary arch – lends precision to observation and memory. Naming is a powerful mnemonic device; it allows for specificity, enabling the artist to record each feature with accuracy and expressive detail. This anatomical lexicon, once committed to long-term memory, serves as a checklist, guiding the successful observation of each new subject.

Canonical head structures and templates also serve as valuable mnemonic aids. These templates, etched into the artist's memory through repeated practice, offer a consistent starting point for any portrait. They establish the general proportions quickly, providing a mental scaffolding for accurately placing the unique features of an individual.

In the forthcoming pages, we will first delve into two processes that will bolster your innate visual memory: comparative measurements and triangulation. These are 'academic observations' representing the systematic, learned techniques of recalling and applying visual data. In contrast, we will also explore 'naive observations', which depend more on intuition and unstructured perception – a raw, unfiltered way of seeing that can sometimes yield insights that the more structured academic approach might overlook.

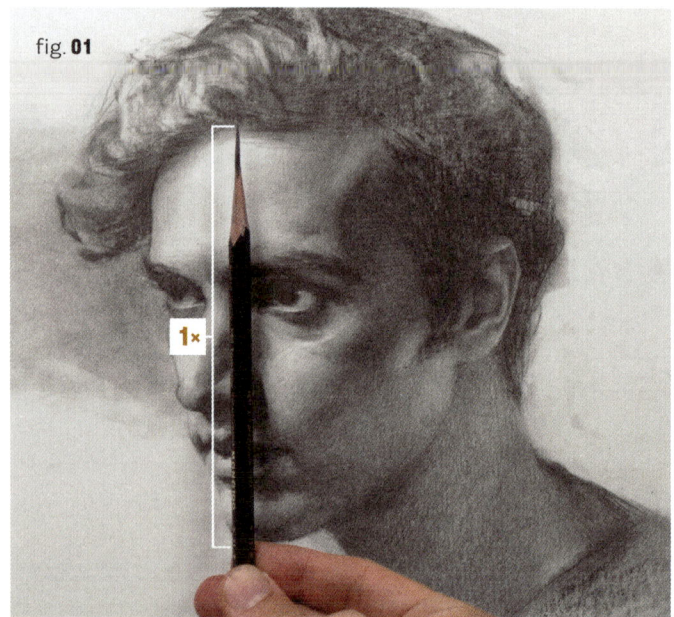

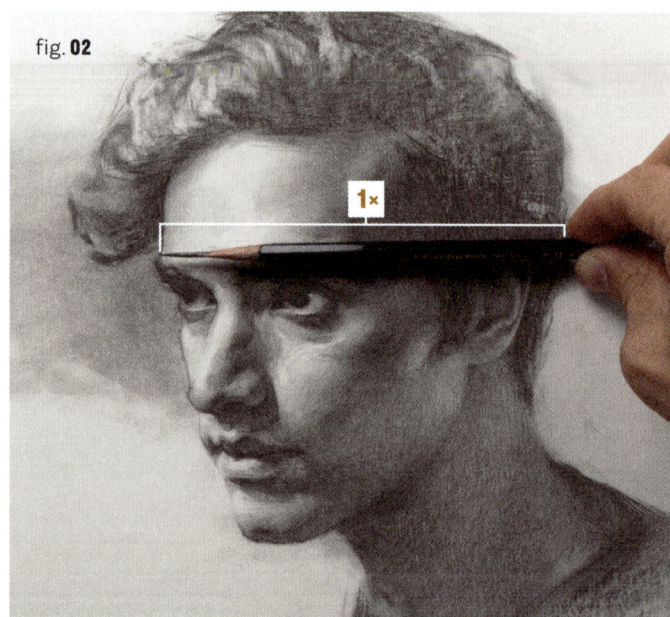

COMPARATIVE MEASUREMENTS

Comparative measurements involve using a consistent unit of measurement – a part of the subject's face or body, or the artist's thumb or pencil – to compare and establish the relative proportions of different elements within a composition. Essentially, it allows you to gauge the size, position, and alignment of one part of your subject in relation to others, thereby ensuring accuracy and coherence.

When you approach the blank paper, these measurements provide a structured approach to initiate your work, reducing the risk of errors that might demand laborious corrections later. As you add layers of complexity, filling in more details and refining the individual features, comparative measurements continue to serve a vital function. They act as an ongoing litmus test, helping you to maintain the proportional and structural integrity of the features.

The benefit of this practice extends beyond the fledgling stages of a portrait. Even when you are adding finishing touches to a piece or engaging in stylistic experimentations, comparative measurements offer a solid fail-safe against disproportionate distortions. They are the checks and balances in your process, allowing you to capture the likeness of your model with a higher degree of certainty.

The images above (**figs. 01** and **02**) show the comparison between the width of the head and its height. By finding the distance from the bottom of the chin to the apex of the light shape of the forehead, and comparing it to the overall width of the head, you can determine the correct relationship between these lengths. Ensuring that proportions like these are accurate is vital, as even slight discrepancies can significantly alter the likeness in a portrait. It is large measurements like this that, in my experience, are most difficult for our eyes to 'remember' without help.

In the image to the right (**fig. 03**), you can see how to select an individual feature to become a unit of measurement, in this case the height of the forehead from brow ridge to hairline, using a pencil. By aligning the top of the pencil with the starting point of the measurement and noting where the feature ends in relation to the pencil's length, you can transfer this measurement to other parts of the face or to the drawing itself. This ensures that the nose's length is depicted in correct proportion to other facial features.

In practising this, it is most useful to decide early on in your drawing process what you will use as a de facto 'point of truth'. The point of truth refers to a length or height you will use as a standard distance when refining other distances throughout the drawing. This convention ensures that you are not changing all of your proportions in relationship to all of your other proportions. Put simply, you are establishing this distance as a constant.

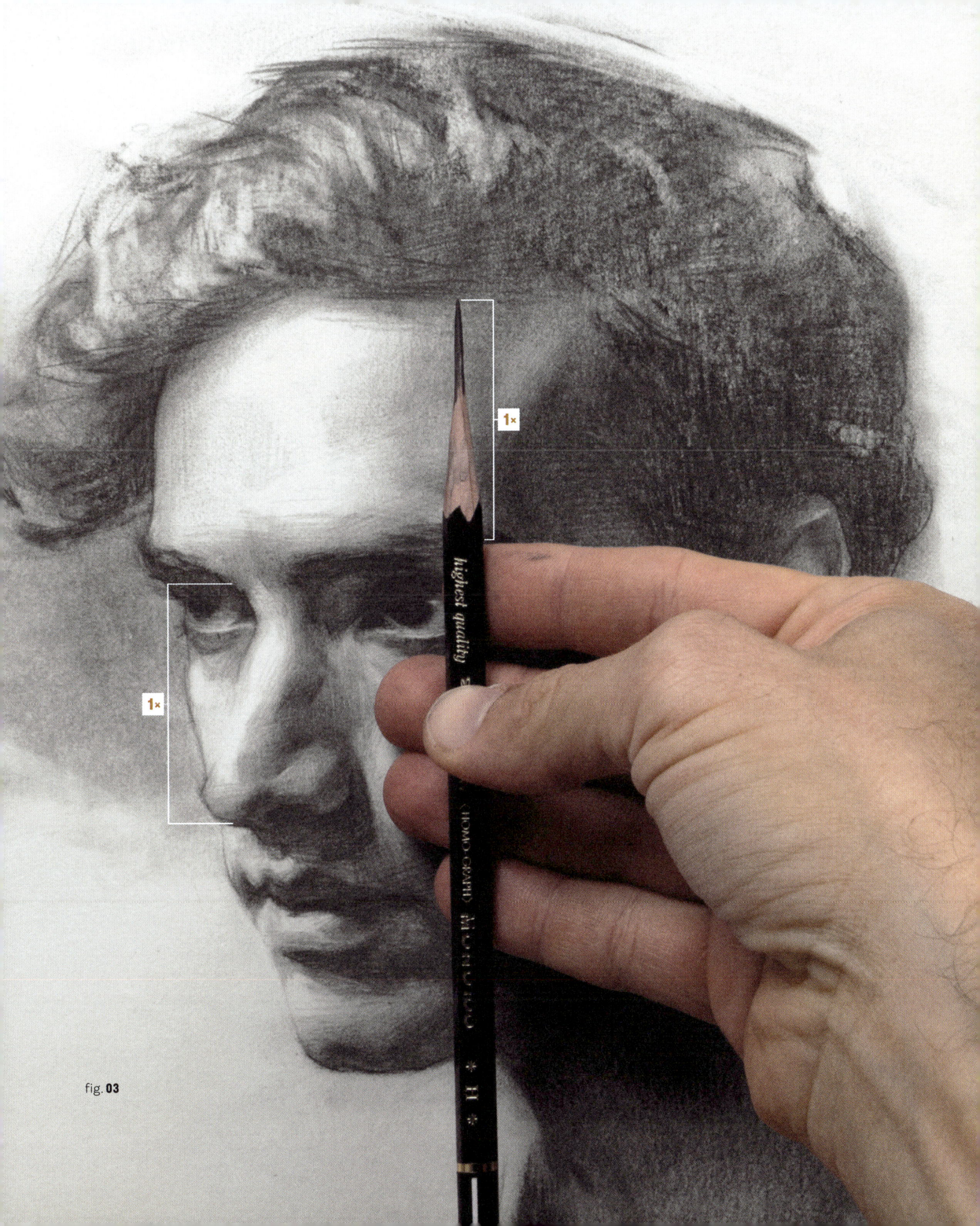

fig. 03

fig. **01**

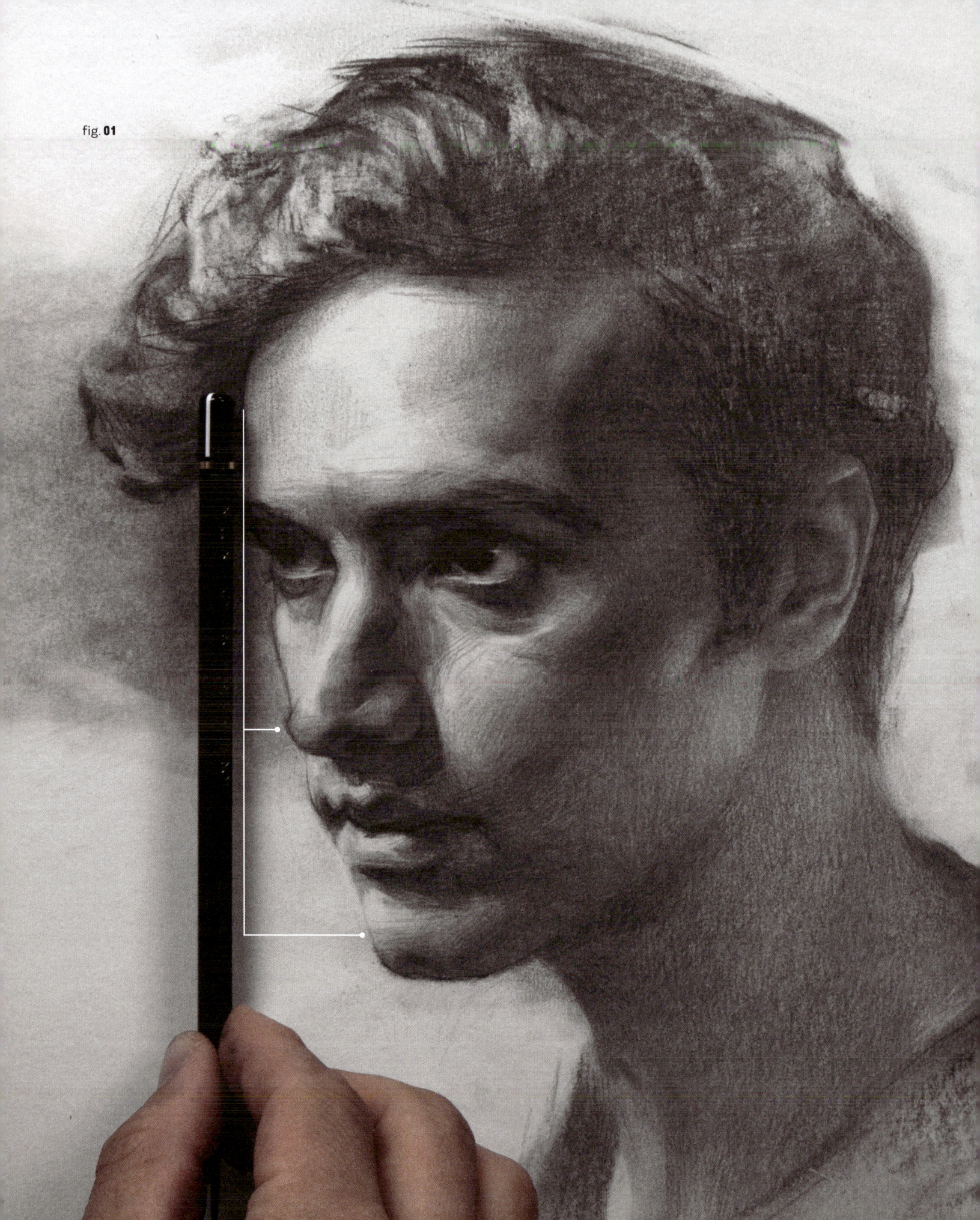

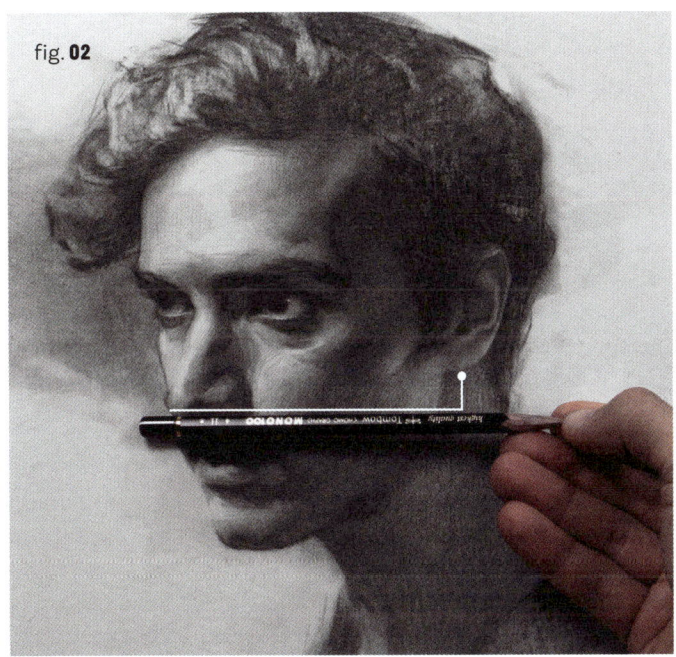

fig. **02**

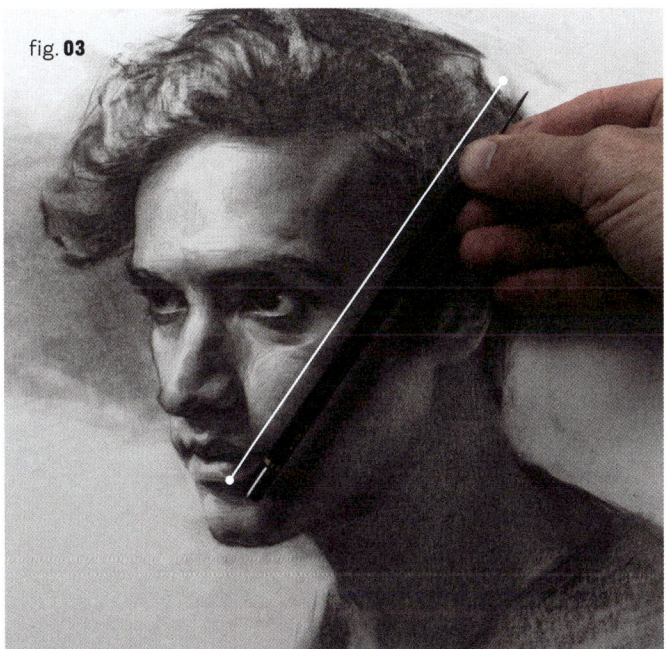

fig. **03**

TRIANGULATION

Triangulation in this context is about harnessing one's tool, often the edge of a pencil, as a visual axis or guide, enabling the artist to measure and relate various points on the face.

The utility of triangulation lies in the establishment of a visual grid, using the pencil's edge as a steady axis. This axis helps the artist ascertain spatial relationships between essential facial landmarks, ensuring that each feature maintains its correct proportion and position. In **fig. 01**, the pencil aligns with the subject's facial contour, indicating three pivotal points: the edge of the forehead, tip of the nose, and base of the chin. This alignment is meant to serve as a visual guideline, helping to judge distances and relationships between these features.

The pencil, in this case, becomes a transitive element – a tool not just for making marks on the canvas, but for understanding the spatial relationships between those marks. The triangulation method has the added benefit of being a dynamic system; that is to say, additional points can be integrated into the existing grid to further refine the drawing. One may extend the line from the eye to the nose and envision a third point, perhaps at the corner of the mouth or the apex of the forehead. These multi-point relationships form a network of points, each aiding in the accurate placement of the next feature, ensuring that every element is in harmonious proportion to its neighbours.

This process of triangulation is not a new concept; indeed, its use goes back to ancient principles of geometry and has been discussed in treatises on art for centuries. Artists such as Albrecht Dürer emphasized the importance of mathematical relationships in art, a notion that has been echoed in various teaching methods through history.

It should be noted, however, that while the straight edge of a pencil facilitates a certain precision, it is just a guide. The ultimate objective is not mechanistic reproduction, but rather, the cultivation of a keen eye that can intuit these relationships even when the pencil is set aside. Hence, triangulation serves as both a practical tool and a form of training, aligning the artist's faculties with the principles of proportion and balance.

In the images above (**figs. 02** and **03**), we can see on the left an example of how to use triangulation between two points on a horizontal axis. In this case, the bottom plane of the nose, where it meets the front plane of the face, and bottom edge of the earlobe. On the right, a final-use case-angle comparison. Much like triangulation, this method of comparison involves an axis between two significant points. The degree of angle between the two points can vary in any variety you find useful. Simply find the angle with your pencil on your source image or model, and shift that angle to compare on your drawing surface.

fig. 01

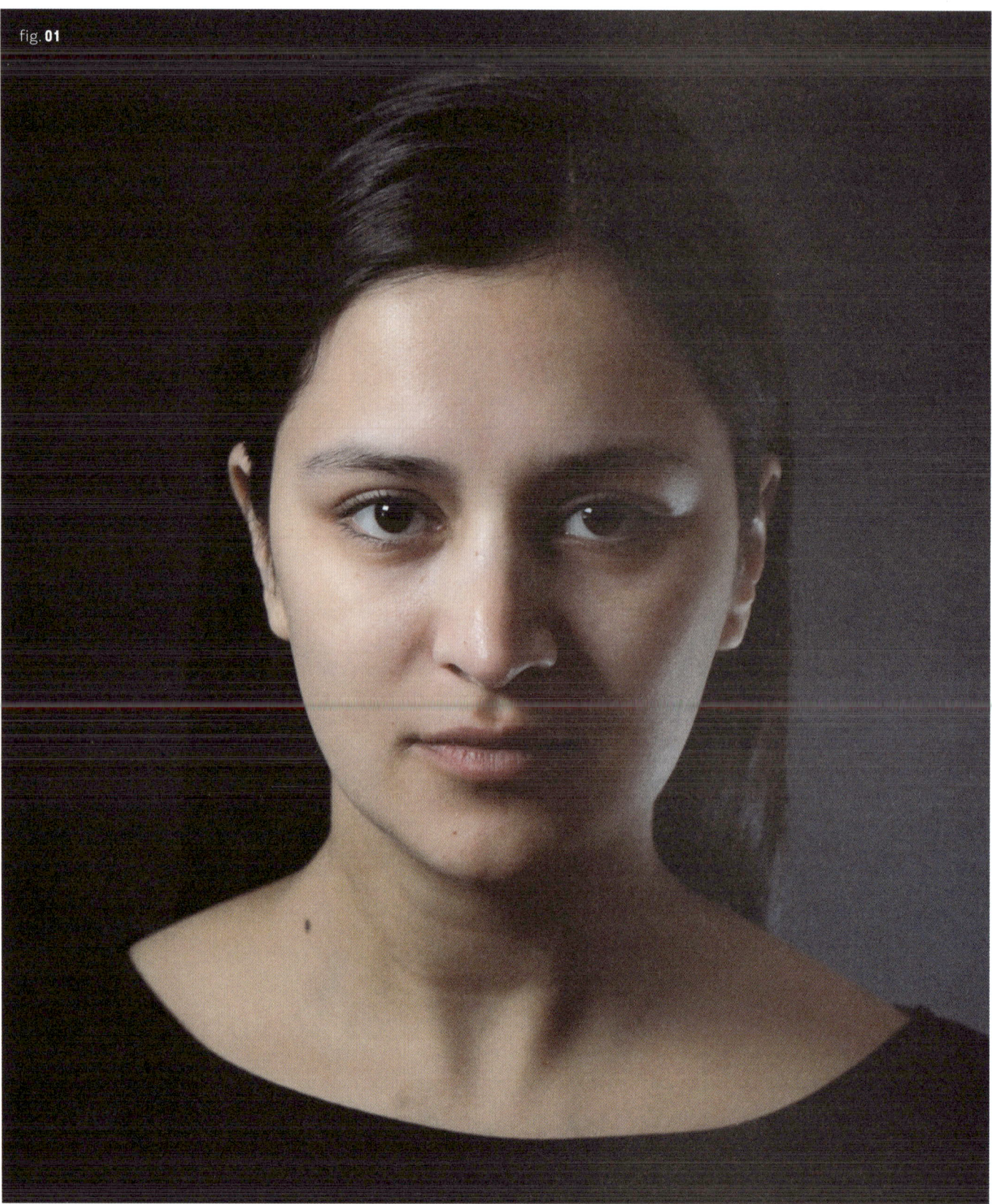

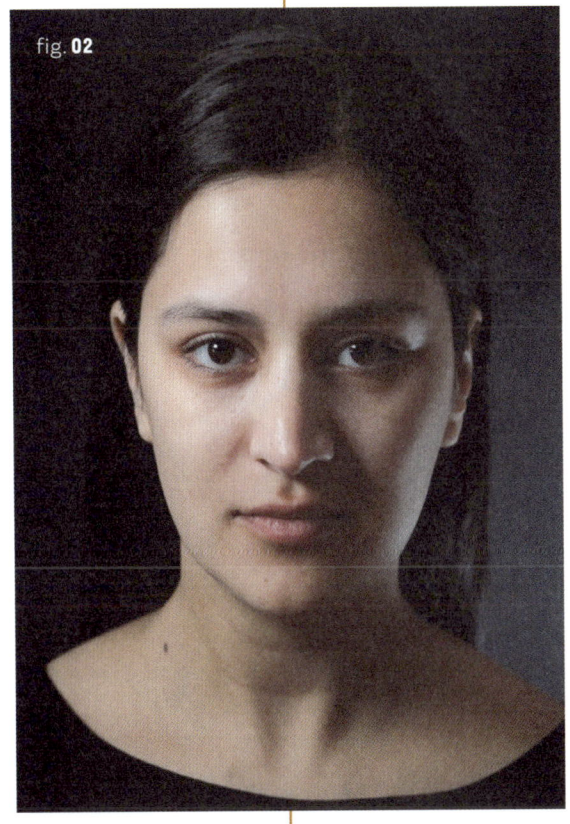

fig. 02

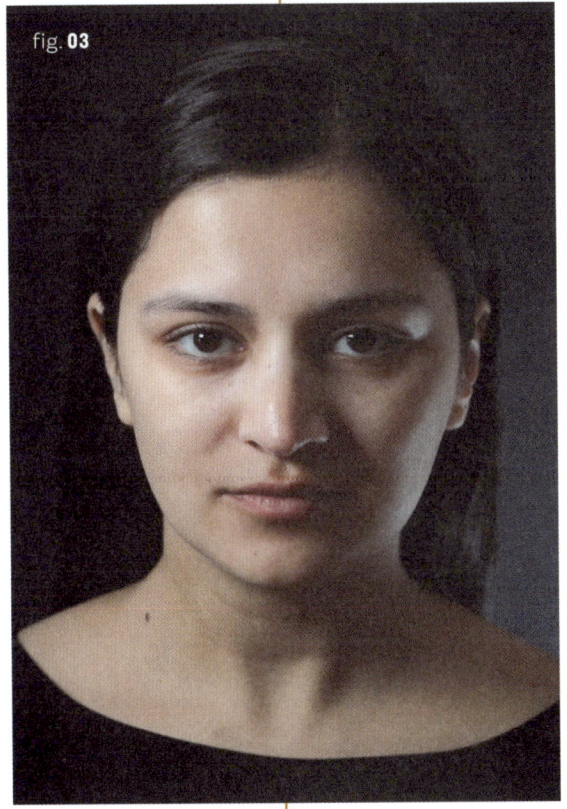

fig. 03

NAIVE RECOGNITION

In the discourse of representational drawing, emphasis is often placed on the structured methodologies of geometric precision that we have already discussed: comparative measurement and triangulation. However, there exists an alternate method, often considered opposed to the methods above, yet entirely complementary. I refer to the alternative as 'naive recognition'. This approach deviates from the strict angular relationships and proportions, and relies instead on an organic, intuitive comparison between the drawn image and the model. The essence is the idea that the closer the drawing approximates the model at any given stage, the easier it becomes to spot differences and adjust them.

Naive recognition depends on a keen sensitivity to what is laid down on the paper, which must be cultivated through a healthy process of simplification. The drawing becomes a mirror of sorts, reflecting not only the model but also the accumulated errors and misjudgements in perception. By contrasting the existing marks on the paper to the subject being drawn, you begin a cycle of perpetual self-correction. Leonardo da Vinci's advice to occasionally view a drawing through a mirror can be understood as an early expression of this method – a way to defamiliarize oneself with the drawing to better recognize its divergences from the model. It's for this reason, in fact, that having a small handheld mirror at your easel is highly advisable for use in checking proportions and general likeness.

This form of observation could be viewed as a marriage between empiricism and intuition. Your eye flits back and forth between the drawing and the model, utilizing the drawing itself as a sort of yardstick for accuracy. One adjusts the lines and tones on the paper in constant relation to the evolving observation of the subject.

It should be noted that naive recognition comes with its own set of caveats. Unlike the systematic approach of triangulation, which can be set down in a series of learnable steps, naive recognition is nebulous and less tangible as a method. It relies heavily on the artist's accrued experience and innate ability to compare and contrast visual elements, which can make it a challenging approach for the novice. Put simply, the closer the drawing looks to the subject, the easier the comparison, meaning it tends to work best at the end of the drawing process, which naturally contains more recognizable details. The trick to unlock its greatest usefulness is to have a recognizable enough block-in that it is easily comparable to your model.

Comparing **fig. 01** to **figs. 02** and **03**, it is possible to immediately notice proportional differences between the model as she is seen in each image. These differences can be observed without any measurement devices or techniques, simply by addressing them with a cursory glance. In a drawing scenario, individual features like the nose or eye socket should be assessed for these same proportional differences.

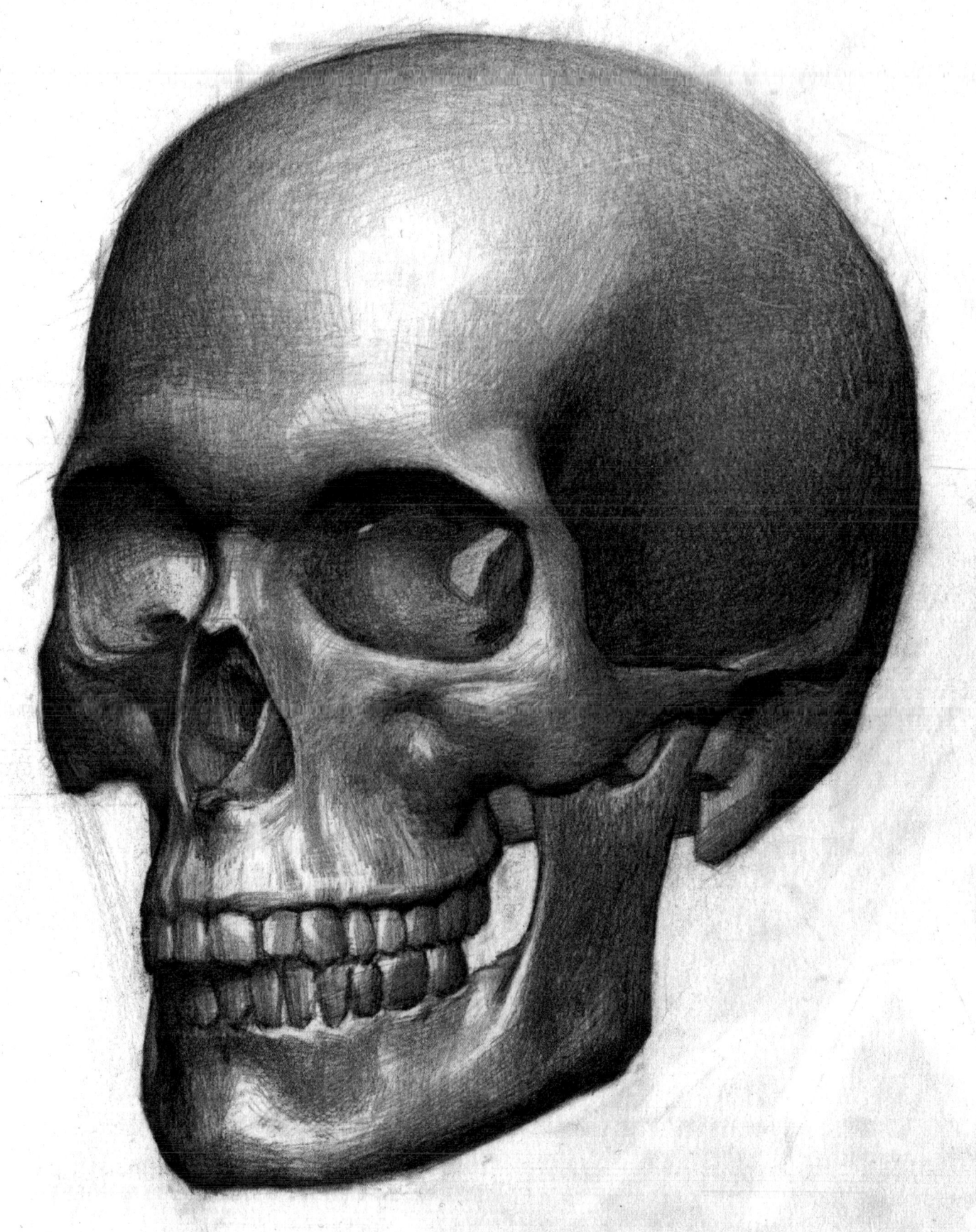

Anatomy

The study of anatomy for the artist is a specialized pursuit, markedly different from its exploration in scientific or medical contexts. Whereas for a physician the anatomical knowledge serves primarily diagnostic and therapeutic purposes, for the artist, anatomy is not an end in itself, but a means to achieve greater sensitivity in representation. The anatomical understanding must be so internalized that it manifests 'in your hands', finding its concrete expression in your drawings. In this vein, our inquiry into human anatomy is particularly tailored to its application in drawing.

The wealth of information on human anatomy is vast, but for the objectives of portraiture, it is not necessary to become encyclopaedic. Of the available information in this area, I have selected with great care only the most significant and useful features. Muscles like the sternocleidomastoid or the masseter, and bony features such as the zygomatic arch and the mandible – these are some of the key elements that most significantly influence the surface forms of the head. When these anatomical landmarks are deeply understood, they serve as guideposts in the drawing process. For example, the placement of the eye is often more accurately captured when one understands the bony structure of the eye socket in the skull.

Moreover, different anatomical features contribute to various stages of the drawing. Take the skull, for instance. While its underlying shape might not be visible except for a few places in a finished portrait, it plays an indispensable role in the initial 'block-in' stage. Understanding the basic form of the skull can guide the artist in establishing the foundational shapes and proportions that will later be refined into a nuanced portrait.

Artistic anatomy, then, becomes a twofold endeavour: it is an academic subject to be studied, yes, but more importantly, it is a practical skill to be honed. It involves not just the memorization of names and forms, but their active application in the medium of choice. In the section that follows, we will proceed with the specific aim of distilling this complex subject into its most essential elements, those that will visibly and directly impact the quality of a portrait drawing. The aim is not merely to know anatomy, but to wield it as a tool for better drawing, allowing you to imbue your work with both technical rigour and expressive depth.

Lastly, I want to mention what anatomy will mean to you in your pursuit of getting better at drawing. It is not a cheat code. Alone, it will not allow you to effortlessly construct the human body on paper. In fact, without learning first the basics of drawing, the quality of the drawings you produce will not noticeably improve through anatomical study. However, coupled with basic drawing skills, an understanding of anatomy will provide you with an infinitely useful tool. You will be able to truly understand the forms and values that you're drawing. You will be able to manoeuvre between abstract construction and a soft but specific visual statement. In short, you will have the key to true specificity in drawing.

fig. **01**

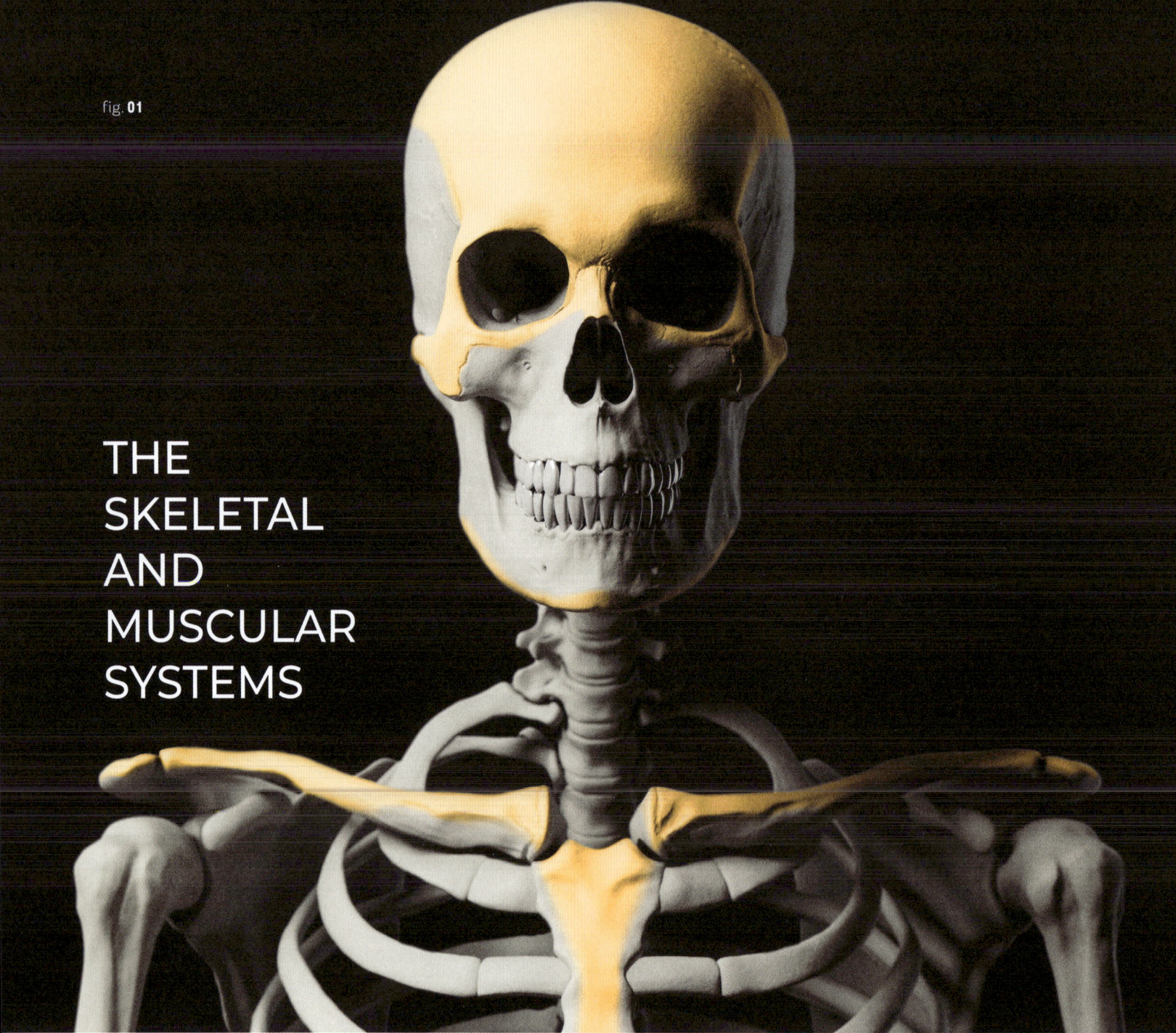

THE
SKELETAL
AND
MUSCULAR
SYSTEMS

The scaffold upon which the entire body is constructed can be broadly divided into two core systems: the skeletal (**fig. 01**) and the muscular (**fig. 02**). The skeletal system provides an armature, while the muscular system, as it is attached to the skeleton, provides the body with a mechanism for animation. When we examine illustrations of these anatomical features, they are frequently depicted in the 'standard anatomical position', as shown here – a pose that offers a consistent and comparative baseline from which to study the human form.

Understanding the relationship between a muscle's points of origin and insertion is also useful. These connections represent the boundaries of that muscular form. So, in cases where we might not see the skeleton, it may still be making a noteworthy impact on the surface form. Therefore, it's not enough to study only what is superficially visible; you must also interpret the unseen structural elements that give rise to the visible form.

fig. **02**

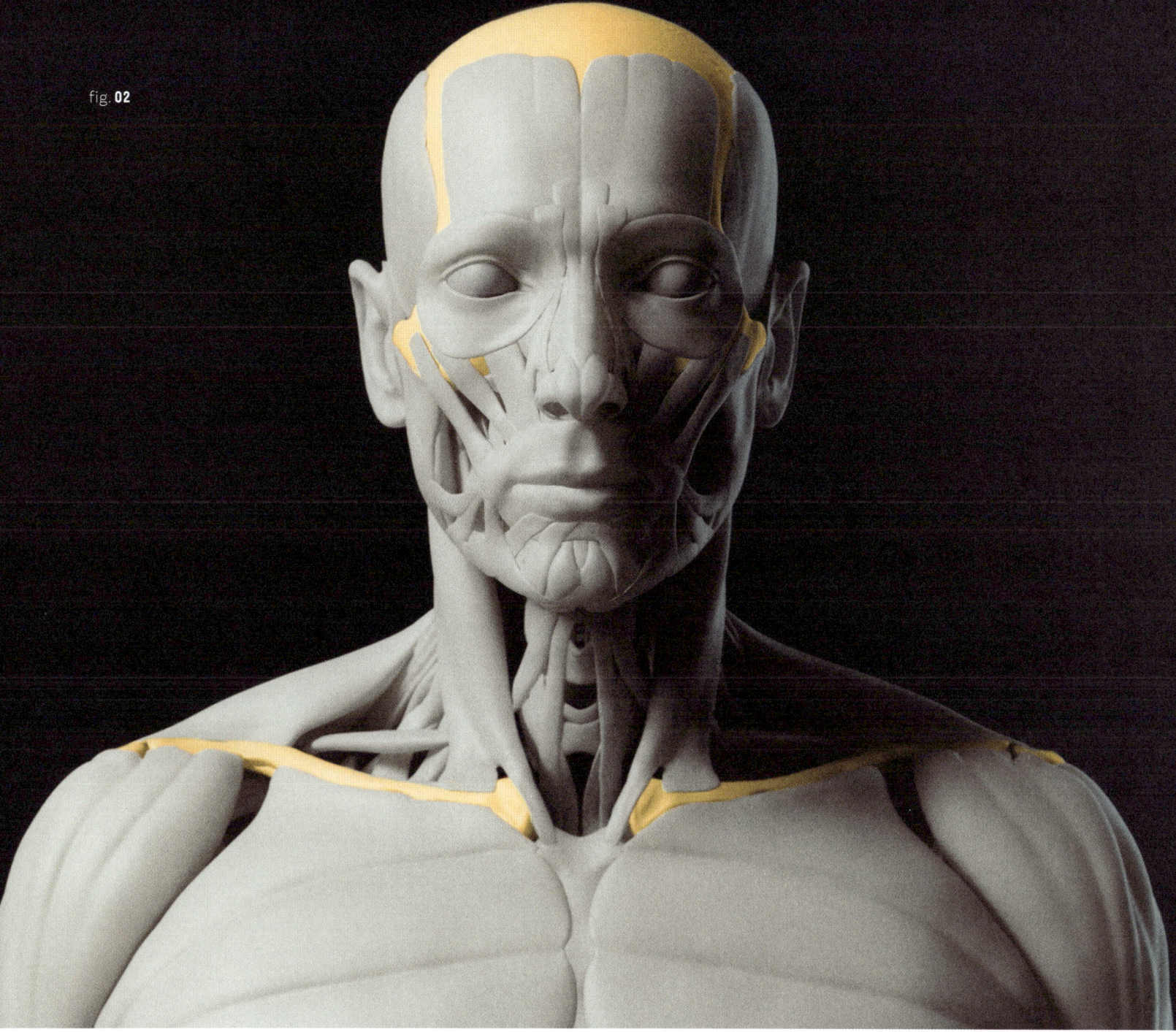

Furthermore, the concept of subcutaneous bony points is a significant one. These are areas (highlighted in **yellow** above) where the bone lies in close proximity to the skin, offering little padding from muscular or fatty tissue. Such points – like the forehead, zygomatic bones, and the mental protuberance – serve as invaluable landmarks. George Bridgman, an influential teacher, emphasized the importance of these anatomical landmarks as a means to measure proportion and establish spatial relationships within the composition.

When applied to drawing, anatomical knowledge functions more like a compass than a map. What is portrayed in medical diagrams, designed explicitly for the detailed exposition of anatomical structures, may appear starkly different when observed 'in the living'. The human form in life presents a more fluid, dynamic interplay of these systems, a nuance that the artist must decipher if they are to usefully apply their hard-won anatomical knowledge.

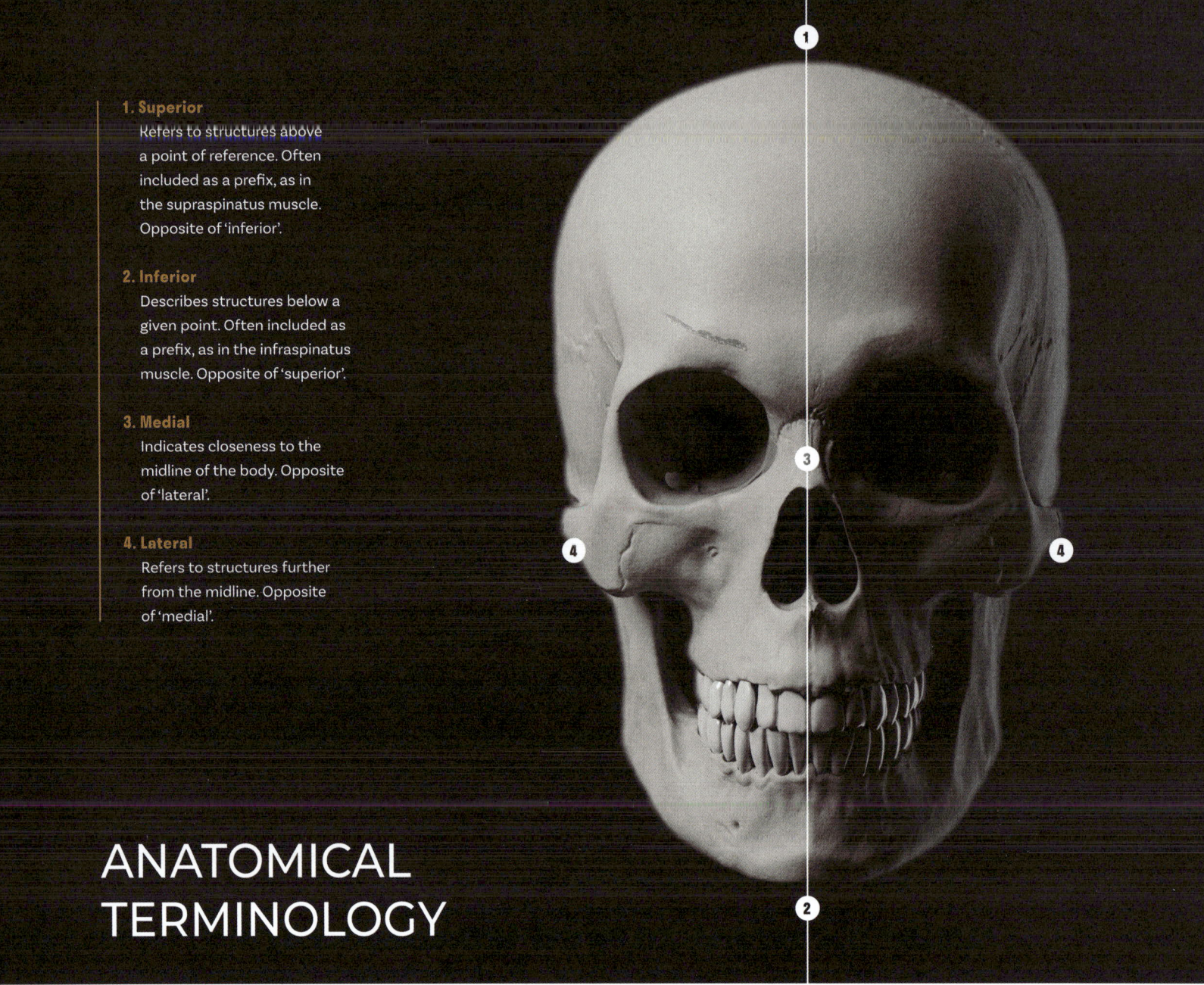

1. Superior
Refers to structures above a point of reference. Often included as a prefix, as in the supraspinatus muscle. Opposite of 'inferior'.

2. Inferior
Describes structures below a given point. Often included as a prefix, as in the infraspinatus muscle. Opposite of 'superior'.

3. Medial
Indicates closeness to the midline of the body. Opposite of 'lateral'.

4. Lateral
Refers to structures further from the midline. Opposite of 'medial'.

ANATOMICAL TERMINOLOGY

Directional terms

As a portrait artist, it's a good idea to learn and use the directional terms that are the cornerstones of anatomical language. Instead of referencing the 'top' and 'bottom', use the terms 'superior' and 'inferior', respectively. This naming practice avoids the ambiguity inherent in everyday language and provides a standardized frame of reference.

'Medial' denotes the middle-most aspect of the body or structure (represented as the 'midline'), whereas 'lateral' refers to the portion most distant from the middle. These terms are invaluable in describing the spatial relationships between muscles, bones, and other anatomical features.

The great French anatomist, Paul Richer, utilized this language in his seminal works to clarify the complex architecture of the human form in a way that was understandable to artists and medical professionals alike.

These terms are often used in the description of individual muscles, such as 'the anterior section of the deltoid' and 'the posterior section of the deltoid'. Through these descriptors, you gain insight into not only the location of a muscle, but often its function as well, facilitating an understanding that can be directly applied to artistic practice.

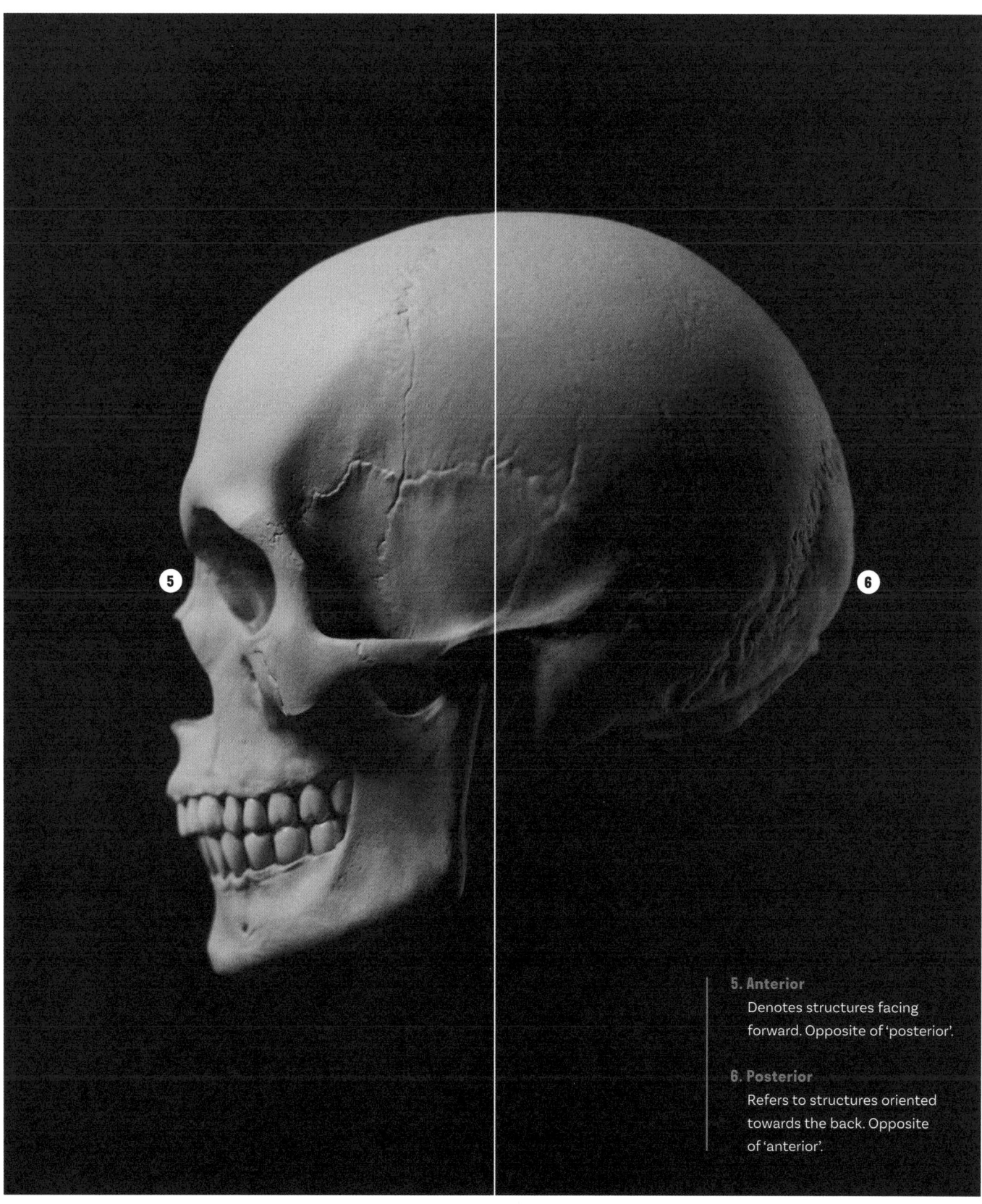

5. Anterior
Denotes structures facing
forward. Opposite of 'posterior'.

6. Posterior
Refers to structures oriented
towards the back. Opposite
of 'anterior'.

Anatomical terms

The vocabulary of anatomical description extends beyond the directional. The terms below will add a further layer to your understanding of human anatomy. These descriptors offer invaluable clarity when one delves into the intricacies of bones, muscles, and other tissues, allowing for a more precise understanding and representation of their form and function.

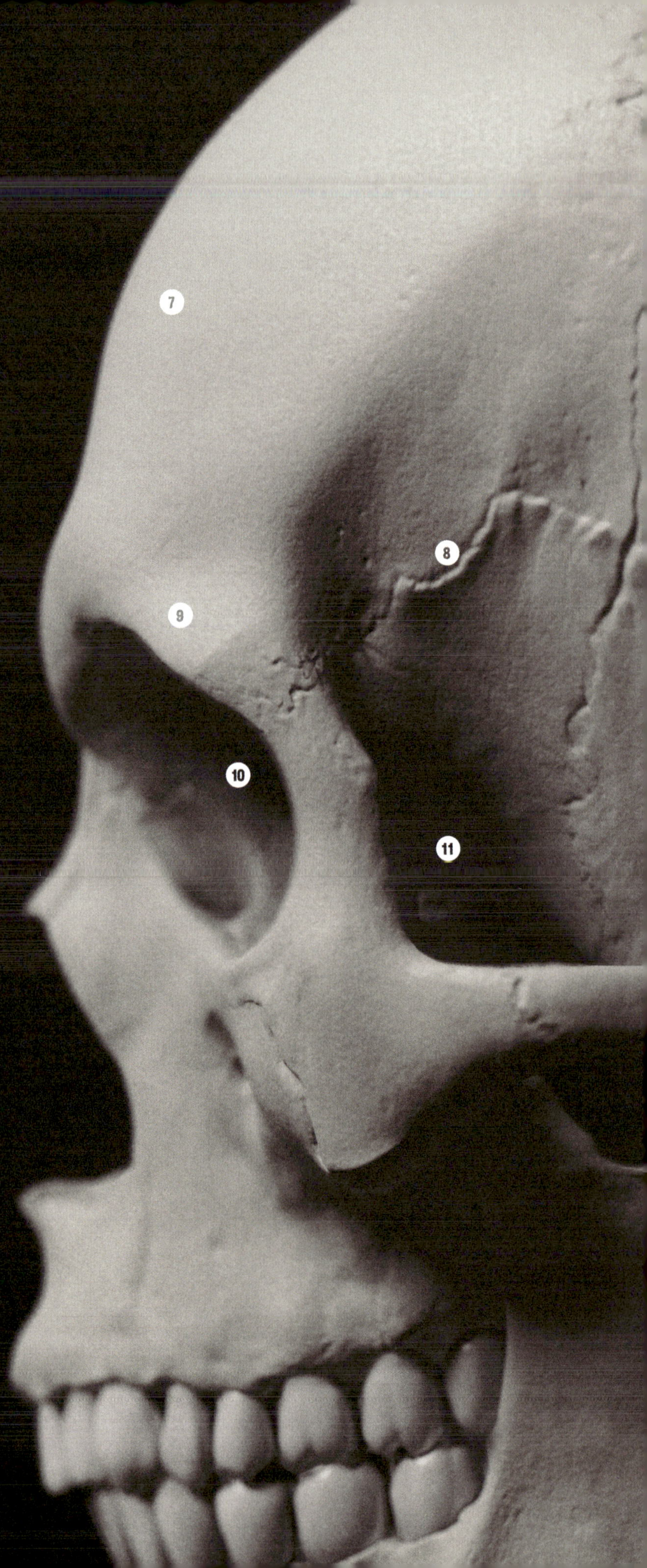

7. Eminence

A raised area or protrusion on the surface of a bone, often the site of muscle attachment and named for its rounded shape.

8. Suture

A line of union between bones, especially of the skull.

9. Apophysis

A natural outgrowth or projection.

10. Cavity

A hollow space within a bone or other body structure, often serving as a chamber for an organ.

11. Fossa

A shallow depression or hollow in a bone.

12. Meatus

A natural body passage or canal.

13. Process

A general term for any bony prominence or projection.

14. Spine

A sharp, slender projection on a bone.

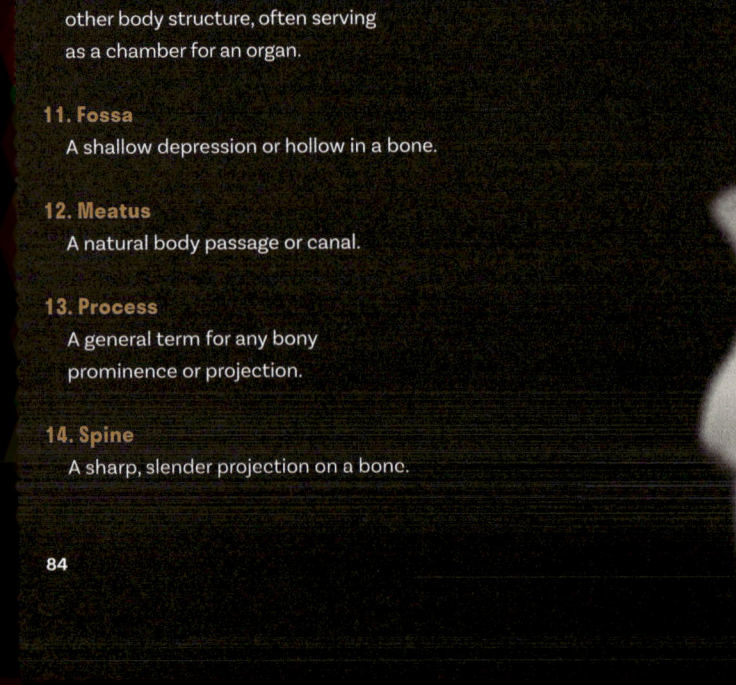

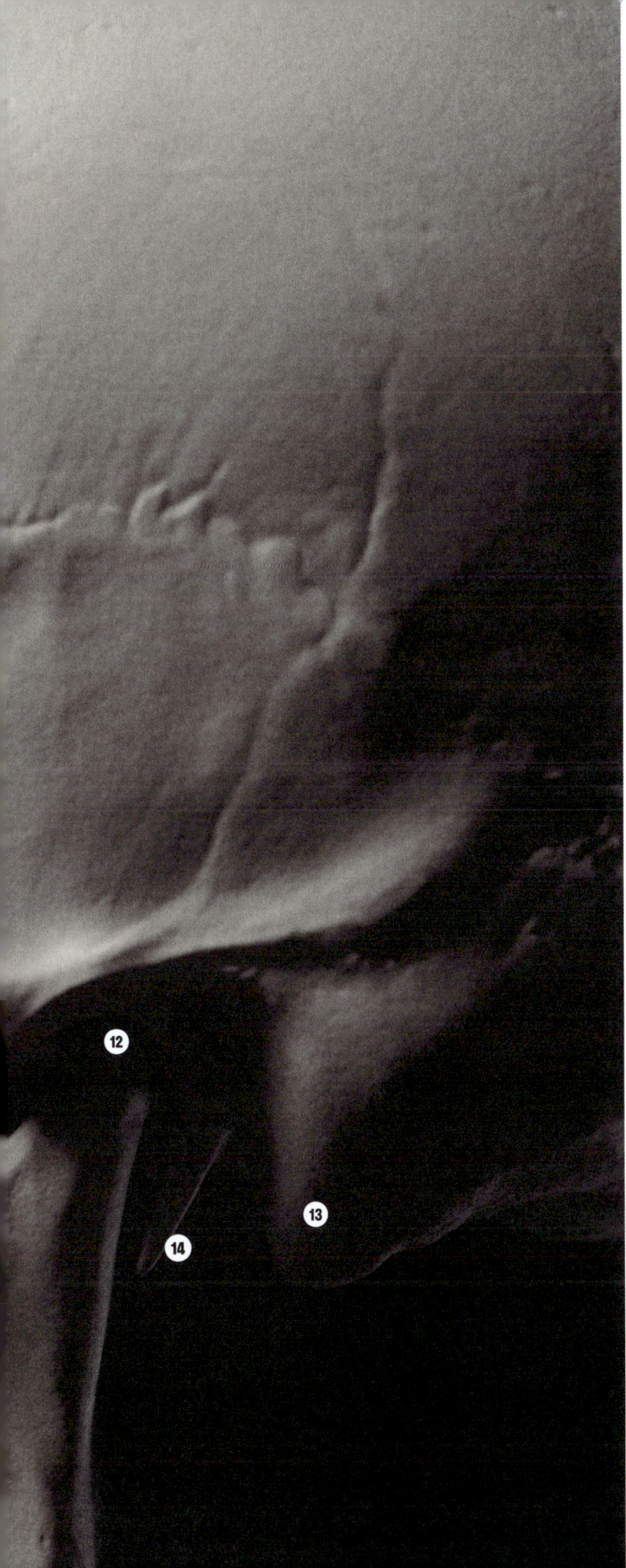

Additional terms (not labelled)

Condyle
A rounded prominence at the end of a bone, usually for articulation with another bone.

Foramen
An opening or hole in a bone, often serving as a passageway for nerves or vessels.

Sulcus
A groove or furrow on a bone.

Crest
A prominent ridge or elongated projection on a bone.

Superficial
A structure that is situated near the surface of the body or closer to the skin.

Deep
Something situated away from the surface of the skin.

Fascia
A band or sheet of connective tissue, primarily collagen, beneath the skin that attaches, stabilizes, encloses, and separates muscles and other internal organs.

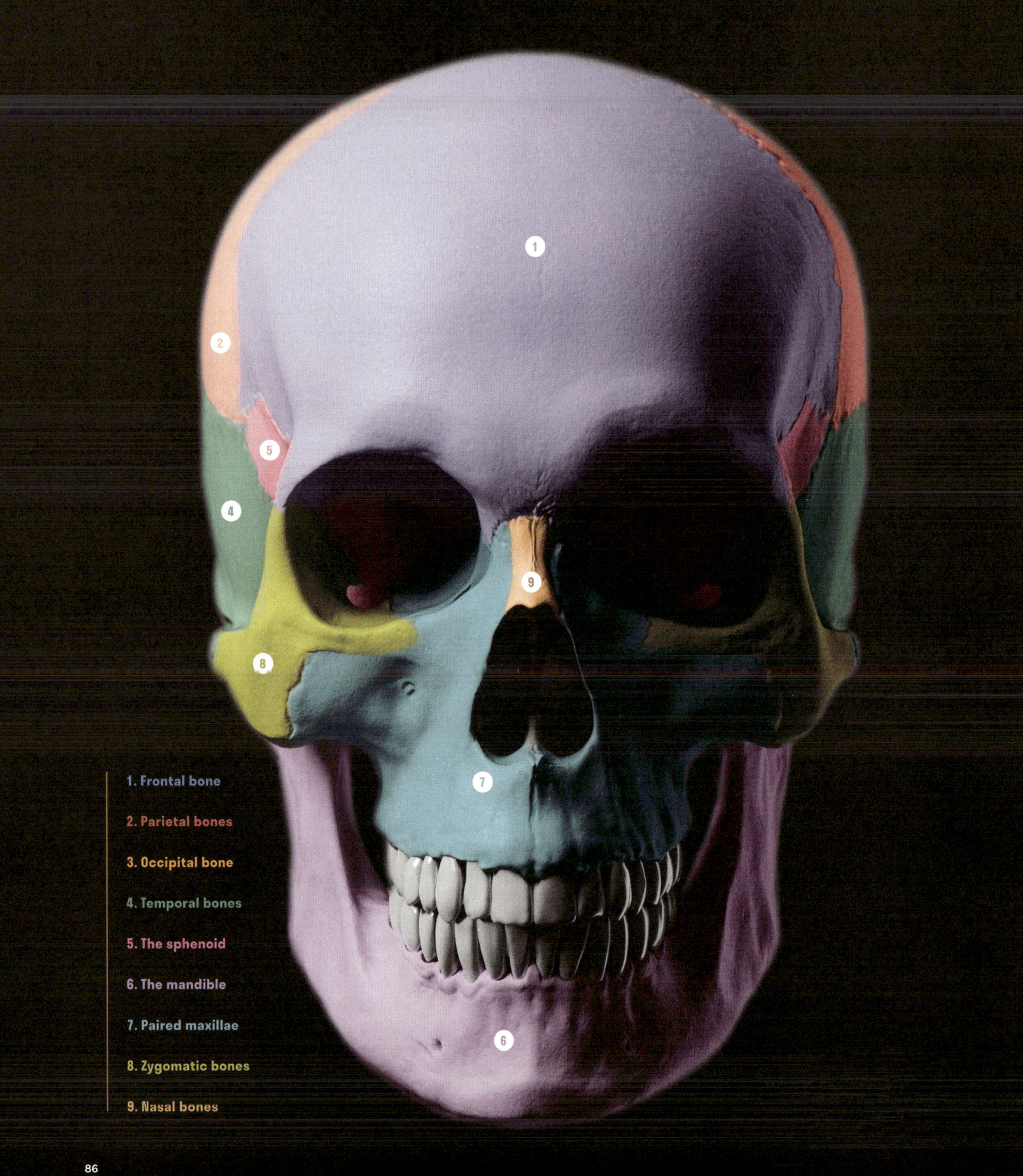

1. Frontal bone

2. Parietal bones

3. Occipital bone

4. Temporal bones

5. The sphenoid

6. The mandible

7. Paired maxillae

8. Zygomatic bones

9. Nasal bones

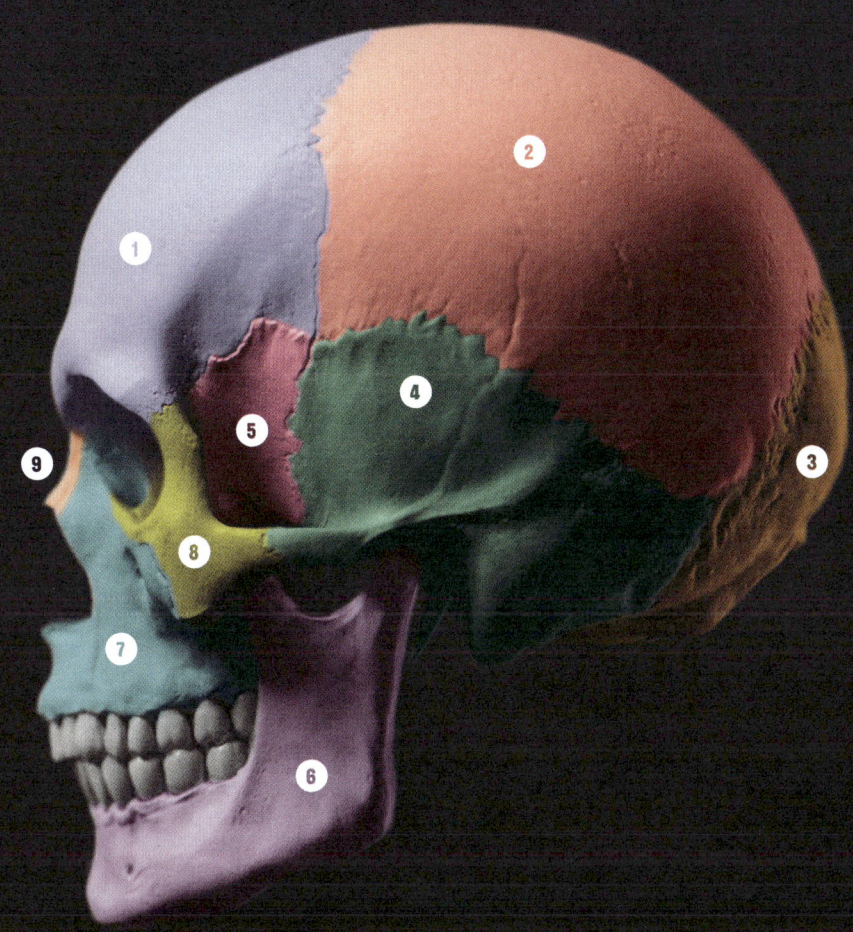

THE BONES OF THE SKULL

The cranium, often referred to as the braincase, is composed of eight bones. The frontal bone (1), singular in its existence, forms the forehead and the upper portion of the eye sockets. Adjacent to this, on either side, are the parietal bones (2), which shape the top and sides of the head. The occipital bone (3), located at the posterior, cradles the back of the head and is intricately articulated with the first vertebra. Temporal bones (4), found on both sides of the skull, contain the inner ear structures and play a significant role in defining the sides of the head. The sphenoid (5), deeply seated, is often likened to a butterfly due to its unique shape. It lies at the base of the skull and provides a junction for several other cranial bones.

Lower down, the face consists of fourteen bones, only a few of which are relevant to the visual artist. The mandible (6), colloquially known as the jawbone, is the only movable bone of the skull. Paired maxillae (7) form the upper jaw and roof of the mouth. Zygomatic bones (8), more commonly recognized as cheekbones, contribute to the prominence of the cheeks and the outer eye sockets. Finally, the nasal bones (9) are responsible for shaping the bridge of the nose.

MUSCLES OF THE HEAD AND NECK

The movements of the head and neck are orchestrated by a complex network of muscles, each contributing to the nuance of facial expressions and appearance.

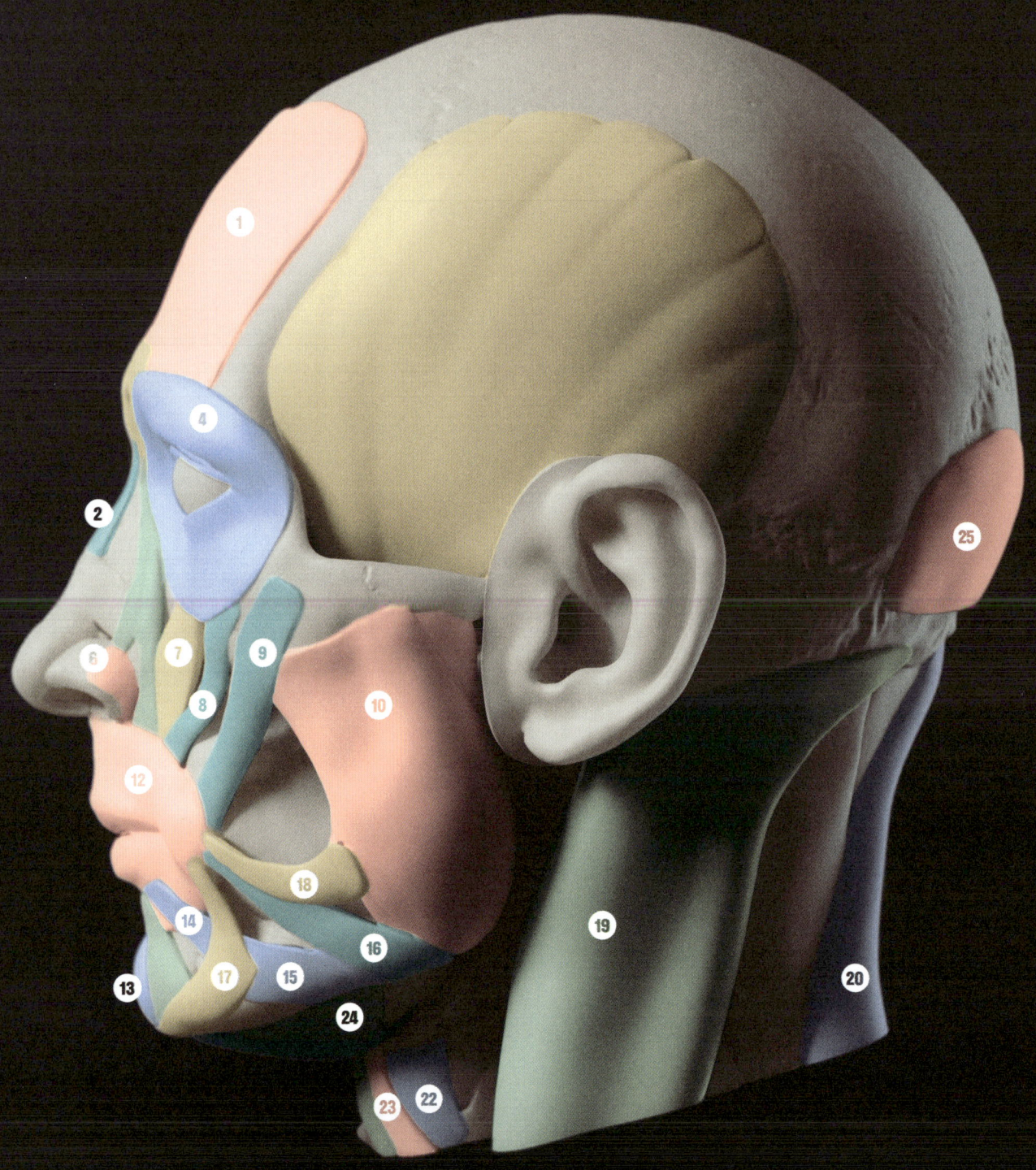

1. Frontalis
Resides beneath the skin of the forehead, with horizontal fibres that elevate the brow.

2–3. Procerus and depressor supercilii
Responsible for drawing the eyebrows downwards; situated medially on the brow.

4. Orbicularis oculi
Encircles the eye and functions to close the eyelids.

5. Levator labii superioris alaeque nasi
Positioned along the upper lip and nose; raises the lip and dilates the nostrils.

6. Nasalis-alar
Compresse the nasal bridge and flares the nostrils.

7. Levator labii superioris
Elevates the upper lip.

8–9. Zygomaticus minor and major
Extend from the cheekbone to the corners of the mouth to raise the lip, primarily in smiling.

10. Masseter
Situated on the side of the jaw, a prime mover in jaw closure.

11. Temporalis
Located at the temple; assists in chewing by elevating the jaw.

12. Orbicularis oris
Encircles the mouth, playing a key role in lip movement.

13. Mentalis
At the chin; protrudes the lower lip.

14. Depressor labii inferioris
Pulls the lower lip downward.

15–16. Platysma (labial and modiolus portions)
Covering the neck and influencing mouth tension.

17. Depressor anguli oris
Draws the corners of the mouth down.

18. Risorius
Stretches the mouth laterally.

19. Sternocleidomastoid
Facilitates head rotation and flexion along the neck.

20. Trapezius
Extends over the shoulders; involved in scapular movement.

21. Levator scapulae
Located at the back and side of the neck, lifting the scapula

22, 23, 24. Omohyoid, sternohyoid, digastric
Positioned in the lower jaw and neck area; involved in swallowing.

25. Occipitalis
At the back of the skull; works with the frontalis to retract the scalp.

SUBCUTANEOUS FORMS OF THE SKULL

The skull, serving as the fundamental volume of the head, only reveals its specific forms in a few subcutaneous areas when observing a live model. These regions, characterized by the hard counterpoints of the bony structure against the softer muscular or fatty tissues, are essential for portrait artists as they provide the underlying framework around which the facial features are constructed.

The cheekbones, brow ridges, and jawline are particularly prominent, providing critical landmarks for the artist. Their visibility and the shadows they cast lend depth and clarity to a drawing's final rendering. In subjects with leaner faces, these landmarks are more pronounced, while in fuller faces, though they may be less evident, they remain critical for understanding the structure around which the face is built.

The structure of the skull serves as the foundation upon which the soft tissues of the face reside. This knowledge, paired with the understanding of the skin, muscles, and other tissues, equips the artist to render a face with confidence.

On the opposite page we'll look at the anterior (frontal) view of the skull. On the following two pages you'll find the lateral (profile) view, superior (top) view, and three-quarter view.

ANTERIOR (FRONTAL) VIEW

1. Eye sockets (orbits)

Directly influenced by the frontal bone's arc, the eye sockets are two bony cavities housing the eyes. The bottom edge of the frontal bone (see superior view on page 93) establishes the upper boundary of these sockets. A pronounced arc to the frontal bone can lead to more recessed and deep-set eyes, while a flatter frontal bone arc may result in shallower orbits. This interplay of bone structure and cavity depth has a significant impact on the play of light and shadow.

2. Glabella

Positioned between the eyebrows, just above the nose bridge, the glabella is a slightly raised, smooth section of the frontal bone. In this anterior view, the glabella is easily discernible, serving as a critical anatomical landmark that gives the forehead its shape.

3. Nasal bone

Situated at the bridge of the nose, this bone dictates the nose's projection and is a determinant for the descending angle. It forms the starting point of the nose, a central feature in the anterior view.

4. Superciliary arch

Found just above the eye socket, the superciliary arch gives depth and dimension to the forehead. It creates a subtle shadowing effect leading to the downward-turning plane of the eye sockets, accentuating the eyes.

5. Maxillary bone

Making up the upper jaw, this bone is responsible for setting the character of the muzzle form, upon which the lips rest. In the three-quarter view on page 93, note the apparent roundness of the maxillary bone, which contributes directly to the roundness of the muzzle form and lips.

6. Mandible and mental protuberance

The mandible sets the face's lower boundary, its contour shaping the jawline. The mental protuberance, more commonly known as the chin, projects forward and gives character to the lower face.

7. Zygomatic bones

Representing the cheeks' high points, the zygomatic bones or cheekbones are also clearly visible in the anterior view (page 90) and slightly visible in the superior view (opposite page). They set the face's lateral boundary and, when prominent, distinctly define the face's silhouette.

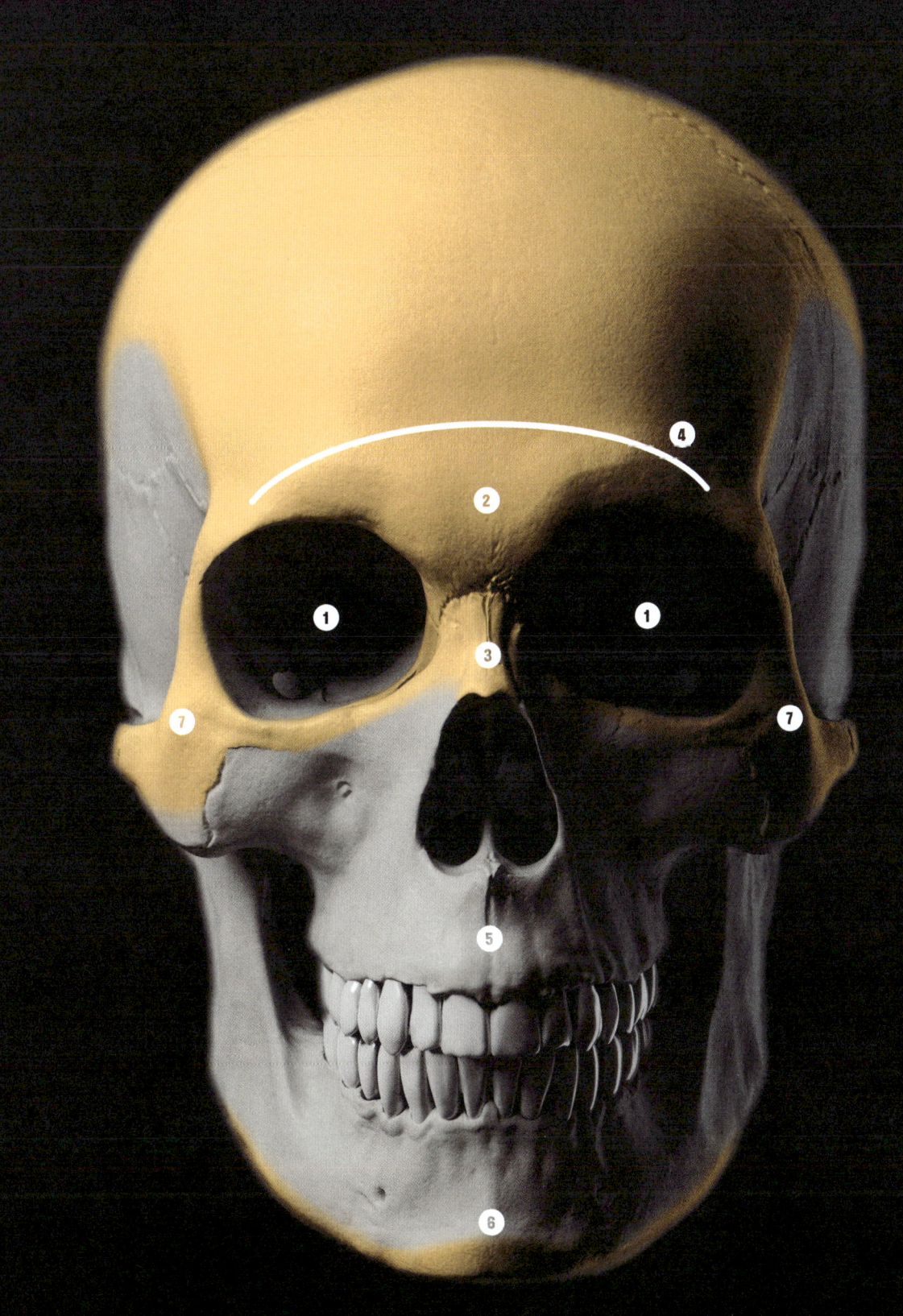

LATERAL (PROFILE) VIEW

8. Temporal fossa

The recession of the temporal fossa is keenly observable in the profile view. It determines the depth and shading around the temple, playing a crucial role in the overall form of the head.

9. External auditory meatus

While not explicitly visible in the living, its relevance in determining the disposition of the zygomatic arch cannot be undermined. It sits just below the space where the arch lands on the parietal bone.

10. Mastoid process

A substantial bony projection found behind the ear, the mastoid process is distinctly visible in the profile. It serves as a landmark for the posterior boundary of the jaw and neck. Significantly, it is the origin of the sternocleidomastoid muscle (see page 120).

11. Temporal line

The temporal line is a linear bony ridge extending along the side of the skull. It marks the attachment of the temporalis muscle and is a key structure in the temporal region. This line begins near the external orbital apophysis and extends superiorly in an arc across the parietal bone. Its position is instrumental for artists to understand the shift between the front of the head and the side plane.

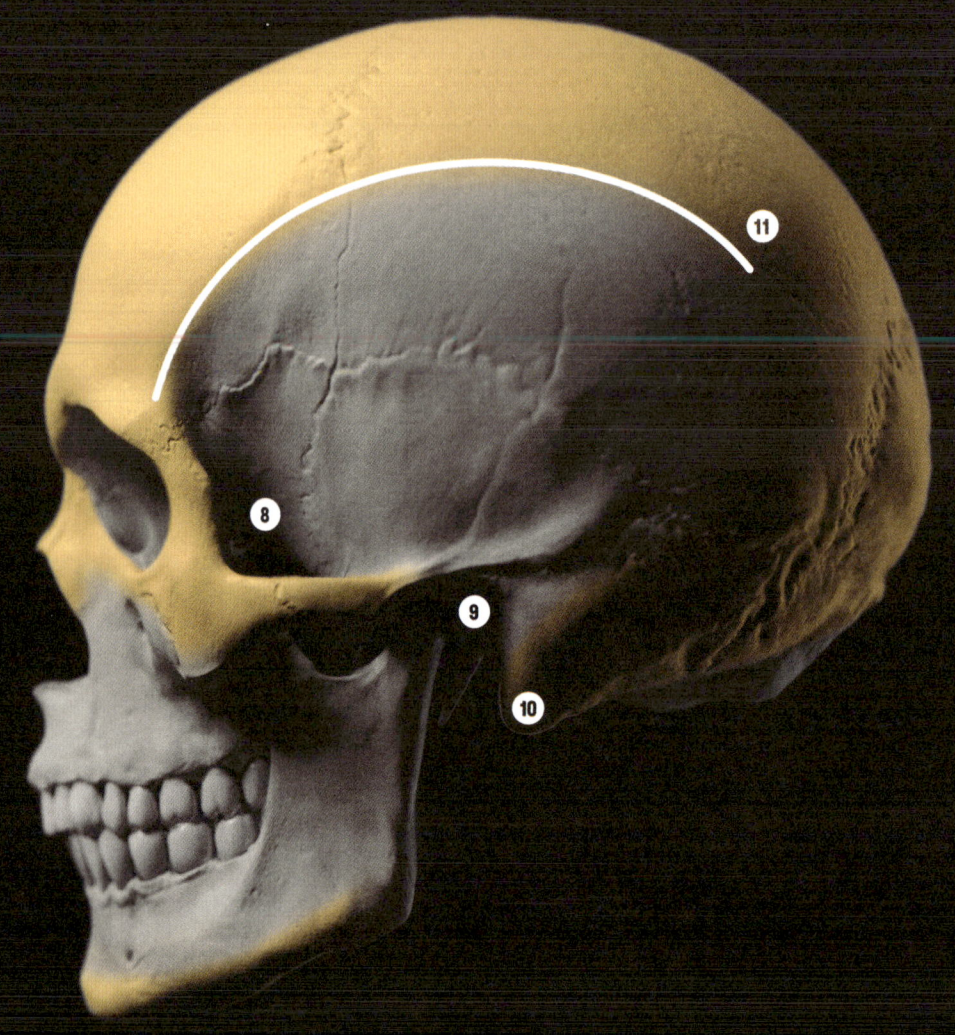

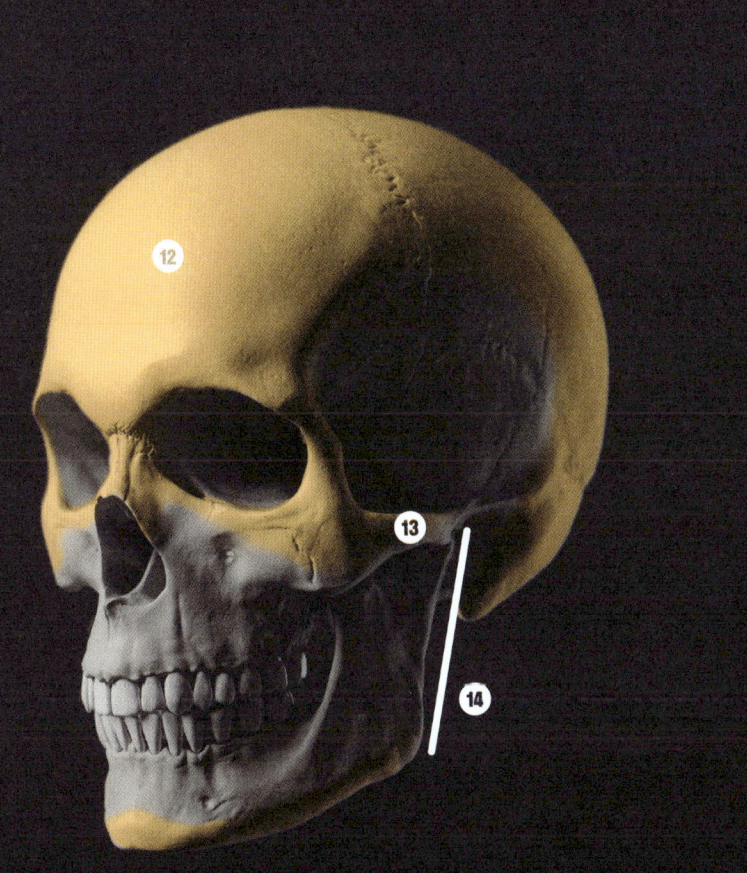

THREE-QUARTER VIEW

12. Frontal bone
While the frontal bone (forehead) can be appreciated from various angles, its breadth, curvature, and the way it transitions into the superciliary arch and temporal lines are best captured in this three-quarter view.

13. Zygomatic arch
The zygomatic arch is prominently showcased here. Originating from the temporal process of the zygomatic bone and connecting with the zygomatic process of the temporal bone, this slender arch acts as a bridge on the skull's side. It serves as the delineation between the cheek and the temporal region. The zygomatic arch is a crucial landmark because of its role in defining the face's width and the transition from the cheek's fleshy region to the temporal hollow.

14. Ramus of the mandible
The ramus of the mandible is the vertical extension of the lower jawbone that rises to meet the temporal bone. It provides structure and form to the sides of the face and is the point of articulation for the temporomandibular joint, allowing for the movement of the jaw. It represents the posterior boundary of the jaw, aligns with the lowest attachment of the ear, and approximately aligns with the conceptual midline of the head when viewed in profile.

SUPERIOR (TOP) VIEW

15. Parietal eminences
These are the broadest points of the skull when seen from above. Their prominence influences the cranium's silhouette, guiding you while blocking a drawing in, to carve out the head's proper width.

16. The occipital bone
Located at the posterior, the occipital bone (see page 87) cradles the back of the head and is intricately articulated with the first vertebra.

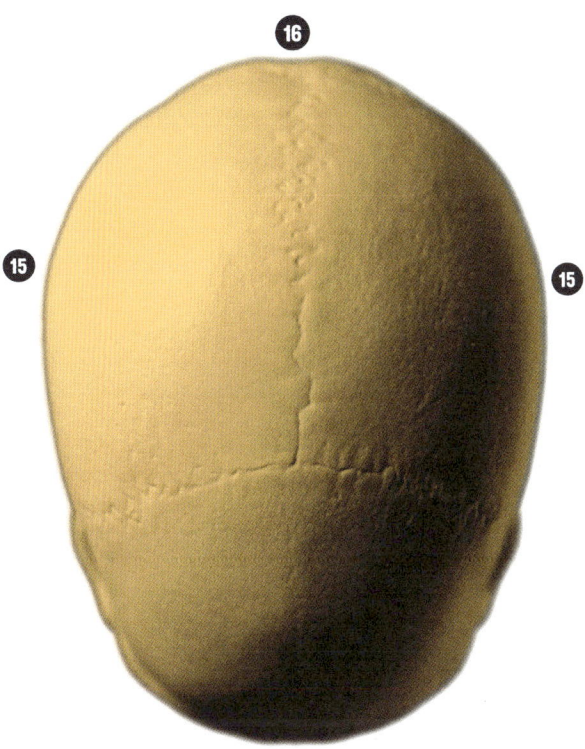

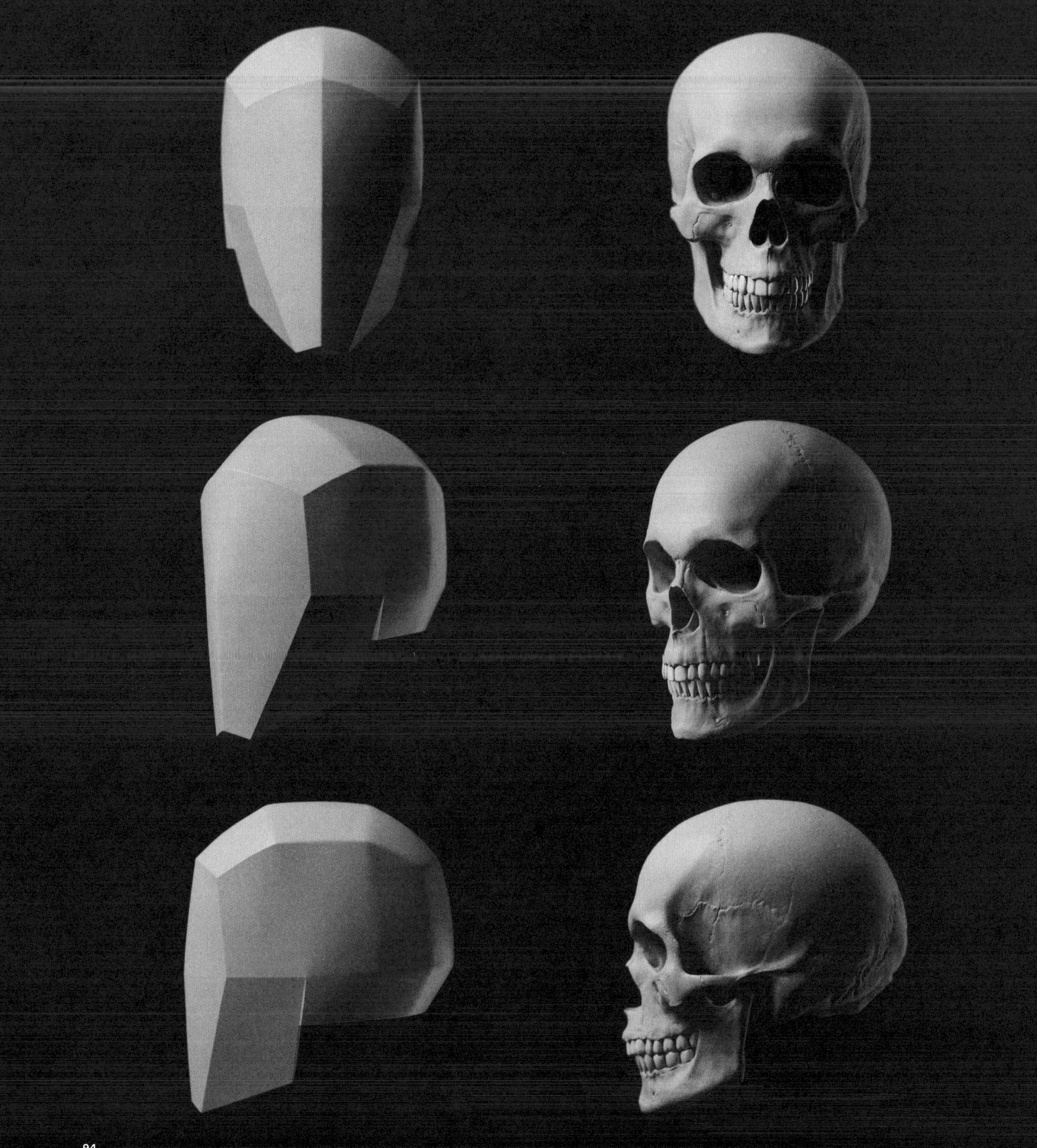

THE SIMPLIFIED MODEL OF THE HEAD

Structural templates serve as the scaffolding upon which the intricate and nuanced forms of portraiture are built. They are the underlying armatures that provide both stability and a point of reference for artists as they navigate the complexities of the human head. In the history of portrait drawing, these templates have evolved and taken various forms, embodying the philosophies and methodologies of their creators.

One of the most eminent examples of such a template is the Loomis head, devised by Andrew Loomis. The model itself stands as a testament to Loomis' teaching approach, which emphasizes understanding the head as an assemblage of simpler shapes that can be easily grasped and manipulated by the artist. Loomis' head employs a block-in method that reduces the head to its most rudimentary geometric forms, thereby allowing the draughtsperson to lay down the foundational proportions with relative ease.

Each artist who aims to capture a human likeness in a portrait, particularly an artist who seeks to teach, inevitably cultivates their own perspective on the most effective methods of simplification and representation. The simplified head model shown here advocates for the use of primarily straight edges that converge at clear, distinct angles. The straight line and angle-break system is not only a stylistic choice, but a strategic simplification that allows for the rapid establishment of proportion, planes, and structural landmarks of the head. By utilizing straight lines and clear angles, a draughtsperson can swiftly capture the essential character of a subject's features without being ensnared in the complexity of curves and subtleties, which can often lead to distortions or a loss of proportion in the early stages of drawing.

This method, like any artistic strategy, is not the definitive answer to the many challenges of portraiture, but rather a powerful tool to be wielded in the pursuit of capturing human likeness with clarity and conviction. It is an artist's conceptual blueprint that can particularly help with the alignment of structurally symmetrical points in relation to the twist and tilt of the central axis of the head. Track these points correctly through the block-in phase of a drawing, and what follows will be as simple as adding the features where they belong.

The transition from the simplified block-in to a more nuanced portrait is a gradual process. At an intermediary stage, the artist begins to soften the rigidity of the initial geometric lines, integrating curves and organic forms that more accurately reflect the natural human anatomy. The stark angles of the block-in serve as anchors from which the contours of the flesh are hung. Muscles wrap around the bony landmarks, skin stretches across the underlying structure, and features begin to emerge. We'll move on to these stages later in the book.

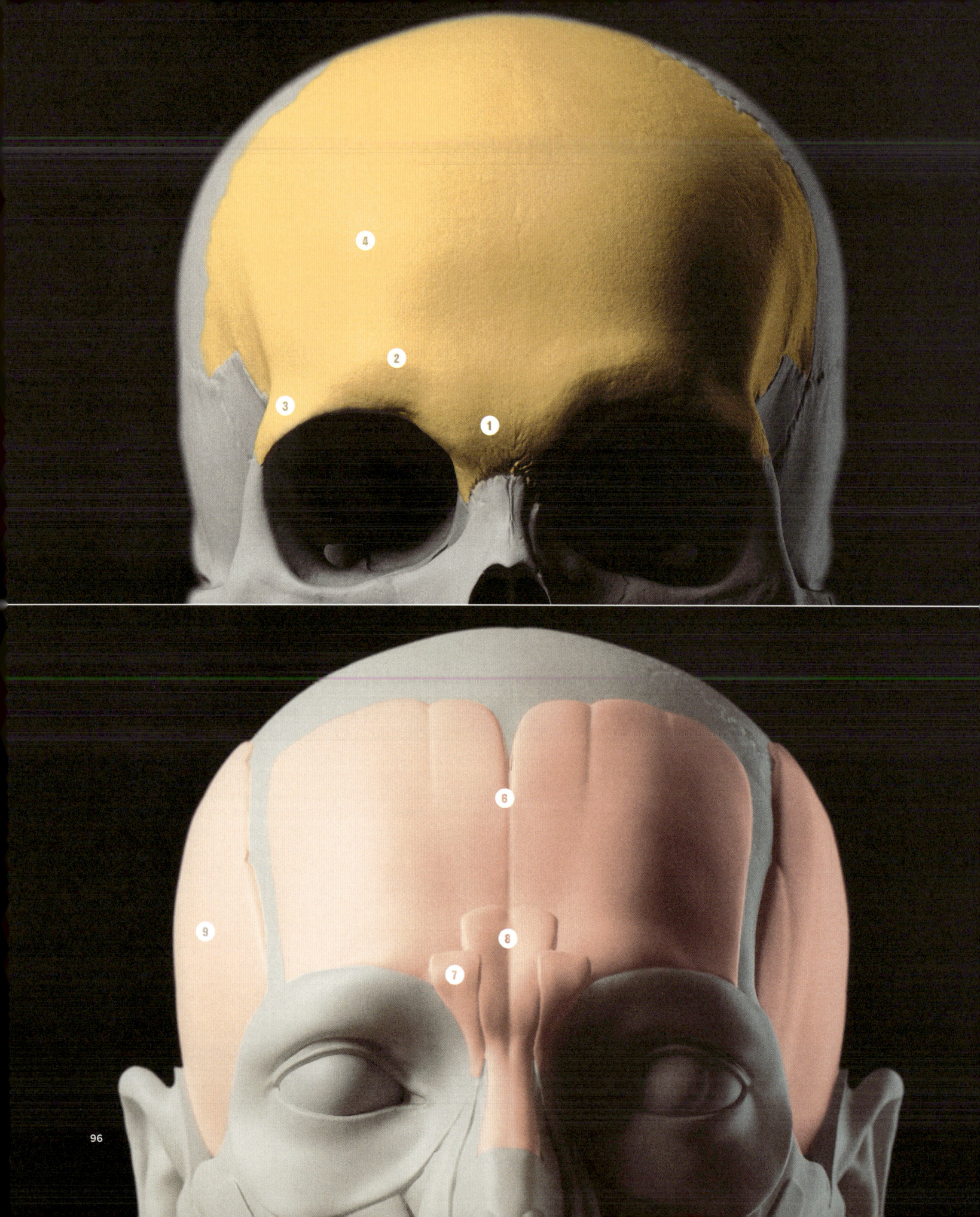

96

THE FRONTAL BONE

The frontal bone arches from the upper orbit of the eye sockets to the coronal suture (the juncture at which it adjoins the parietal bones), delineating the uppermost region of the face. It forms the forehead, which is typically among the lightest planes in a portrait set-up, and plays a significant factor in the reading of an individual's likeness.

When artists approach portrait drawing, their understanding of this bone is not merely academic, but practical too. The bone's curvature forms the forehead's dome, across which the rendering of values is a strong indicator of the overall roundness of the head.

Parts of the frontal bone

1. Glabella

At the juncture above the eye sockets, this part presents itself as a prominent marker. This slightly raised part of the frontal bone is situated between the eyebrows, and in some individuals, it projects more distinctly. It can be observed as a subtle mound or a pronounced downturning plane, often dictating the shadow patterns in the lower-central region of the forehead.

2. Superciliary arches

Moving upwards and laterally, you'll find the superciliary arches. These bony ridges define the upper limits of the eye sockets. Their prominence can vary greatly among individuals, influencing the appearance of halftone in this region. In their most prominent expression, these arches contribute to the expression and character of the face, as light glances off their convexity or settles into the concave hollows below them.

3. External orbital apophysis

Flanking the outer edge of the superciliary arches, this area is less discussed but equally significant. At the point where the zygomatic process of the frontal bone meets the zygomatic bone, it serves as an anchor for the lateral canthus of the eye, and is a contributor to the major three-quarters edge of the head, so is therefore often referenced in the block-in stage. Its subtle protrusion can affect the perceived depth and angle of the eye socket.

4. Frontal eminences

These rounded prominences are often symmetrical and impart a gentle convexity to the forehead, which is crucial for capturing the volume of the head overall. The well-observed rendering of halftones across these eminences can suggest the bone's subtle protrusion and the soft tissue that overlays it.

5. Temporal line

Lastly, this is an arcing ridge that traverses the bone's lateral aspect, and marks the boundary where the temporalis muscle attaches. It is not always visible, but can become a defining contour in a three-quarter view of the head. The challenge lies in indicating this line with minimal contrast, ensuring it complements the head's overall form without overpowering the portrait's subtler features.

Muscles on the frontal bone

6. Frontalis muscle

With its origin on the galea aponeurotica and insertion into the skin of the eyebrows, this muscle elevates the brows and creates horizontal forehead wrinkles. When contracted, its action is pivotal in shaping the topography of the forehead.

7. Depressor supercilii

A compact muscle originating from the medial orbital rim and inserted above the eyebrow, it pulls the brow downwards and inwards. Its function shapes the glabellar region, creating a furrow that deepens with frowning or concentration.

8. Procerus

Starting at the nasal bone and lateral nasal cartilage, and inserting into the forehead's skin, this muscle draws the skin between the eyebrows downwards, producing horizontal lines across the nasal bridge and lower forehead. Its contraction distorts the form of the brow and the bridge of the nose, as it contributes to the creases and furrows that can signify a stern or scrutinizing expression.

9. Temporalis

Arising from the entire surface of the temporal fossa and attaching primarily to the coronoid process of the mandible, this muscle is instrumental in jaw elevation. Its presence is implied on the forehead by the temporal line, which can subtly alter the side plane of the forehead, particularly when the jaw is clenched.

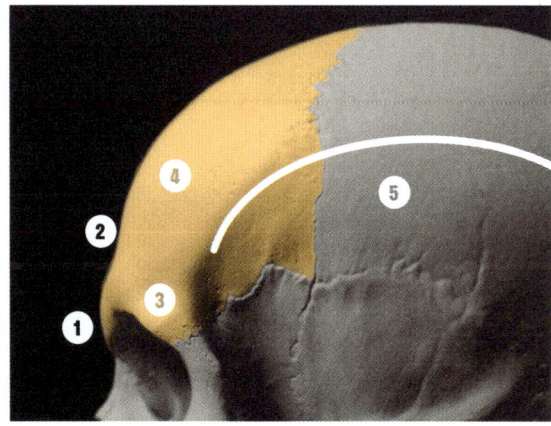

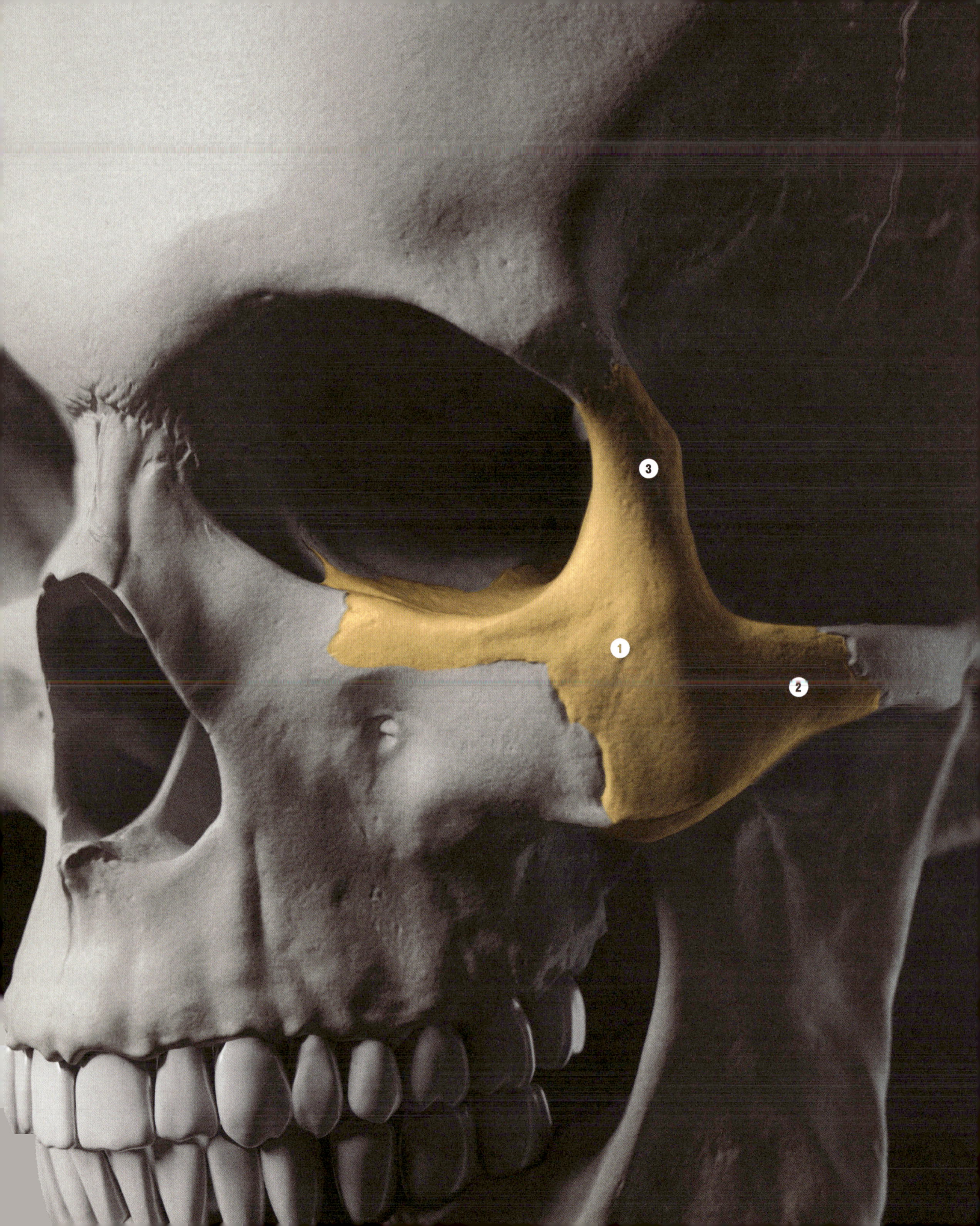

THE ZYGOMATIC BONE

The strategic position and structural complexity of the zygomatic bone, or cheekbone, plays a pivotal role in the form and function of the face. Anatomically superior to the maxilla and lateral to the nasal bones, it articulates with its partners to form the prominence of the cheek, the inferolateral margin of the orbit, and part of the lateral wall and floor of the orbit.

Parts of the zygomatic bone

1. The 'body' of the bone

This part is most visible beneath the skin, giving rise to the cheek's elevation and fullness. The major plane break found here defines the cheek's roundness and the face's width.

2. Temporal process

Projecting from the body of the bone, this process joins with the zygomatic process of the temporal bone, culminating in the zygomatic arch. This slender yet sturdy bridge is a critical anchor for muscle attachment and a defining feature in the silhouette of the face, marking the transition between the face and the cranium.

3. Frontal process

This reaches up to articulate with the frontal bone. It forms a significant part of the lateral orbital rim, contributing to the orbital cavity's structure and influencing the eye's protective bony encasement. It plays a vital role in determining the breadth and form of the orbit, impacting the eye's recess or prominence within the face.

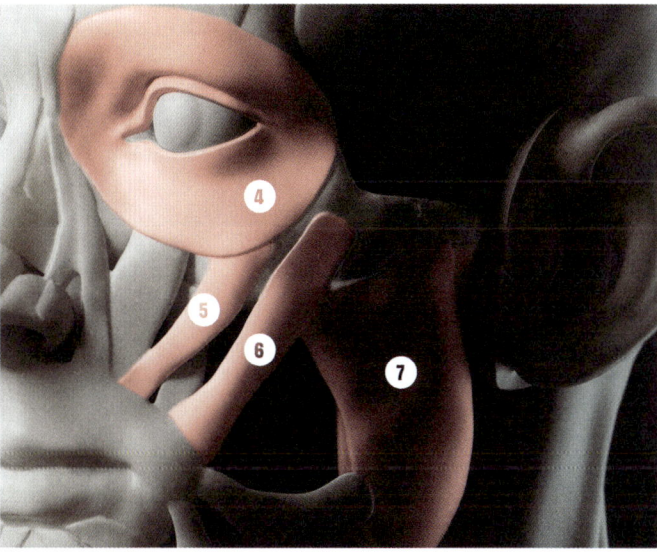

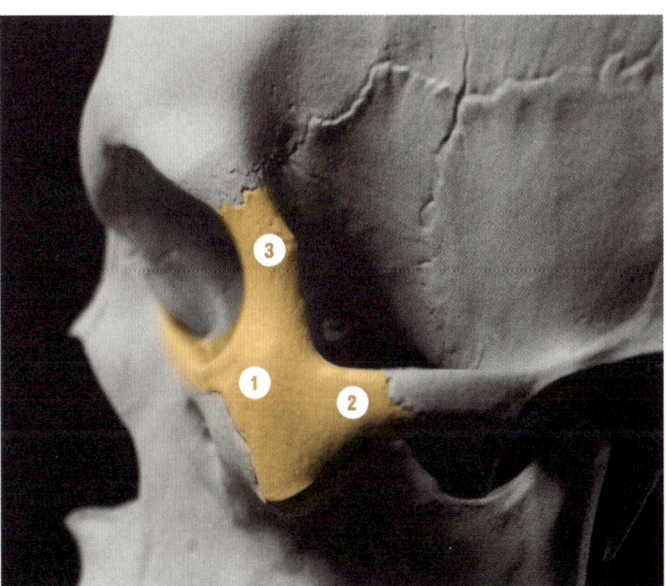

Muscles on the zygomatic bone

4. Orbicularis oculi muscle

Partially encompassing the orbital rim, this is a sphincter muscle that orchestrates the closing of the eyelids. It operates over the surface of the zygomatic bone, contributing to the subtle undulations seen around the eyes during expressions such as blinking or squinting. Through its contractions, the orbicularis oculi can create fine lines or 'crow's feet', indicating a person's habitual expressions and adding a level of depth to the ocular area in portraiture.

5–6. Zygomaticus minor and major muscles

These are critical for the animation of the upper lip and the cheek, both originating from the zygomatic bone. The zygomaticus minor, taking a path slightly above its major counterpart, inserts into the node at the corner of the mouth, accentuating the nasolabial fold. Its action is more subtle than the major, but equally important, adding nuance to the curvature and elevation of the lip. The zygomaticus major inserts into the node at the corner of the mouth, pulling the lip upwards and outwards to craft a smile.

7. Masseter muscle

This muscle originates from the inferior edge of the zygomatic arch and inserts into the lateral surface of the mandible. It bulges when engaged, as seen during chewing or clenching of the teeth, affecting the lower facial contour. The masseter shapes the jawline's form, tone, and bulk, contributing to the facial profile. Its portrayal can communicate not only the act of mastication, but also emotions related to determination or aggression.

THE MANDIBLE

Parts of the mandible

1. Alveolar process
A significant bony ridge holding the sockets for the lower teeth.

2. Mental protuberance (chin)
A forward projection that is palpable beneath the skin.

3. Ramus of the mandible
A vertical bony plate that rises to meet the cranial base.

4. Condylar process
A rounded protuberance that's part of the temporomandibular joint, which facilitates the opening and closing of the mouth.

5. Coronoid process
A thin, triangular eminence where the temporalis muscle is attached, facilitating the elevation and retraction of the jaw.

6. Angle of the mandible
The external angle where the ramus joins the body. It can vary in inclination, influencing the shape of the lower jaw in profile.

7. Oblique line
A ridge that starts near the angle and extends to the area below the coronoid process.

8. Base of the mandible
A thick, bony edge that extends from the angle to the mental region, providing strength and support to the lower jaw.

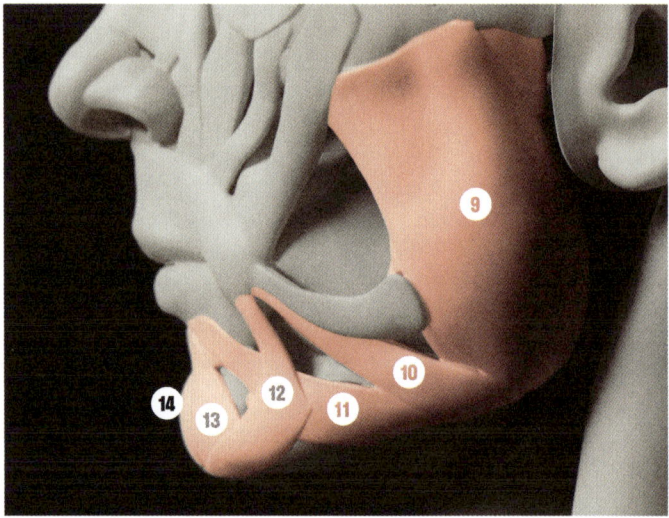

Muscles on the mandible

9. Masseter muscle
Originates from the posterior edge of the zygomatic arch and inserts along the angle and lateral surface of the ramus. Its powerful contraction is essential for elevating the mandible to enable chewing.

10. Nodular portion of the platysma
Originates from the fascia overlying the pectoralis major and deltoid muscles, with fibres running upwards into the muscular node at the corner of the mouth. Involved in subtle movements of the lower jaw.

11. Labial portion of the platysma
Originates from the same fascial layer as above, and ascends to insert into the lower lip and the fibres of the orbicularis oris muscle, affecting the downward movement of these areas.

12. Depressor anguli oris
Originates from the oblique line of the mandible and inserts at the muscular node at the corner of the mouth. It pulls the corners of the mouth downward in expressions such as a frown or grimace.

13. Depressor labii inferioris
Originates from an oblique line outside the body of the mandible and inserts into the skin of the lower lip, drawing the lip downward in expressions of sorrow or concentration.

14. Mentalis muscle
Begins at a vertical line on the front of the lower jaw just below the roots of the teeth, and inserts into the skin of the chin. This muscle is responsible for elevating the chin and protruding the lower lip.

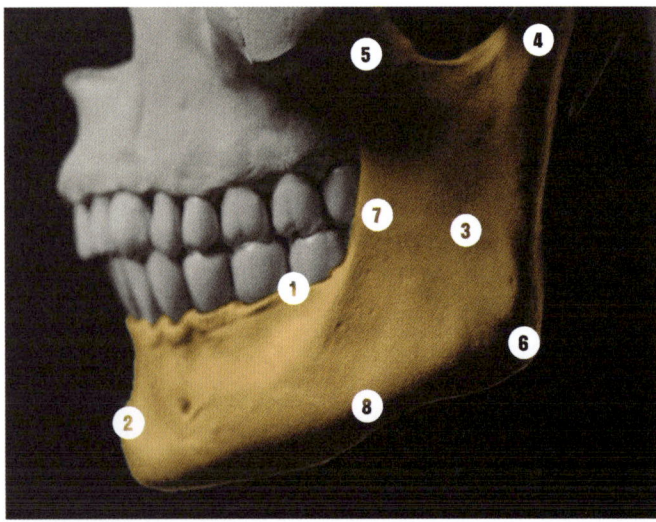

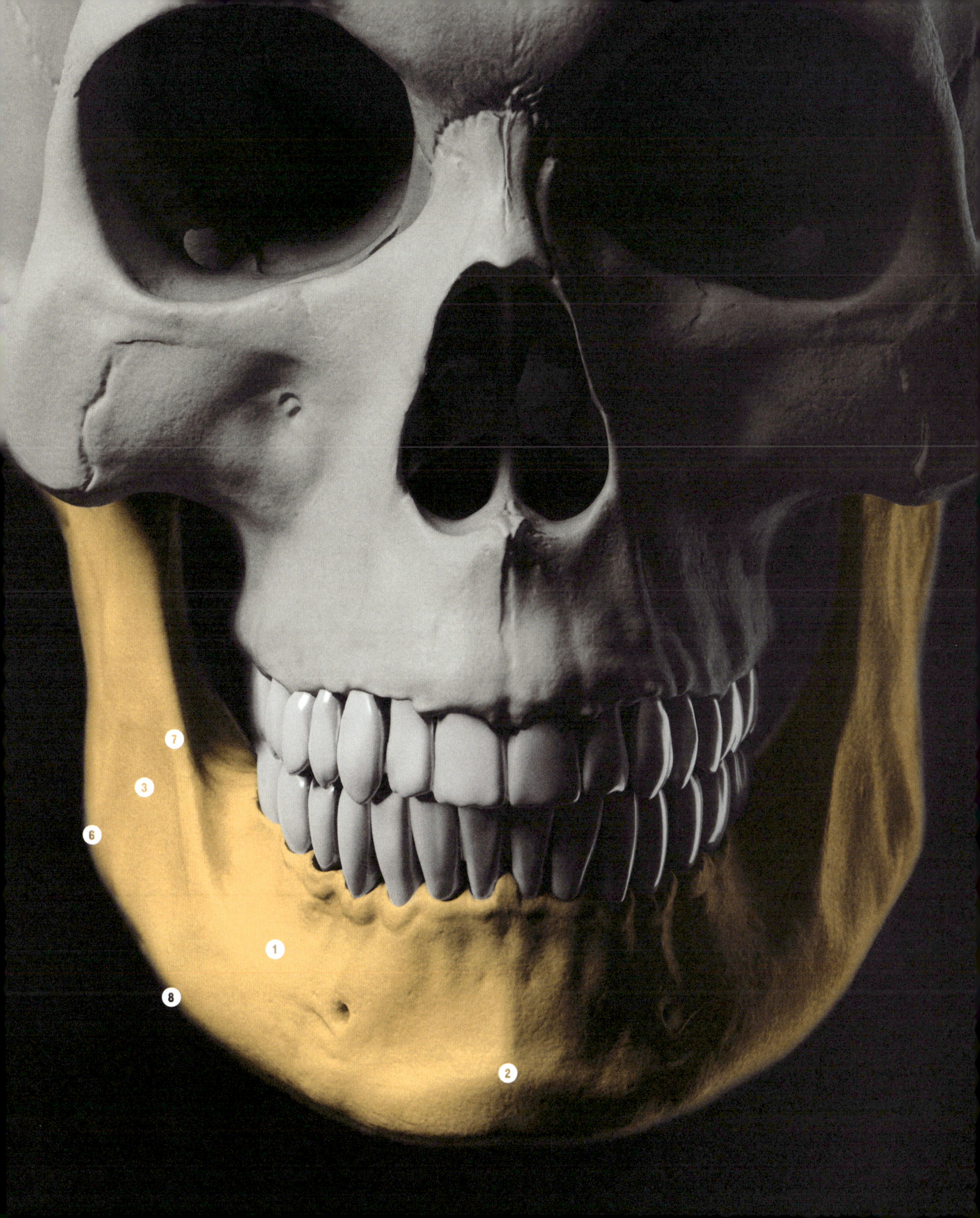

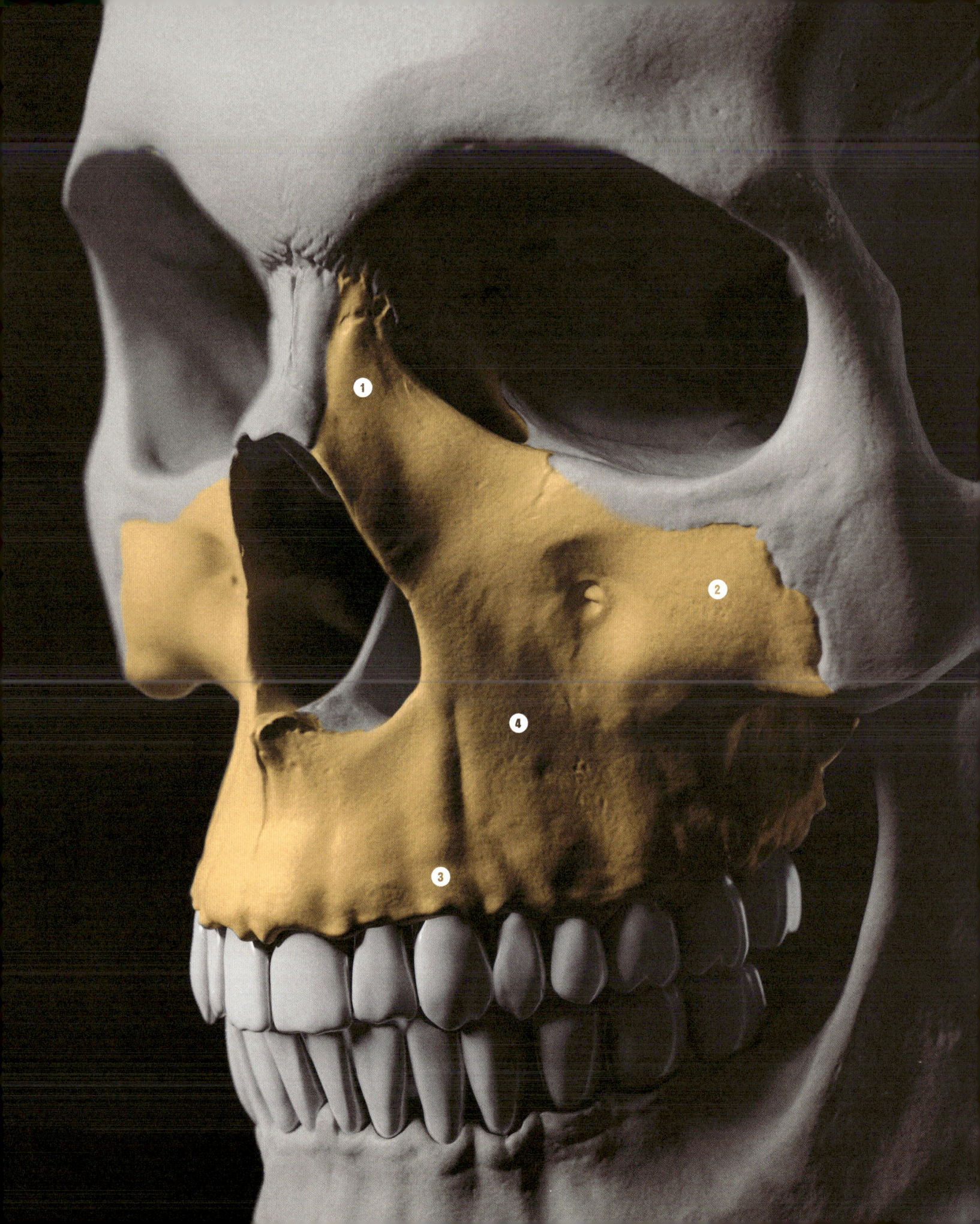

THE MAXILLAE

The maxilla, a core component of the facial skeleton, serves as a fundamental influence on the surface form of the face.

Parts of the maxillae

1. Frontal process

This is a vertical extension that articulates with the frontal bone. It's a critical contributor to the formation of the medial boundary of the orbit, delineating the recess in which the eye sits. The prominence and extent of this process influences the depth of the eye socket and the subsequent appearance of the eyes within the facial structure.

2. Zygomatic process

This is a bony projection that extends to articulate with the zygomatic bone. It is a defining factor in the width and contour of the face, giving rise to the cheekbone's characteristic prominence.

3. Alveolar process

This lies on the anterior aspect of the maxilla and contains the alveoli – the sockets for the teeth. It defines the curvature and contour of the mouth region. Its prominence, or lack thereof, can affect the fullness of the lips and the outward appearance of the lower face.

4. Body of the maxilla

This is the large central portion of the bone, with a convex curvature responsible for the curved volume of the muzzle form (along a similar curvature of the mandible). This is likely the most significant feature for artists.

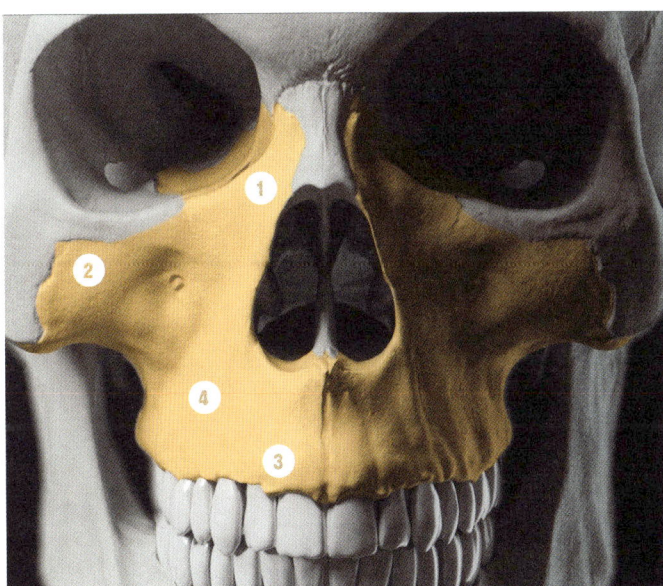

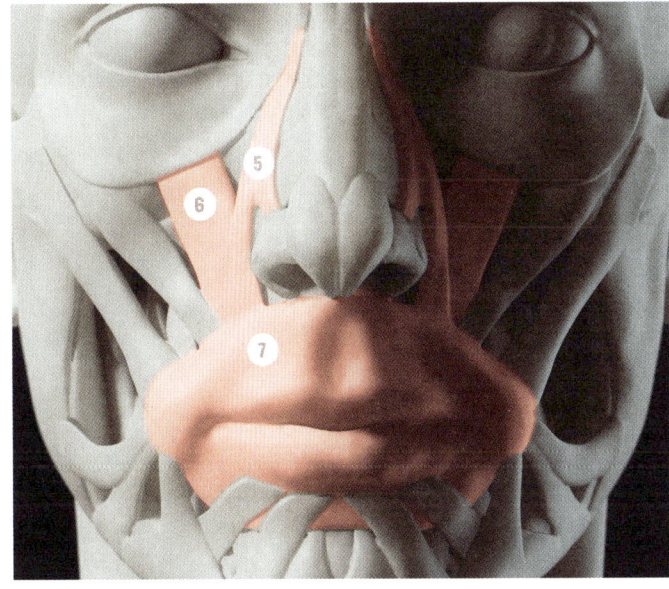

Muscles on the maxillae

5. Levator labii superioris alaeque nasi

This muscle is responsible for elevating the upper lip and flaring the nostril, and has one of its origins in the frontal process of the maxilla. Dividing into three slips, it inserts into the uppermost end of the nasolabial fold, the posterior end of the wing of the nose, and along a line extending from below the posterior end of the wing of the nose to the lower end of the ridge of the philtrum. It is the most medial of the muscles that are involved in lifting the upper lip. This muscle's placement and function have a direct impact on the nasolabial fold, creating subtle changes in expression that can denote emotions ranging from disdain to elation.

6. Levator labii superioris

This also originates from the maxilla along a long thin line at the lower border of the orbit. Its insertion, at the superficial level, is into the skin of the nasolabial furrow just lateral to the wing of the nose. This muscle acts to elevate each central half of the upper lip, drawing it superiorly and laterally, and is integral in forming expressions such as a smile or a grimace.

7. Orbicularis oris

A complex, multi-layered muscle that encircles the mouth. The lower lip connects slightly deeper than the upper, causing the upper lip to overlap the lower at the mouth's angles. Its muscle fibres intermingle with those of the levator muscles, allowing for the diverse range of motions of the mouth, from the pursing of lips in contemplation to the wide expanse of joy.

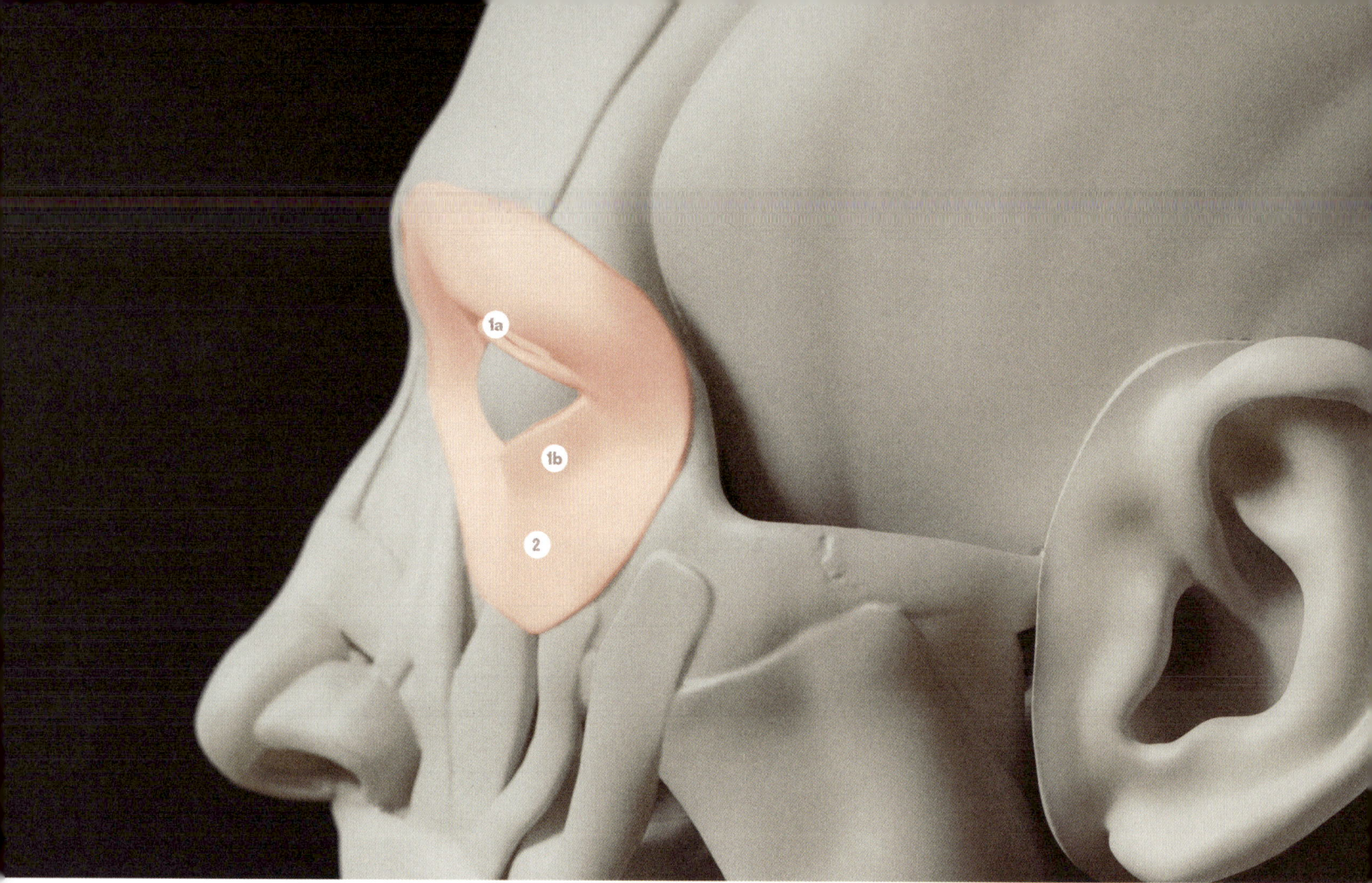

ORBICULARIS OCULI

The orbicularis oculi is a muscle that encircles the eye socket and lies directly beneath the skin's surface. This complex muscle is divided into several portions, with the orbital and palpebral being the most prominent.

1. The palpebral portion

This thin and delicate part is located within the eyelids, and is primarily responsible for the gentle closing of the eyelids, as in blinking. It is divided into superior (a) and inferior (b) parts, each named for their anatomical location relative to the fibrous membrane and tarsal plates of the eyelids. The superior and inferior tarsal plates are like the firm backing inside the upper and lower eyelids. They give your eyelids their shape and strength, and help them move properly when you blink or close your eyes.

2. The orbital portion

This part is more substantial, encircling the orbit and lying over the orbital rim. It is responsible for the forceful closure of the eyelids, as seen in squinting or protecting the eyes from bright light.

Both the palpebral and orbital portions originate from the medial canthal tendon – which is attached to the bony orbit near the nose – and insert into the lateral canthal tendon, which is affixed to the outer part of the bony orbit.

From a frontal view, the gentle curvature of the eyelids and the radial pattern of creases that can form during squinting or smiling indicate the muscle's presence. The tightening and bunching of the skin around the eye when the eyelids close forcefully showcase the orbital portion's activation.

From a side view, the thickness of the eyelids, the tautness when the eyes close, and the slight bulge of the lateral canthal tendon provide visual cues to the muscle's structure and function. The contraction of the palpebral portion can be seen in the quick, subtle motion of a blink, whereas the orbital portion's contraction is more pronounced, often causing crow's feet – those characteristic lines that fan out from the lateral corners of the eyes.

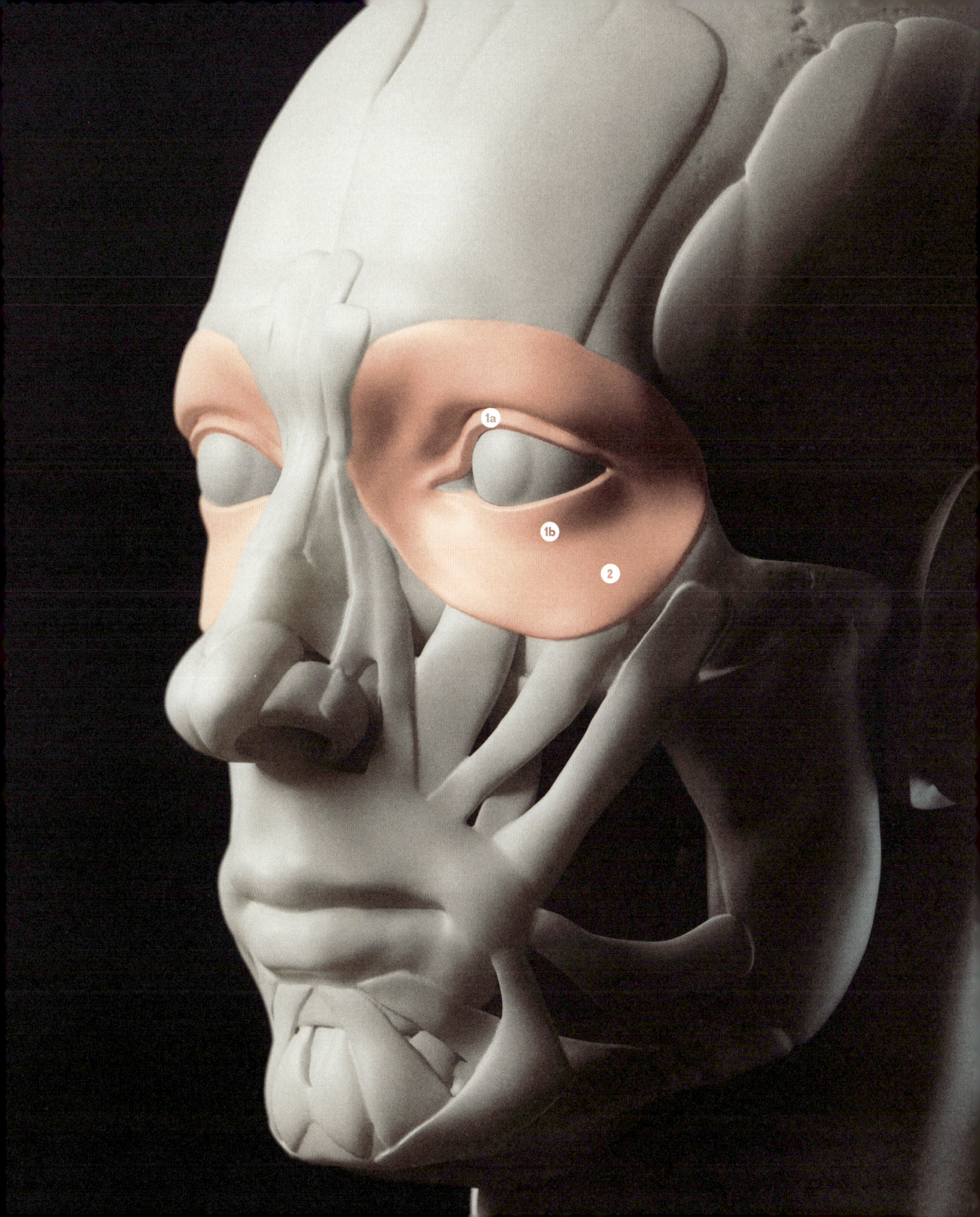

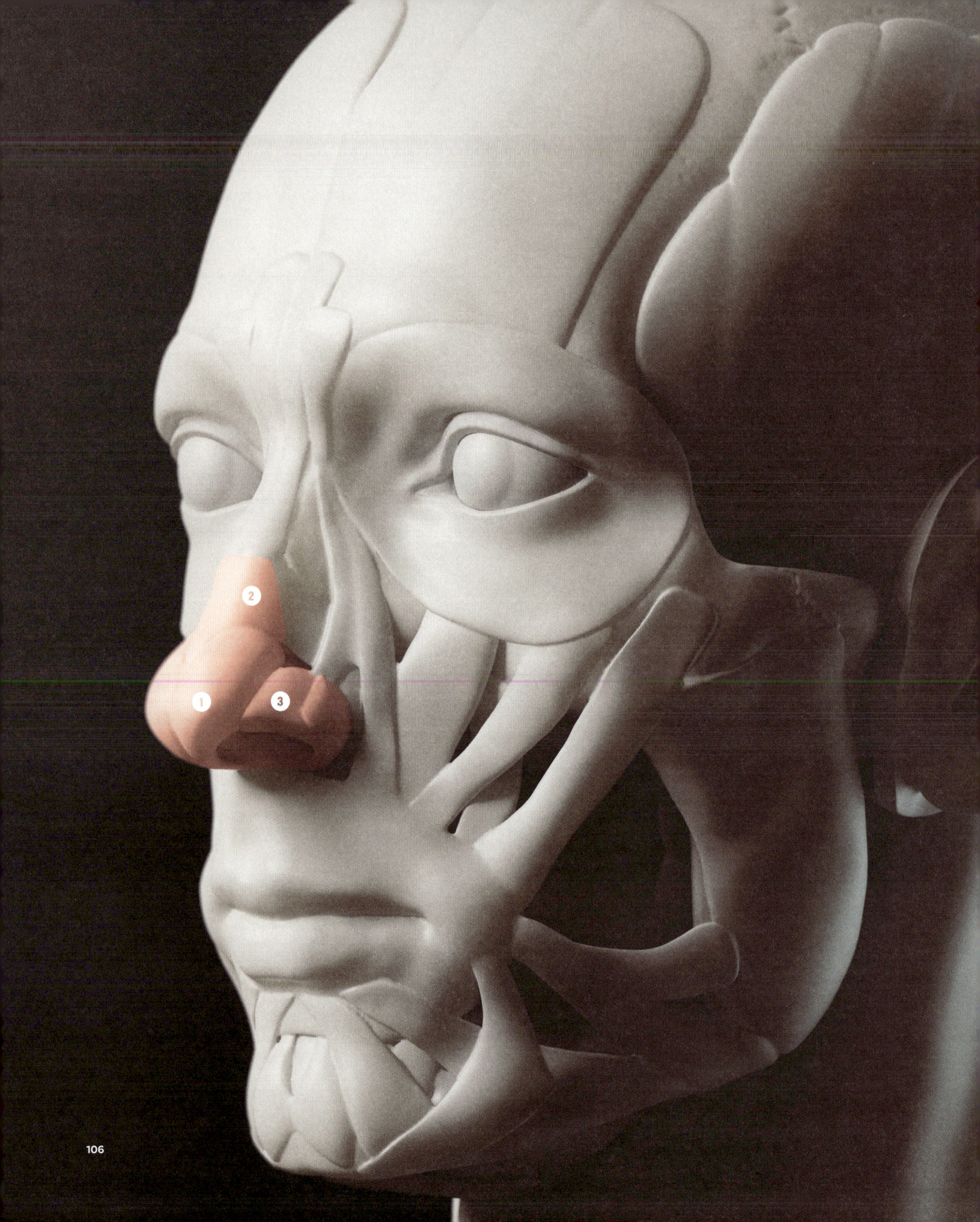

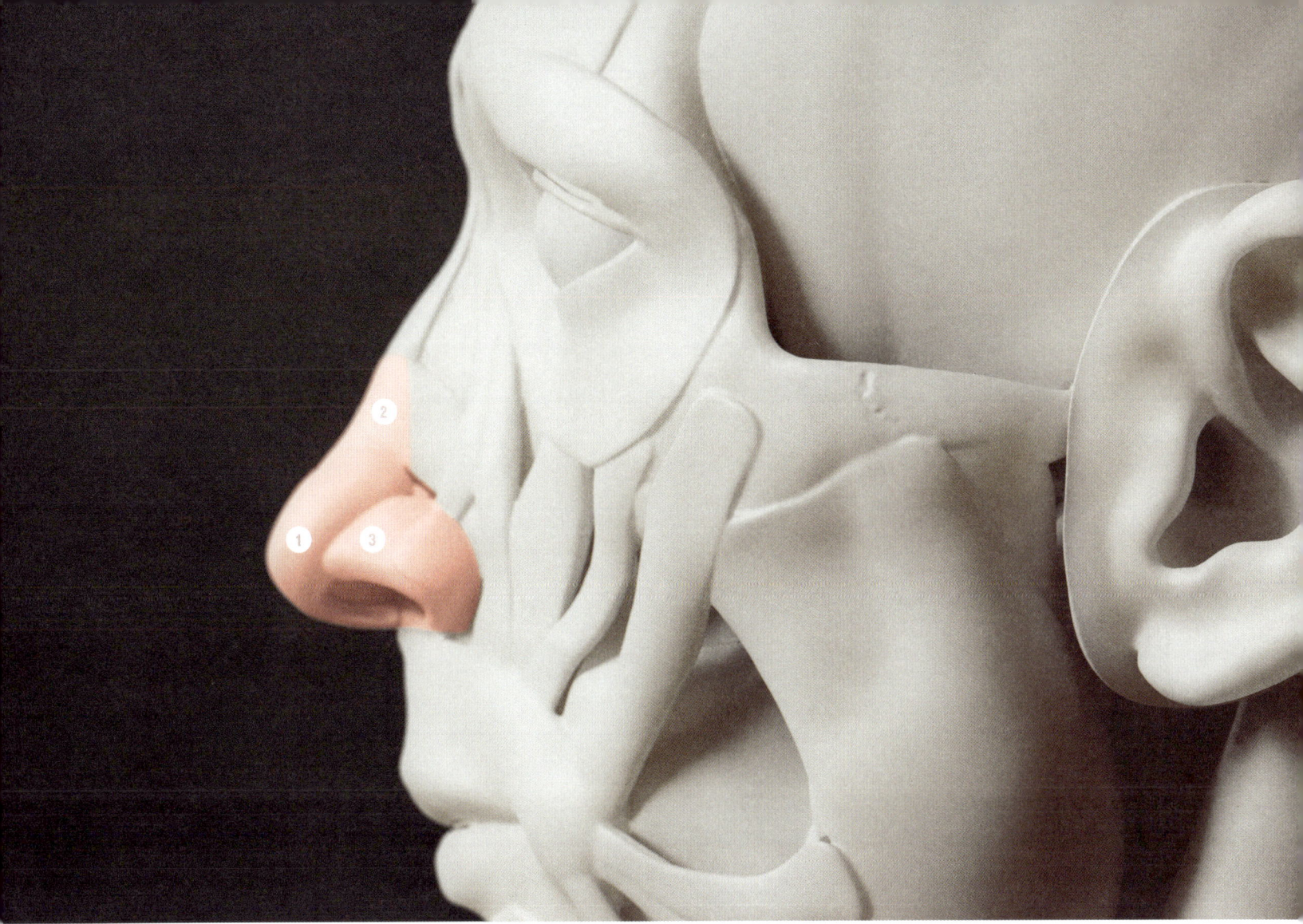

STRUCTURES OF THE NOSE

The greater alar cartilage, the lateral cartilage, and the fibro-fatty tissue of the wing of the nose play distinctive roles in shaping the nose's appearance and functionality.

1. The greater alar cartilage

This is perhaps the most significant in terms of defining the nose's contour. It consists of two pieces of cartilage, one on each side of the nose, which shape the tip and the nostrils. These cartilages are flexible yet resilient, allowing the nostrils to maintain their open form while also enabling them to dilate and contract during breathing.

2. The lateral cartilages

These pair with the septal cartilage and form the sidewalls of the nose. They are somewhat triangular in shape and less flexible than the greater alar cartilages. They provide structural stability to the midsection of the nose and help form the nose's overall architecture.

3. The nasal ala

This is the fibro-fatty tissue of the wing of the nose – the softer part that forms the sides of the nostrils and contributes to the nose's pliability and expressiveness. This tissue allows for the slight movement and flexibility of the nostrils, which is necessary for facial expressions and the regulation of airflow during respiration.

Together, these cartilages and tissues determine the shape, size, and functionality of the nose. They are covered by skin and muscle, which conform to their underlying shapes, creating the varied contours and profiles seen in the human nose. The greater alar cartilage especially influences the nose's aesthetic by defining the tip's shape and the nostrils' flare.

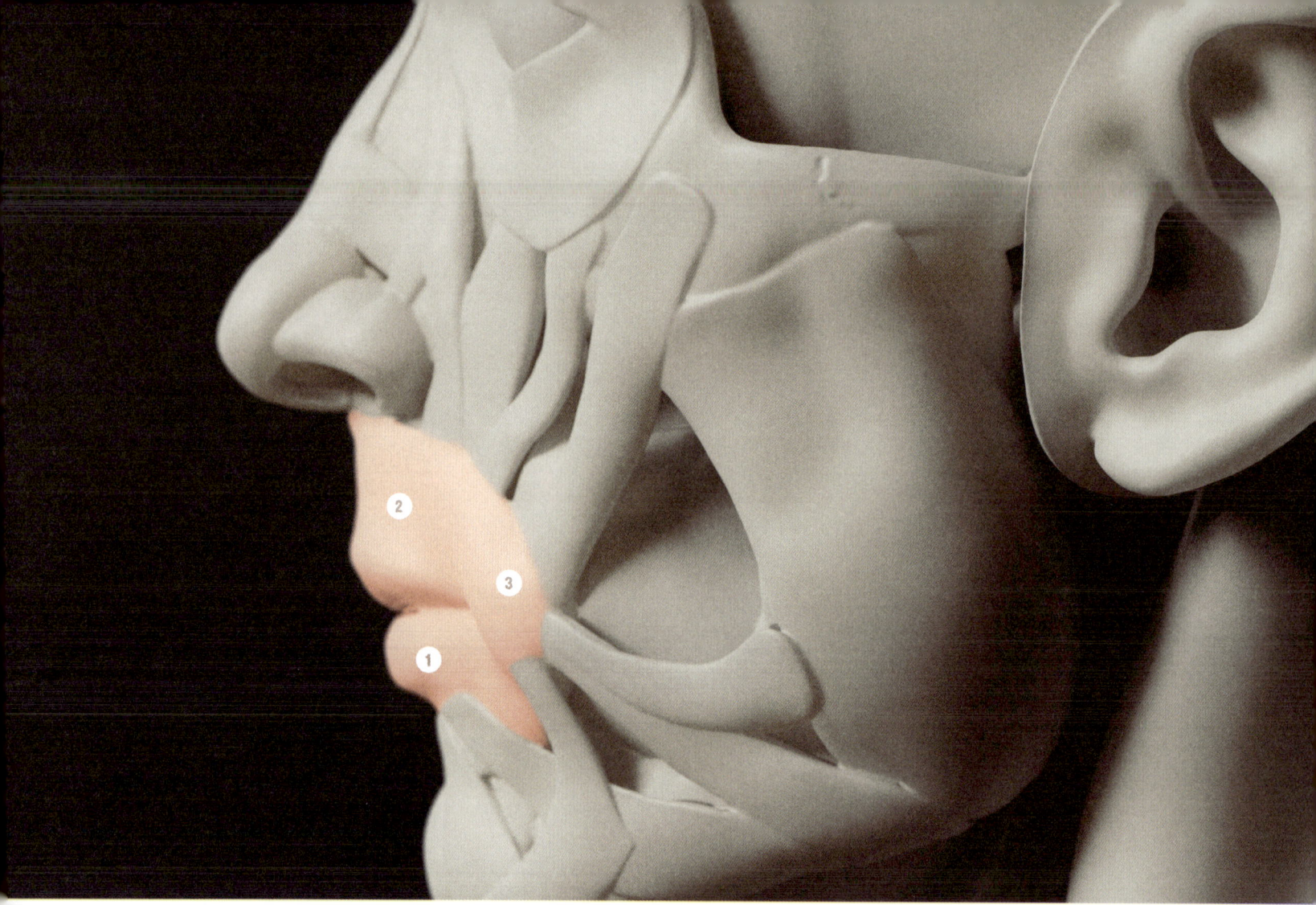

THE ORBICULARIS ORIS

The orbicularis oris is a complex, multifunctional muscle that encircles the mouth. It does not have a bony origin or insertion like many other muscles. Instead it consists of fibres that intertwine around the mouth, originating and inserting into the skin and other muscles in the area. This muscle is unique because it forms a continuous loop, which is critical for its primary function: manipulating the shape and movement of the mouth.

1. The marginal part

This is the inner part of the muscle, also known as the labial part, which directly controls the lips.

2. The peripheral part

This is the outer part, more associated with the structure of the mouth region.

3. Nodes

These are small concentrated areas at the outer corners of the mouth where muscle fibres converge or overlap. In particular, the many muscles that control lip movement – the orbicularis oris itself, buccinator, zygomaticus major and minor, levator anguli oris, risorius, and depressor anguli oris. When the orbicularis oris contracts, these nodes become more pronounced, enhancing certain expressions.

On a living model, the orbicularis oris can be identified in both frontal and side views through the movements and contours it creates. From the front, when the muscle contracts, you can often see the lips purse or tighten, forming a rounded shape for actions like kissing, or the flattening and spreading that occurs during a smile. From the side, the puckering of the lips or the pressing together in a tight seal is visible, with the nodes sometimes creating small dimples or creases at the corners of the mouth.

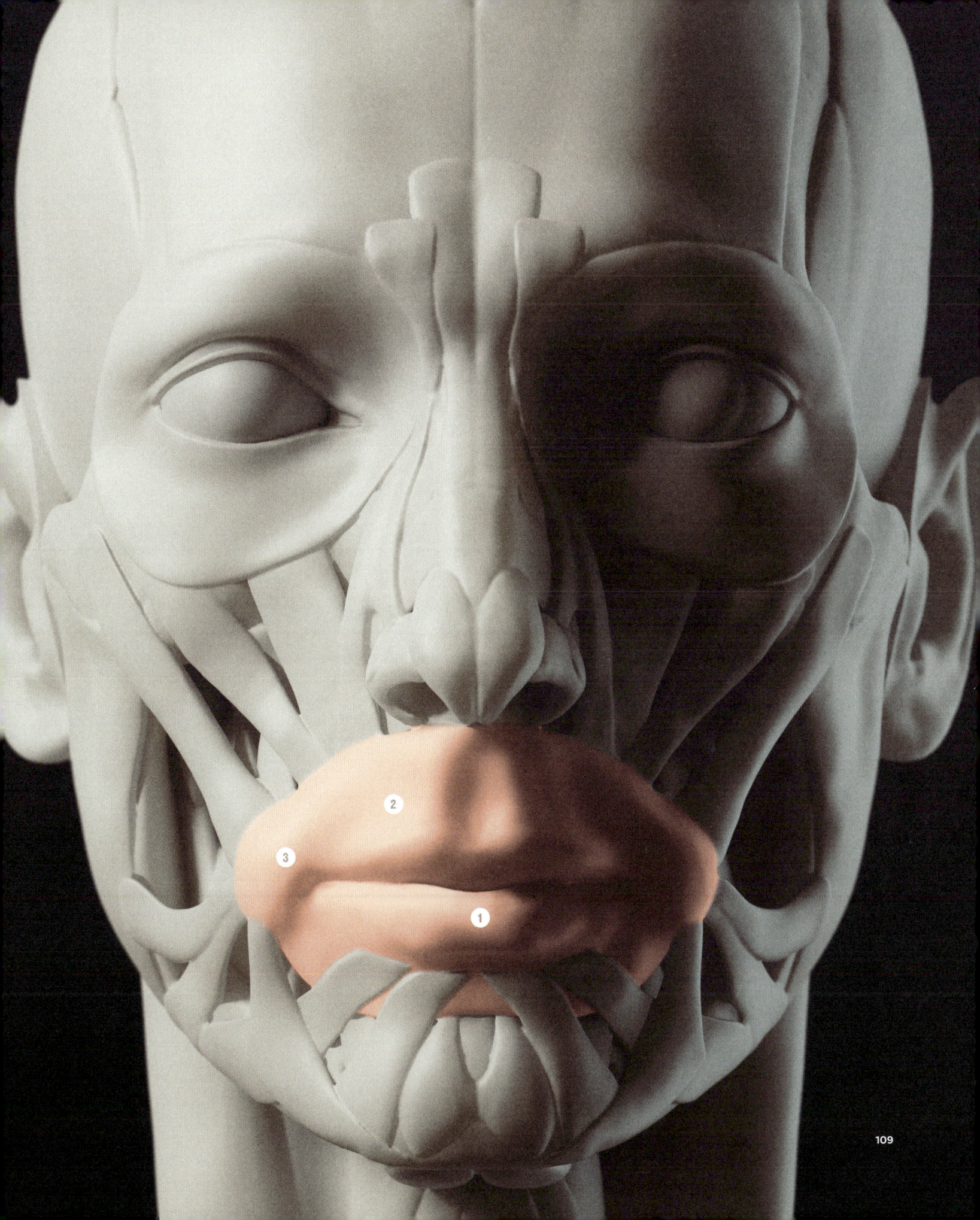

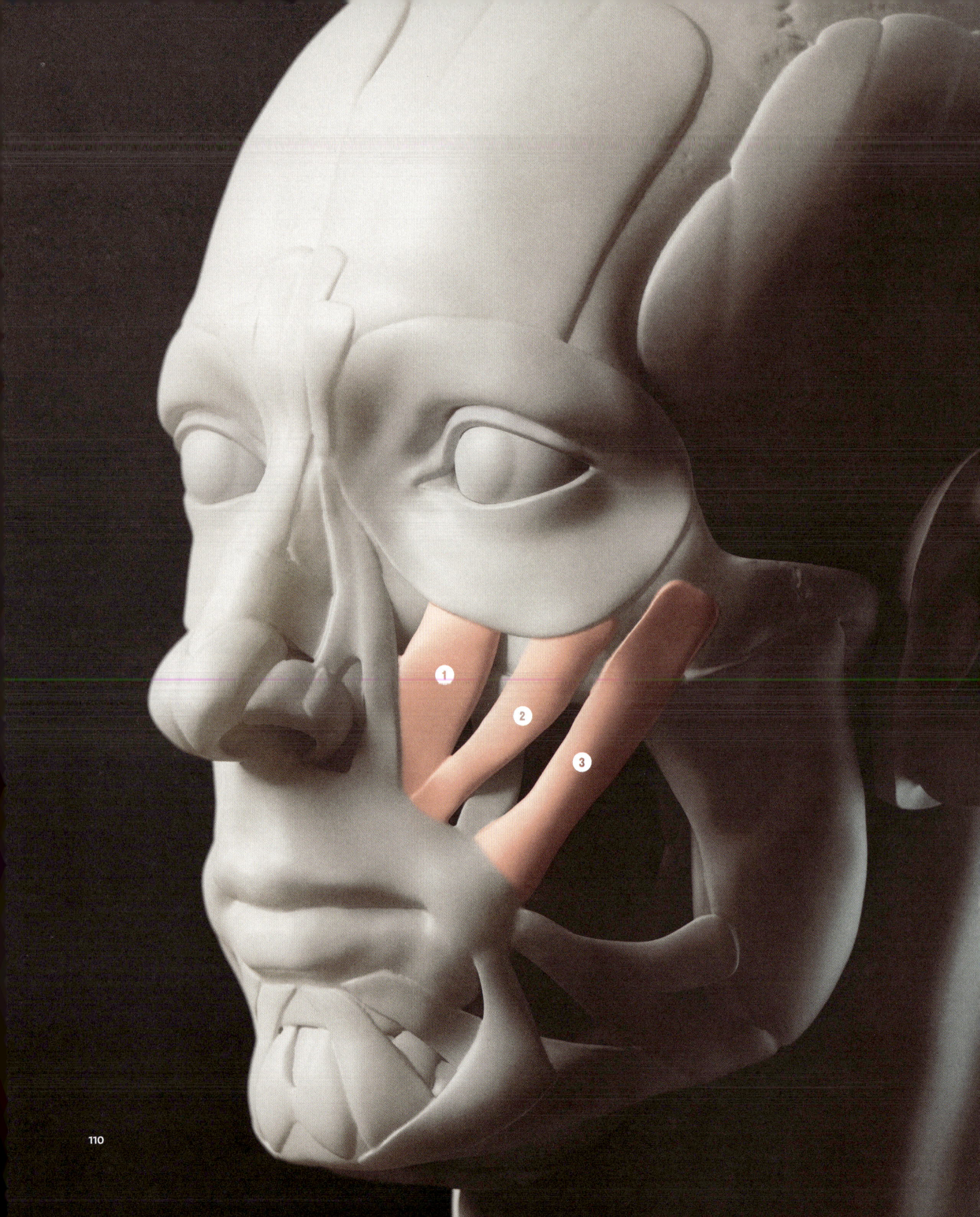

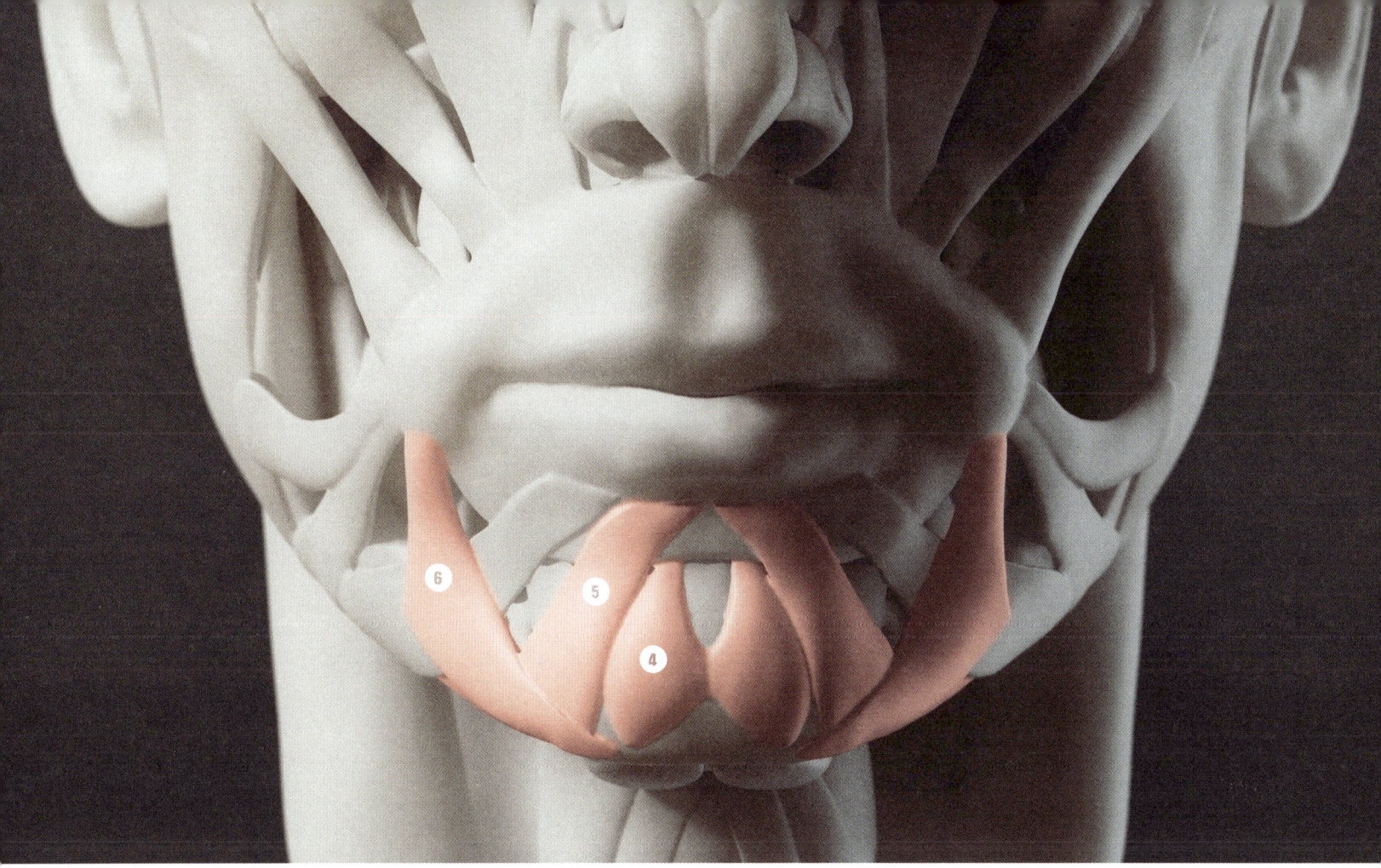

MUSCLES OF THE CHEEK AND CHIN

1. Levator labii superioris

This originates from the upper part of the frontal process of the maxilla, near the infraorbital foramen. It inserts into the skin of the nasolabial fold and continues down into the deep surface of the skin of the upper lip, blending with the orbicularis oris. Its action creates deep nasolabial folds, enhancing the emotional intensity displayed.

2. Zygomaticus minor

This muscle finds its origin on the front surface of the zygomatic bone, extending to the angle of the mouth where it inserts into the skin of the nasolabial furrow, and continues on into the marginal portion of the orbicularis oris muscle. When contracted – when smiling – it draws the corner of the mouth upwards and laterally.

3. Zygomaticus major

Although similar and parallel in function to the minor version, the major is larger and originates from the zygomatic bone's outer surface, inserting above the upper-lip's corner at the node. It assists in the same actions.

4. Mentalis

Often referred to as the chin muscle, this originates from a vertical line on the front of the lower jaw, just below the roots of the teeth. It is immediately lateral to the midline and inserts into the skin of the chin. It is responsible for protruding the lower lip and wrinkling the chin skin, as in expressions of doubt or displeasure.

5. Depressor labii inferioris

This arises from an oblique line on the mandible's body and inserts into the lower lip. It acts to lower the bottom lip and is crucial for sad expressions such as frowning.

6. Depressor anguli oris

This originates from the outer surface of the mandible near the angle and, superficially, the fascia covering the platysma – extends to insert at the muscular node at the corner of the mouth. It depresses the corner of the mouth, contributing to expressions of sadness.

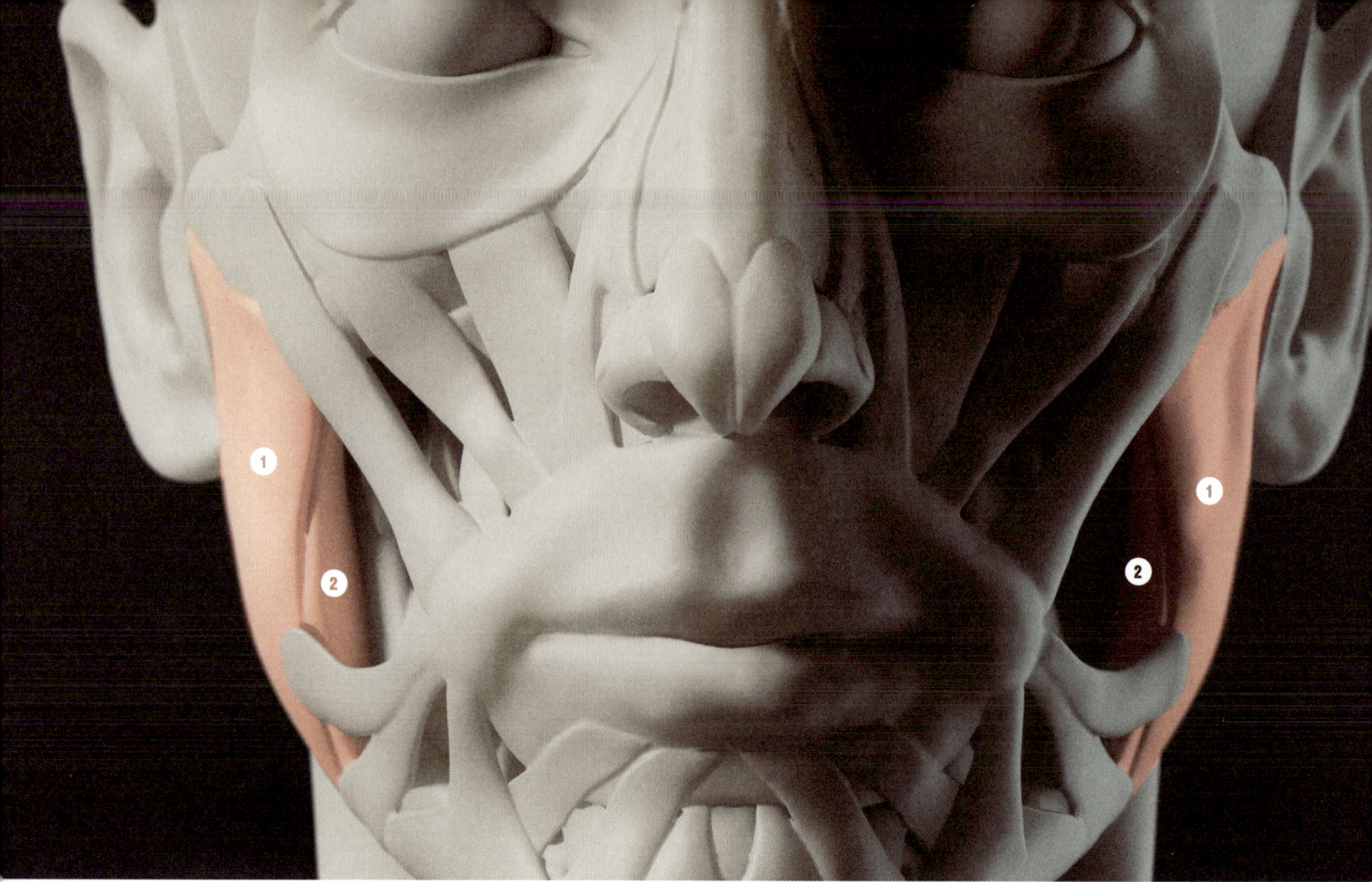

THE MASSETER

The powerful masseter muscle is a prominent facial muscle, critical for the function of chewing, and plays a significant role in defining the form of the lower face. Its nature and positioning make it one of the most easily identifiable muscles in the facial anatomy. Originating from the zygomatic arch's inferior border, the masseter muscle spans downwards to insert along the angle and lateral surface of the mandibular ramus. It is divided into two distinct layers.

1. The superficial part
This arises from the anterior two-thirds of the lower border of the zygomatic arch.

2. The deep part
This originates from the posterior third and the whole of the medial surface of the arch.

The masseter muscle is primarily responsible for the elevation of the mandible, or the closing of the jaw, and plays a secondary role in the protraction and retraction of the mandible.

On the surface, it gives the cheek and posterior section of the jaw their characteristic fullness and can significantly influence facial contour, especially in the lower region. In individuals with well-developed masseter muscles, this can manifest as a pronounced width in an area of the jaw that is inferior to the zygomatic arch.

Identifying the masseter on a living model requires observation of the muscle's surface landmarks. From a frontal view, the muscle can be seen most clearly when the teeth are clenched, creating a subtle bulge at the sides of the face, extending from the cheekbone down to the lower jaw.

From a side view, the masseter's form is more distinct. The anterior border of the muscle can often be seen just posterior to the oral cavity, presenting as a vertical definition that may be more prominent in individuals with a strong musculature or when the muscle is tensed. The lower edge of the zygomatic arch provides a visual guide to the upper origin of the masseter, and the angle of the mandible indicates its lower insertion.

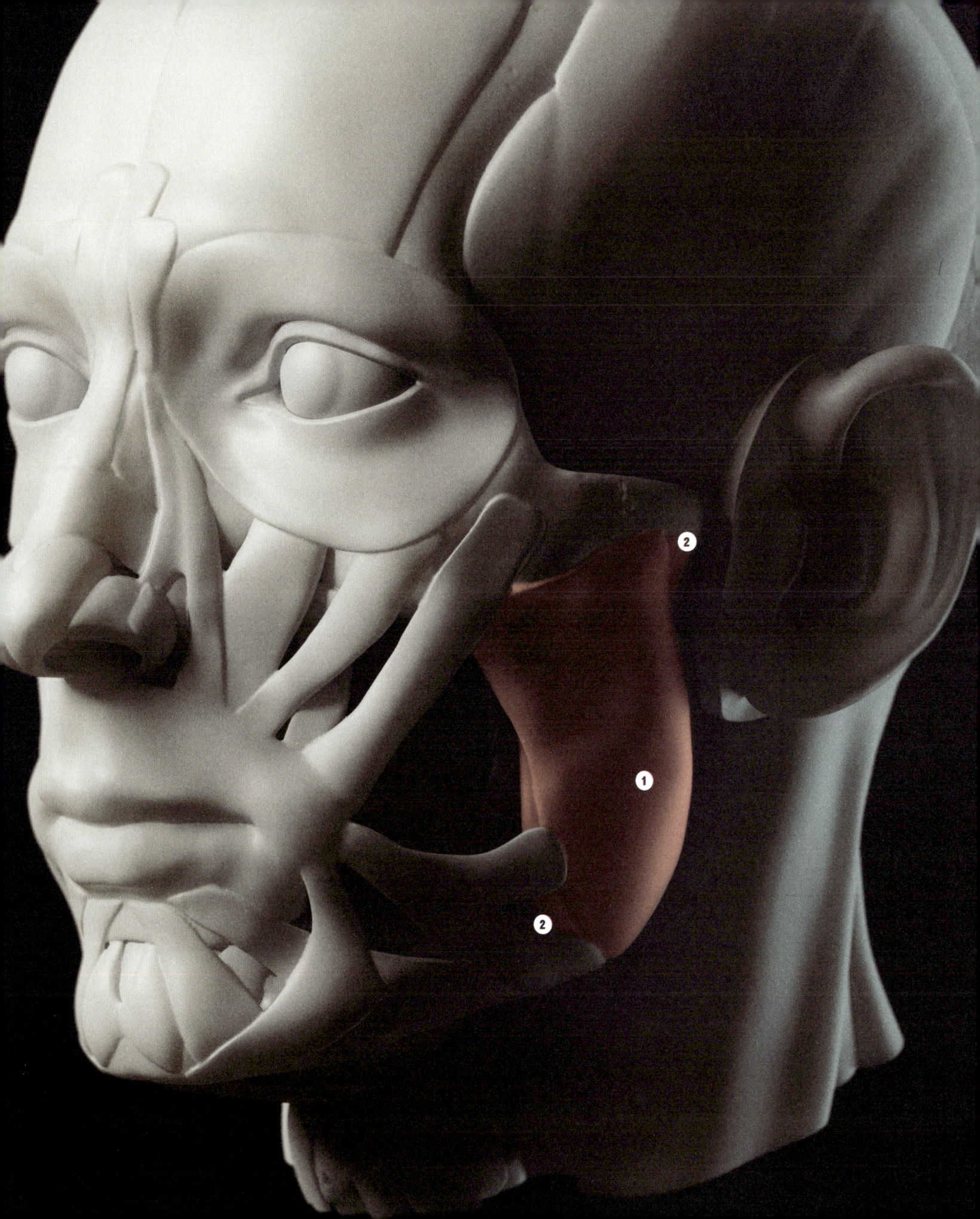

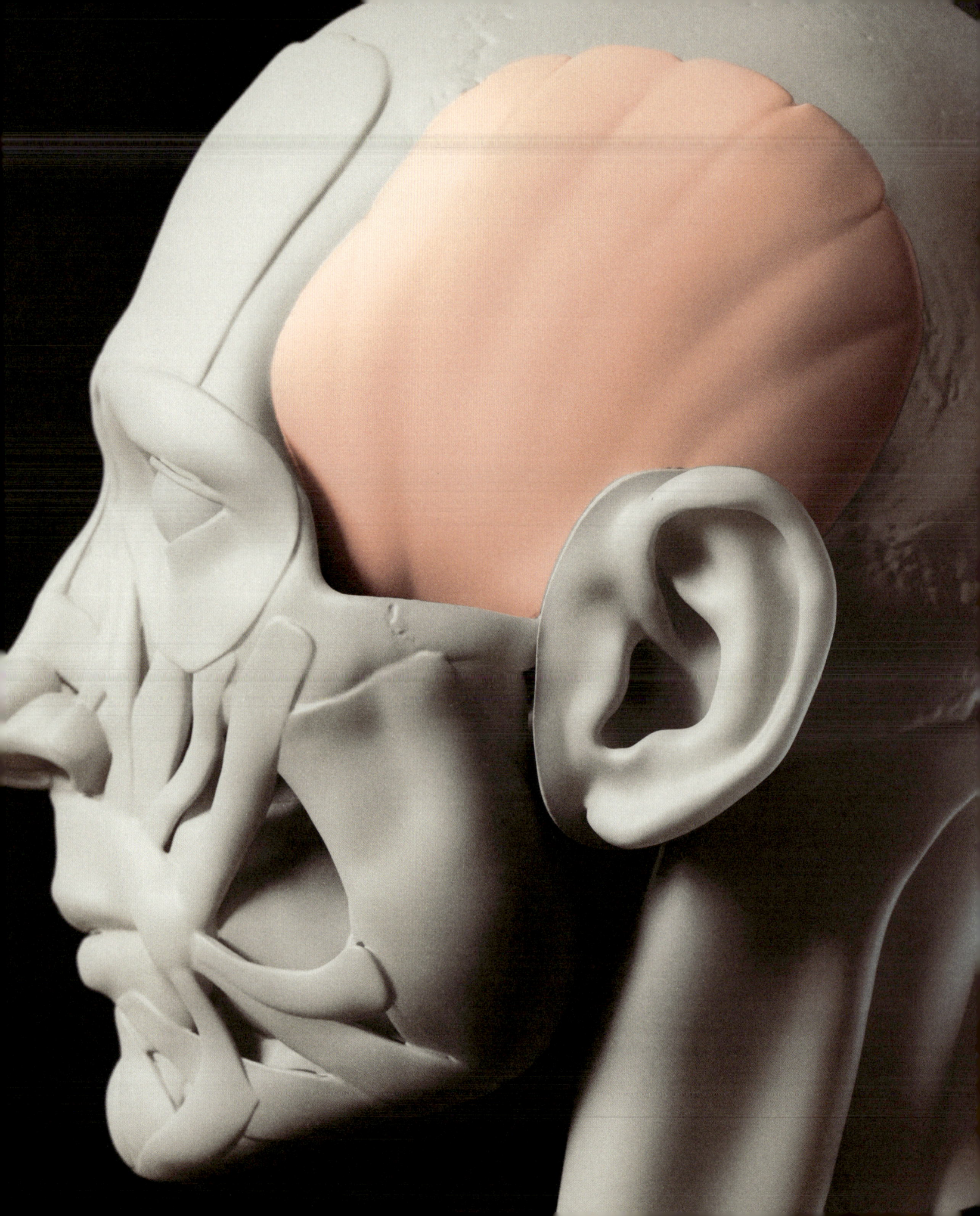

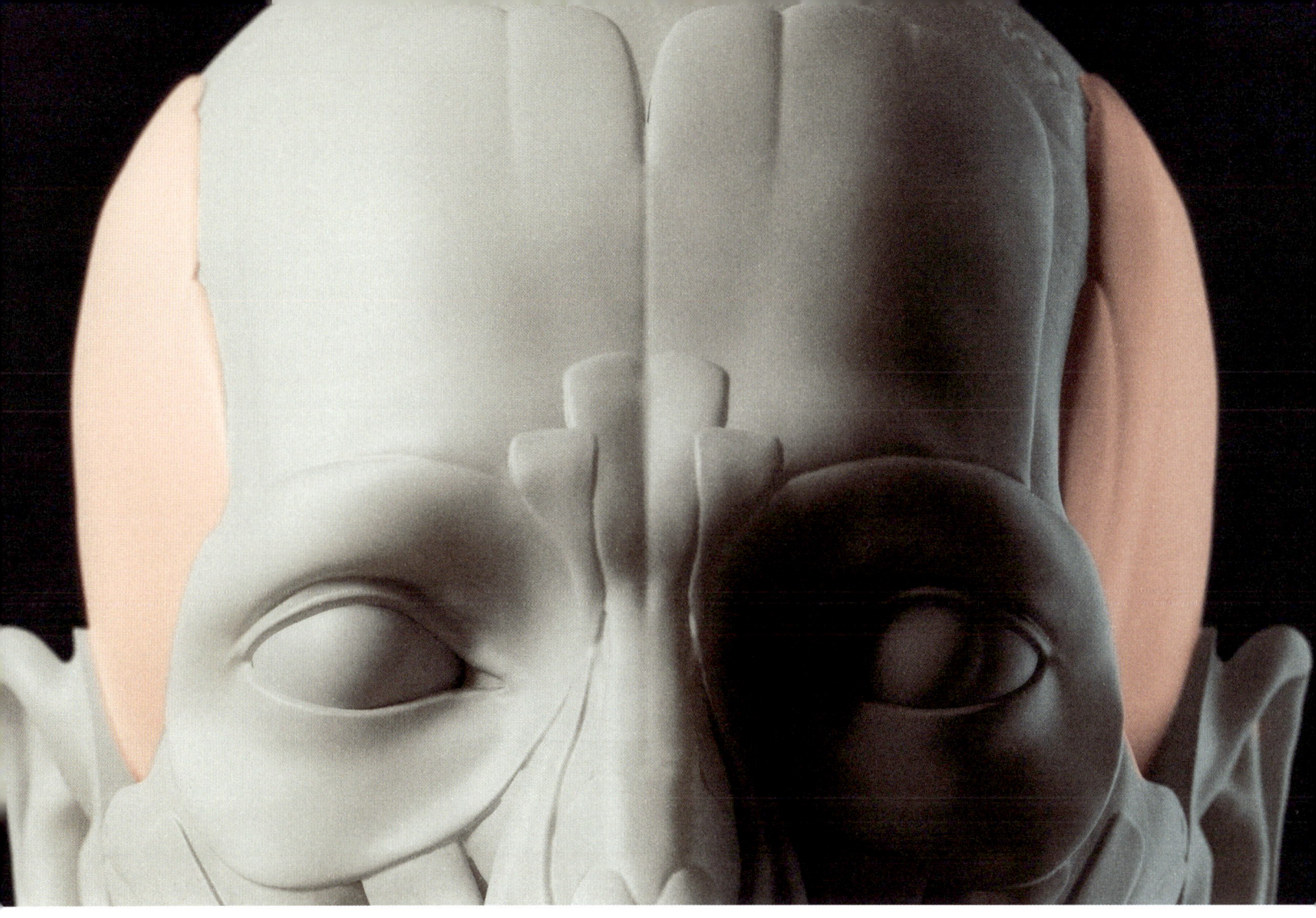

THE TEMPORALIS

The temporalis (highlighted in the images) is a broad, fan-shaped muscle positioned on the side of the head, covering much of the temporal bone. This muscle is responsible for elevating the mandible, which closes the jaw, and retracting the mandible, pulling it backwards. Its action is essential for biting and grinding food, making it one of the primary muscles of mastication.

Given its size and strength, the temporalis can generate considerable force, which is transmitted to the mandible. Originating from the temporal fossa, a shallow depression on the side of the skull, the temporalis extends down beneath the zygomatic arch, where it converges into a tendon that inserts onto the coronoid process of the mandible.

Covering the temporalis is the temporal fascia, a strong, fibrous sheet of connective tissue. This fascia attaches to the superior temporal line of the skull and spans down to the zygomatic arch, effectively concealing the upper part of the muscle and the division between the temporalis and the zygomatic arch.

On a living model its form can be more or less pronounced depending on the individual's anatomy and the muscle's development. From a frontal view, this bulge is subtle, seen as a slight convexity at the temple, just above and behind the eye. From a side view, the muscle's outline is more discernible, especially when the jaw is clenched.

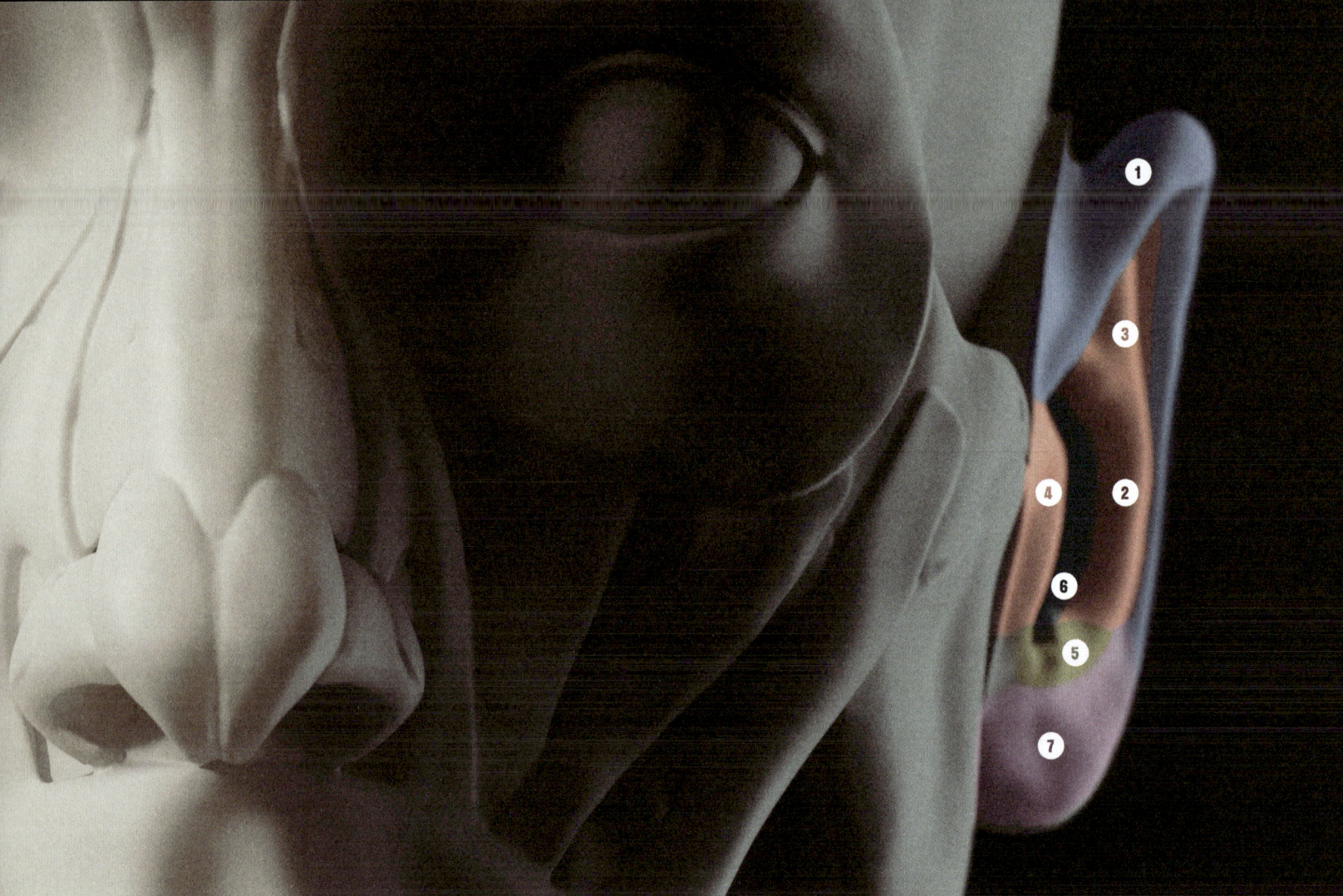

THE EAR

The human ear captures and funnels sound into the auditory canal as well as serving an aesthetic purpose. Its structure is composed of intricate folds and contours, each with a designated term and function.

1. Helix

At the outer rim of the ear, this is the prominent, curved ridge that travels down from the top of the ear to the lobe. It forms the outermost margin and acts as a protective boundary for the rest of the ear's delicate structures. The helix starts just above the ear canal in a thickened area known as the crus of the helix, which then continues to form the main curve of the helix itself.

2. Antihelix

Parallel to the helix, this is the Y-shaped ridge that branches out below the upper part of the ear. It serves to reinforce the ear's structure, providing a firmness to the cartilage that helps to maintain the ear's shape.

3. Fossa triangularis

This is a small depression nestled between the branches of the antihelix. It adds to the ear's complex topography and is bordered by the two crura of the antihelix.

4–5. Tragus and antitragus

Lying below the antihelix, towards the front of the ear, this is a small, pointed eminence of cartilage that protrudes over the ear canal and aids in collecting sound waves from the environment. Opposite it is the antitragus, a smaller mound of cartilage above the earlobe.

6. Concha

The hollow, bowl-like space just next to the ear canal entrance. It is the largest depression in the external ear and plays a role in gathering sound and funnelling it into the auditory canal.

7. Earlobe

The soft, fleshy part hanging below the rest of the ear. It lacks the cartilage that gives the rest of the ear its firm structure.

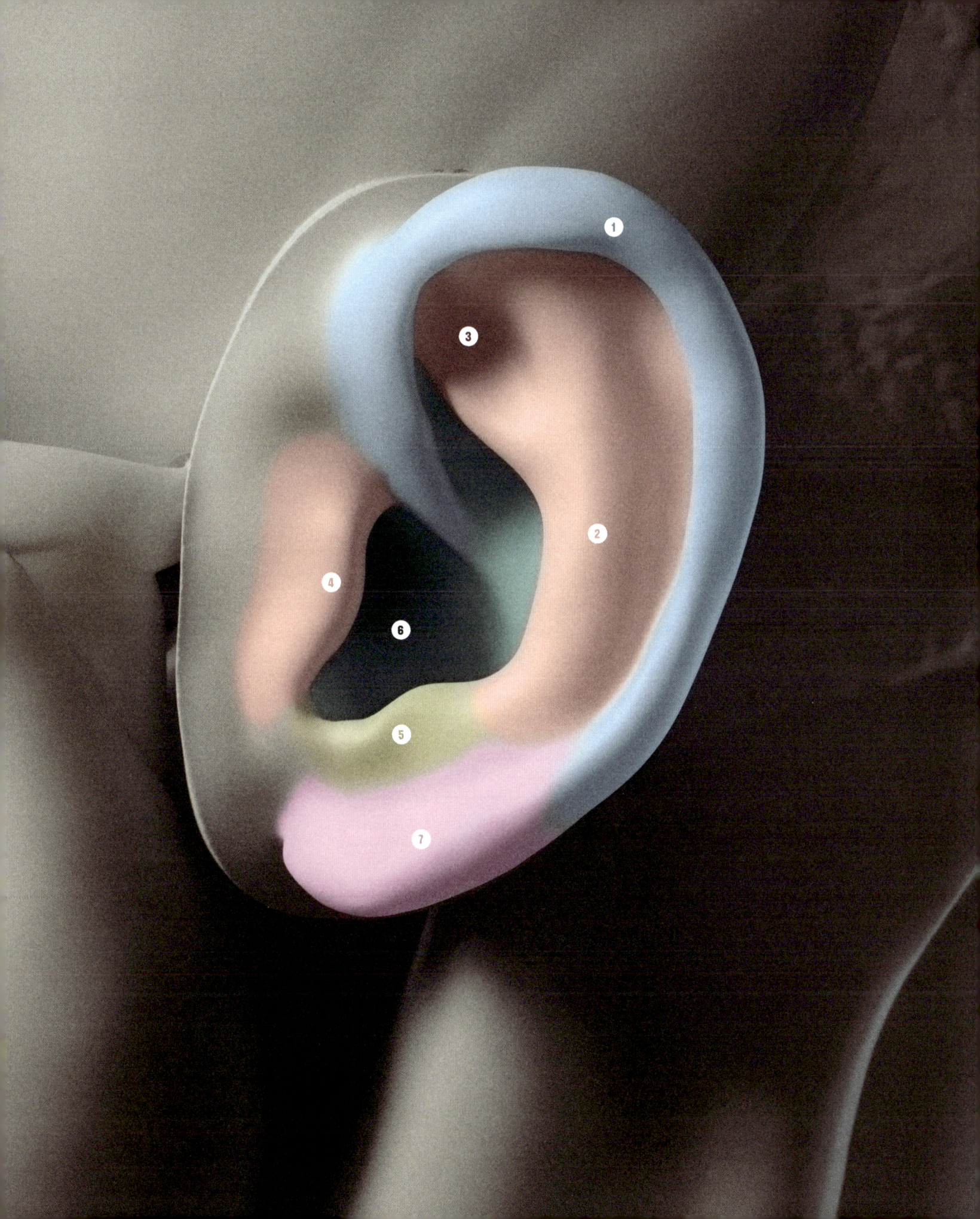

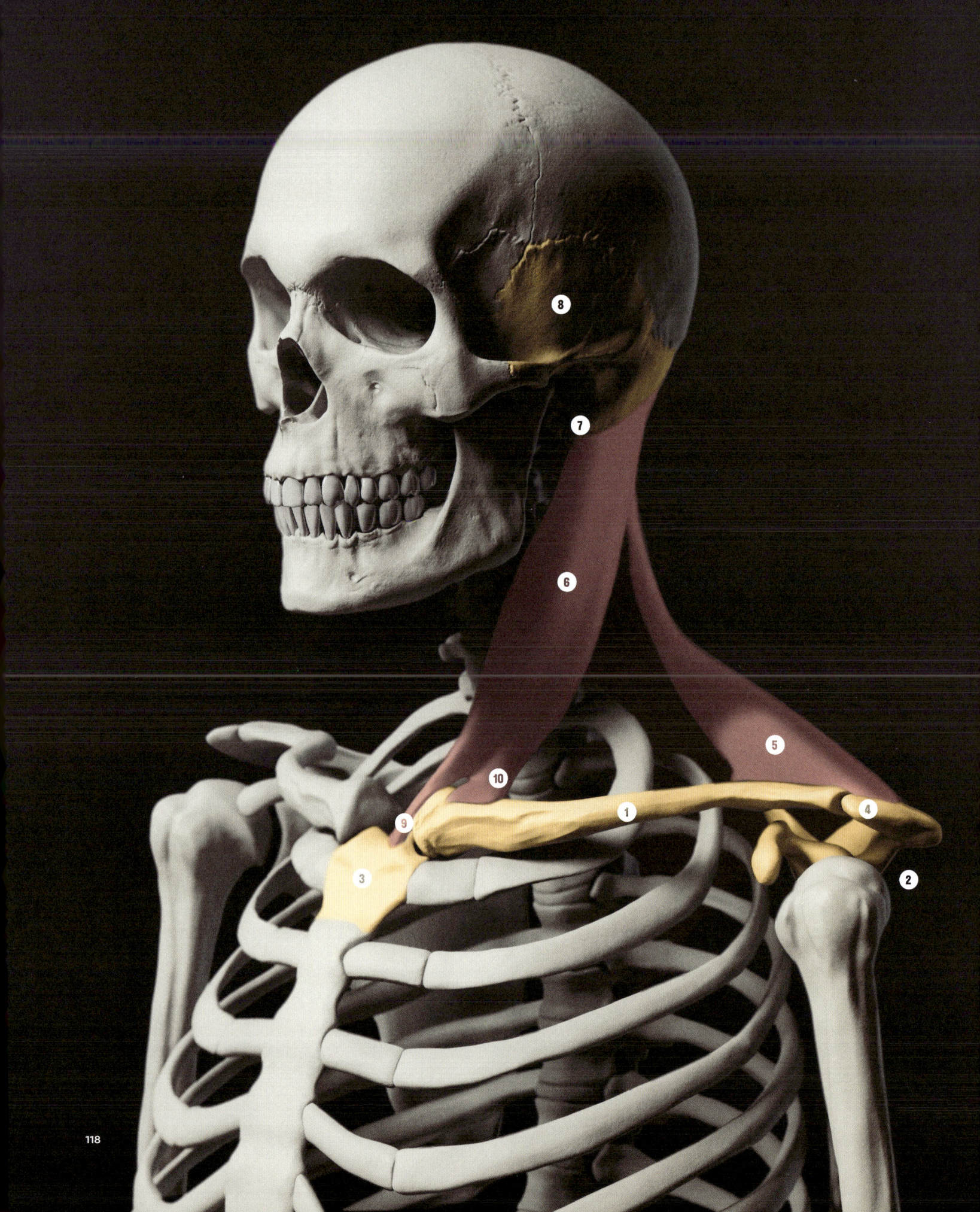

ATTACHING THE HEAD TO THE BODY

The anatomical structures connecting the head to the body include several prominent muscles and bones that facilitate movement and provide support.

The clavicles, scapulae, and sternum collectively form the shoulder girdle, a bony framework that provides attachment points for numerous muscles and supports the arms' motion.

Important bones in this area

1. Clavicles

Also known as collarbones, these are long, slender bones that stretch horizontally between the sternum at the base of the neck and the **scapulae (2)**, otherwise known as the shoulder blades. At their medial end, the clavicles articulate with the manubrium of the **sternum (3)** at the sternoclavicular joints. Laterally, the clavicles connect to the scapulae at the acromioclavicular joints, where a small projection of the scapula, the **acromion process (4)**, meets the outer end of the clavicle. This joint facilitates the movement of the scapulae, allowing them to glide over the rib cage.

2. Scapulae

These are flat, triangular bones positioned on the back of the ribcage. While not involved in the vast majority of portrait poses, they are relevant particularly for their articulation with the clavicles and support for the points of insertion for the **trapezius (5)**.

3. Sternum

This long, flat bone in the centre of the chest consists of three sections: the manubrium at the top, gladiolus in the middle, and xiphoid process at the bottom. A central keystone of the shoulder girdle, it anchors the clavicles and provides indirect support for the scapulae through the muscular and ligamentous structures attached to it.

4. Acromion Process

A bony prominence at the top of the shoulder.

5. Trapezius

This is a broad, flat muscle that spans the upper back and extends to the neck. It originates along the occipital bone at the base of the skull, the ligamentum nuchae, and the spinous processes of the cervical and thoracic vertebrae. It then fans out to insert on the lateral third of the clavicle, the acromion process, and the spine of the scapula. The trapezius muscle moves the scapula and supports the arm, and the upper fibres also contribute to extending the head backward.

6. Sternocleidomastoid (SCM)

This is a thick, cable-like muscle that is easily noticeable on either side of the neck. It originates from the **mastoid process (7)** of the **temporal bone (8)**, just behind the ear. From this origin, the SCM extends diagonally downward across the neck, where it separates into two heads, inserting into two points: the **sternal head (9)** inserting on the anterior surface of the manubrium and the **clavicular head (10)** inserting along the superior edge of the clavicle's sternal end. The muscle's primary action is to rotate and flex the head. When one side contracts, the head tilts towards the shoulder on that side and rotates to face the opposite side; when both sides contract together, the head flexes forward.

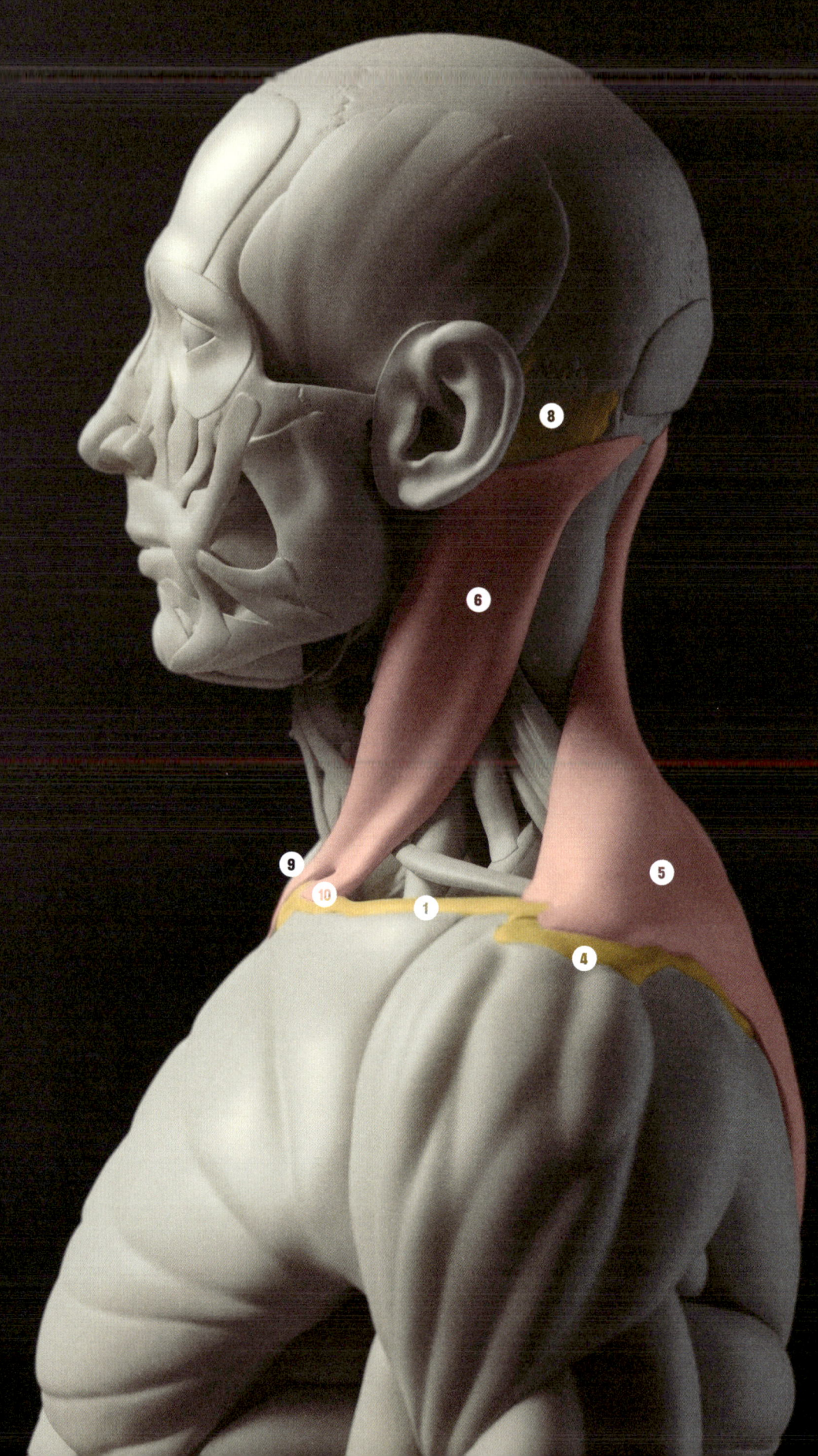

On a living model, both muscles are discernible, providing characteristic contours to the neck and shoulders. From the front, the SCM frames the neck, creating a V-shape that starts at the base of the neck and extends diagonally towards the ear. The clavicles form a horizontal line beneath the SCM, their subtle ridges leading towards the sternum at the centre of the chest. From the side, the SCM is more prominent, standing out as it stretches from behind the ear down to the clavicle and sternum. The muscle's twin insertions (at the manubrium and the clavicle) are visible under the skin, especially when the head is turned or flexed.

The trapezius shapes the upper back and the neck's posterior. Its upper fibres can be seen sloping from the neck down to the shoulders, where they meet the acromion process: a bony prominence at the top of the shoulder. The muscle's presence is accentuated when the shoulders are shrugged or when the arms are moved upwards from the side.

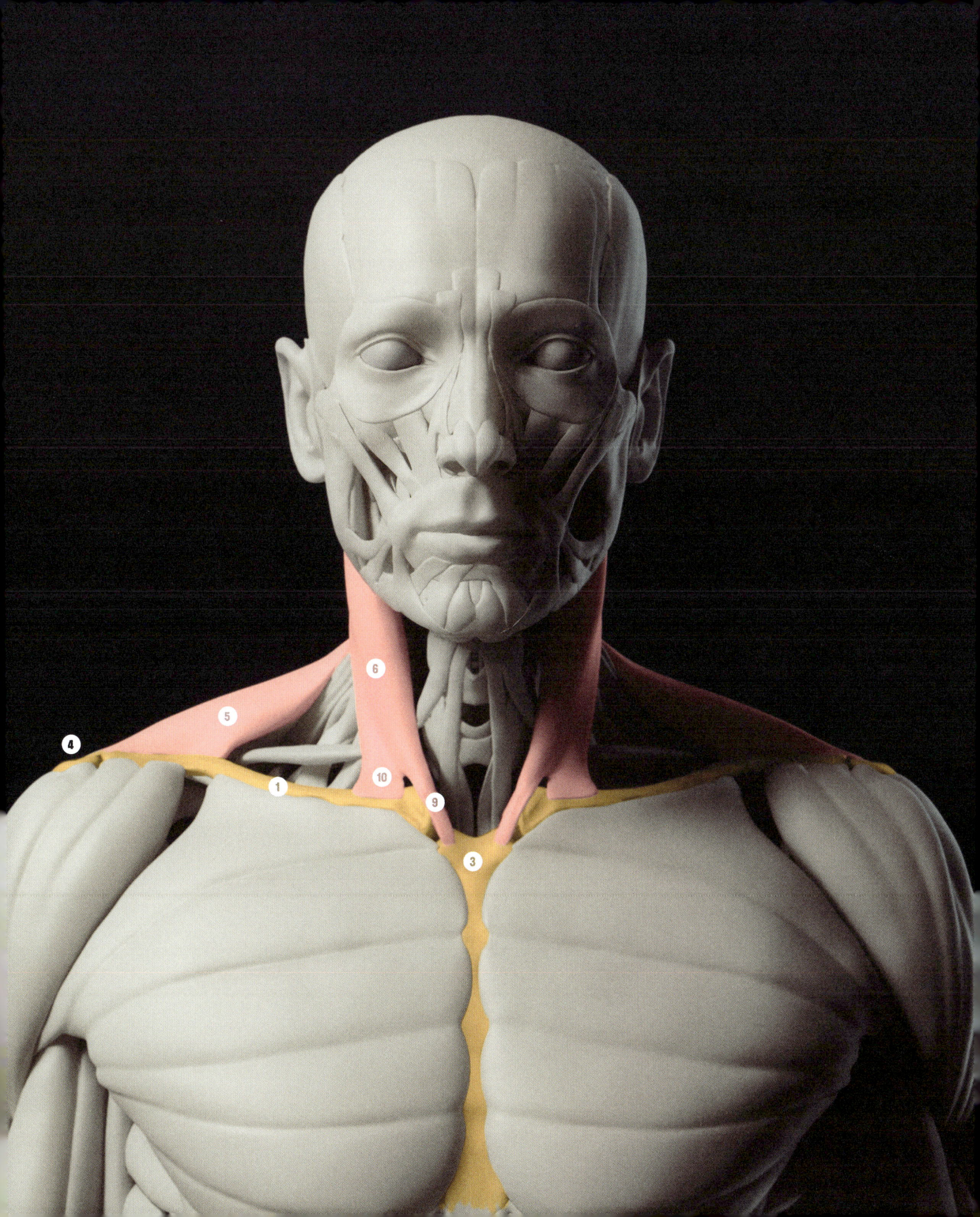

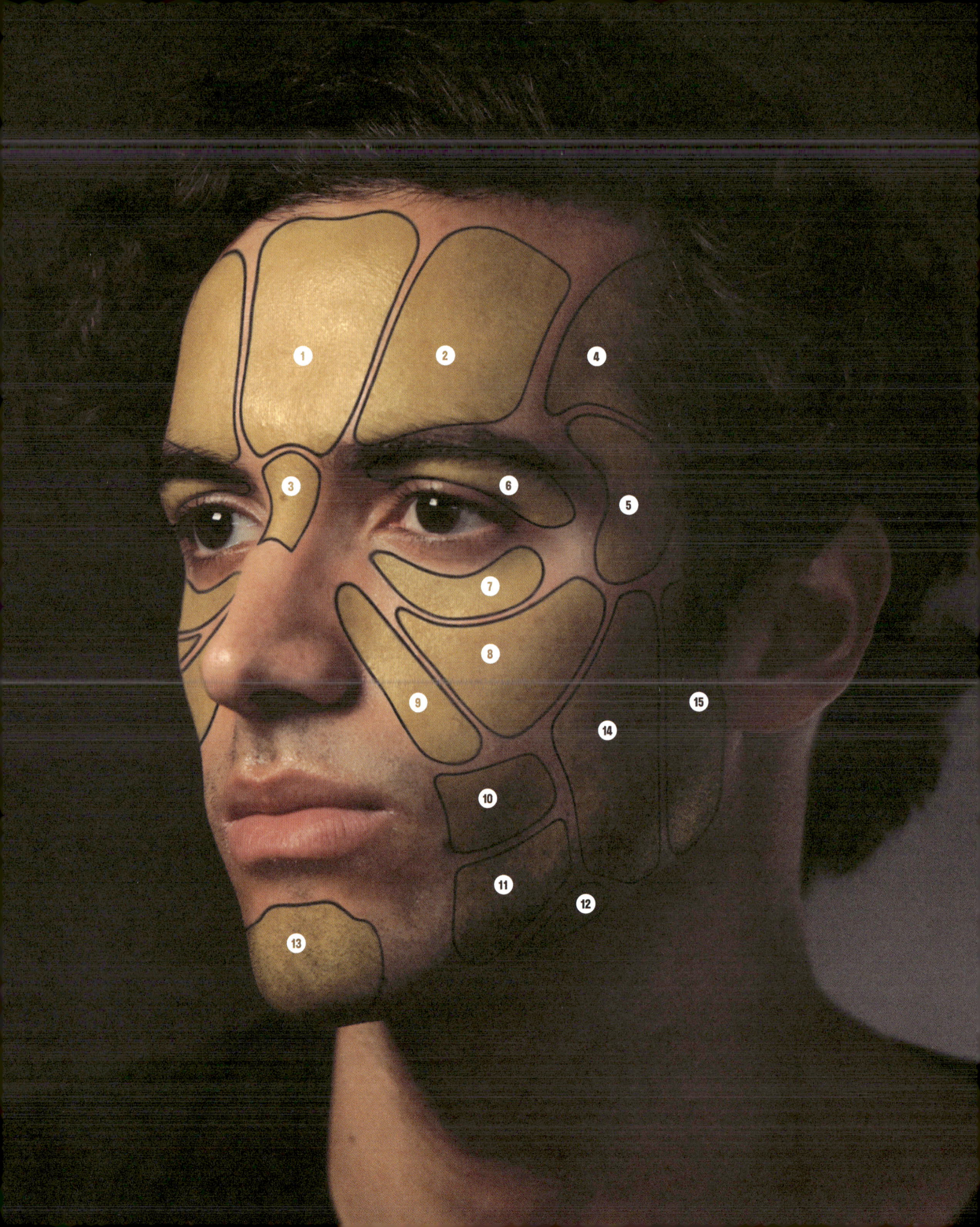

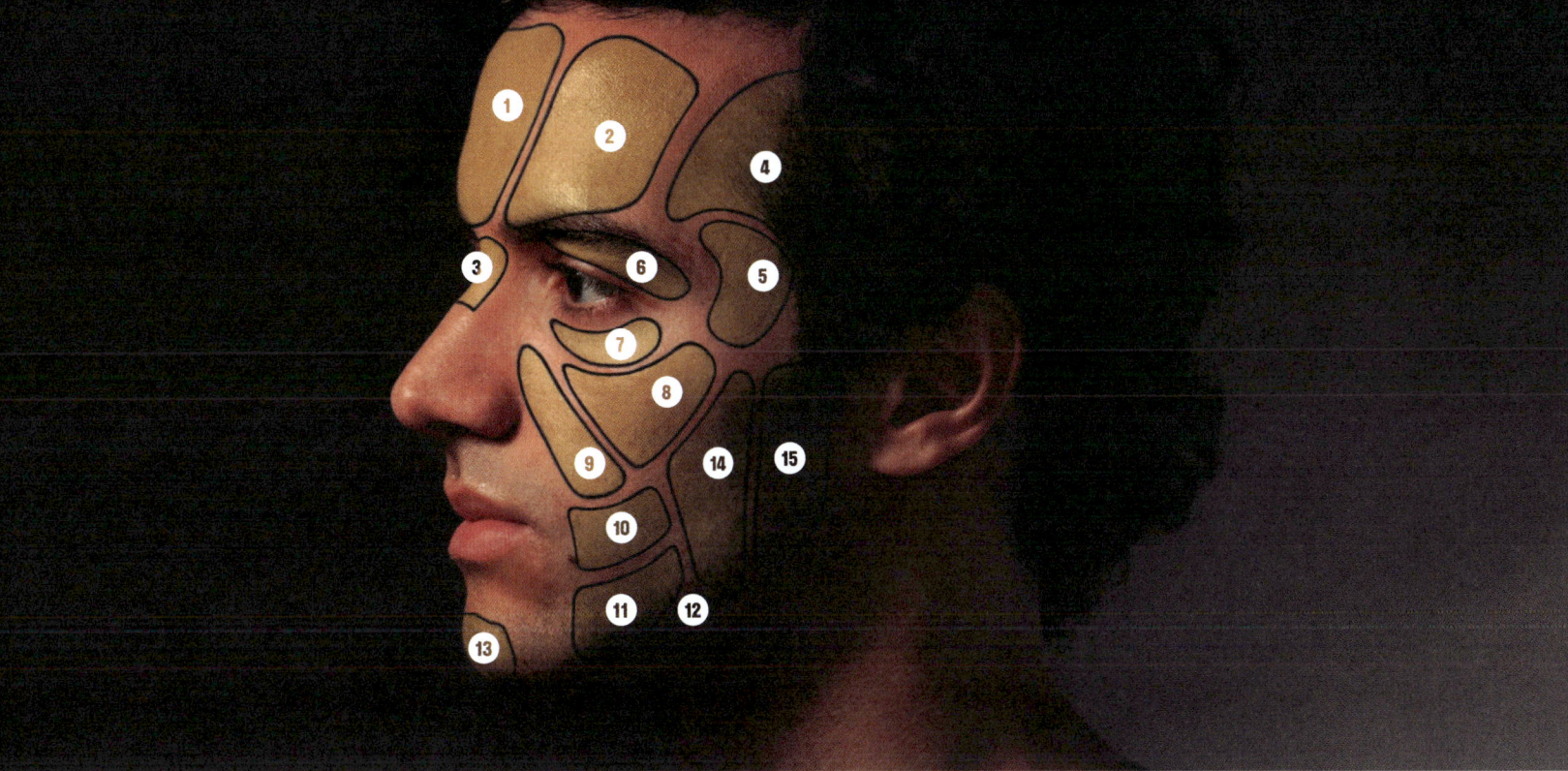

FAT DEPOSITS OF THE FACE

The face is not only defined by its muscles and bones, but also by the distribution of its fat deposits.

1. Central forehead fat pad

Situated in the middle of the forehead, this provides a smooth contour, and its prominence can be seen when the brows are furrowed.

2. The lateral forehead fat

Located at the sides of the forehead, this contributes to the rounded appearance of the temple region.

3. Radix fat

Found at the root of the nose, between the eyes. It fills the area where the nose meets the forehead and can be seen clearly in profile, softening the angle between the nasal bone and the forehead.

4-5. Lateral and inferior temporal cheek fat

These are situated around the temples. The lateral temporal cheek fat fills the space over the zygomatic arch, contributing to the softness of the cheek's contour, while the inferior temporal fat sits below this, giving fullness to the lower temple.

6. Superior orbital fat

Located within the orbit, above the eye.

7. Infraorbital fat

Just below the eye, giving volume to the lower eyelid and upper cheek.

8. Medial cheek fat

A significant volume contributor to the midface, filling the area beneath the infraorbital fat. This fat pad is important for a youthful appearance and can be identified as the fullness seen across the front plane of the cheeks.

9. Nasolabial fat

Located between the nose and the mouth, contributing to the nasolabial fold. More commonly referred to as the 'smile line'.

10-12. Superior, inferior, and submandibular jowl fat

Superior jowl fat (**10**) contributes to the fullness just anterior to the masseter muscle. The inferior jowl fat (**11**) is lower, contributing to the shape at the jawline, and the submandibular jowl fat (**12**) is under the jaw, which can affect the definition of the neck.

13. Mental fat

Localized around the chin, providing shape and prominence to the lower face.

14-15. Middle and lateral temporal cheek fat

These round out the posterior jaw directly below the zygomatic arch.

Composition

In the most general sense, composition refers to the group of ideas that we use to understand how to make a good picture. The use of 'good' here does not refer to any one type of idealized quality, rather it means the best version of the subject and intent of the artist. Composition has its own vocabulary and many of the practical ideas are contained within these terms. Take 'negative space', for example. There is not an objective way to use it or a predestined outcome when applying it to design. One merely needs to raise their awareness of its existence and evaluate its implication in the drawing to get the value of it as a tool.

'The discipline of accurately rendering will form a foundation for whatever you wish to build upon it.'

Charles Bargue

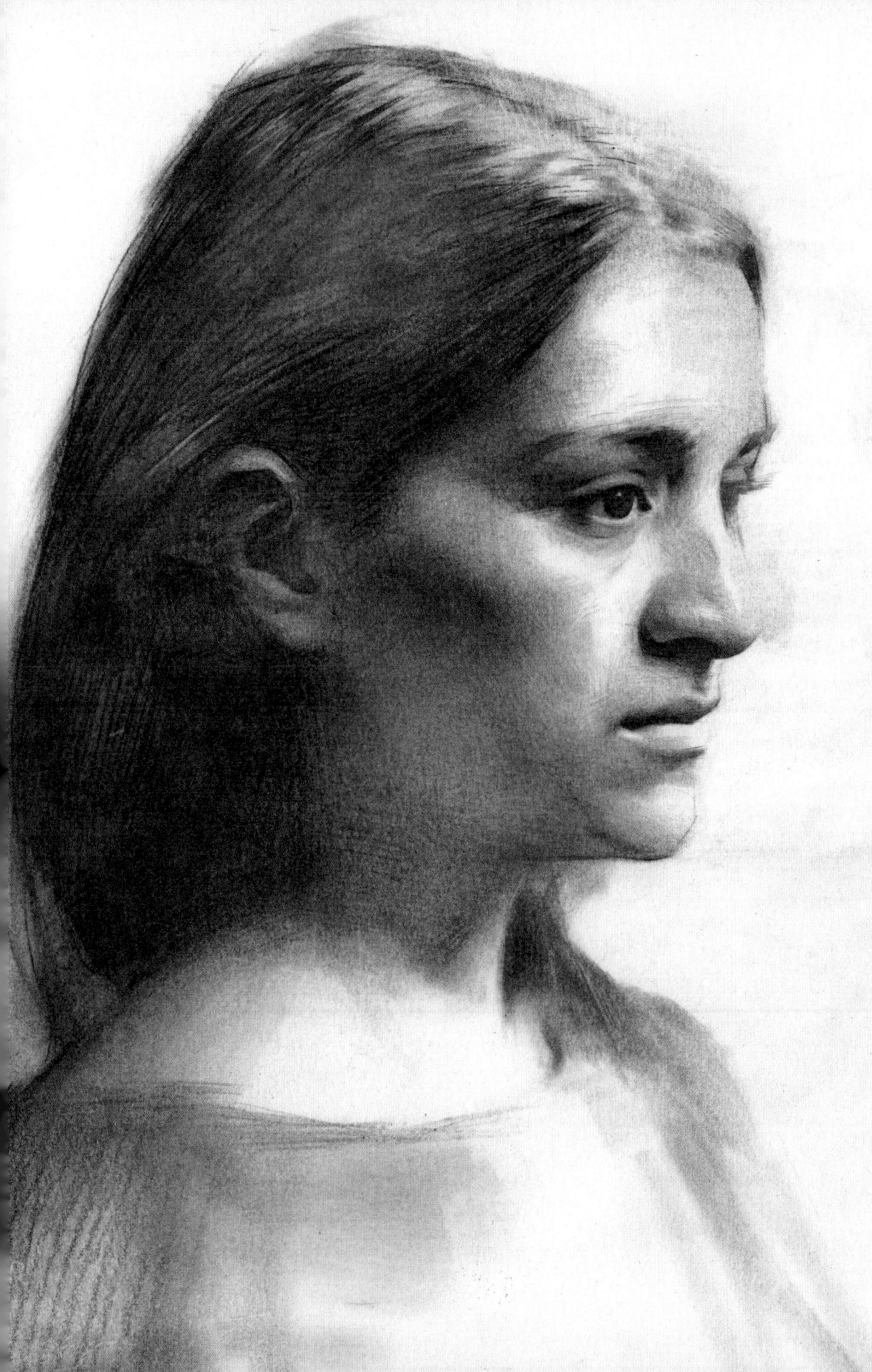

THUMBNAILING

Thumbnail sketches serve a utilitarian function in the art-making process. Their primary value lies in efficient use of your time, though they shouldn't be underestimated for the confidence they can bring to your process. By working out compositional challenges on a small scale, artists can explore multiple ideas rapidly without the commitment of time and resources that a full-sized drawing demands. This preliminary step reduces the likelihood of extensive reworking later or, even worse, abandoning the project altogether, as compositional elements are resolved early in the conceptual phase.

There is no set rule for the optimal number of thumbnails to create, but producing a range often proves beneficial. A series of two to three thumbnails allows an artist to explore a breadth of possibilities, from the most conventional to the more experimental. Whenever possible, aim to make each one noticeably different. This variety can stimulate creativity and provide a clearer direction for the final composition. The final piece will often incorporate aspects from two, or perhaps all three of the initial thumbnails.

Implementing a ratio of large, medium, and small shapes can imbue the composition with a sense of balance and interest. Large shapes typically serve as the foundational elements within the composition, setting the general tone. Medium shapes can link the large and small shapes, often forming the mid-ground that connects the subject with the background and helps to guide the viewer's eye through the drawing. Small shapes add complexity and detail, serving as focal points or areas of interest that draw the viewer in for a closer look.

fig. **01**

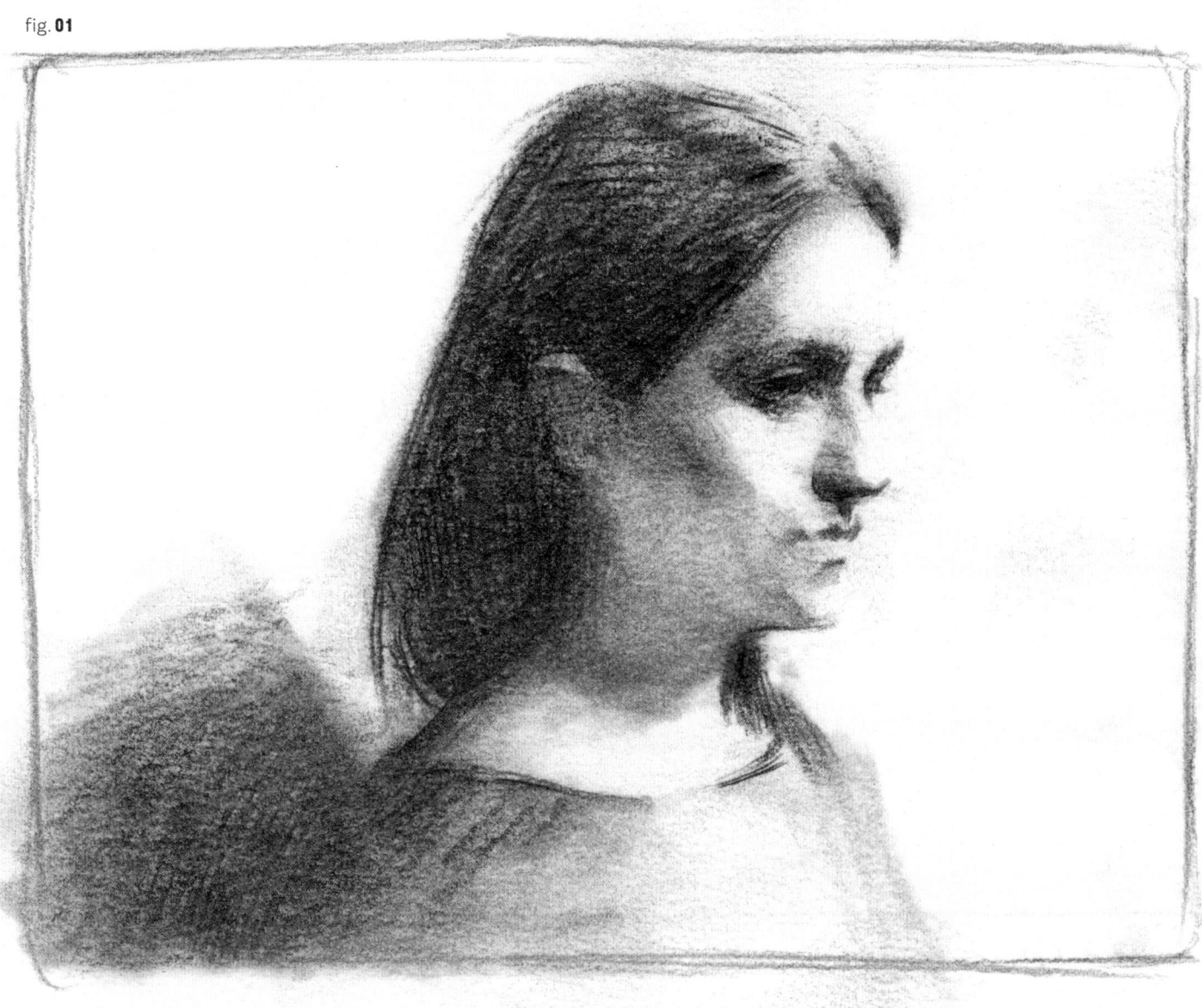

fig. **02**

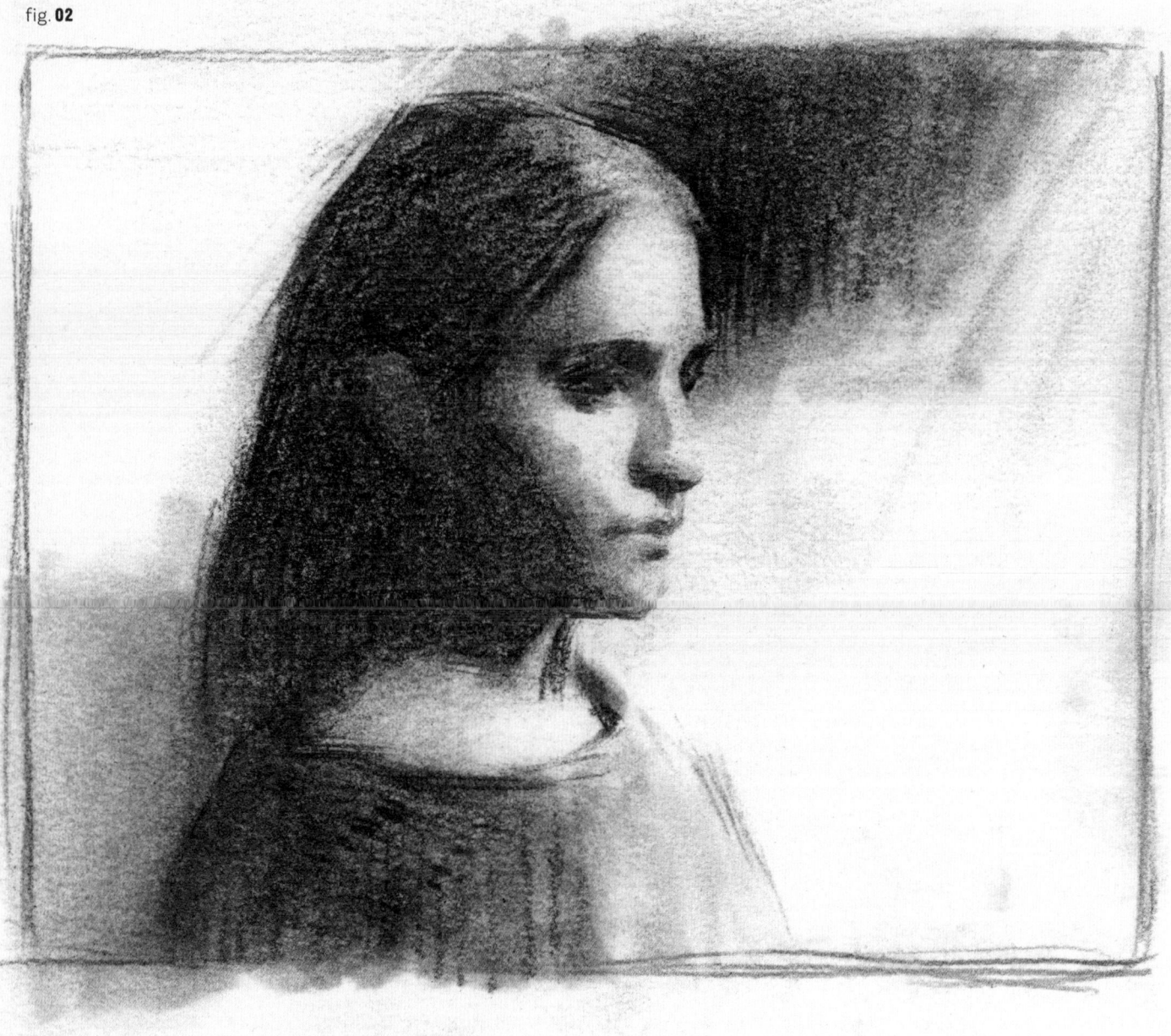

The quality of a thumbnail is measured by its effectiveness in composition. A successful thumbnail will have a clear focal point and a balanced distribution of value shapes that work harmoniously to support the portrait's theme. It should naturally guide the viewer's eye to the areas of interest without confusion or visual competition from less significant areas.

To draw a successful thumbnail, there are a few immutable laws to remember. Elements that attract the viewer's attention include strong contrasts, sharp edges, and rich details. Conversely, low contrast, soft edges, and generic simplified design deflect attention. Use these elements well and you'll be able to direct your viewer's attention anywhere you like, ideally towards the aspect you find most compelling about your subject.

The first thumbnail is less successful in conveying the intended meaning (**fig. 01**). This is primarily due to a lack of clear definition in the value shapes, which causes the facial features to blend into the shadows. The values are mid-range and the contrasts are not as pronounced, resulting in a flatter appearance with less depth. The distribution of light and dark does not adequately guide the viewer towards the focal point of the face (the eye). Additionally, the edges in this sketch are somewhat ambiguous, failing to define the forms of the face compellingly.

Conversely, **fig. 02** is more effective. The distribution of light across the subject's profile is managed with greater contrast, providing a clear hierarchy of values that guide the viewer's eye to the face, which is the intended focal point. Moreover, the edges are more decisive, which helps to separate the figure from the background and creates a better sense of three-dimensional depth.

In **fig. 02**, there is a strategic balance of value shapes, with the darkest tones placed behind the head, medium tones within the shadow, and the lightest tones highlighting the forehead, nose, and neck. This distribution creates a visual path that naturally draws the eye, making the composition more dynamic. In contrast, **fig. 01** fails to establish a focal point with the same effectiveness, resulting in a composition that feels somewhat stagnant and less compelling.

COMPOSITION TERMS

Composition
The arrangement of elements within a work, encompassing the use of space, balance, and interaction of forms.

Balance
The distribution of visual weight in a composition, creating a sense of equilibrium. In portraiture, balance can be symmetrical or asymmetrical, influencing the viewer's perception of the subject.

Contrast
The use of opposing elements (such as light and dark, warm and cool colours) to create visual interest or draw attention to specific areas of the portrait.

Focal point
The area in a composition that attracts the most attention. In portraits, this is often the subject's eyes or face.

Proportion
The relative size of elements within a composition. Accurate proportions are essential in portraiture for realism.

Scale
The size of an object in relation to other objects within a composition, or to the size of the composition itself.

Hierarchy
The arrangement of visual elements to signify importance. In portraiture, certain features or aspects of the subject might be given prominence.

Rhythm
The repetition of visual elements to create movement or a sense of flow within the composition. This can guide the viewer's eye through the portrait.

Unity and variety
The balance between consistency and diversity in a composition. Unity creates a cohesive look, while variety adds interest.

Negative space
The space around and between the subject(s) of an image. In portraiture, negative space can dramatically affect the composition's mood and readability.

fig. **01**

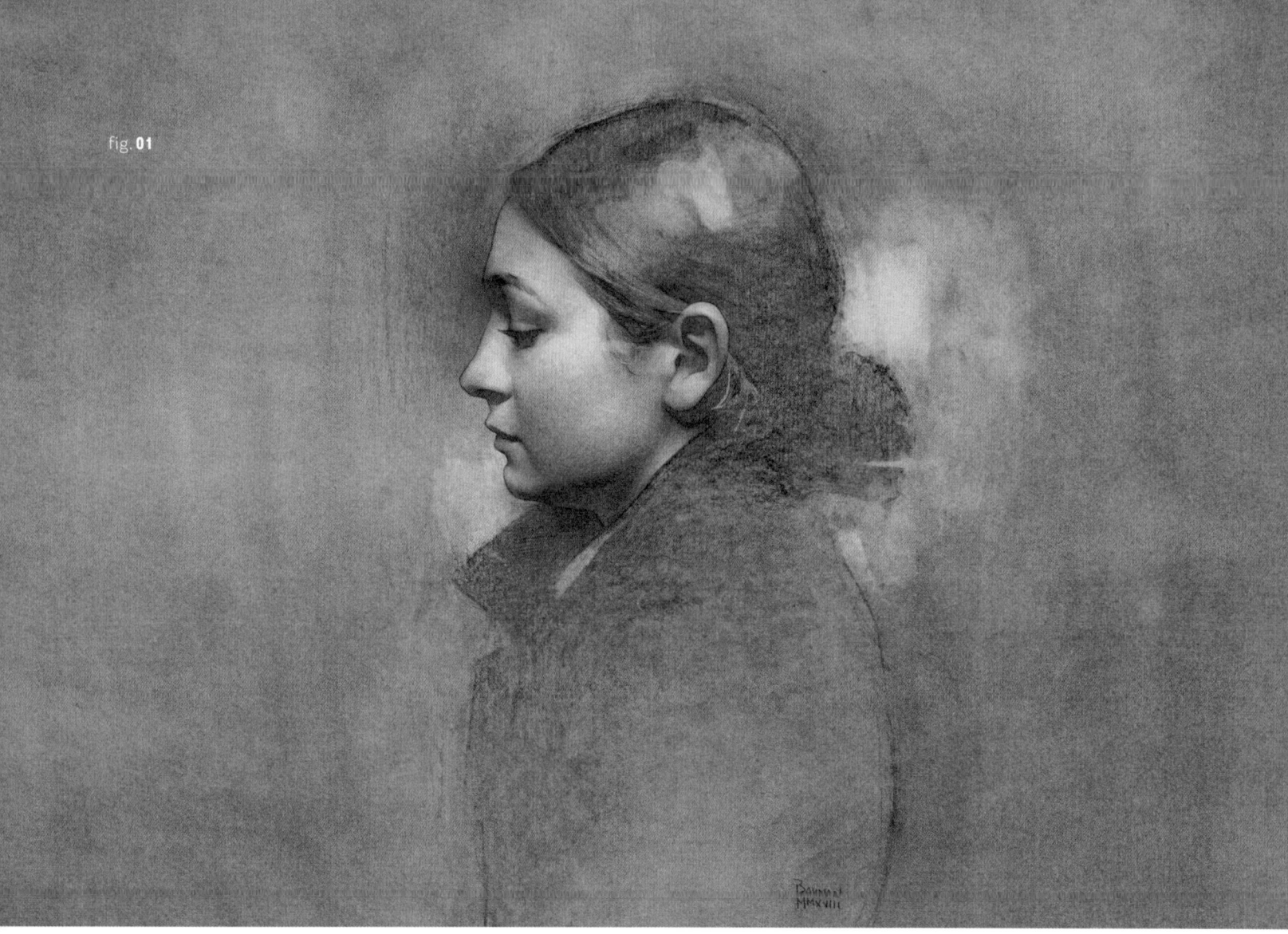

START WITH A FEELING

These two distinct drawings provide a study in contrast, both in technique and in the mood they evoke.

In the first portrait (**fig. 01**), there is a conservative shape-scale ratio, with the subject's profile modestly set against a vast, mostly unified background. This ratio, the model's pose (a profile effectively hides half of the face), along with the subject's placement towards the upper edge of the frame, conveys a sense of solitude and introspection. The moderate contrast between the figure and the background ensures that the subject is perceived gently, without the starkness that a higher contrast might impart. The edges are carefully arranged in a hierarchy to support this subtlety; soft edges around the periphery and more defined lines that carve out the profile and features. Detail is deliberately reserved for the facial features, the focal point, allowing the rest of the composition to recede into soft focus. The substantial scale of the background relative to the subject further emphasizes the feeling of introspection, while the interplay of positive and negative shapes enhances the sense of depth in the scene. The overall atmosphere is one of quietude and reflective stillness.

Conversely, the second portrait (**fig. 02**) commands immediate engagement through its dramatically different scale and framing, the subject's face occupying a significantly larger portion of the pictorial area. The central placement of the model and the direction of her gaze creates a forthright and personal encounter with the viewer. High contrast between the values used in the form of the figure and the darkest dark behind accentuates the curvature and features of the face,

fig. **02**

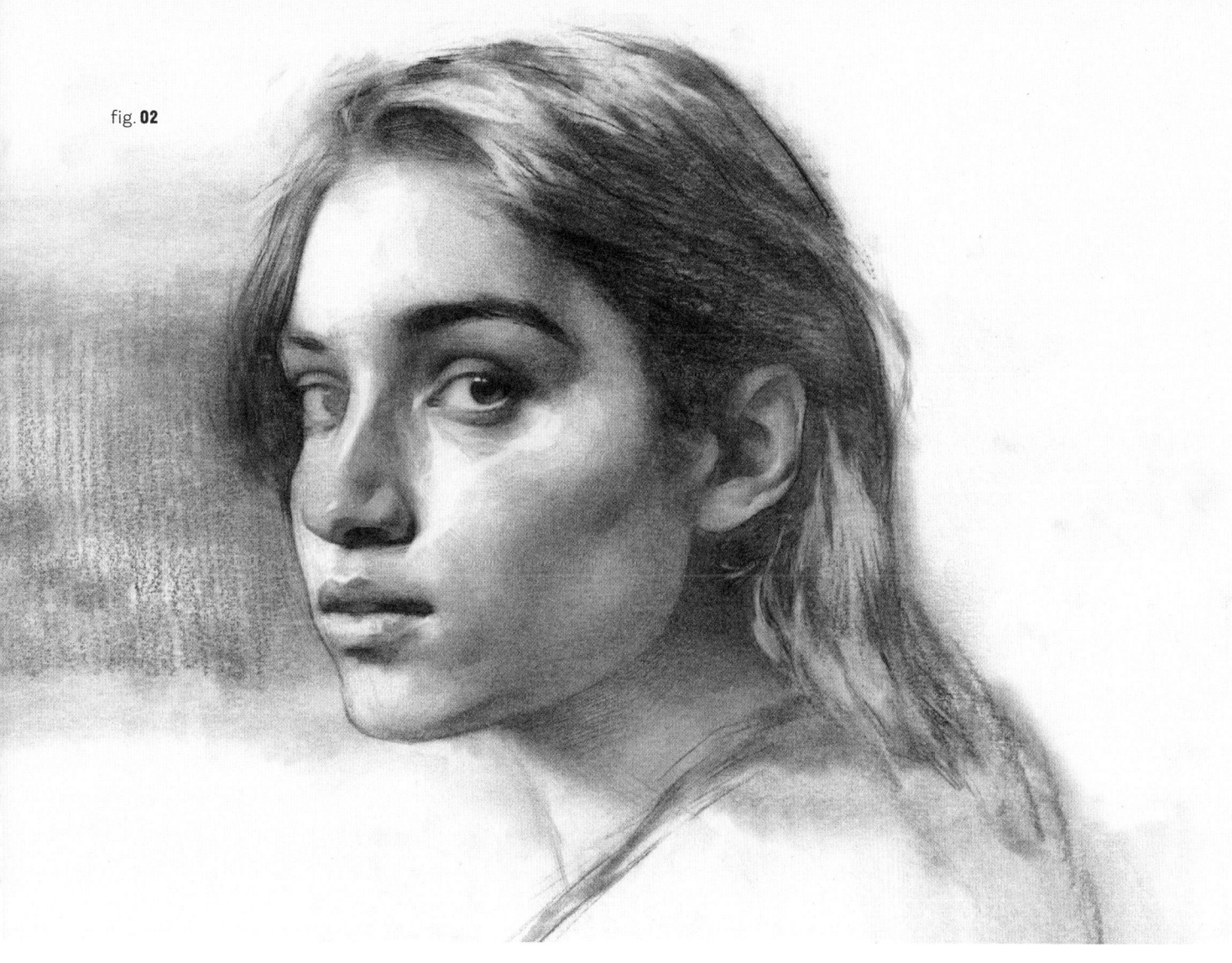

lending the image a vivid, sculptural quality. The edges in this drawing are also intentionally organized, with sharp, focused lines drawing attention to the model's striking gaze and softly contoured lips, which are central to the composition. Fine details are rendered with precision, inviting the viewer to a closer examination; establishing a connection with the subject. The scale of the subject against the background is pronounced, making the figure's presence undeniable and immediate. Positive shapes are dominant, leaving less room for negative space, which intensifies the portrait's immediacy. The mood is one of dynamic intensity and potent presence.

Each portrait, through the application of these formal elements (value, scale, placement, edges, etc.), establishes the mood and guides the viewer's emotional experience.

Fig. 01, with its spacious framing and soft transitions, offers a moment of quiet contemplation, while **fig. 02**, with its immediacy and clarity, conveys an undeniable intensity and connection. Many of these effects can be achieved simply by manipulating thc formal elements mentioned here. However, in the process of making these drawings, the application of formal compositional ideas was made specifically to 'rhyme' with the pose and lighting situation. Put simply, always start your compositional search with a feeling. Does the model look towards or away from you? Can you look them in the eye? Are they looking past you with an upturned nose, or up at you with a bowed head? What does that say about them? Even small variations can begin a process that culminates in a dramatic final composition. Asking questions of your subject will reveal the story in your drawing.

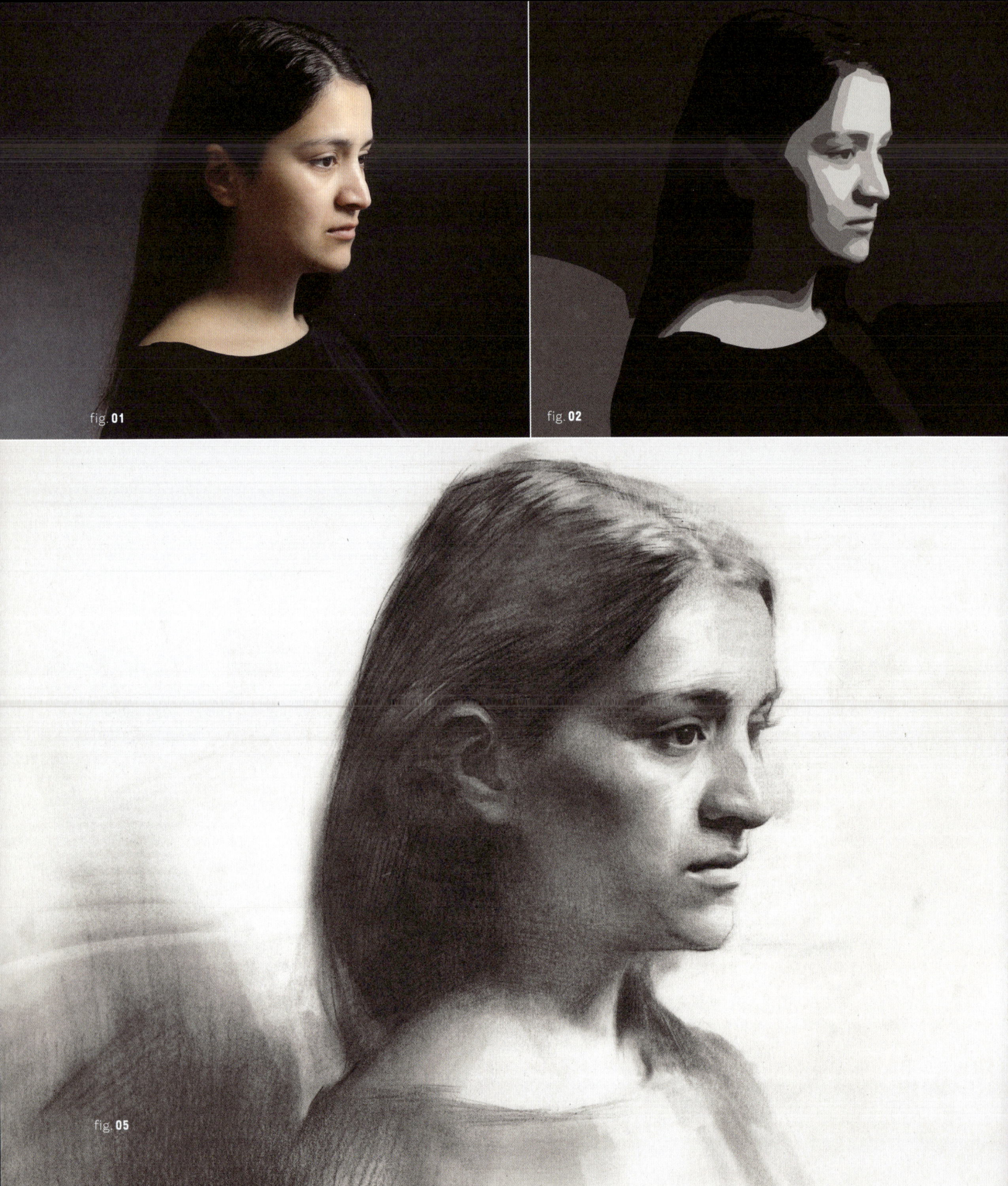

fig. 01

fig. 02

fig. 05

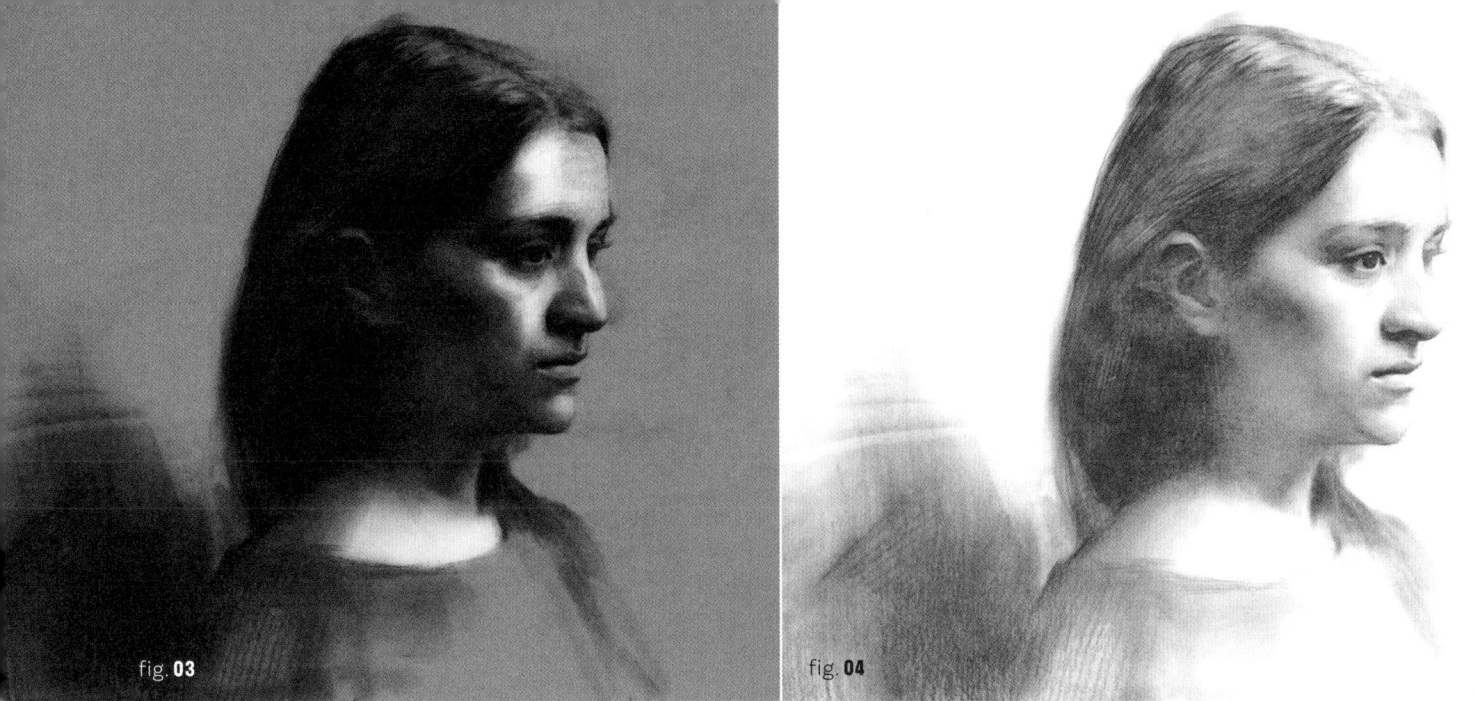

fig. 03

fig. 04

KEYING AND CHOICES

Keying a drawing is a nuanced process that involves more than the mechanical replication of lights and darks. It is a deliberate orchestration of values to not only depict form but to also evoke a particular emotional resonance. The essence of the endeavour lies in the artist's ability to discern and manipulate the value scale – the range from white to black and all the greys in between – to serve the narrative they seek to convey.

To key a drawing, you must first observe the subject carefully, noting where the darkest darks lie, and the same for the lightest highlights. This observation establishes the 'value key', or the range within which all other values will fall. This implies a certain kind of simplification of values as seen in **fig. 02**. This raw and mechanical tone mapping can be seen as the baseline for what keying represents – in reality, it is so much more than that.

But first, let's go over a few different keying concepts. A high-key drawing has more light values and fewer darks (**fig. 04**). A low-key drawing, conversely, emphasizes the use of darker tones (**fig. 03**). And a mid-key drawing leans heavily into halftones – this is often found in drawings aiming for a realistic representation, which will inevitably incorporate a light and dark accent to frame the middle values.

An artist manipulates the key by adjusting the value range to control the mood. For instance, in a portrait, the artist may choose to lower the key by compressing the overall shadows and dark halftones, reserving the true whites for only the most specular highlights (**fig. 03**). This can create a sense of

drama, making the subject appear more serious or intense. Alternatively, by lifting the key and utilizing a preponderance of lighter values, the mood becomes brighter, imparting a sense of hopefulness or purity (**fig. 04**).

The process of keying is a dynamic one. The artist does not simply lay down one value next to another until the drawing is done; rather, they organize and arrange values according to what is needed with an eye towards the intended end result (see page 126). For example, all of the images on this page are taken from the same source photograph (**fig. 01**), yet each one is quite different. The value choices taken in **figs. 03**, **04**, and **05** to compress various value groups all hold together as being 'realistic' – but why is that? The key is relativity. In the value hierarchy of each drawing the various compression concepts applied never subvert the overall lightest light and darkest dark. Operate within the parameters of this rule and just about any keying solution is available to you, while staying well within the boundaries of a realistic result.

In any example we could choose, there is one consistent point that is necessary to make: keying a drawing is a thoughtful exercise in storytelling as well as a practical exercise in observation. It is a process of fine-tuning the values and contrast to harmonize with the narrative the artist intends to communicate, and to coincide with the lighting situation the model is arranged in. How an artist keys their drawing to their theme and intent can transform the viewer's experience from observation to emotional participation.

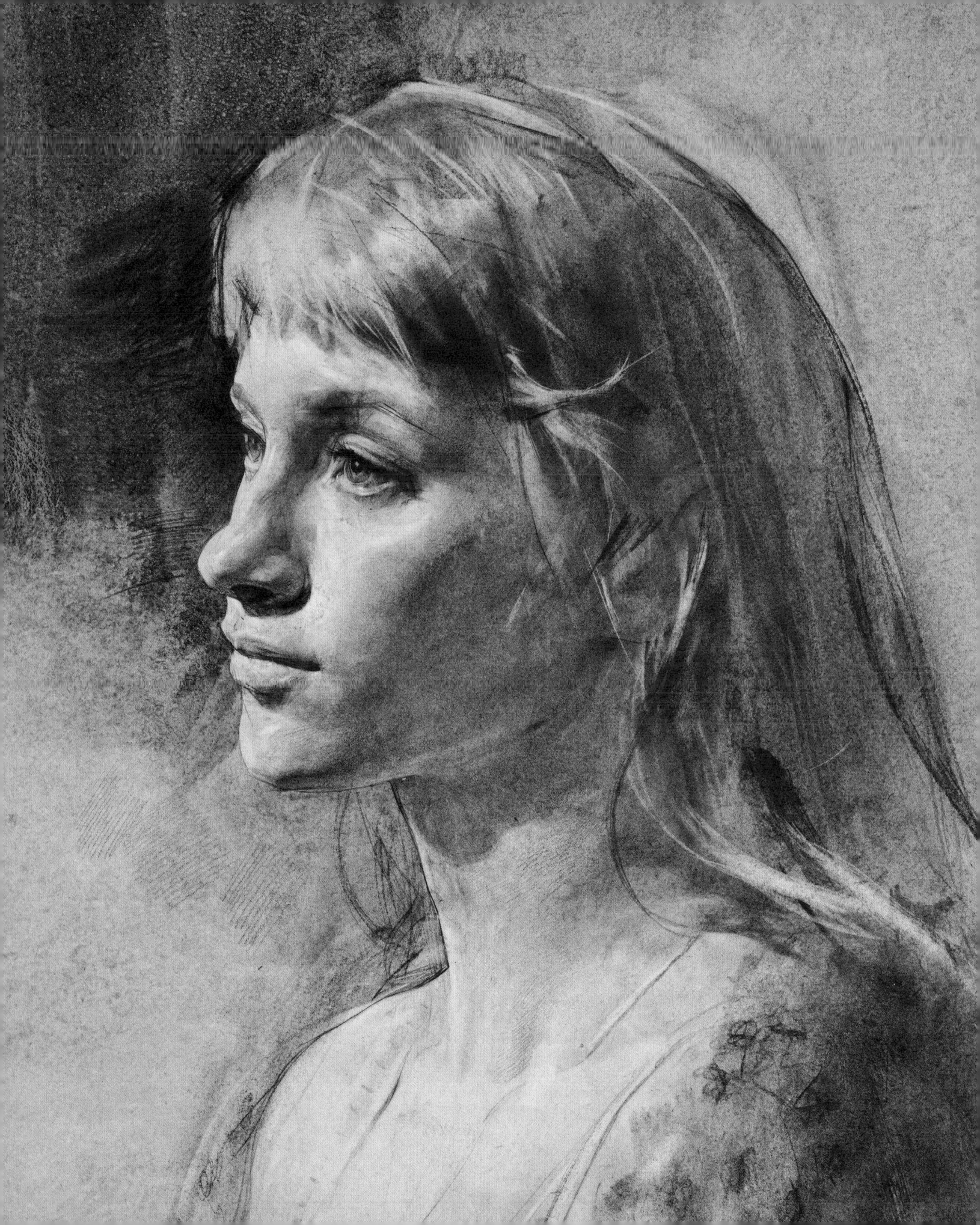

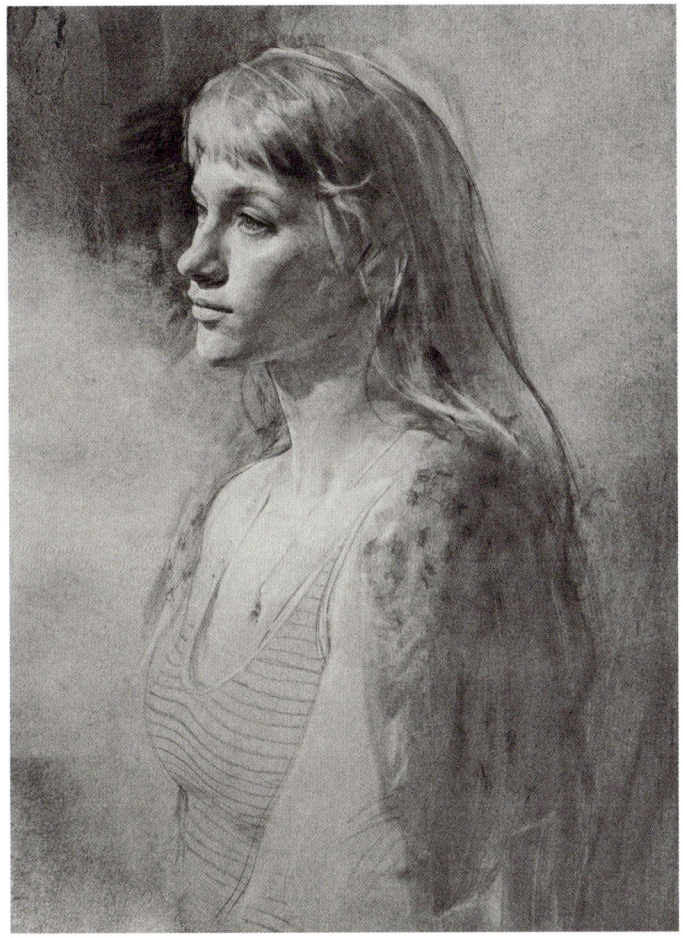

COMPOSITION ANALYSIS IVAN LOGINOV

This composition benefits greatly from the strategic use of negative space, which serves as a quiet expanse that the subject's contemplative gaze seems to explore. The lines are rendered with a delicate touch in places, soft enough to maintain the ethereal quality of the drawing while still providing sufficient definition to key features. Textural details are approached with finesse. Hair, skin, and clothing are differentiated between with subtle variations in technique, contributing to the overall sense of realism without distracting from the portrait's gentle ambience.

There exists a compelling balance between the assertive definition of the subject's profile and the unrendered and unrefined quality that envelops the rest of the composition.

The artist has skilfully delineated the profile with hard, crisp edges, capturing the precise curvature of the cheek, the sharpness of the chin, and the delicate contour of the nose. This clear demarcation imbues the figure with a presence that is both commanding and intimately focused. Contrasting this, the surrounding elements are rendered with a gentler touch; the hair, neck, and shoulders have softer edges, lighter lines, and the background is a subtle wash of gradated tones. This juxtaposition not only enhances the three-dimensional form of the subject, but also imparts a dreamlike quality to the scene. The softness elsewhere invites the viewer into a deep, quiet, and contemplative space, while the distinct profile anchors the composition, creating a portrait that is as poignant in its presence as it is delicate in its execution.

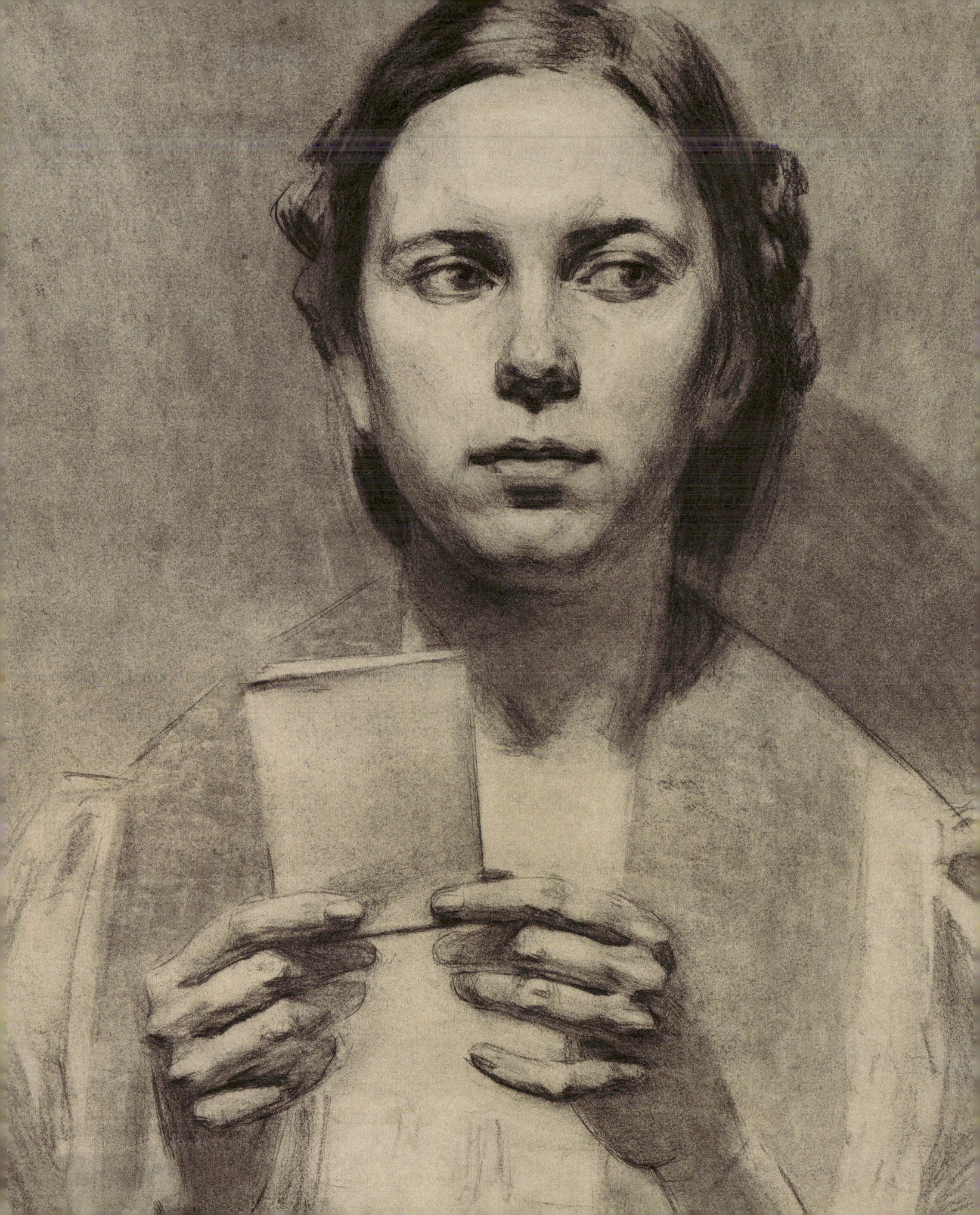

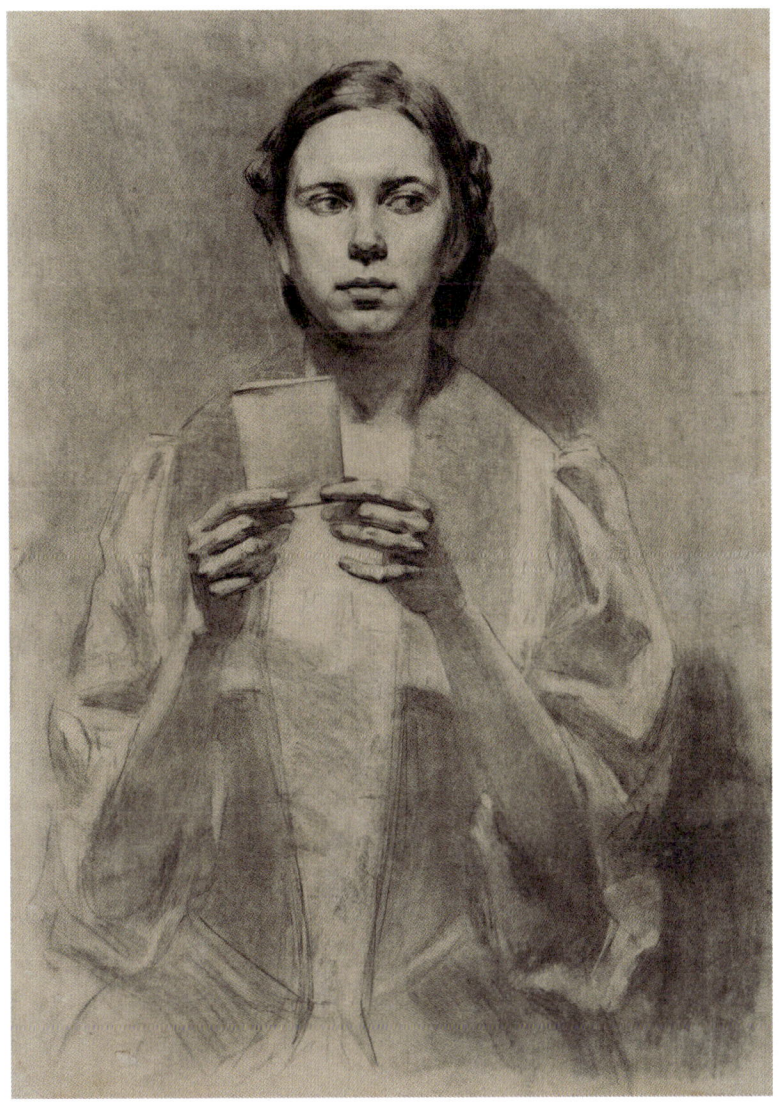

COMPOSITION ANALYSIS KSENIA ISTOMINA

Sharp edges around the subject's face and hands draw attention to these focal points, while softer edges in the clothing and background suggest a secondary plane, allowing the subject to emerge with a gentle dominance.

The subject is positioned centrally with a gaze directed away from the viewer, establishing a sense of narrative, or internal action. This central placement of the model is balanced by the ample negative space around the figure, and the scale of the subject is substantial yet not overwhelming, anchoring the composition without overpowering the surrounding space.

While the face and hands are rendered with a higher degree of complexity, showcasing the artist's ability to capture subtle variations in texture and form, other areas are treated with a looser hand. This selective focus, emphasizing areas of importance, allows less critical areas to blend harmoniously into the background.

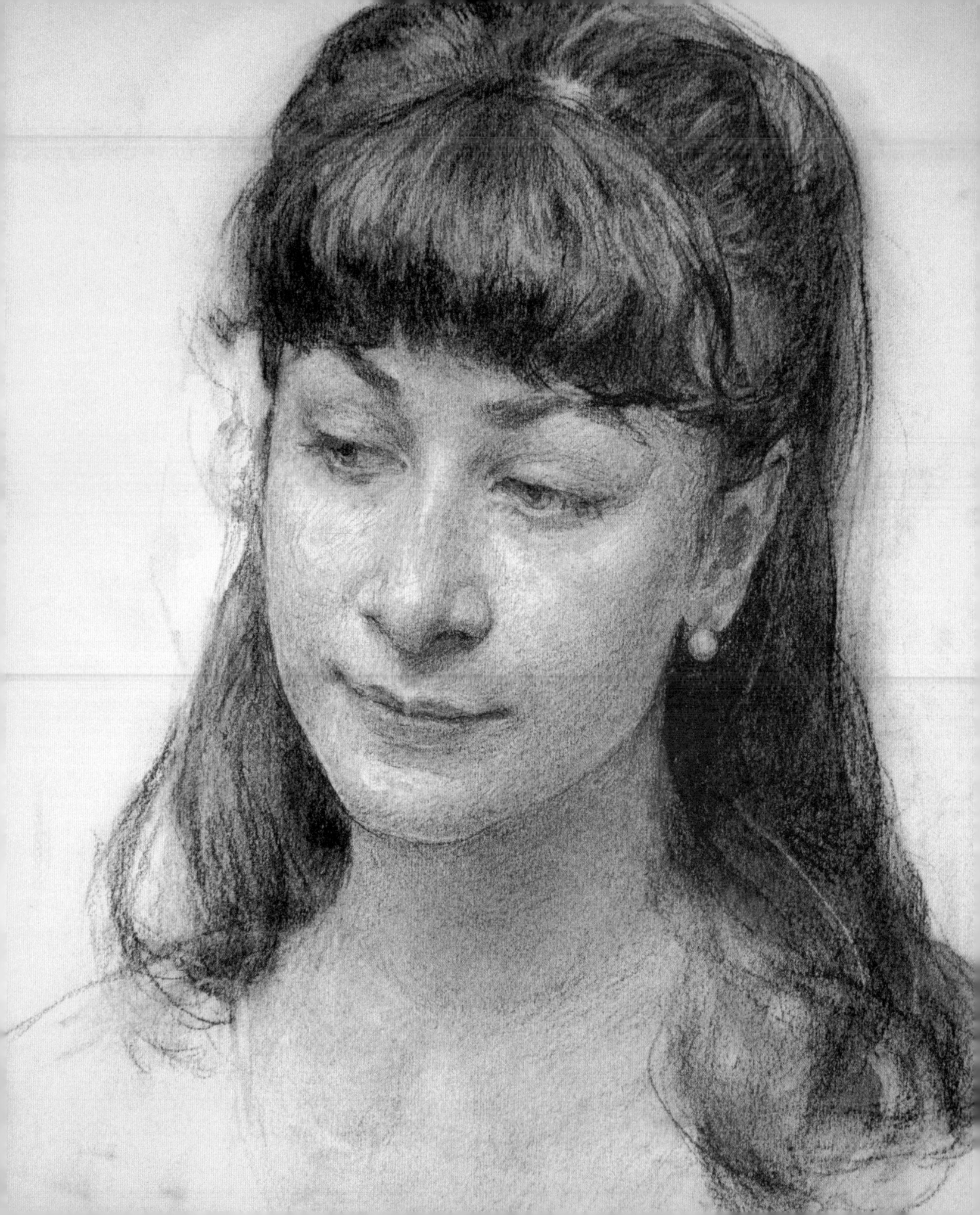

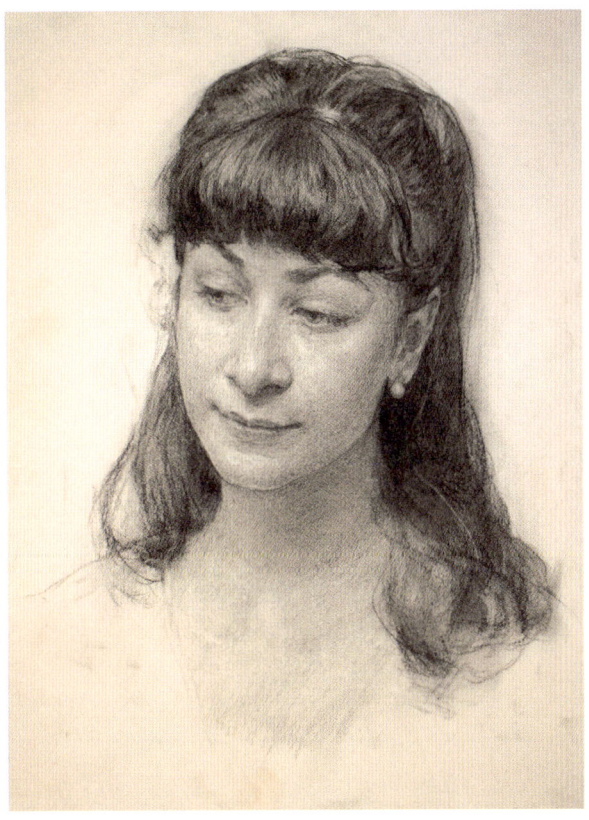

COMPOSITION ANALYSIS DARIA NOVIKOVA

A study in the subtle interplay of light and shadow, precise control of line, and the delicate rendering of form. The use of midtones is particularly adept, suggesting the curvature of the cheeks and forehead without stark contrasts. The shadows under the chin and neck provide weight and grounding to the head, while the highlight along the cheekbone and the bridge of the nose suggests a soft, yet directional light source.

Line quality in this drawing is varied and intentional. The artist has used firmer, more defined lines to outline the profile and features such as the eyebrows, lips, and nose, which draws attention to these areas. Softer, more diffused lines are employed to suggest the texture of the hair and the softness of the skin, especially around the cheeks and neck. The outline of the face is distinct but not harsh, allowing the figure to emerge softly from the background. The hair is treated with a combination of definite strokes and softer edges, suggesting texture and depth without overwhelming the subtlety of the face.

The unfinished areas of the drawing contribute to a feeling of emergence, as if the subject is materializing from the paper, or perhaps fading back into a memory. This quality gives the portrait a temporal dimension, with the figure anchored in a specific moment, yet timeless in its execution. The composition is intimate, with the subject's head placed centrally and occupying a significant portion of the frame, bringing the viewer into a close, personal space with the subject. The downward gaze adds an introspective quality.

In this portrait, Daria hints at the character beneath the appearance. There is a balance between the solidity of the features and the ephemeral quality of the expression, capturing a convergence of the external appearance and the internal world of the model.

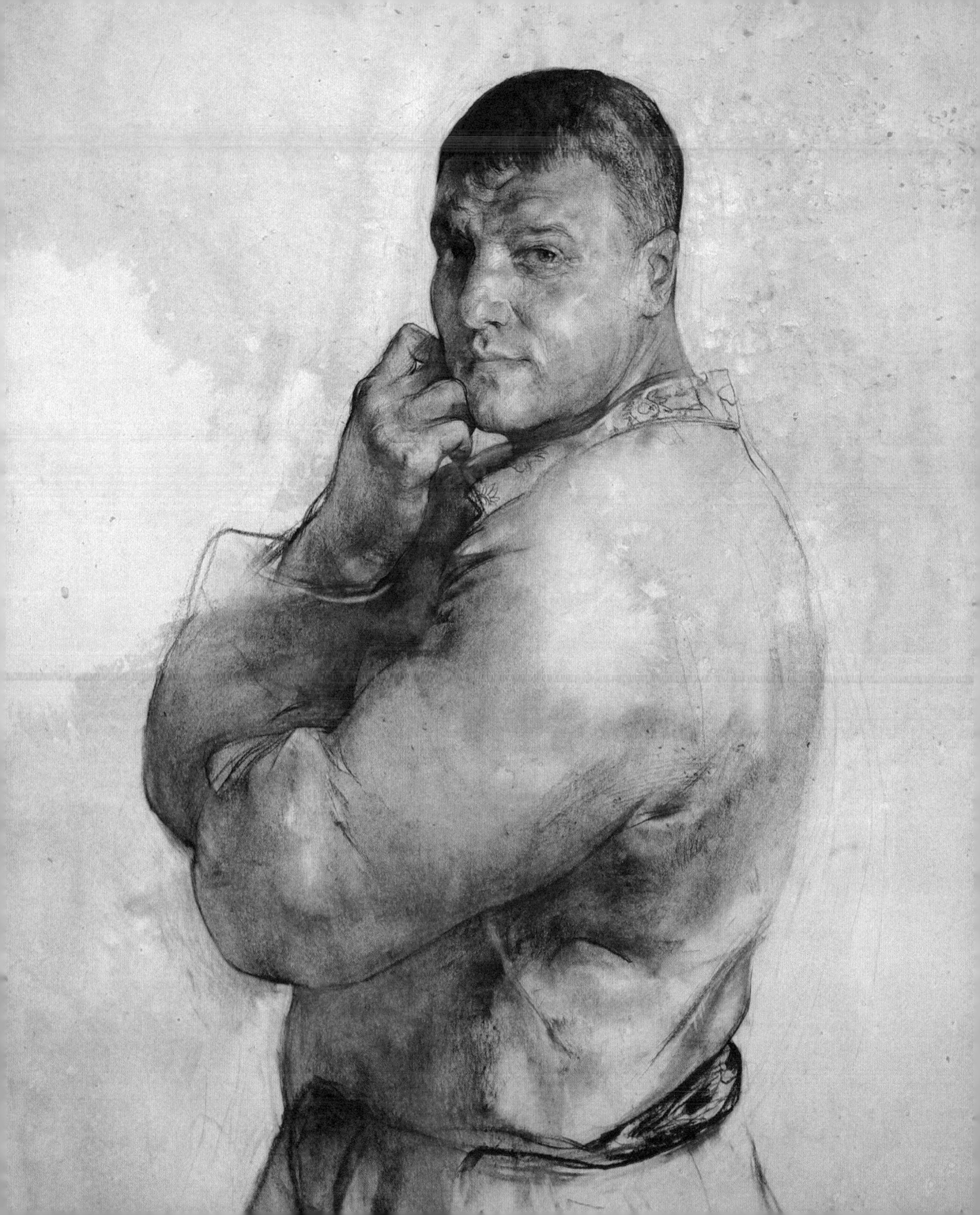

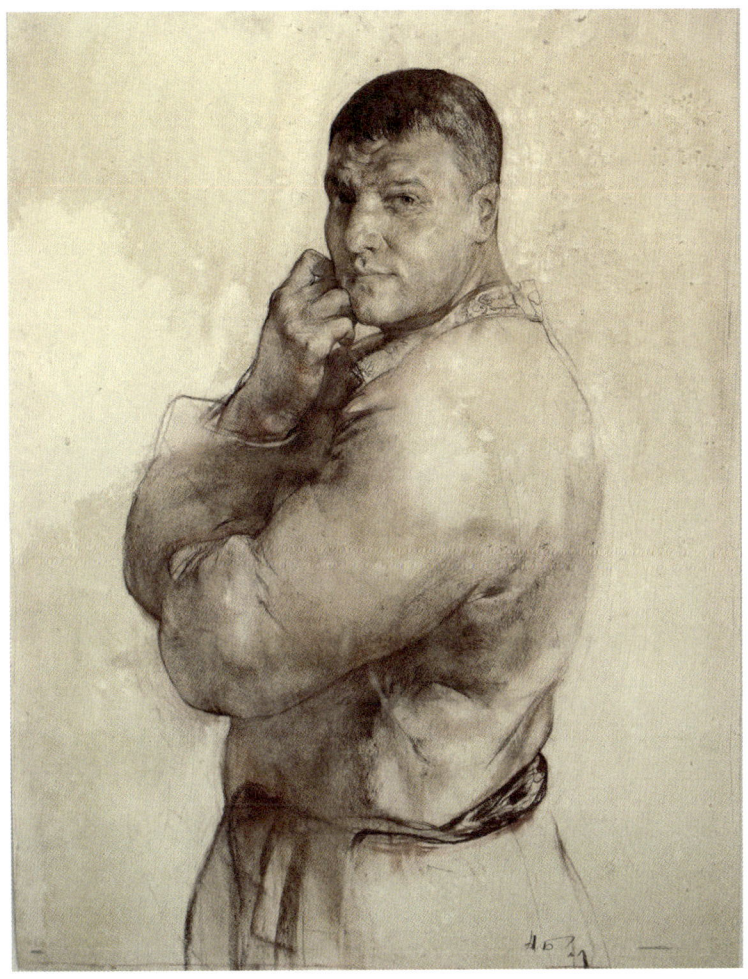

COMPOSITION ANALYSIS NIKOLAI BLOHKIN

The edges in this work function as silent narrators of form and substance, employed with varying degrees of softness and assertiveness. The robust outline of the subject's jaw and the crisp delineation of the knuckles speak to a certain forthrightness and resolve. Contrasting this, the gentle softness with which the shirt collar and distant contour of the back are rendered imparts a sense of atmospheric depth, imbuing the composition with a dynamic tension between the tangible and the transient.

The chiaroscuro applied here speaks of volume and weight. The stark contrast between the light striking the subject's cheekbone and the cavernous shadows beneath the folded arms imbues the figure with a monumental quality, reminiscent of the grandeur found in classical sculpture.

Dominating the space, the figure is an anchor, a focal point around which the composition seems to pivot. The scale ratio, in its generous allocation, celebrates the physicality of the subject, granting a heroic stature to the form that is both powerful and poised. This is not a figure to be overlooked; it demands attention, not through flamboyance, but through the sheer force of its sculptural presence.

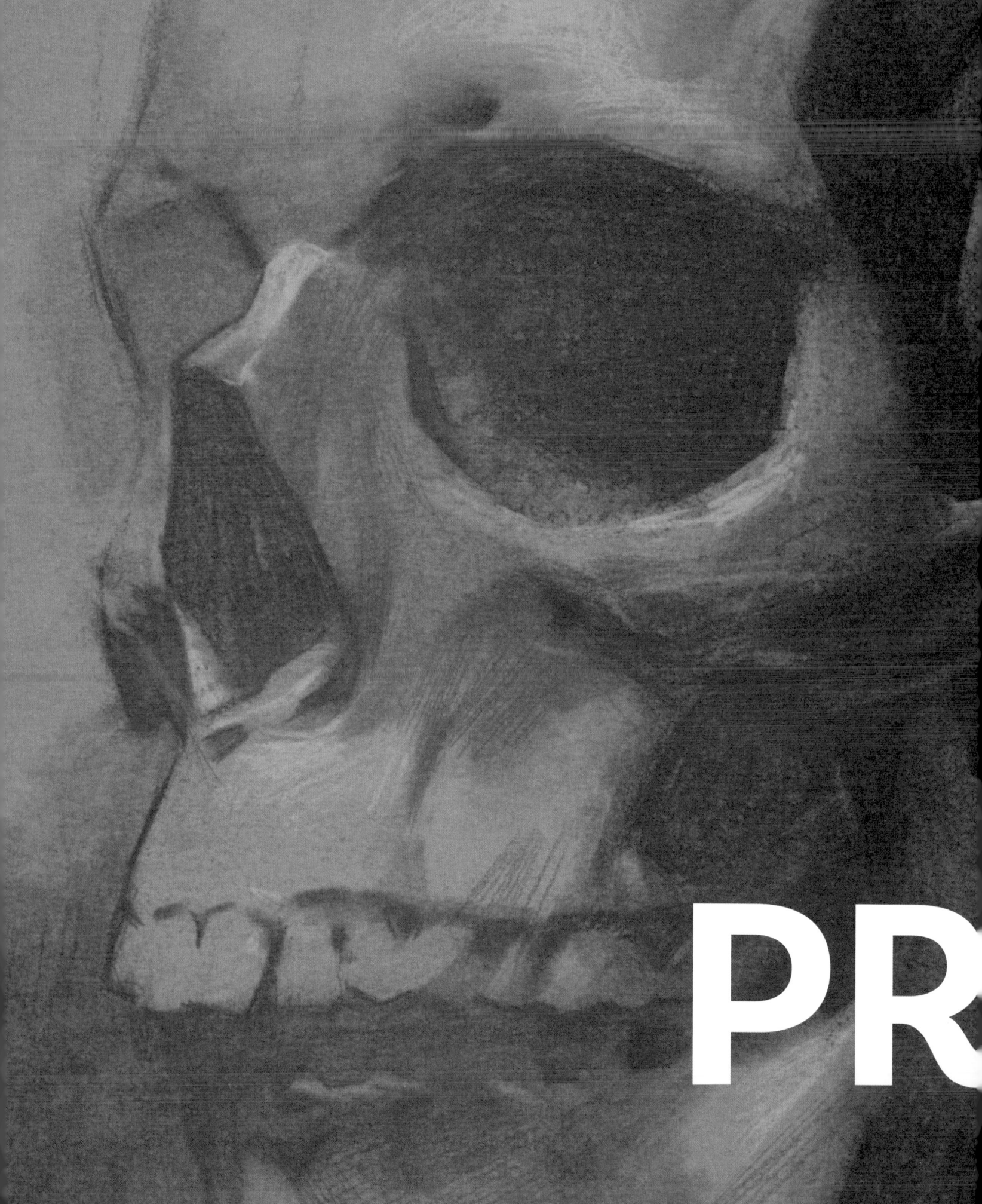

ACTICE

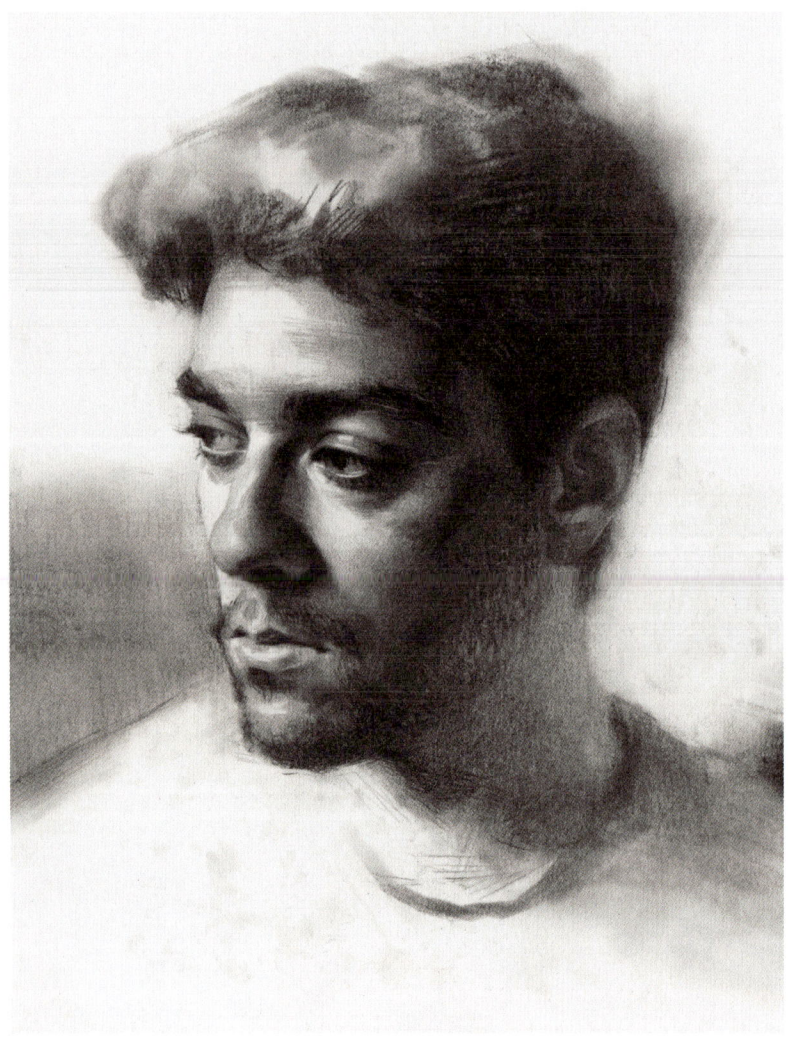

'Practice what you know and it will help you to make clear what you do not know.' **Rembrandt van Rijn**

On my first day as a student at the Florence Academy of Art, my peers and I were tasked with making a relatively small, visual-style block-in of a nude model. It was around nine inches high on a white or off-white sheet of Stonehenge paper. The drawing tools were only a rather hard H or 2H pencil and a kneaded eraser. It was a simple enough assignment, not that any of us did a very good job of it. This most basic drawing practice was repeated a minimum of twice a week for the next four years. Many other projects populated the curriculum, from Charles Bargue drawings to cast drawings and paintings, still life, and portraiture, but none were repeated in this way. This focus was meant to instil at least two things in the collective student body. The first, that the block-in stage is the most easily repeatable and important ingredient in the optimized progression of drawing skills. The second, that learning the fundamentals of drawing is not unlike the development of muscle memory.

Understanding how to practice drawing might be the most important discipline of all. Misunderstand it and you may be inclined to give up drawing altogether. Recognize that any practice, however modest, is superior to none. Yet to achieve the highest level, practising the right way is imperative. This means that your drawing materials, source images (lighting situations), degree of resolution, and target of the exercise must all be aligned in order to maximize your progress.

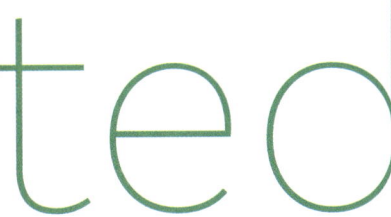

Drawing materials

The instruments you choose – the pencils, paper, erasers – should be in step with the quality that you eventually mean to produce. The habits that you develop during this skill-building endeavour will grow out of the materials you work with. For example, if you learn to render form efficiently using a cheap variety of paper, you will then have to relearn it on a better one. There is a caveat here: do not let a lack of access to great materials stop you from practising. However, I recommend using the best materials you can consistently obtain.

Source images and lighting

Starting with clear, unambiguous lighting situations is best. The primary dominant light-source situations used in this book represent a logically accessible lighting concept that will adapt well to translation into drawing.

Degree of resolution

At first, broad strokes and simplified shapes are what is needed, capturing the essence without getting bogged down in detail. As proficiency is gained, the focus can narrow, resulting in more and more detailed drawings. Together with the target of the exercise, it is wise to consider the degree of resolution a drawing needs to internalize that lesson. To fully understand portraiture, for example, it may be necessary to make quite an elaborate drawing that takes dozens of hours to complete. To understand and recall the placement and shape of the mandible, however, requires merely a sketch. Put simply, understanding where you are going will be the best aid in understanding how to get there.

Target of the exercise

Purposeful practice is key. Each drawing should have a specific aim, whether it's to better understand how to key values, study the fall of light across a subject's face, or internalize the relevant anatomical features in a pose. This understanding ensures that practice time is not just spent, but invested.

As one progresses in the art of drawing, the complexity of the exercises should increase. Move from a simple sphere to the subtle dynamism of the human skull; from simple studies of shadow and light to the challenges of a full-value portrait composition. Drawing practice should be thoughtful and cumulative. It is a craft where incremental steps lead to true progress, where the alignment of the right elements cultivates a progression that is both rewarding and profound. With each new level of complexity, the artist builds a richer understanding of this visual language.

Finally, as you are introduced to the exercises that follow in this section, remember that they will reach their peak utility only through repetition. By design, they are as simple as possible – and that simplicity belies an immense depth.

STUDIO SET-UP AND EFFECTIVE PRACTICE

Creating a dedicated space for drawing is essential, not only for the practicality of having a consistent place to practise your craft, but also for the psychological benefits it brings in developing and sustaining the habit of drawing regularly. A well-organized studio space can reduce 'start-up friction', the resistance often encountered when initiating a task, thereby fostering a conducive environment for productivity.

There are some key things you can do to ensure your workspace and practice is as effective as possible:

Cue-routine-reward loop

Establish a cue for your drawing practice, such as a specific time of day or a pre-drawing ritual like making a cup of tea. This signals to your brain that it's time to engage in the routine of drawing. Following your practice with a reward, such as a small treat or some fresh air, helps to solidify the habit loop.

Minimize decision fatigue

Make as many decisions ahead of time as possible. Pre-plan your drawing subjects or exercises for the week so that when you sit down to draw, you can dive right into the process.

Visibility

Place your drawing area in a spot you'll see often. The visual reminder of your drawing space can serve as a prompt to engage in your practice.

Consistency

Try to draw at the same time each day. The consistency reinforces the habit, making it a regular part of your routine.

Track progress

Keep a log of your drawing sessions or maintain a progress chart. Seeing your dedication and progress visually can be a powerful motivator.

Community

Share your workspace and progress with a community, whether it's through social media or within a group of fellow students. Accountability can be a strong incentive to maintain your practice.

Comfort

Ensure your seating and lighting are comfortable. Discomfort can be a significant barrier to long drawing sessions. Good lighting is crucial, not just for seeing your work clearly but also for avoiding eye strain.

Equipment shown in the photographs

1. M/34 tabletop easel from Mabef

This is my preference for small-to-medium-sized drawings. Its design satisfies two specific requirements. First, it allows me to draw on a vertical surface, which is imperative for the kind of drawing I do. Second, unlike almost all H-frame easels or pochade boxes, it is made with a de facto drawing board as its body, making it ideal for working with panels and loose papers.

2. A vari-pole

Also known as a variable tension pole, this is a movable post that allows you to affix almost anything (lights, cameras, tablets, palettes, and so on) while having the smallest footprint possible. This is an incredible space saver when compared to alternatives like a tripod.

3. Aputure Light Storm LS 60d Daylight LED

This is by no means the only light you can have that will work, but it has all of the features required. It's also cost effective and compact. Most importantly, the colour rating is 95+ CRI (a wide spectrum of colour in the light), 54,300 lux (think of luminous flux, with the unit lumen, as a measure of the total 'amount' of visible light present), and is made with an attachment for a soft box.

4. Soft box

This final piece is critical. A soft box (seen here is a 24-inch octagonal soft box with a white interior) effectively spreads the otherwise focused light beam to cover a larger area.

5. Stonehenge White from Legion paper

All of the drawings in this book were made on this paper. It comes in a wide variety of tones and colours, and is quite versatile in the media that it proficiently accepts. Importantly, it comes in loose sheets from A4 up to 22 inches × 30 inches, mounted to aluminium panels in a variety of sizes, and rolls at 50 inches × 360 inches. If you get used to working with it, you will not have a barrier regarding the size of your drawing.

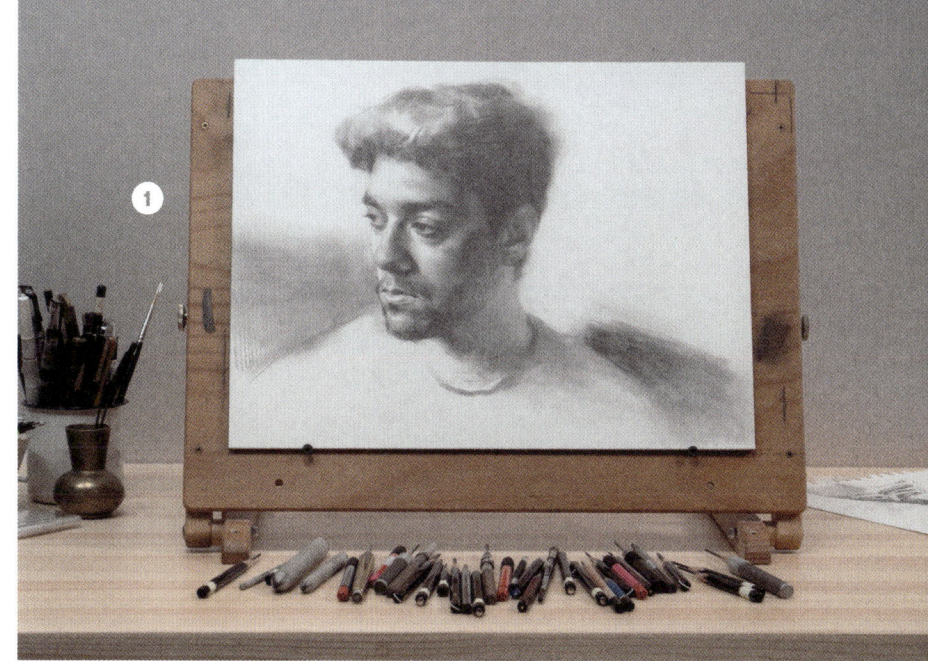

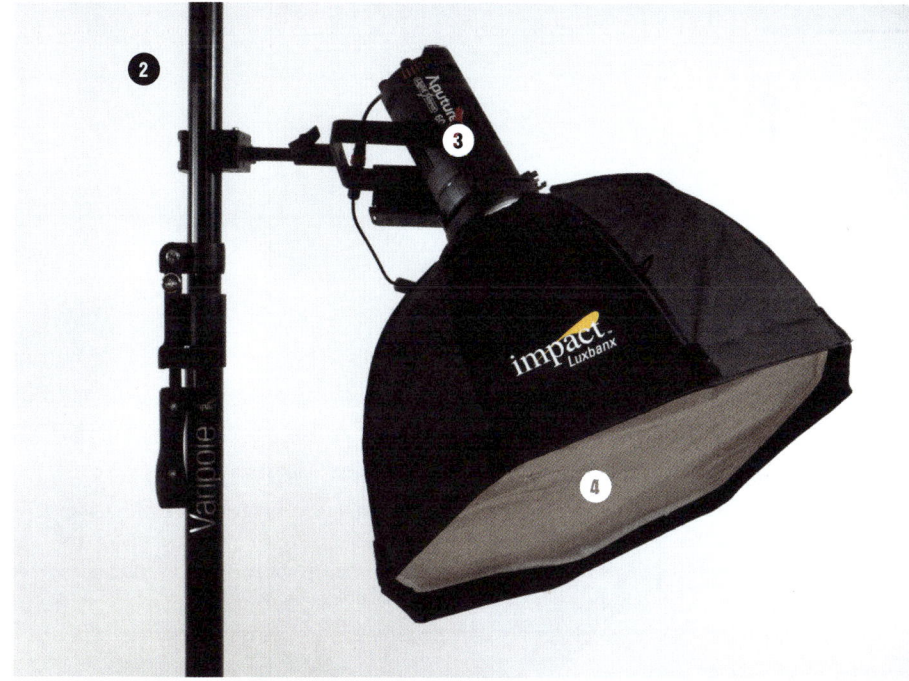

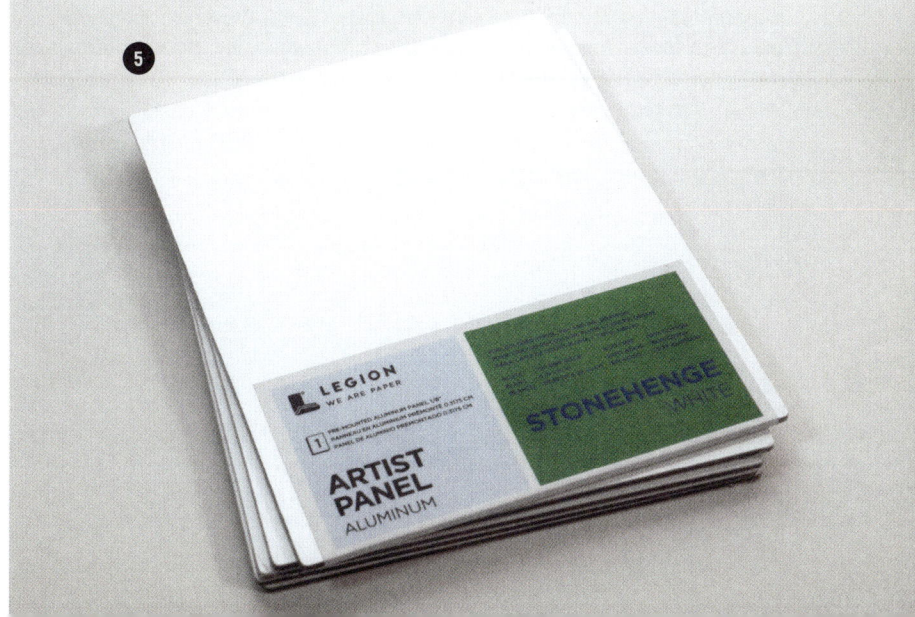

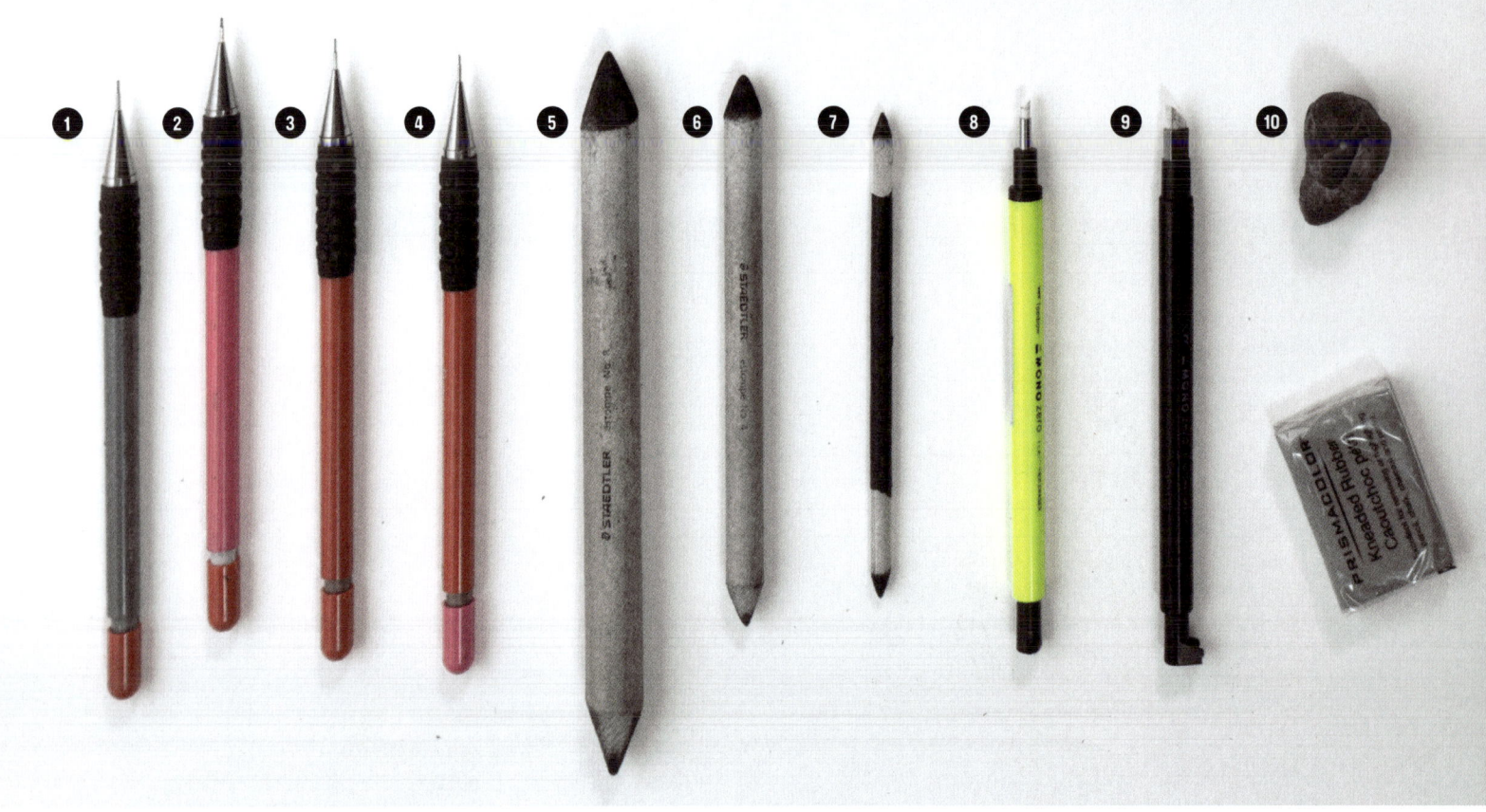

MATERIALS

After fifteen years of dedicated work with graphite, exploring every conceivable combination of materials, I have refined my understanding of what is essential for rendering a portrait drawing to a high degree of finish. This distillation of experience is offered here to guide you in selecting tools that are not just effective, but conducive to achieving the nuanced detail and texture vital to high-quality portraiture.

My preferences for materials are not minimalistic. I look at these as tools, much like a hammer or a screwdriver. Each one is designed to achieve a purpose; in the same way you wouldn't use a screwdriver to hammer a nail, you would also not grab a 6B graphite stick to render your lightest halftones. With that said, there is a risk of having too many preferences – at least at first. You will want to use and eventually totally inhabit this equipment. While observing your model and reflecting on what to add next to your drawing, your hand should instinctively reach for the appropriate tool for the job.

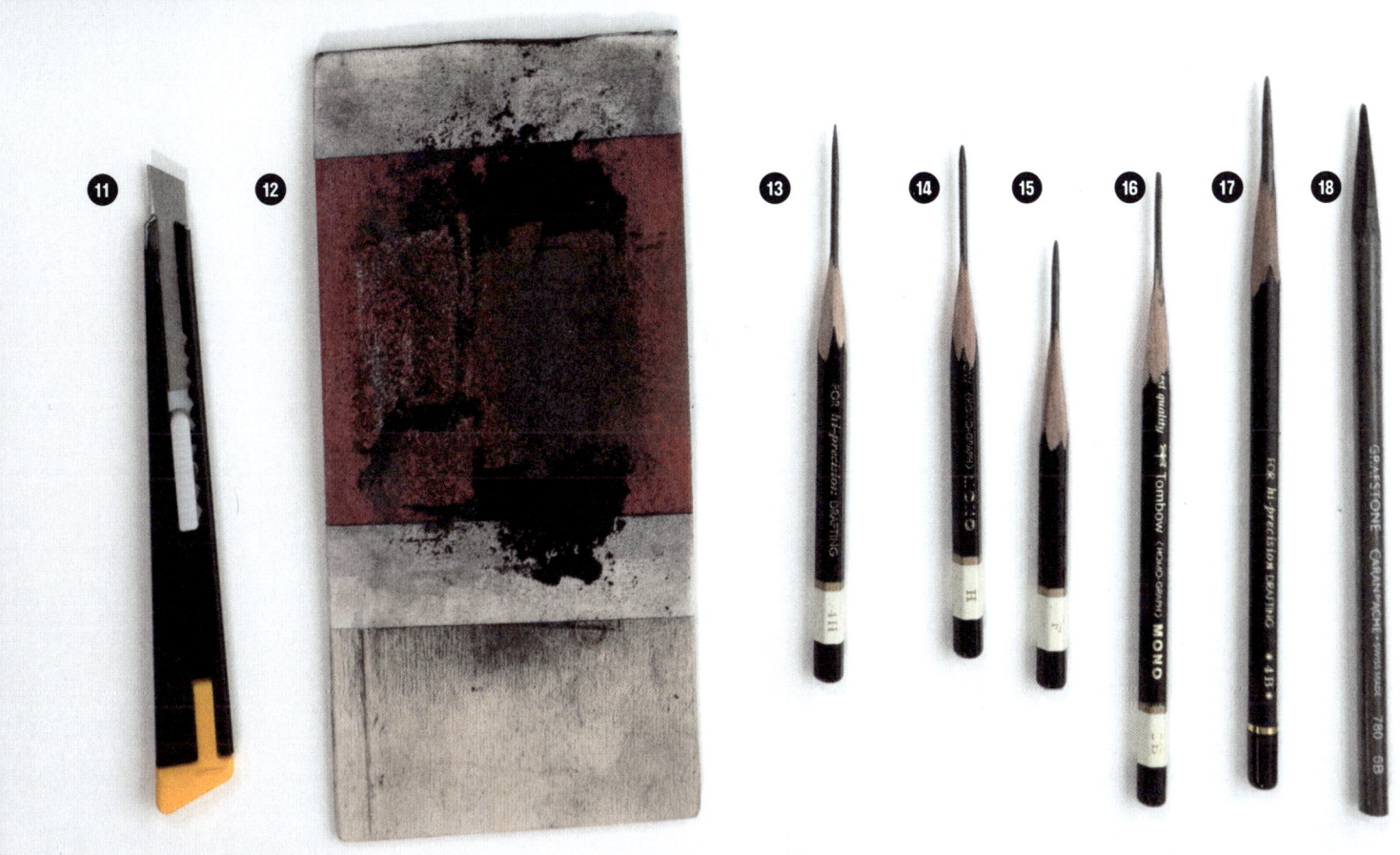

1–4. Pentel 120 A3DX, two 0.3mm and two 0.5mm pencils, each one with different grades of graphite

In the 0.3mm pencils, there is H and 2B, and in the 0.5mm pencils, there is HB and 4B. Some of these grades can be hard to find commercially, but this is less important than having different levels of hardness in the same diameter.

5–7: Rolled paper stumps saturated on at least one side with very soft graphite

These are used for drawing and applying values more than for 'blending'. Think of them as pencils that apply very soft diffuse lines. They are also helpful for applying light value, or smoothing out value at the beginning of the drawing process.

8–9: MONO Zero erasers, one cylindrical and the other chisel-tipped

These are best understood as a mechanical pencil, but with an eraser instead of lead. Useful for general erasing, but more specifically for carving out shapes, from halftones to the darkest shadows. Also useful for creating hair-like textures.

10: Kneaded rubber eraser

Applicable to most types of erasure required in drawing. From removing points of graphite build-up to shaping the broadest shapes of value, this is really the only eraser you need. The other erasers listed are merely more convenient ways to create the desired effects.

11: Olfa utility knife

Almost any variety like this will do. I have chosen this one as it is the sharpest, most durable, and easily replaceable one that I've found. Its primary use is shaving down graphite sticks and removing the wood from pencils to reveal the graphite within. Its next-best use is cutting papers to size from larger sheets.

12: A sharpening block for wood pencils

This is a very fine-grit piece of sandpaper affixed to a flat surface like a block of ¼ inch birch panel, as seen here, or a sturdy piece of cardboard. It's used for sharpening wool pencils, white chalk, or charcoal to a fine point. It's less useful for graphite sticks as the grain of the sandpaper fills up too easily.

13–17: Tombow MONO and MONO 100 pencils, from 4H to 4B

More can be added to this set, if desired. In general, this is what I use throughout this book.

18: Graphite stick from Caran d'Ache 6B

Excellent for the broadest application of values, as in mass drawing, for example.

THREE LEVELS OF DRAWING

It is crucial to recognize and differentiate between the three tiers of drawing development: the sketch, study, and finished drawing. Each serves a unique purpose and requires a distinctive approach tailored to the needs and goals of the project.

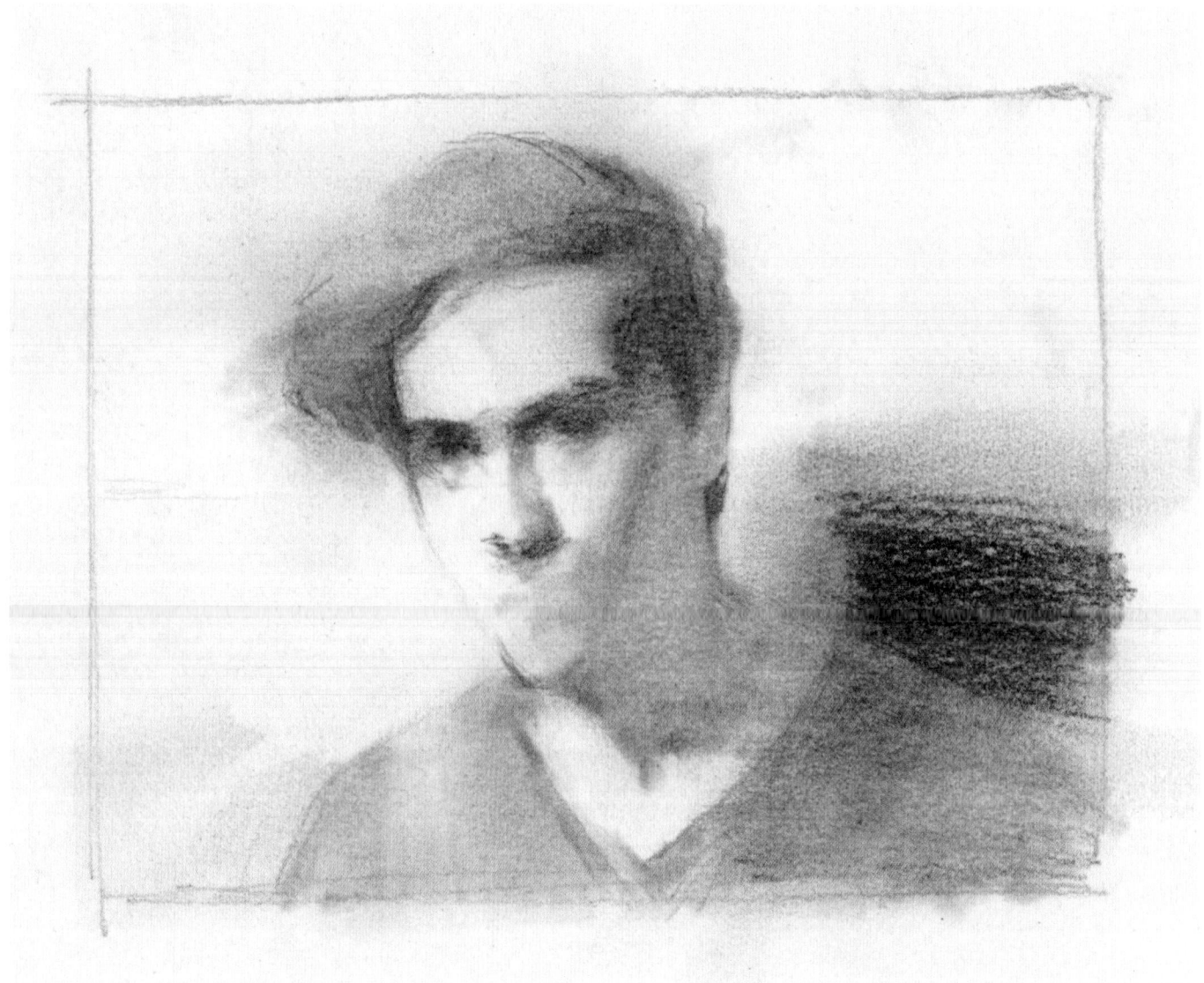

Level one: The sketch

Sketching is the most immediate and instinctive of the three. It is a tool for exploration and experimentation; a casual endeavour where ideas begin to take form. As such, it is perfect for on-site practice as you would in a museum or a public square in a beautiful city. Sketching allows the student to play with composition, quickly capture gestures, and experiment with the interplay of light and shadow without the commitment to detail. It's an invaluable exercise for internalizing concepts and translating observations into visual language. As such, sketches are often spontaneous, unrefined, and full of potential; a visual-brainstorming session that sets the foundation for more intricate work.

Level two: The study

Moving into deeper waters, the study is a focused examination of a particular subject or aspect of drawing. Here, you can discover the intricacies of the subject, whether that is the complex overlapping forms of human anatomy, subtle textures of fabric, or strictures of perspective. Studies are methodical and deliberate, often repeated to gain a thorough understanding. They are about honing skills, refining technique, and building a visual vocabulary that can be called upon in the creation of more developed works. Though their appearance can be rough or unrefined, studies demand patience and a critical eye, as they are about learning through repetition and incremental improvement.

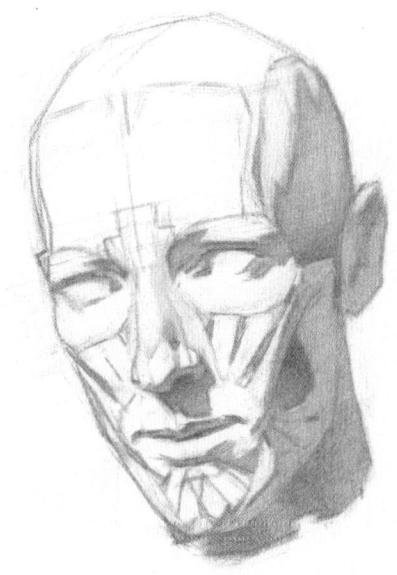
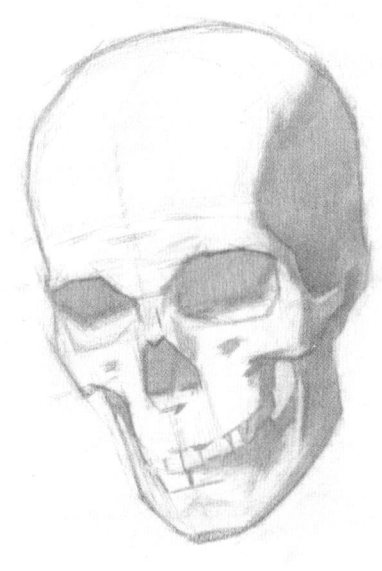

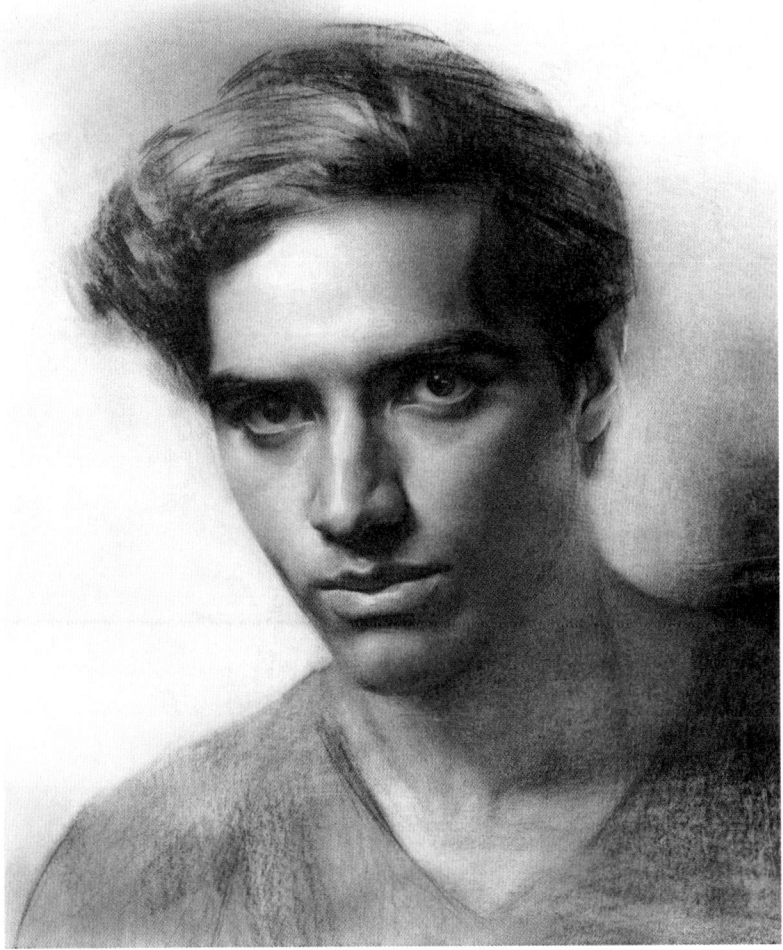

Level three: The finished drawing

A finished drawing is the culmination of the knowledge and skill accrued through sketching and study. It is an orchestrated piece where each mark is intentional and every detail is considered. It is also worth noting that this orchestration should leave the appropriate room for improvisation, without which there is a risk of a bland or unfeeling result. The creation of a finished drawing often follows a series of stages, starting with a simplified block-in that outlines the general proportions and composition. This foundation gradually evolves, with each subsequent stage building upon the last, integrating more detail and refining the image until it reaches its final form. The finished drawing is not merely the sum of its parts, but a cohesive entity where each element, from the broadest strokes to the finest details, works in concert to convey the artist's vision.

THE IMPORTANCE OF AN EVEN TONE

A golfer chooses a specific club based on factors like distance to the hole, terrain, and wind conditions. For instance, drivers are used for long distances on open fairways, while irons are chosen for precision in shorter shots. Bottom line, you would not putt with a 6-iron. This decision-making process mirrors an artist's choice of graphite hardness. Artists select different grades of graphite depending on the darkness and texture they wish to achieve in their drawings. Softer B-grade pencils produce darker, richer values, ideal for shading and bold marks, while harder H-grade pencils offer lighter, more precise values, suitable for fine details. Just as a golfer assesses the course before choosing a club, an artist considers the visual effect they desire before selecting a graphite grade.

The usefulness in being able to render even tones across a spectrum of values cannot be understated. It is not only the dark, rich blacks that require a smooth application, but the entire value scale too. The variance in value is partly a product of the graphite density (4H, H, HB, 4B, and so on), but also down to the artist's control and technique.

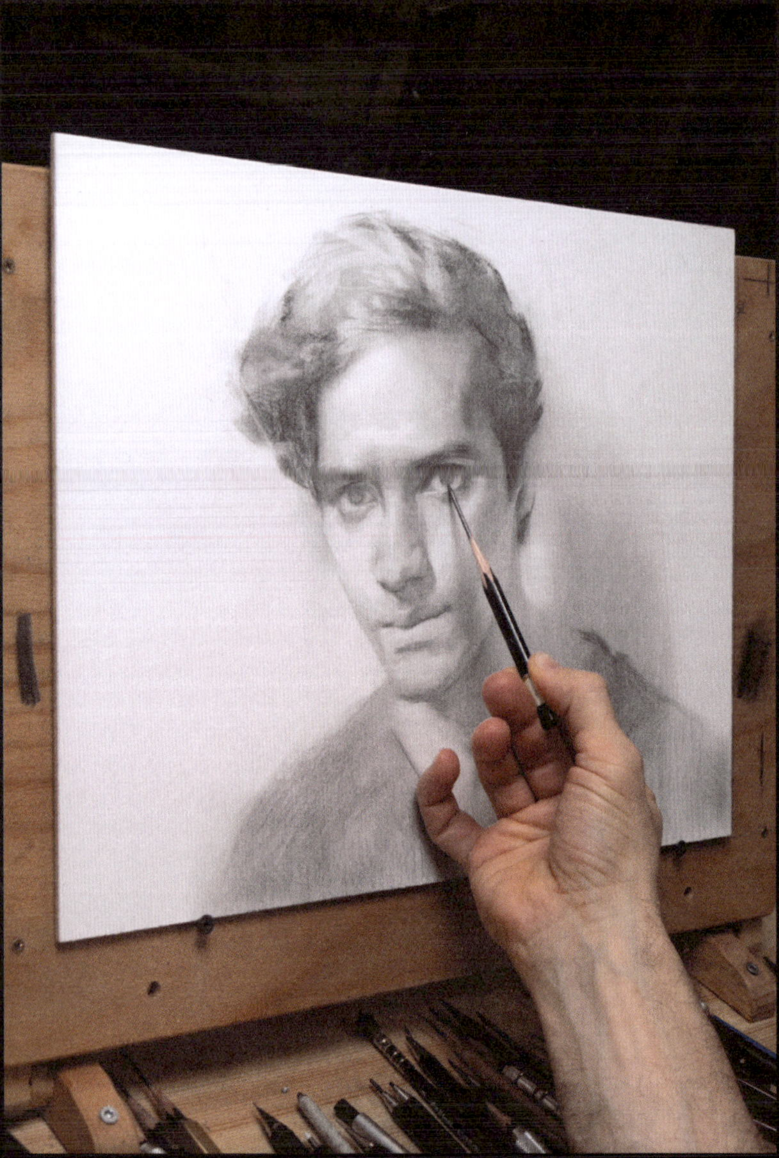

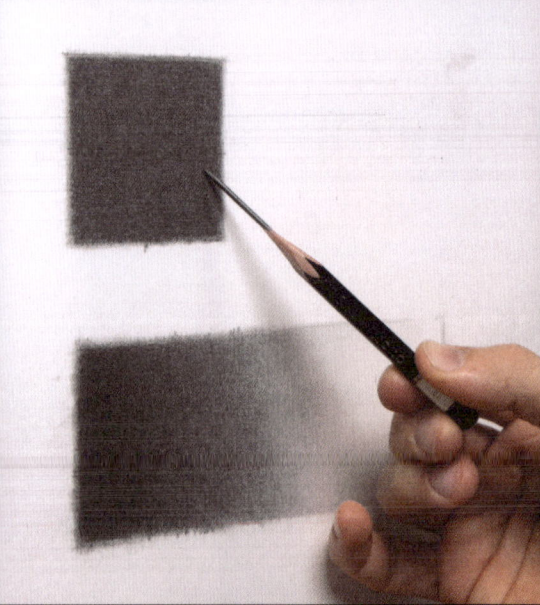

Maintaining an even pressure is crucial

The pencil should be held in such a way that the weight of the hand is distributed evenly. This can be achieved by balancing the hand or resting it on a part of the paper where you are not currently applying graphite. Notice in these images how the weight of the hand is balanced on the pinkie finger rather than on the point of the pencil. In addition, the pencil is held towards the back, which also creates a lighter touch. The aim is to avoid heavy-handed marks that can create unevenness in value.

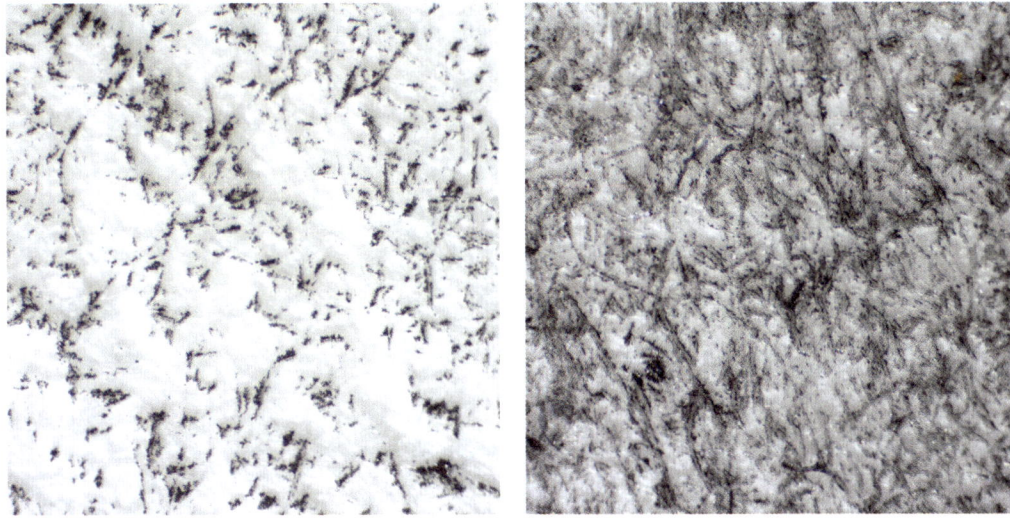

fig. **01**

fig. **02**

The texture of the paper provides the tooth that holds the graphite, but it also presents a challenge: the 'holes' or gaps within the paper's texture that must be filled to achieve a uniform value.

Fig. 01 shows a light application of HB pencil on Stonehenge paper, as seen through a microscope.

Fig. 02 shows the same paper after some stumping and further pencil application.

Solving this problem isn't a matter of simply pressing harder with the pencil to attain darkness, but rather a deliberate process of layering, working graphite into the texture of the paper to eliminate white spots without compromising the specificity of the value.

Creating an even gradient is a seamless extension of this skill. It demands the same meticulous attention to the pressure and movement of the pencil, ensuring that the transition from one value to another is smooth and free from abrupt changes or banding. The gradient is the ultimate test of value control, a demonstration of the ability to manipulate graphite with precision and intention. Layering is the cornerstone of this technique, a method that allows for gradual build-up of value.

Using a paper stump can expedite this process, blending the graphite into a cohesive tone with greater speed than layering alone. However, it is not merely a tool to hasten the work; it requires its own form of skill and understanding of pressure and motion to avoid a muddy or overly smooth appearance that lacks the vitality of a carefully built-up surface.

It is essential to recognize that an even value does not equate to a mechanical or sterile application. It is a *harmonious resolution of value* within a given area that is sought after.

Much like the pixels in digital graphics, where 8-bit illustrations, though comprised of larger, more distinct blocks of value, can achieve a cohesive and pleasing aesthetic, so too can a drawing with a less-refined value application. Conversely, a drawing with a finer 'resolution' of value, akin to a 4k graphic, contains a higher level of detail and smoothness. Both are even in their execution and harmonious within the context of their respective mediums.

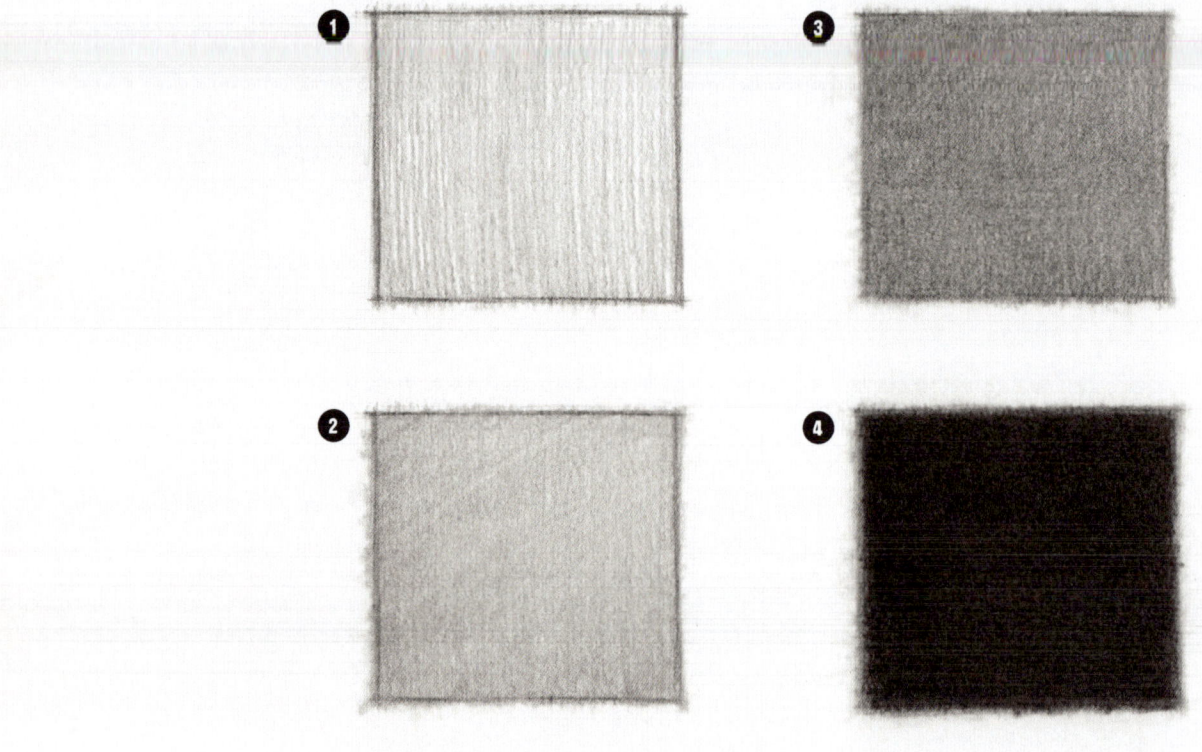

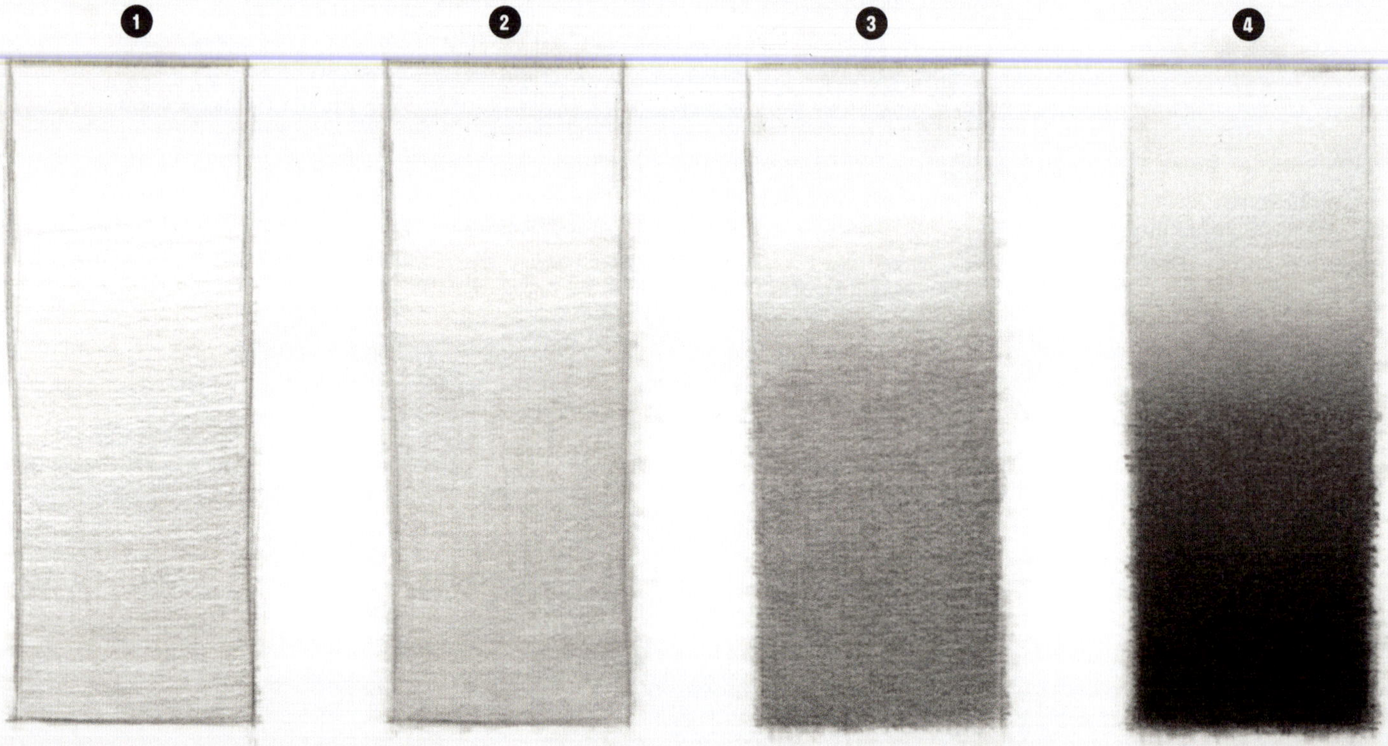

EXERCISE:
EVEN TONE PRACTICE

Target of the exercise: To discover the extent of evenness in tone

that is possible with a specific combination of materials.

Step 01. Initial layering

Begin with a pencil that is slightly harder than the desired outcome. For instance, if a 4B look is the goal, start with a 2B pencil. This initial layer should be applied uniformly across the area. The lighter touch of a harder pencil ensures that the texture of the paper is not overly compressed, which allows subsequent layers to adhere better. This step creates a foundation, a sort of 'primer', for the subsequent layers of graphite.

Step 02. Blending with a stump

Once the initial layer is down, use a blending stump (a piece of tightly rolled paper or a felt tool) to smooth out the graphite. This tool should be rolled gently over the applied graphite to blend it into the paper's texture. The gentle pressure will push the graphite into the nooks of the paper's surface, resulting in a more uniform application.

Step 03. Application of target grade

Over the blended layer, apply the graphite pencil that is capable of reaching the target value –

in this case, a 4B pencil. This layer should be as even as the first, with the same careful attention to pressure to ensure smoothness. Now do the second blending, using the stump again to blend this layer. This step further smooths out any variations and integrates the layers of graphite to create a cohesive tone.

Step 04. Refining and achieving value

Inspect the value for inconsistencies. Use a harder pencil, such as an H, to fill in any areas that appear lighter, where the paper's white is showing through. These 'holes' need a lighter touch, and a harder pencil provides the precision required. Concurrently, use a kneaded or Tombow MONO Zero eraser to lift off any spots that may have become too dark or prominent. This erasing technique is not just for correcting mistakes; it is also a drawing method that helps to refine the value and bring a drawing into balance. If, upon inspection, this has not resulted in the desired outcome, a repetition of the refining stage is most likely required.

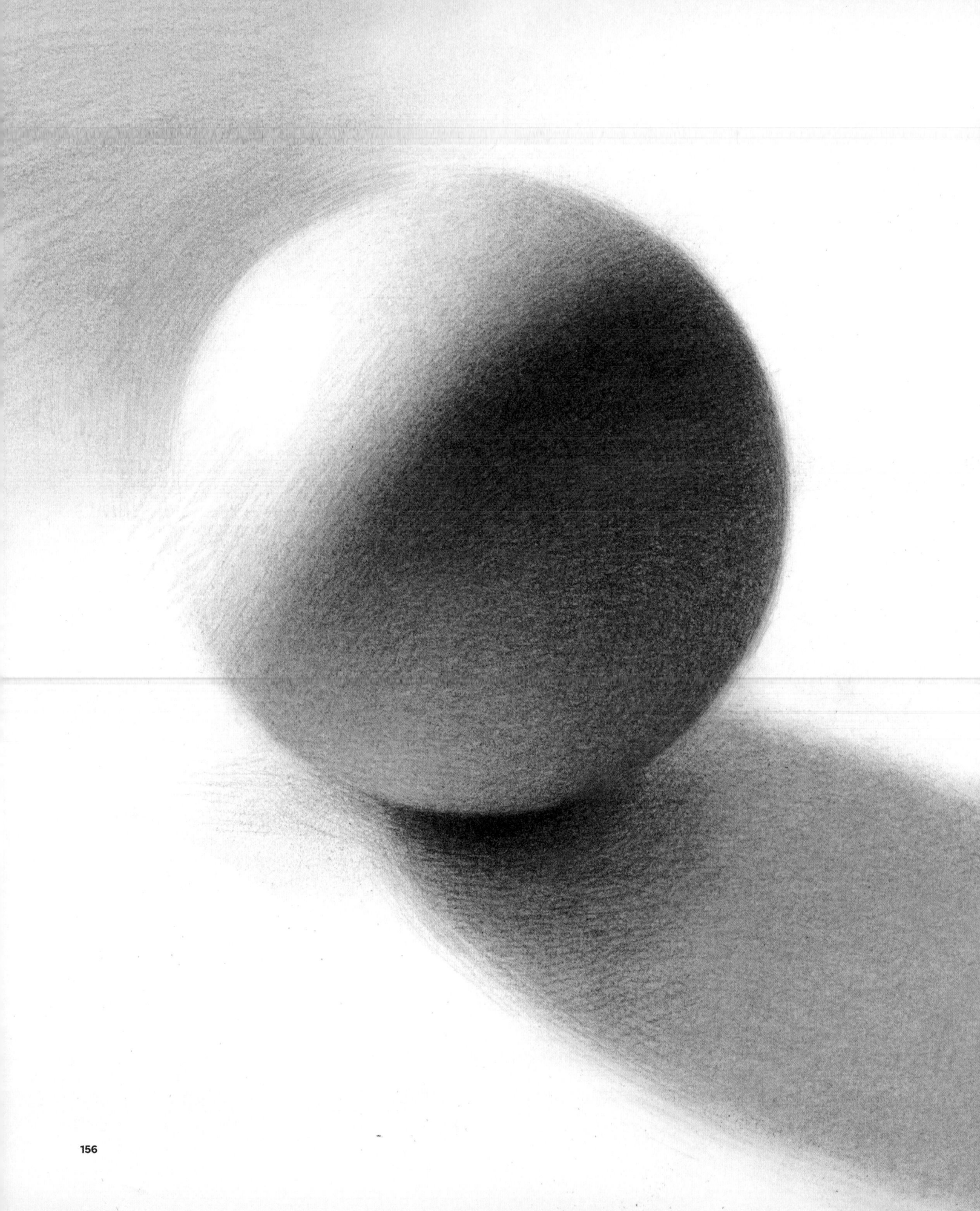

WHAT CAN YOU LEARN FROM DRAWING A SPHERE?

In short, you can learn everything that is essential to mastering realistic drawing by drawing a sphere. This humble shape encapsulates the fundamental principles of light, shadow, and form. The act of turning a flat circle into a convincing sphere serves as an indispensable exercise for any artist, helping to refine many skills.

The concept of form and how light falls

The three-dimensionality of the sphere requires the artist to think beyond the flatness of the paper. Artists must learn to understand how light falls on an object, creating highlights, midtones, and shadows. These components are crucial in conveying depth and volume.

A useful building block

More complex objects can often be broken down into basic shapes, such as a sphere or cube, and mastering those simpler forms equips an artist with the skills needed to tackle more intricate ones. This is integral to creating realistic representations of varied subjects.

The skill of creating gradations

The transition from light to dark on a sphere is gradual and smooth. Learning to replicate this effect with pencil is a foundational skill for creating realistic forms on more complex subjects, such as the human face or rippling fabric.

Edges and edge control

Varying the softness or hardness of edges is vital in drawing, as the nature of edges, whether sharp or soft, greatly affects the compositional focus within a piece.

Observational skills

As an artist you must carefully observe the direction of the light source and how it creates reflections and casts shadows, and influences the perceived value of the object. Beyond objective observation, the simplicity of the sphere makes it an ideal subject for artists to critically evaluate their own work. By comparing their rendering to the actual form and understanding where deviations occur, artists can develop a critical eye for self-assessment, an essential skill for continuous improvement in their practice.

Precision and control

The process of meticulously rendering a sphere, with its subtle gradations and delicate shifts in tone, demands patience and technical skill. This precision is indispensable in portraiture as a slight deviation can significantly alter the likeness and character of the subject.

Simplicity

In its unassuming form, the sphere does not distract with complex textures or intricate details. This allows the artist to focus on the core principles of light, shadow, and form. It's a reminder that mastery of basic forms is the foundation upon which more complex and detailed work is built.

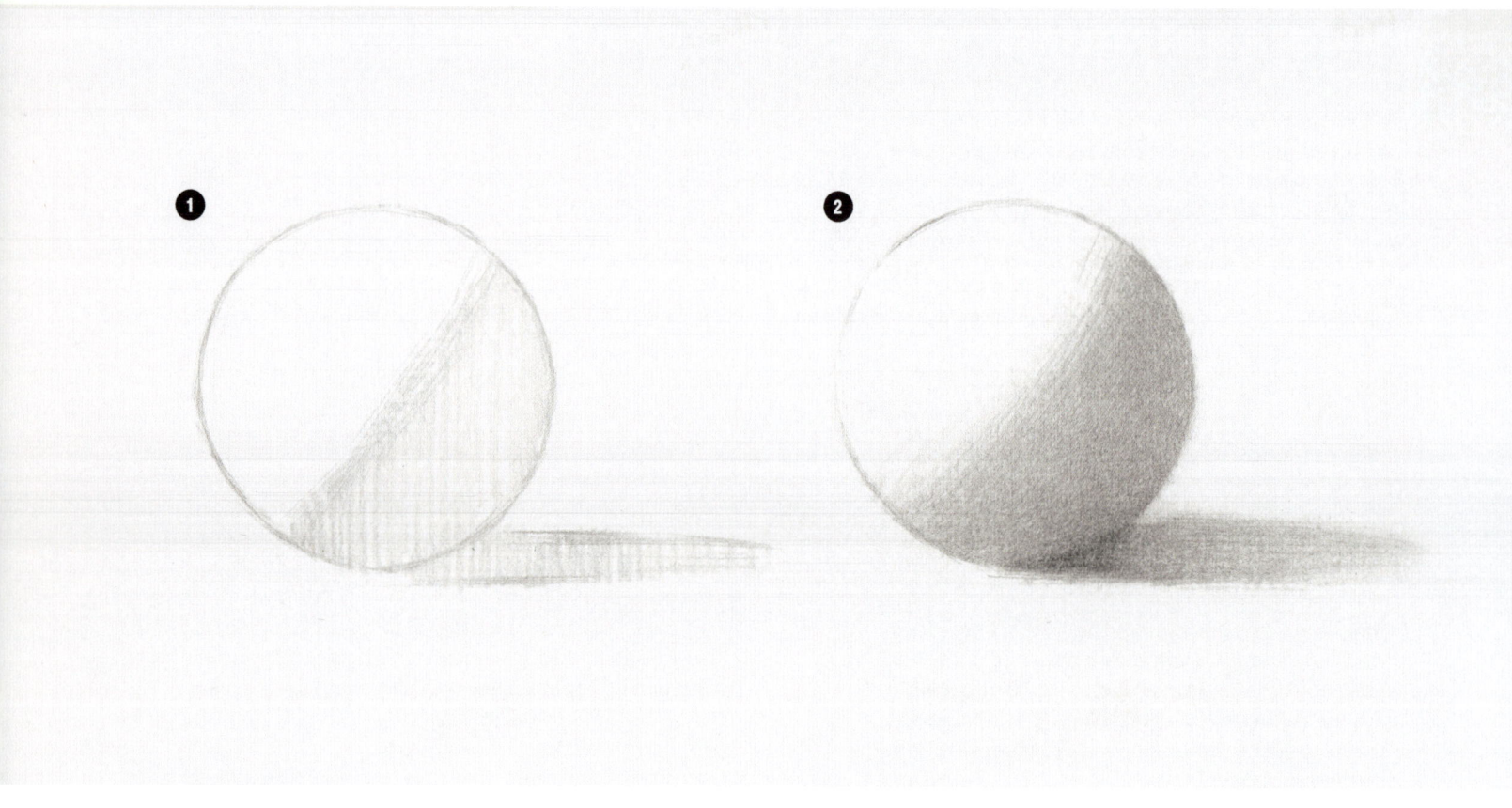

EXERCISE:
SPHERE-DRAWING PRACTICE

Target of the exercise: To practise and perfect skills such as value application, edge control, gradient resolution, understanding of materials, and general means of representation.

Step 01. Outline and axis

First establish the initial height versus width of the sphere, which requires a simple comparative measurement to ensure these two axes are equal in length. The addition of a shadow edge serves as the equator of the sphere and helps in establishing the direction of the light and its orientation in relation to the sphere in space. Additionally, the cast shadow extends to the right in accordance with the trajectory of the light rays hitting the sphere.

Step 02. Shading gradient

Introduce a basic gradient to the sphere. The light shape at the top left, where the light hits the form directly, is totally unified in accordance with the relative value scale present at this stage. This soft edge between the light shape and the shadow shape indicates the curvature of the sphere and begins to give it a three-dimensional appearance. The cast shadow on the ground also becomes more prominent through the addition of darker ambient occlusion, anchoring the sphere on its plane.

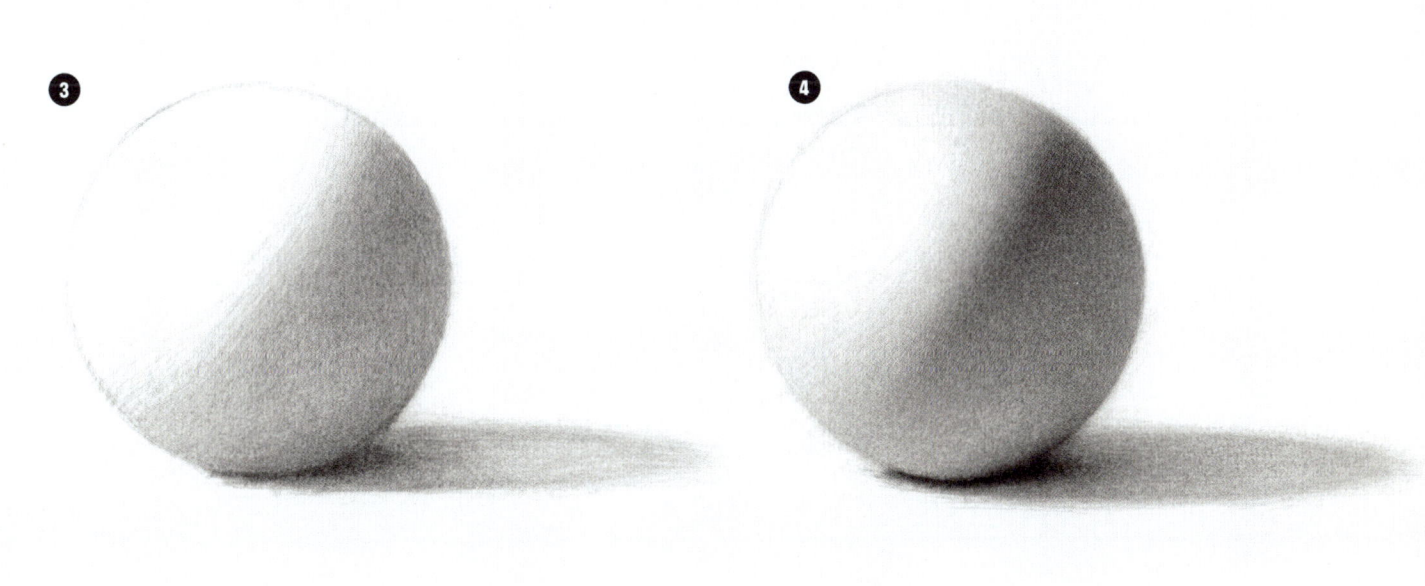

Step 03. Refining shading and shadow

Refine the shading on the sphere. The value range is expanded, with the light shape remaining mostly untouched, while the shadows grow deeper, providing a more dramatic sense of the sphere's volume. The transition between light and dark is further resolved to create a more realistic representation of how light falls across a rounded surface. The shadow on the ground is also more defined, with a softer edge where the penumbra is located, indicating the crossing rays of the light source.

Step 04. Halftone and contrast

The shading is now fully realized, with high contrast and subtle transitions between light and shadow. The centre light is more defined, and there is a clear indication of the planes of the sphere within the light shape through the application of a halftone value. The distinction between the light shape and the shadow shape, known as the 'core shadow', achieves a slightly darker value than the rest of the form shadow, with the exception of the lowest edge of the sphere, which is darker due to the ambient occlusion effect. This further contrast gives the sphere a solid, tactile presence. The cast shadow on the ground is consistent with the light direction and has a soft edge, suggesting a diffuse light source.

Each step builds upon the last, moving from a flat circle to a fully rendered sphere with a believable sense of form and depth. This methodical process of layering tones is essential in creating the illusion of three-dimensionality on a two-dimensional surface.

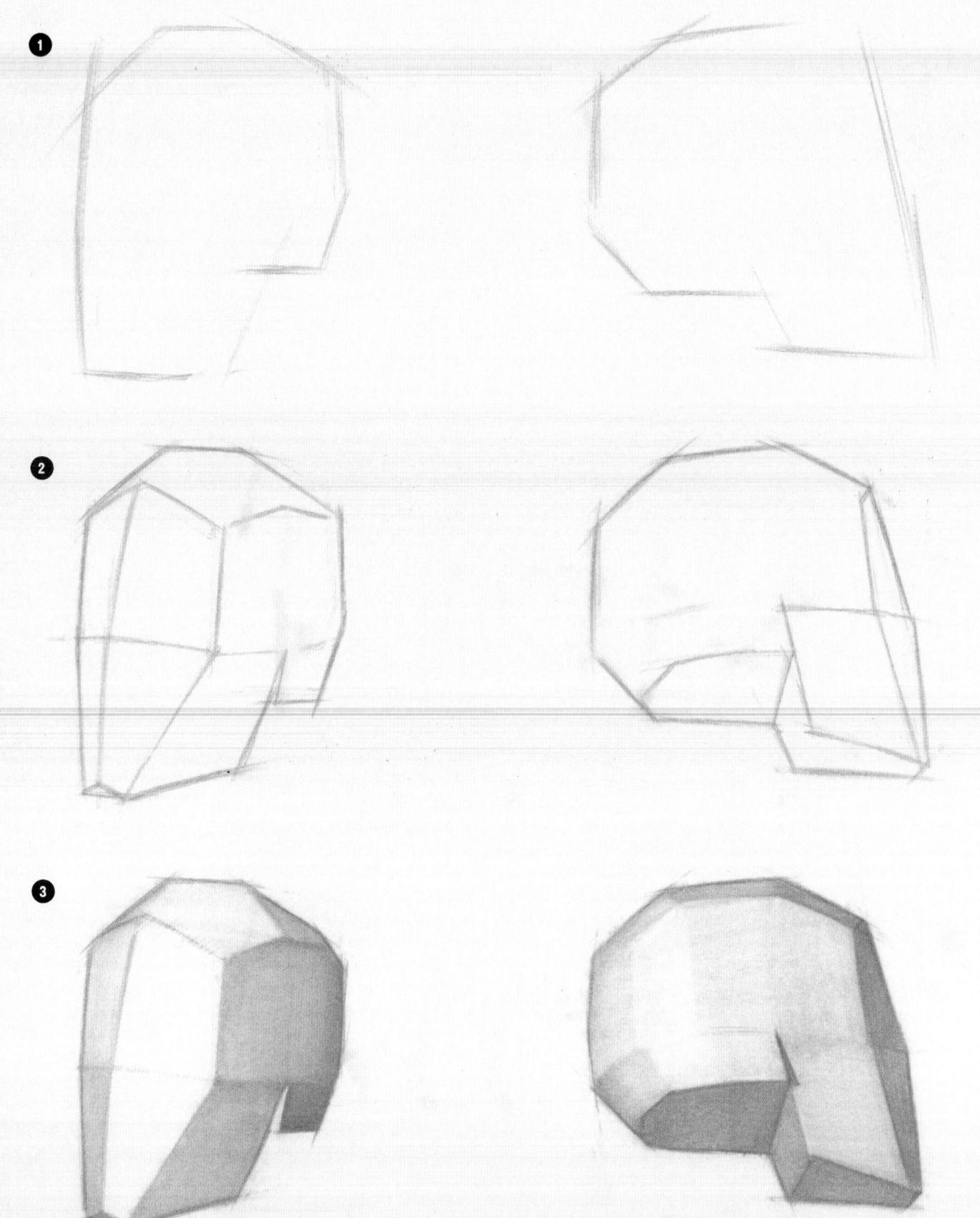

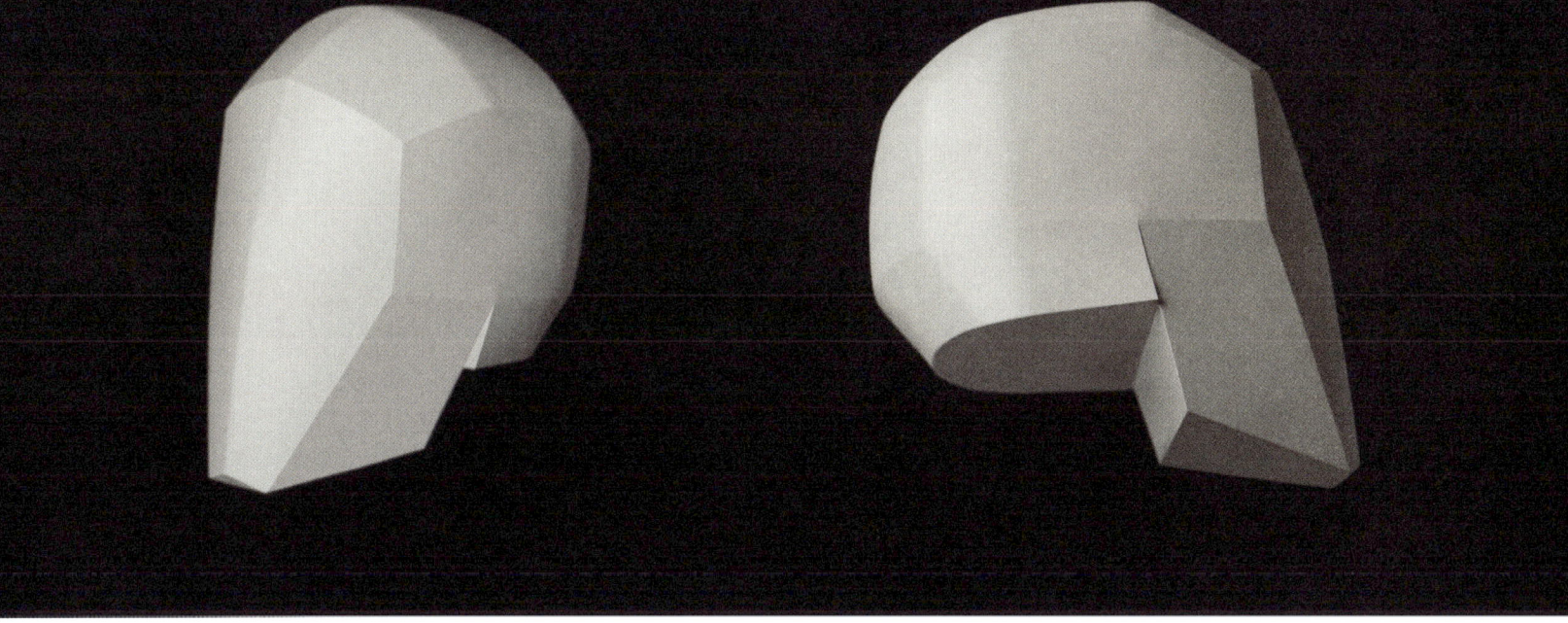

EXERCISE:
SIMPLIFIED BLOCK-IN PRACTICE

Target of the exercise: To develop an understanding and memorize the appearance of the simplified head from any angle.

This simplified head template (as discussed on page 95) represents an incremental increase in complexity. For this exercise, the level of drawing only needs to be a sketch. The goal is to become familiar with the basic construction of the head, its major planes and proportions, and, in particular, how it aligns with the anatomy of the skull. Unlike the sphere, it will take some practice to understand how it looks from any direction. I refer to this as being able to 'tumble' the form.

Step 01. Basic shapes and proportions
Draw the basic dimensions and outlines that will form the foundation of the subject. The emphasis here is on capturing the correct proportions and angles without any concern for light and shadow. The objective is to observe and simplify complex forms into more manageable geometric shapes. Consider that there are several opportunities at this stage to make comparative measurements and triangulations based on the present angle breaks. Whatever you fix and make certain now will only benefit your drawing later.

Step 02. Geometric form
Moving to a more detailed breakdown, the subject is subdivided into planes. Each plane is defined by its orientation in space, which will later inform the light it receives. Think about the structure of the subject in three dimensions and how it is oriented in this space. The tilt and rotation can be compared and well observed.

Step 03. Light and shadow application
This process of applying light and shadow starts to give the subject volume and depth. This is where you will apply your knowledge of light-source direction and how it interacts with form, translating it into varying values on each plane. This stage reinforces the concept that the value on each plane is determined by its angle, relative to the light source.

DRAWING FROM MEMORY

When first introduced, memory drawing can seem like a somewhat exotic or separate discipline from standard drawing exercises. However, it is worth mentioning that all drawing exercises are in fact memory drawing exercises, as it is not possible to simultaneously observe your drawing and your subject – you are forced to commit different aspects of what you see to memory. Accepting this as true, we can delve into all of the techniques that can be used to enhance the retention of those memories.

Observe the subject carefully for a significant amount of time before you start to draw. This isn't just casual looking, but instead a deep, analytical observation. Take comparative measurements and commit the proportional ratios to memory, such as 1 width = 1.5 height, and so on.

Simplify the subject into basic geometric shapes. Often used in academic drawing, this technique helps in understanding the general structure and proportions of the subject. By reducing complexity, you make it easier to recall the subject when drawing from memory.

Identify key features or landmarks in your subject that can act as anchors in your memory. These could be distinctive shapes, specific features, or strong contrasting edges.

By creating these mental anchors, you can build the rest of the image around them when recalling the subject (the bottom edge of the ear aligns with the bottom edge of the nose on a horizontal axis, the back edge of the eye socket aligns with the front plane of the neck on a vertical axis, and so on).

Narrate the process of creating the image in your mind. This verbal or mental walkthrough can help to solidify the memory of the subject. As you observe the subject, describe it to yourself; it could be the process of how one part connects to another, or the relationship between different elements, and so on. This method echoes the teaching strategies used in classical-art training where students are encouraged to articulate their process. Assigning language to a visual marker is a powerful way to integrate additional memory pathways into your drawing process.

Practice drawing the same subject multiple times with intervals between sessions. This spaced repetition is an important tool for memory training. As advocated by educational theorists like Hermann Ebbinghaus, repetition over spaced intervals significantly enhances memory retention. Drawing the subject multiple times over a certain period allows the brain to consolidate the memory, making it more likely to be remembered in the long term.

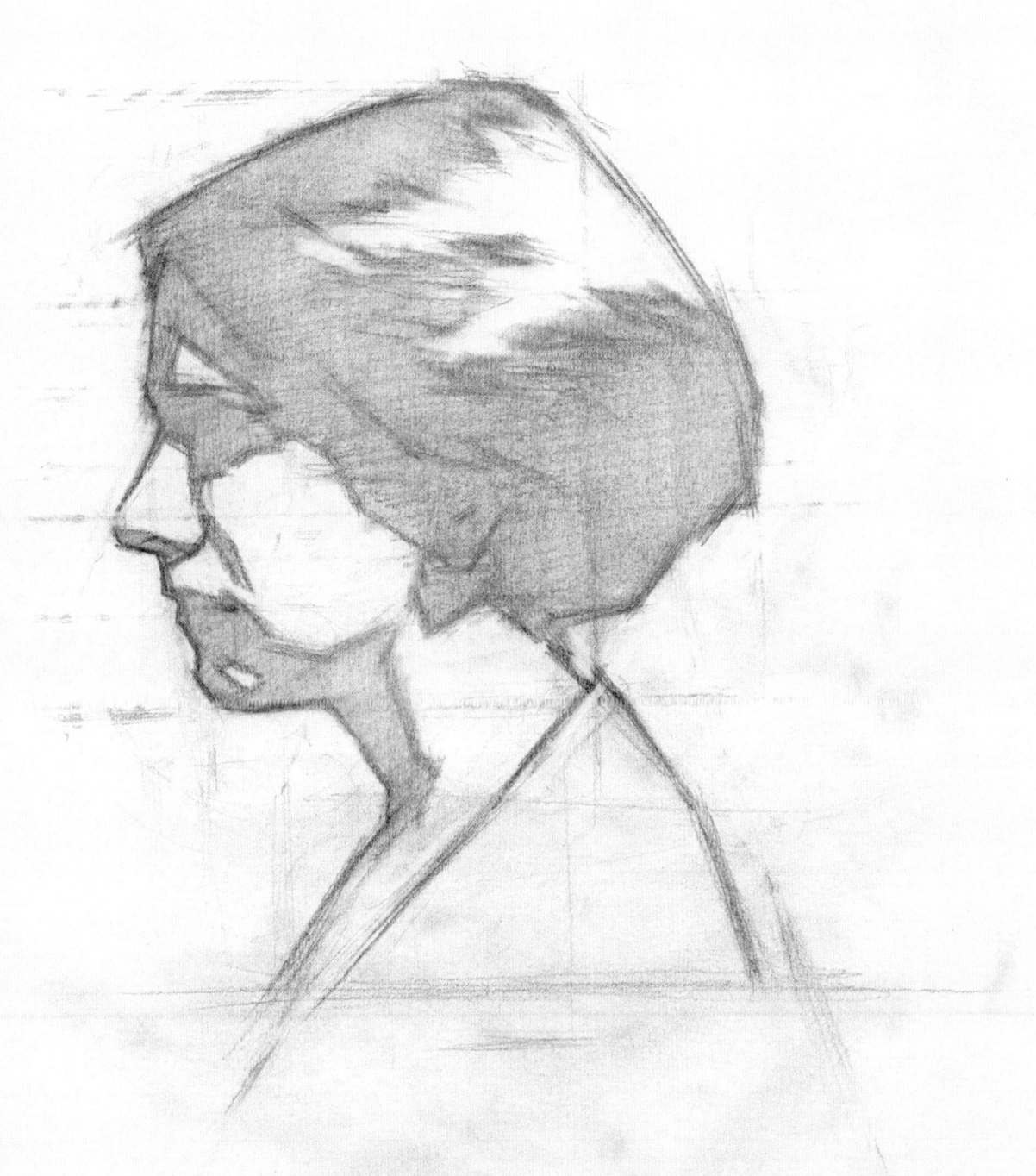

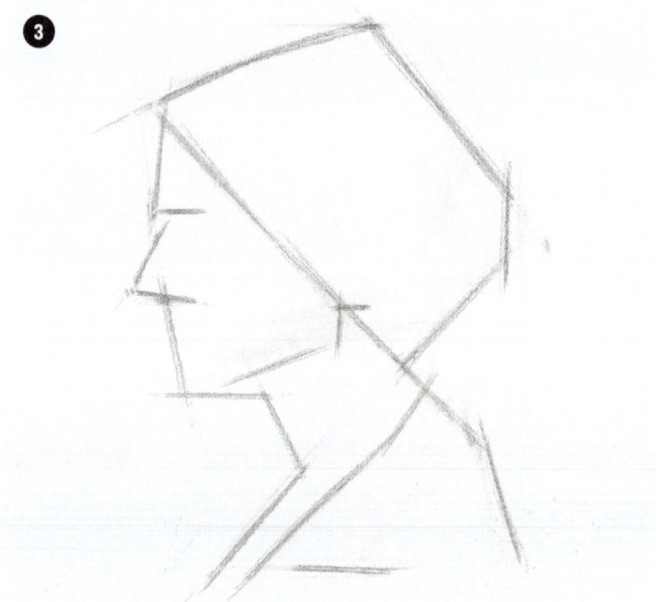

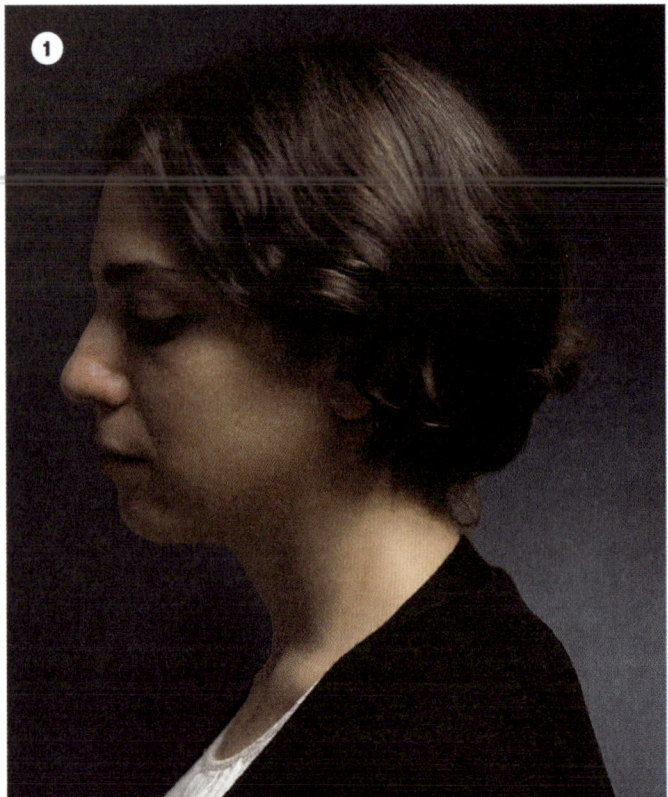

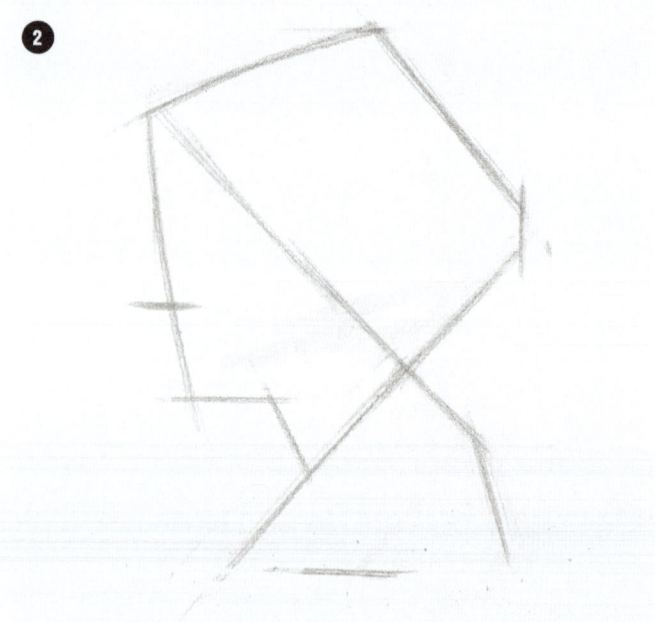

EXERCISE: MEMORY-DRAWING PRACTICE

Target of the exercise: Strengthen the process by which measurements and visual organization are utilized to enhance visual memory.

Step 01. Initial observation (five minutes)

Start by focusing on the reference image for five minutes. Absorb as much detail as possible, noting the general composition, key forms, and values. Break down the subject into simple geometric shapes, and make mental notes of proportions and angles. Create associations that link different parts of the image. For instance, the width of an eye might relate to the distance between the nose and the ear. Observe the direction of the light source, noting where the highlights and shadows fall. Pay attention to the negative space around the subject, which can help in gauging distances and relationships between elements.

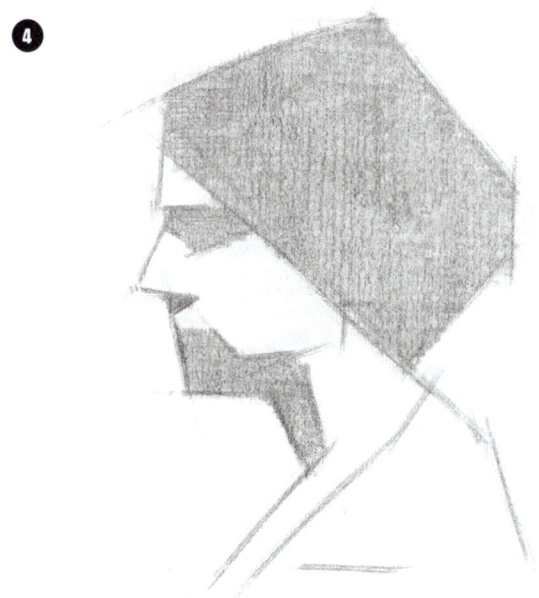

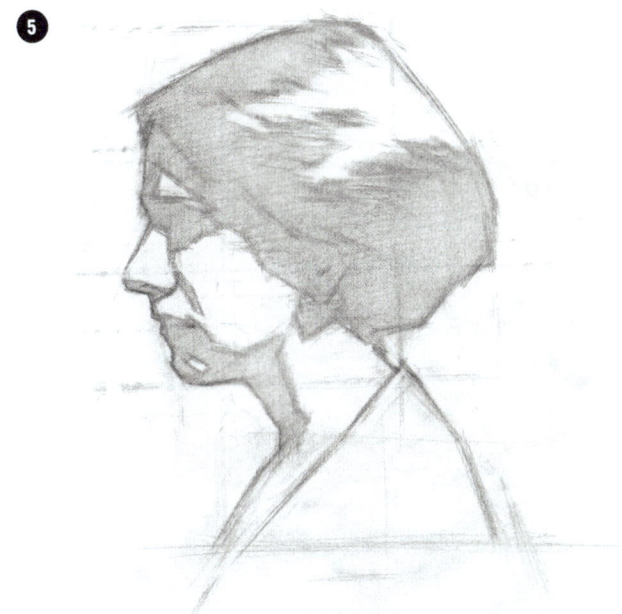

Step 02. First drawing phase (fifteen minutes)
Cover the image and begin drawing from memory for fifteen minutes. Start with the general shapes and proportions noted earlier, sketching lightly and in long, relatively straight lines to allow for adjustments. Gradually refine the drawing, adding details from memory using associations and measurements made during the observation phase. Resist the urge to peek at the image; the goal is to rely on visual memory.

Step 03. Re-observation (five minutes)
Cover the drawing and observe the original image again for five minutes. Look for details and relationships that were missed or inaccurately remembered. Take this time to correct the mental image, making more precise associations and measurements. Compare what you remember of the appearance of the drawing and search for incongruities.

Step 04. Second drawing phase (fifteen minutes)
Cover the image again and continue refining the drawing for another fifteen minutes. Make corrections based on the insights gained during the second observation phase. Focus on areas that were challenging, using the fresh information to improve the representation.

Step 05. Further iterations
Repeat the cycle of observing for five minutes and drawing for fifteen minutes as many times as necessary. With each iteration, the memory should become clearer and the drawing more accurate.

Step 06. Post-drawing session evaluation
Once the final drawing session is complete, compare the drawing to the original image. Evaluate the accuracy of shapes, proportions, values, and spatial relationships. Reflect on what was challenging to remember and why that might have been the case. Analyse the drawing for areas of improvement, and note them down for future reference. Consider the associations that were helpful and those that were not, refining the strategy for the next session. Assess the overall impression of the drawing and whether it captures the essence of the original image.

In this final step, it's best to be both critical and constructive. The aim is to identify gaps in memory and execution to inform future practice. Each session should build upon the last, creating a cumulative effect that deepens your skills in observation, memory, and rendering.

Visual block-in

A visual block-in has its basis in the antique Italian notion of chiaroscuro, which translates to 'light and dark'. This type of study is meant to accurately communicate the most basic elements of the visual phenomena. However, it is practical to take things one step further and say that a visual block-in focuses on how the impression of light and shadow hits your eyes – precisely how you perceive them. This distinction is important as it permits a degree of flatness to the rendering that, in turn, brings out one of the strengths of this approach: two-dimensional shape design.

Popularized during the Renaissance, chiaroscuro involves the dramatic use of contrasting areas of light and dark to achieve a sense of volume in modelling three-dimensional objects and figures. When studying this, you must strip down the complexity of the subject and focus on the basic distribution of light and shadow. This encourages the artist to utilize their sense of naive recognition in evaluating the likeness of their drawing.

Moreover, this technique encourages an efficient workflow. By addressing the broadest aspects of the composition first, artists can avoid getting lost in the nuances of form and halftone too early in the process. This hierarchy of working (general to specific) ensures that light, form, and the overall composition are prioritized before the features of the model are added.

Working in this style also cultivates an artist's skill for abstraction and simplification. To clarify, abstraction is being used here to denote anything flat or two-dimensional, as opposed to a representation of the world. This abstraction is key to translating the nuances of the real world into a compelling and coherent design. Form, or roundness, has a way of distracting attention from the kinds of two-dimensional spatial relationships that are the bedrock for this type of design.

It is worth mentioning that this approach to blocking-in a drawing relies heavily on the lighting situation. In a situation with a primary, dominant light source, or even one in which there is also a dim secondary source, it will work efficiently. However, if too much complexity is added to the lighting, its merit significantly diminishes, along with the appearance of clear-cut light and dark shapes.

Over the next few pages, we'll delve into a visual block-in exercise and the specific stages involved.

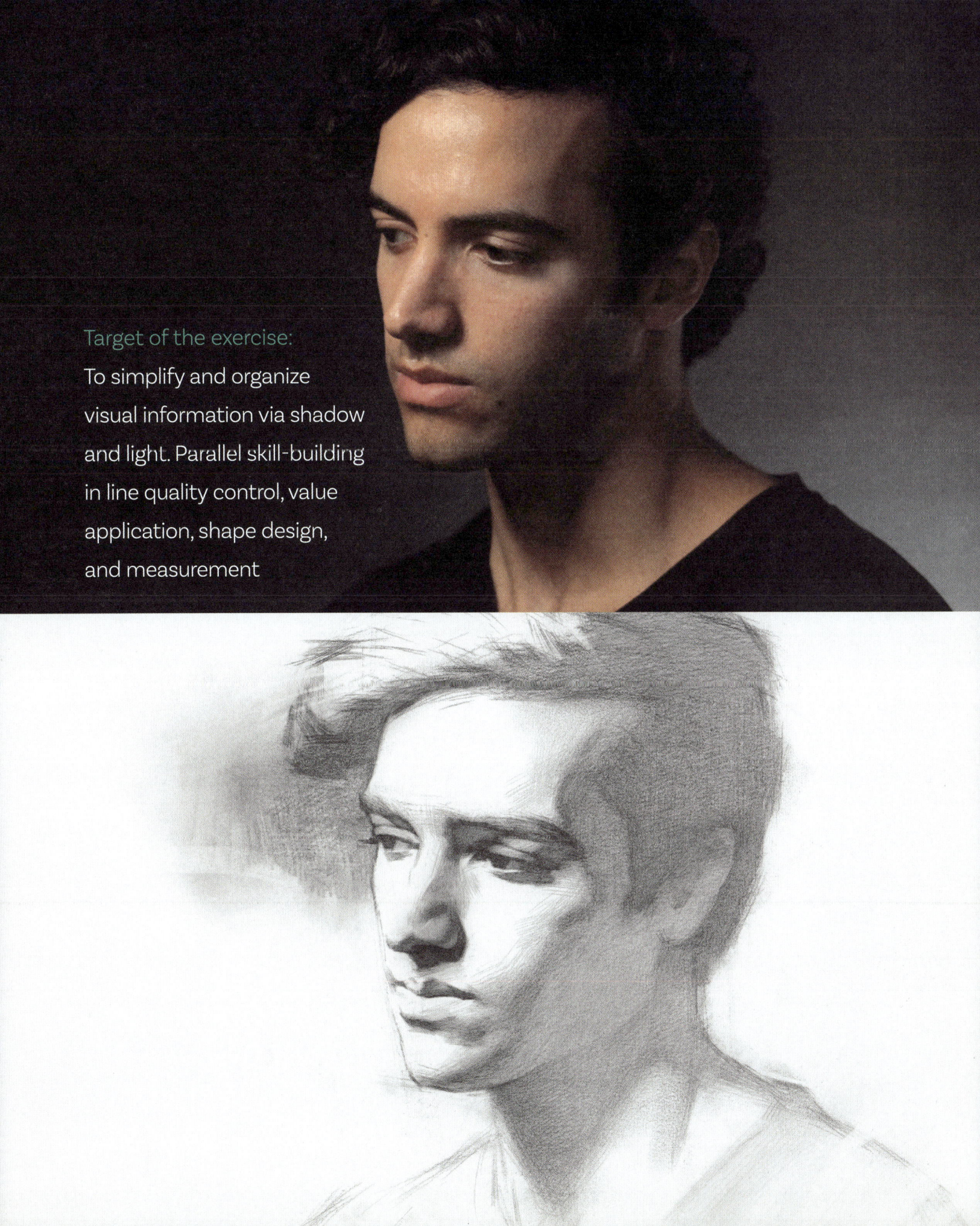

Target of the exercise:
To simplify and organize visual information via shadow and light. Parallel skill-building in line quality control, value application, shape design, and measurement

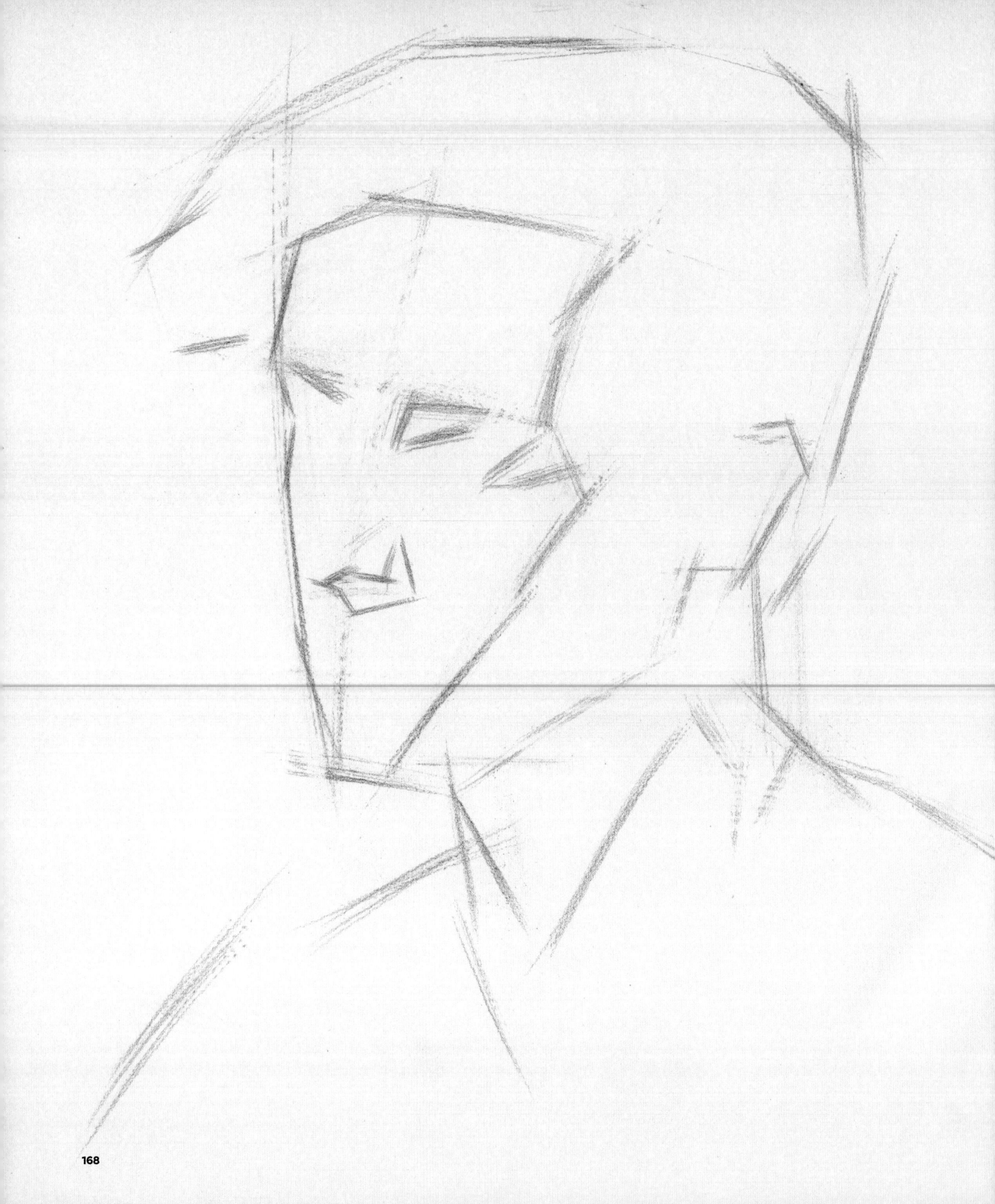

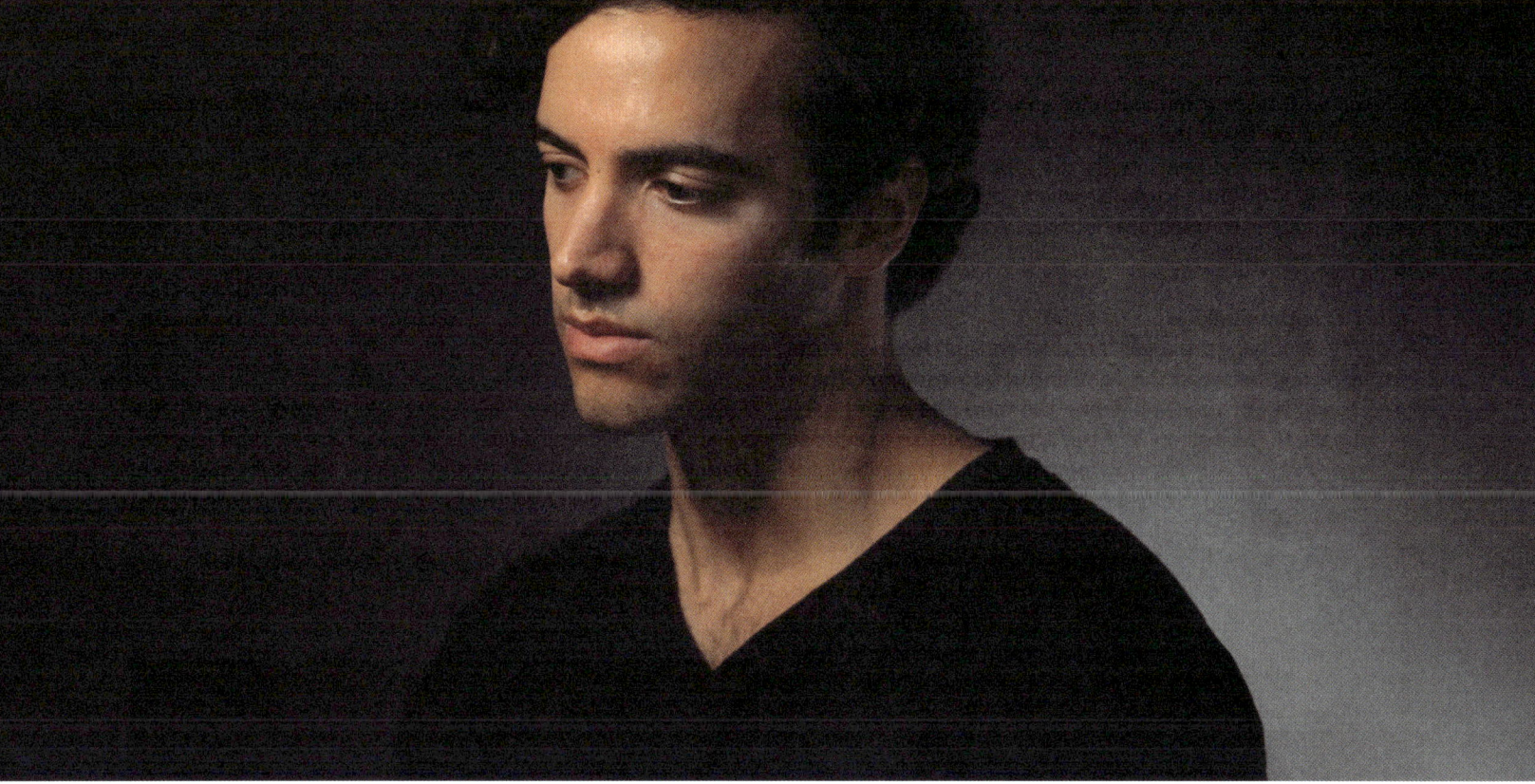

VISUAL BLOCK-IN: STAGE ONE

In the beginning stage, there are a few simple goals. The first is to arrange a series of straight lines and angle breaks for cross-referencing, in order to establish a blueprint-type image of the model's pose and proportions. The second is to indicate the biggest shapes possible that represent the configuration of light and shadow. Finally – and this is more of a guideline than a goal – it is imperative to block in the entire head. The judgement of its proportions is dependent on the assessment of a complete height-to-width ratio.

There are several key-point indicators to note for the biggest proportional relationships in the head, each of which should be used, if visible:

- Width of the forehead from temporal line to temporal line.

- Width of the cheekbones at the widest point of the face.

- Posterior edge of the jaw, especially where it meets the connection of the earlobe.

- Bottom edge of the chin.

- Brow ridge, as indicated by the eyebrows and/or the superior edge of the shadow in the eye socket.

- The hairline.

- The visible extend of the top and back of the head. This will be an indication of the boundary of the hair rather than the head itself, but is nonetheless useful in establishing boundaries for proportional measurement.

VISUAL BLOCK-IN: STAGE TWO

Advancing from the foundational arrangement of lines and angles that establish the pose and proportions of the model, we proceed to the next stage: the introduction of shadow values (**fig. 01**). This stage is where the two-dimensional blueprint begins to transform into an impression that seems three-dimensional.

Applying initial shadows

Begin by identifying the largest areas where light does not reach, distinguishing between the light and shadow regions. These broad swathes of tone will define the form and act as a foil to enhance the appearance of the light shape. Use a midtone value to block in these areas, understanding that this initial layer only sets the stage for further refinement. This blocking-in of shadows unifies the composition, providing a visual anchor for the features of the face. When applying the shadow, consider the character of the light source. The direction and quality of light – whether it is harsh and direct, or soft and diffused – will determine the edge type and value of the shadow. Hard light creates sharp, distinct shadows, while diffused light results in softer, more subtle transitions.

Dual-toned shadows

With the broad shadow areas in place, we can introduce dual-toned shadow values (**fig. 02**). This involves using two distinct values within the shadow areas to bring out the contrast between the darkest darks and the base value of the model's skin. Select a darker tone to represent the deeper shadows, often found where forms turn away from the light source most drastically, as found in an ambient occlusion, or in a locally dark surface such as dark hair or eyebrows. The darker of the two shadow values will be used to fill these shadow areas, allowing for a contrast that increases the readability of the drawing.

The execution of dual-toned shadows requires a careful balance. Each of the values should be unified unto themselves and, when observed while squinting, unify somewhat together. Consider that they should appear to be a group when seen in contrast with the value of the light shape.

Cross-referencing

Throughout this process, it's essential to continually cross-reference the shadows' edges against the established proportional markers. The shadow along the cheekbones in this instance reflects the widest point of the face. The width of the forehead is clearly aligned with the temporal line. The top of the shadow shape of the eye socket shows us the bottom of the brow ridge and also establishes a distance to the beginning of the shadow shape of the nose. The shadow shapes of the mouth create a proportional divider within the overall height of the light shape of the lower third of the face. All of these relationships are new measurements to be taken. Any time that new information is added, an opportunity for more precise triangulation comes with it.

Consider also the key-point indicators mentioned previously – these are your navigational stars as you map the shadows. The posterior edge of the jaw, the bottom edge of the chin, the brow ridge, the hairline, and the visible extent of the top and back of the head – all of these serve as reference points to ensure each shadow is in the correct place and is the correct shape and size.

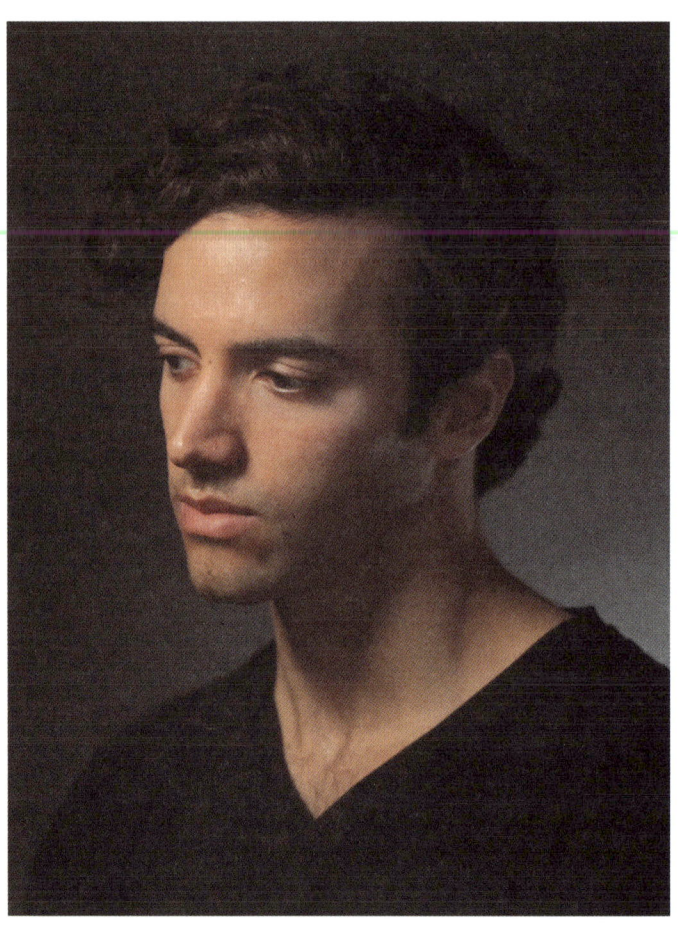

fig. **01**

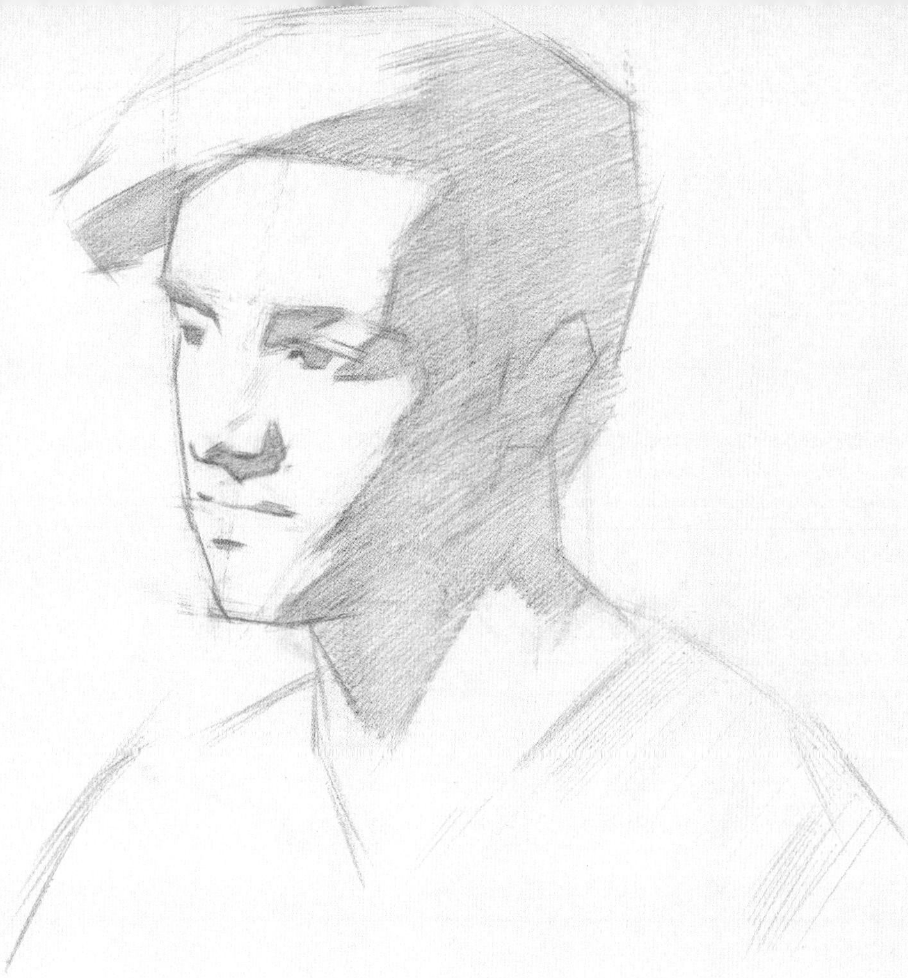

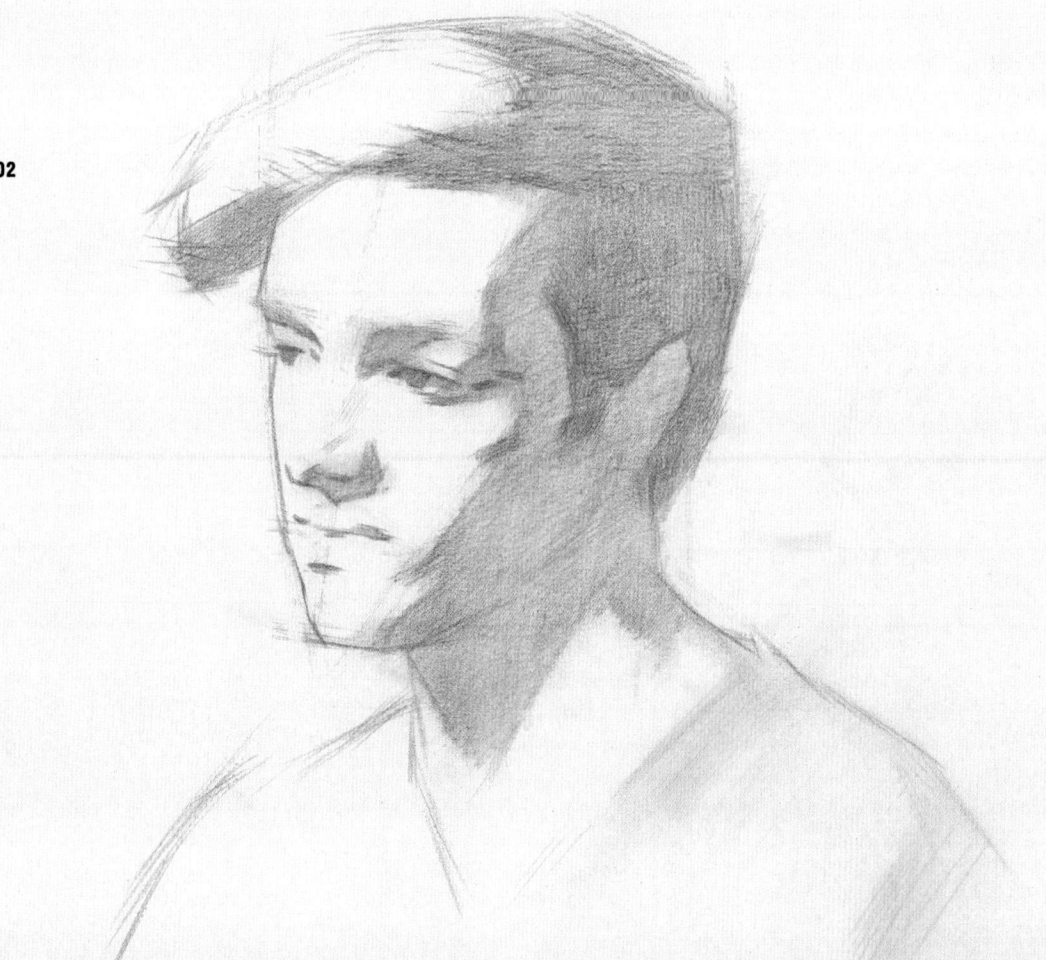

fig. **02**

VISUAL BLOCK-IN: STAGE THREE

The introduction of shadow values and dual-toned shadowing in the previous stage was the prelude to a more intricate arrangement of light and shadow. Stage three is where a greater degree of likeness is achieved by clarifying facial features, enhancing the interplay of light and shadow, and honing the edges to reflect the character of the turning forms.

Defining facial features

Here, the features must be defined not by their outline, but by how they emerge from and recede into the shadows. This pattern of light and shadow satisfies both the visual requirements of the style as well as the abstract quality necessary to be utilized in triangulation and measurement. The eyes, the nostrils, the curve of the lips – all must be delineated with care and intelligence, ensuring that the play of light and dark across them is truthful to the form. Simplify these shapes well and they will lead you to a better and more flexible drawing.

The core shadow

This is a pivotal element at this stage – the darkest part of the shadow where light and shadow meet. It is the defining line of the form, and enhancing it can significantly bolster the three-dimensionality of the drawing. It should be rendered with a varied but generally soft edge, allowing it to transition well into the lighter areas, creating a roundness.

The keying of edges

This is a nuanced task that involves grading the transitions from softest to hardest. Not all edges are created equal; some are sharp and distinct, such as the bridge of the nose against its side plane, while others are soft and subtle, such as the gentle fade of the fatty tissue of the cheek. The artist must assess each edge and decide its sharpness based on its relationship to the sharpest and softest edges. This range of edges provides cues to the viewer about the volume and contour of the subject.

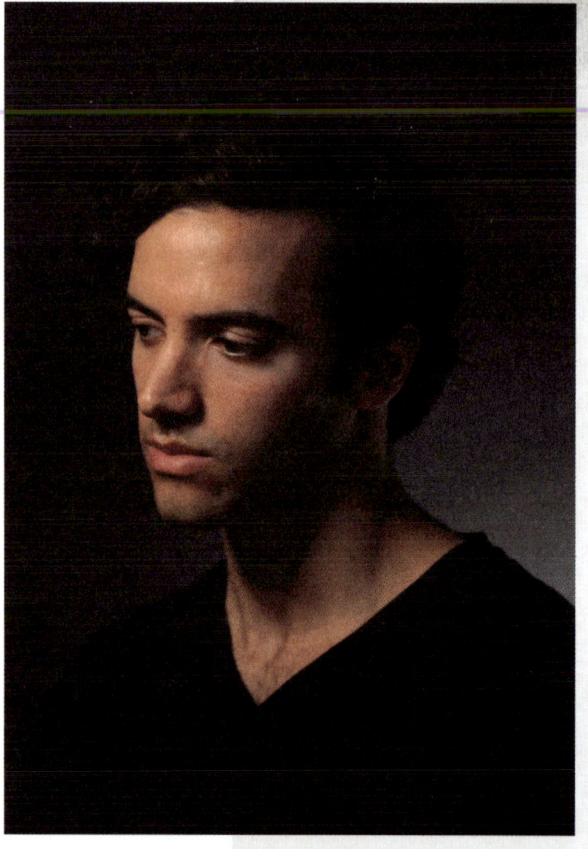

The background

The background plays a more significant role than often credited. The assessment of boundaries where the subject and background meet is vital. A well-considered background can elevate a portrait, giving it space to breathe and reinforcing the mood of the piece. Whether it's a stark contrast that makes the subject pop or a lost edge that suggests a deeper setting, the background should complement and enhance the subject, not compete with it.

Throughout this stage, one must be vigilant, always measuring, always comparing. Every new piece of information added is an opportunity to refine the relationships between the elements of the face. The proportional dividers (the cheekbones, the chin, the brow) become even more critical as the drawing develops. They are the benchmarks against which all else is judged, ensuring fidelity to the subject's unique features.

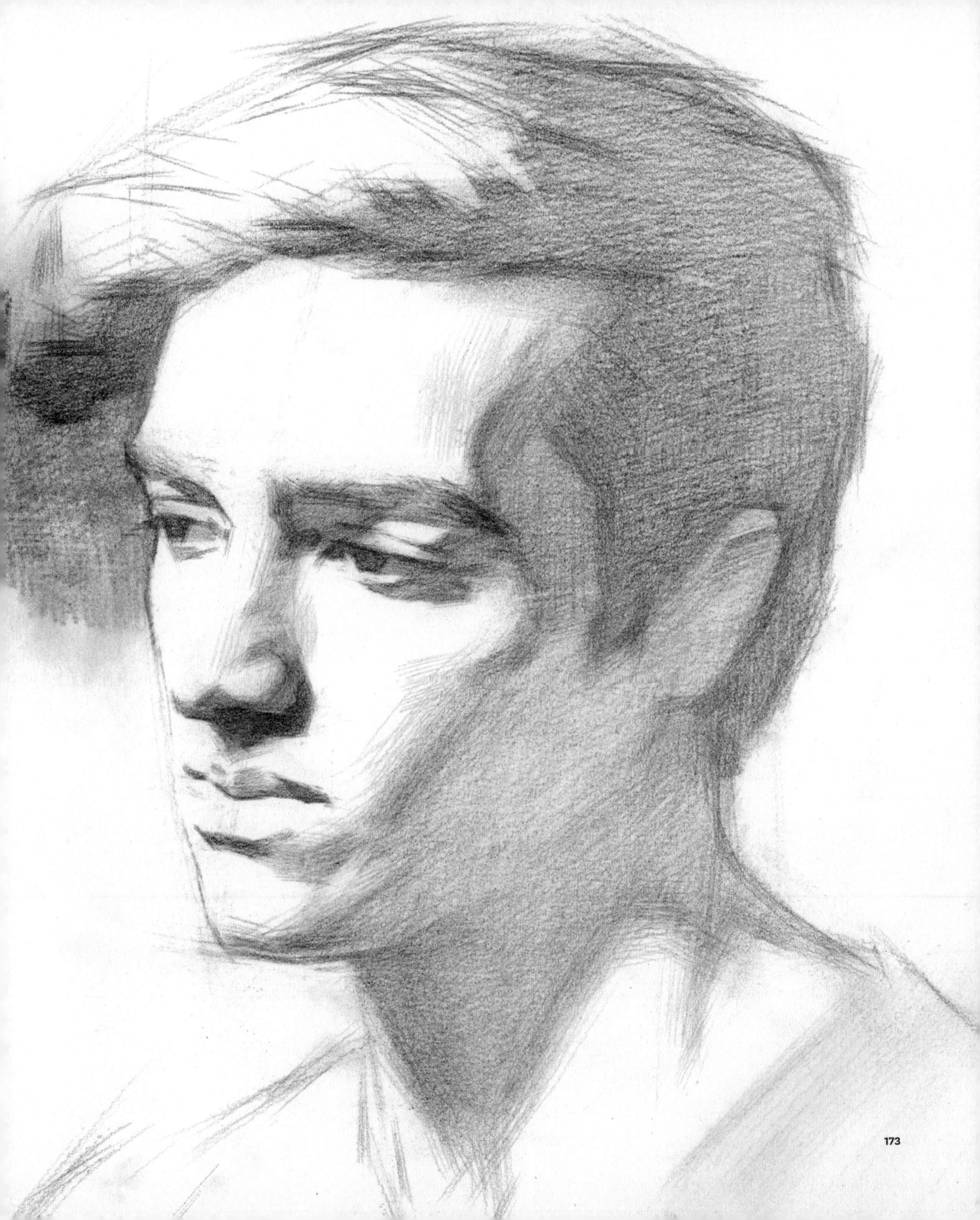

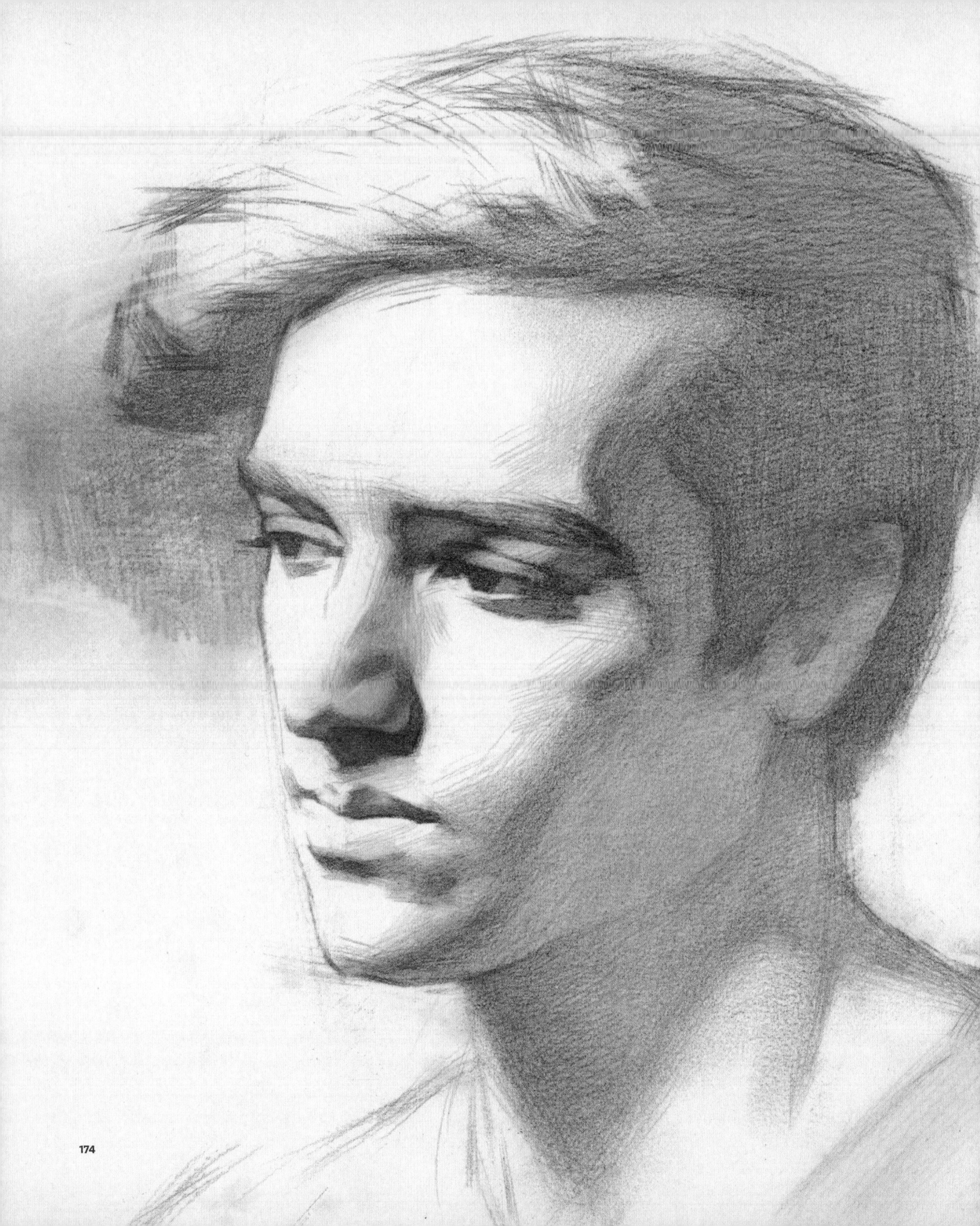

VISUAL BLOCK-IN: STAGE FOUR

As we progress from establishing the basic interplay of light and shadow to refining our visual block-in, the focus now shifts to achieving a harmonious balance and a heightened sense of realism in our drawing. This involves keying the values, evening out value application and gradations, and introducing dark halftones – each step crucial in bringing the drawing to its targeted conclusion. It's worth mentioning here that although it is possible to start a drawing in this style, with the intent of proceeding all the way through to a high degree of refinement, our goal here is to capture our progress at the block-in stage only.

Keying the values to focal areas

The first step is to key the values, particularly in the features of the face or the focal area of your drawing. This means adjusting the values to ensure they correctly correspond to the lightness or darkness of these areas in real life, with the added objective of considering if more contrast here or less contrast outside the focal area would enhance the intent of the composition. For example, if the focal area is the face, observe carefully where the light hits the hardest and where the shadows contrast most deeply, and adjust your values accordingly.

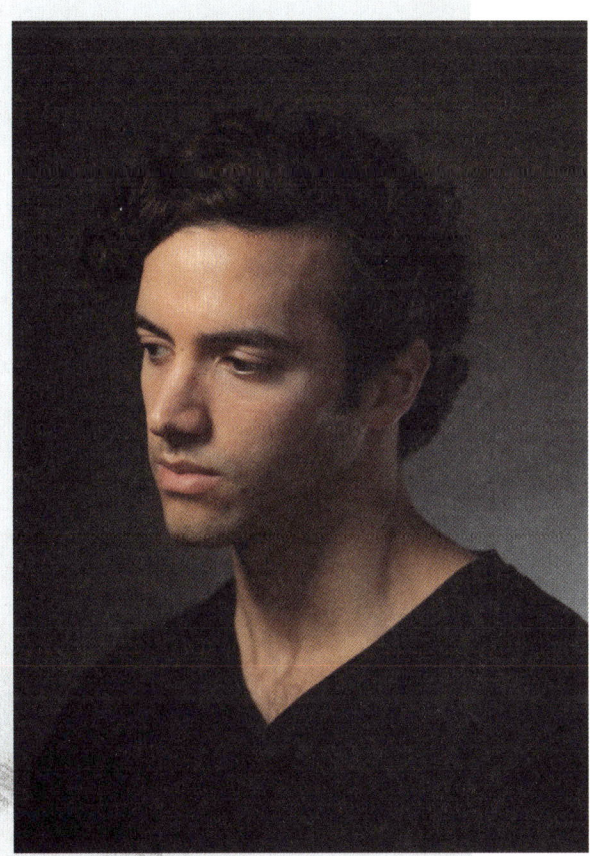

Evening out the values

Once the values are keyed to the features, the next step is to even them out across the drawing. This involves manipulating and adding graphite as needed, much in the same manner as the first exercise on page 155 suggests. This is also the stage for smoothing out any harsh transitions between light and shadow, ensuring that the values change gradually and naturally. This step is critical for creating a cohesive design in the value shapes and the portrait overall.

Adding dark halftones

After evening out the values, introduce dark halftones to areas that are neither in direct light nor in complete shadow. These are the areas where the form turns away from the light source but doesn't fall into complete shadow. The addition of dark halftones adds volume and form to the drawing, making it adhere more easily with the impression seen while squinting. This step requires a subtle touch, as overdoing the dark halftones can result in a loss of form and a flattening of the image.

Continue refining throughout

Throughout this process, continue to refine and adjust. Constantly measure and compare the relationships between the elements of the face and the rest of the drawing. Keep the proportions and spatial relationships in check, ensuring that the drawing remains true to life. Remember, each new piece of information is an opportunity to refine your drawing further, bringing you closer to a finished block-in that not only captures the likeness of the subject, but also pushes your skill level forward.

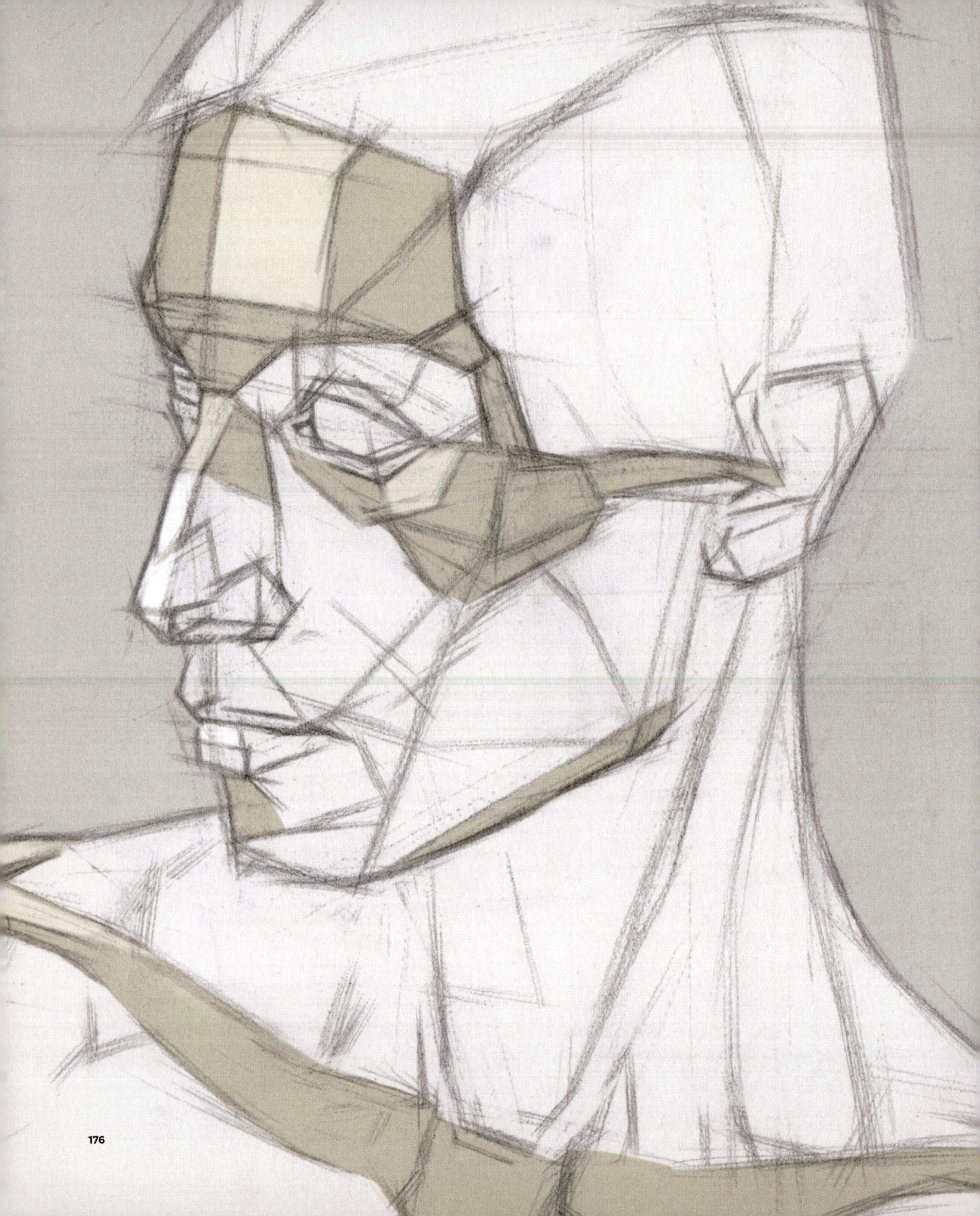

Structural block-in

Target of the exercise: To develop an understanding of three-dimensional form through simplification and analysis.

The structural approach to drawing involves a fundamental shift from viewing the human body solely through its biological form to understanding it through geometric abstraction. This method has profound implications for how artists learn to perceive and depict the human figure.

Structural drawing, as it applies to portraiture, is a method that seeks to understand and capture the underlying framework of the human face. This approach is akin to creating a three-dimensional wireframe, starting with the simplest forms. It's a process that lays the foundation for accurately rendering the complex forms of the face and head, ensuring that the final portrait not only resembles the subject, but also possesses a concrete sense of depth and accountable volume.

Structural drawing also involves a keen understanding of anatomy. Knowledge of skull structure, muscle groups, and how the skin drapes over these forms helps not only in creating a believable finished drawing but, even more so, an effective block-in.

The technique involves drawing lines that trace around the form of the subject, much like the latitude and longitude lines on a globe. Cross-contour lines help in visualizing and depicting the volume of the subject in space.

From a process perspective, creating a hierarchy of forms is a way to understand and organize a complex series of elements based on their significance and role in the overall construction. This can be likened to constructing a building, where the broad structural elements must be established before focusing on the decorative aspects. In portraiture, this involves blocking-in the overall shape of the head and the major planes of the face before refining the features. Once the primary forms are in place, you can then move on to secondary forms. These are the smaller planes and forms that sit within the larger shapes, such as the brow ridge, cheekbones, and the nose in a portrait.

In a structural drawing, lines are the primary means of defining form. They serve to outline the boundaries of shapes and planes, suggesting the edges where different planes meet and the contours that describe the subject's form in space. These lines can vary in weight and intensity: bolder lines may be used to indicate the outermost limits of the form, while finer lines might detail the subtle shifts within the structure of the face.

Values interact with the planes to define the form and turn of the structure within a three-dimensional space. Lighter values represent planes that are oriented towards the light source, while darker values indicate planes that are angled away from the light. The transition between these values is what suggests the curvature of the form. These values emphasize the structure established by the wireframe. By shading according to the planes defined by the wireframe lines, you will reinforce the volume concept.

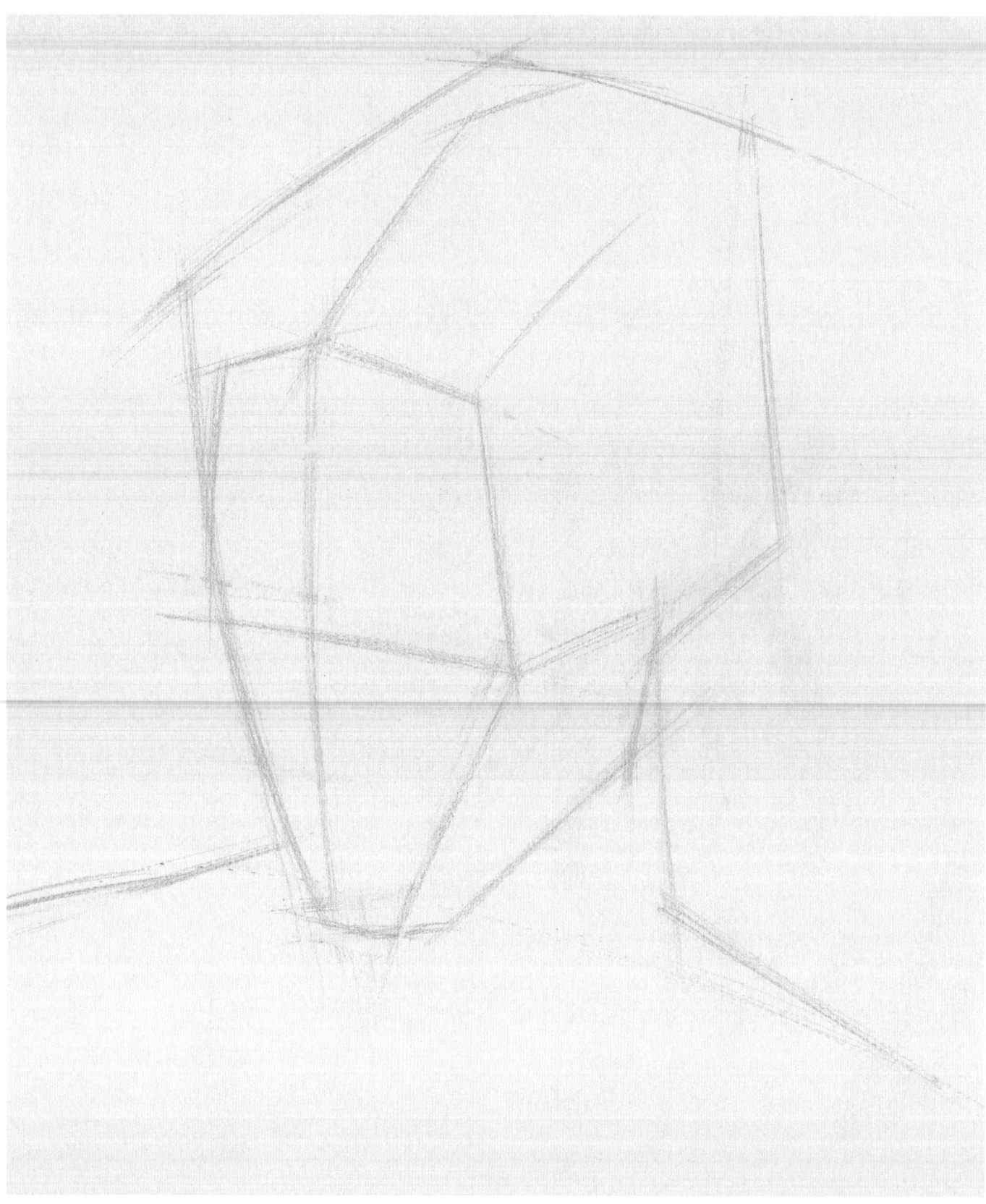

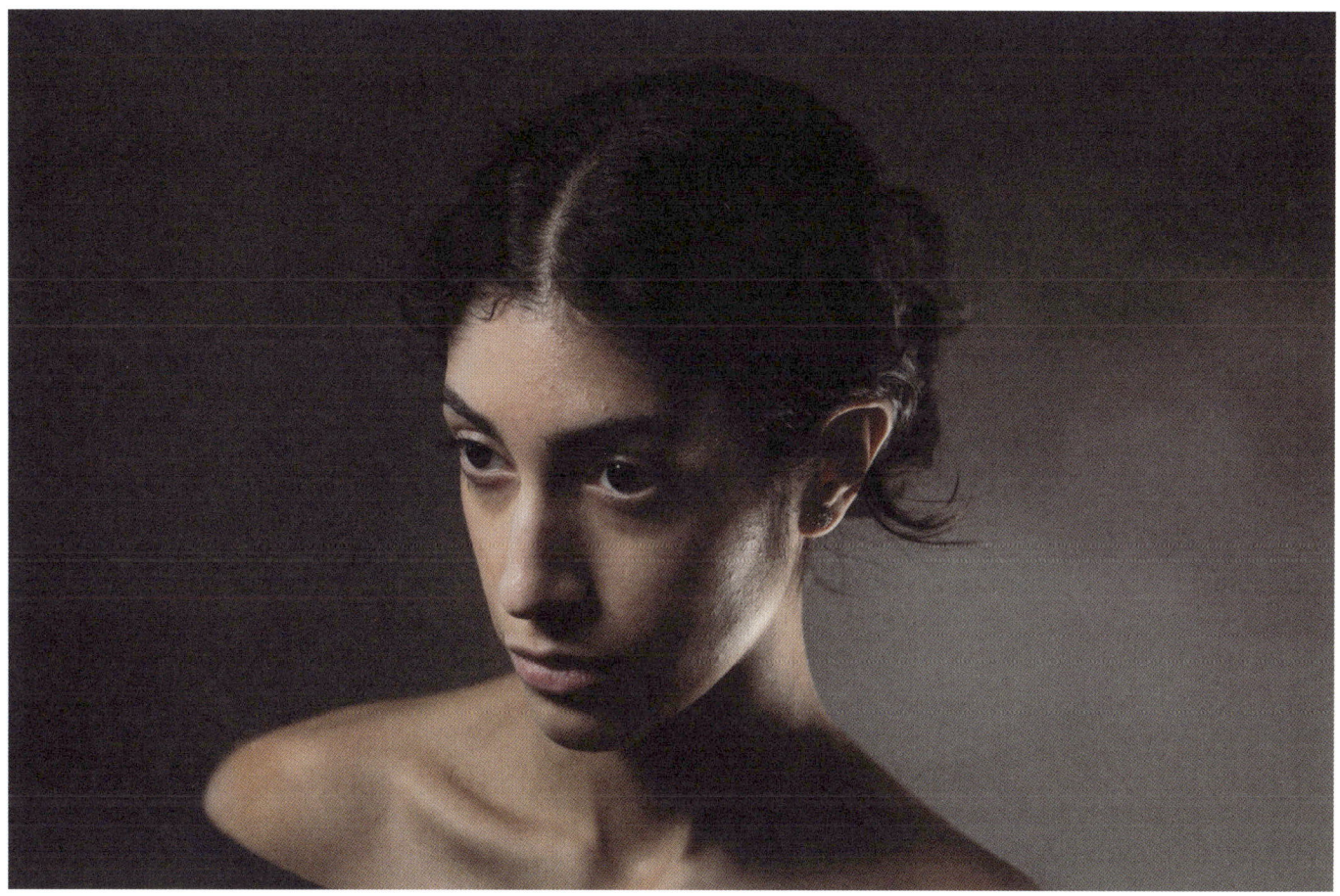

STRUCTURAL BLOCK-IN: STAGE ONE

The overall shape

The process begins with the selection of a simple geometric shape to represent the head's overall mass. This is typically a sphere or an oval, chosen for its similarity to the general shape of the cranium. This shape is not just a flat circle but a three-dimensional form, representing the bulk of the skull. The artist must visualize this shape in space, considering its dimensions in terms of width, height, and depth.

Major proportions

With the basic shape in place, the artist then determines the major proportions of the head. This involves dividing the shape to locate key landmarks, such as the hairline, brow line, nose line, and chin. These divisions are not arbitrary but are based on average human proportions. For instance, the distance from the top of the head to the chin is often divided into equal thirds – from the top to the hairline, the hairline to the brow, the brow to the base of the nose, and from there to the chin.

The jawline

The next step involves extending the basic shape to include the jawline, which gives the head its unique outline. The jawline's angle and length vary significantly from person to person and are crucial for likeness. The artist must also consider the angle of the head – whether it is tilted up, down, or to the side – and adjust the basic shape accordingly.

Throughout this first stage, constant evaluation and adjustment are necessary. The artist must continually step back to assess the overall structure, checking for accuracy in proportions and angles. This stage is less about detail and more about getting the basic structure correct. It's a process of measuring, comparing, and refining.

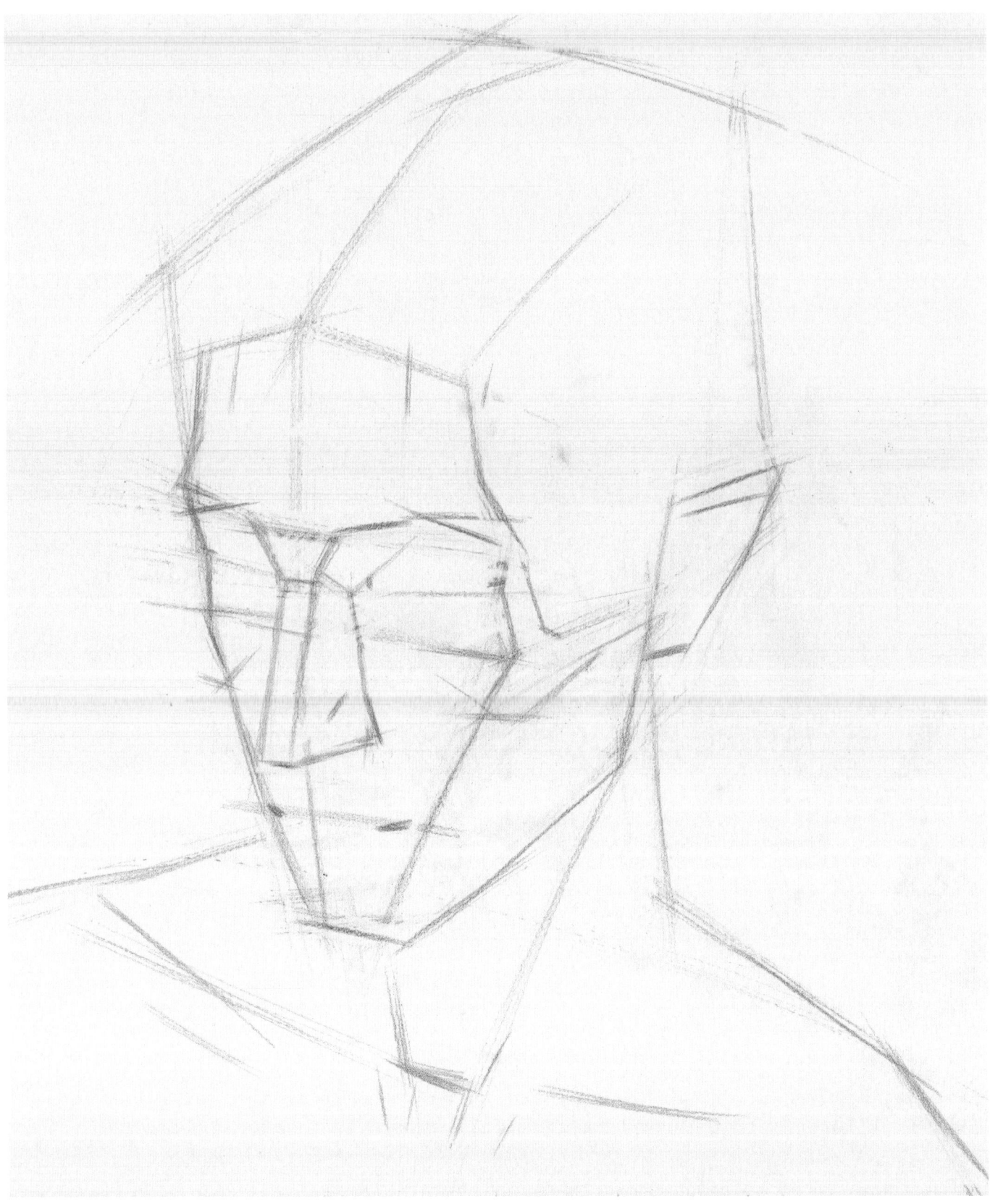

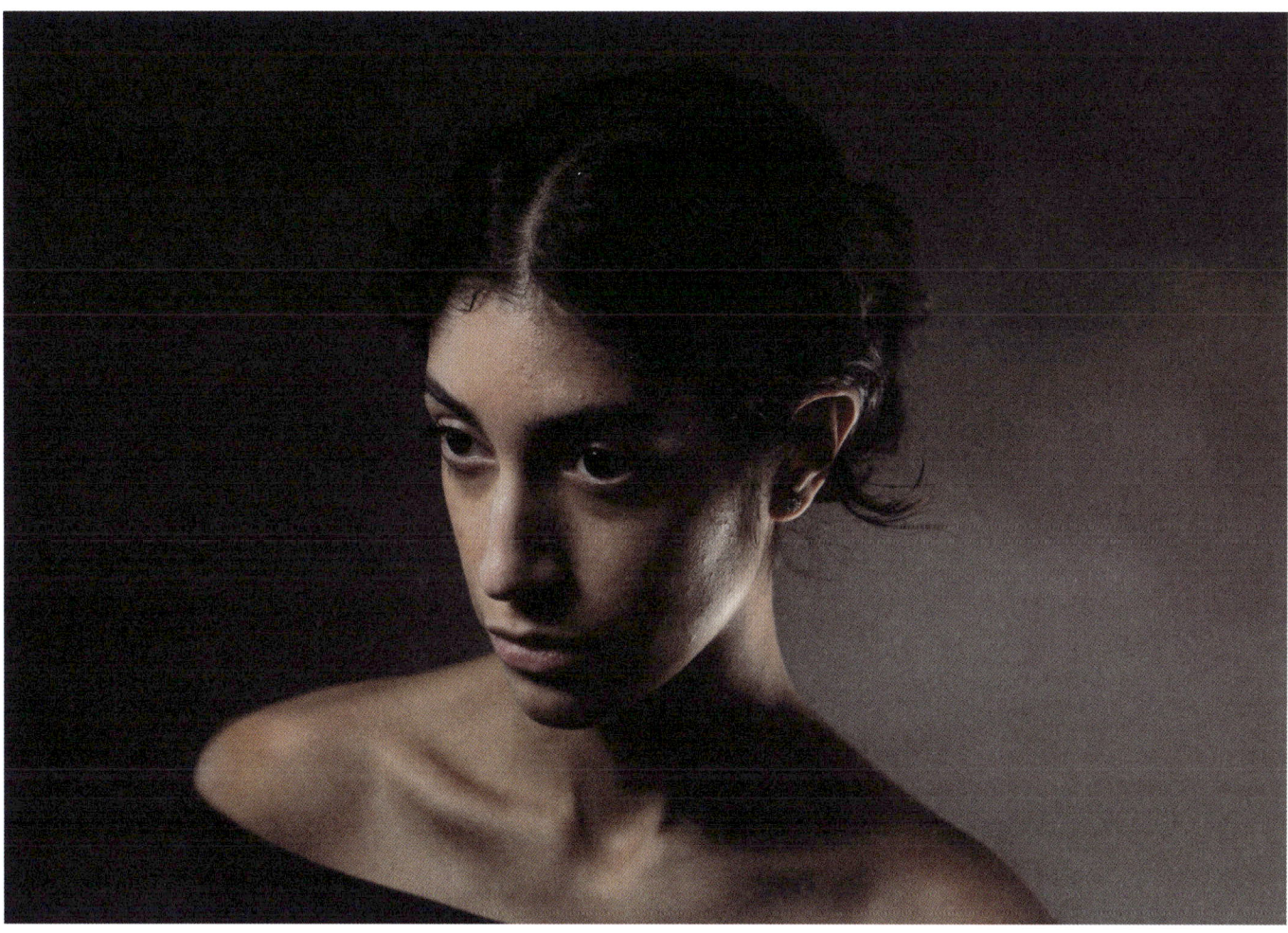

STRUCTURAL BLOCK-IN: STAGE TWO

Depths and projections

The projection of the nose characterizes the evolution of the study in this phase. The previous stage simplified the structure, deliberately excluding certain depths, like the eye sockets, and projections such as the nose and ears. This is a strategic choice to maximize efficiency, focusing on resolving the proportional challenges of the earlier stage. As you progress, it becomes imperative to introduce a new layer of specificity to the drawing, enhancing its realism and depth.

The brow ridge, articulated along the midline with the glabella, marks the start of the downturning plane that forms the eye sockets. In extending these elements laterally, the basic forms of the zygomatic bones and arch are also defined, connecting to the major plane of the ear at the side of the head. Returning to the glabella, the top plane of the nose emerges below it,

angling away from the front plane of the face. This requires the delineation of two side planes and a bottom plane to complete the nose's connection to the rest of the face.

Balance and symmetry

An essential aspect of this stage is the pursuit of structural symmetry. As each new element is added to the drawing, the artist must engage in a continuous search for balance and symmetry. This involves careful observation and a nuanced understanding of human anatomy. Symmetry, however, should not be misconstrued as perfect uniformity; the human face is inherently asymmetrical. Therefore, the long-term outcome of this quest for symmetry is more about achieving a harmonious balance rather than an exact mirroring of features.

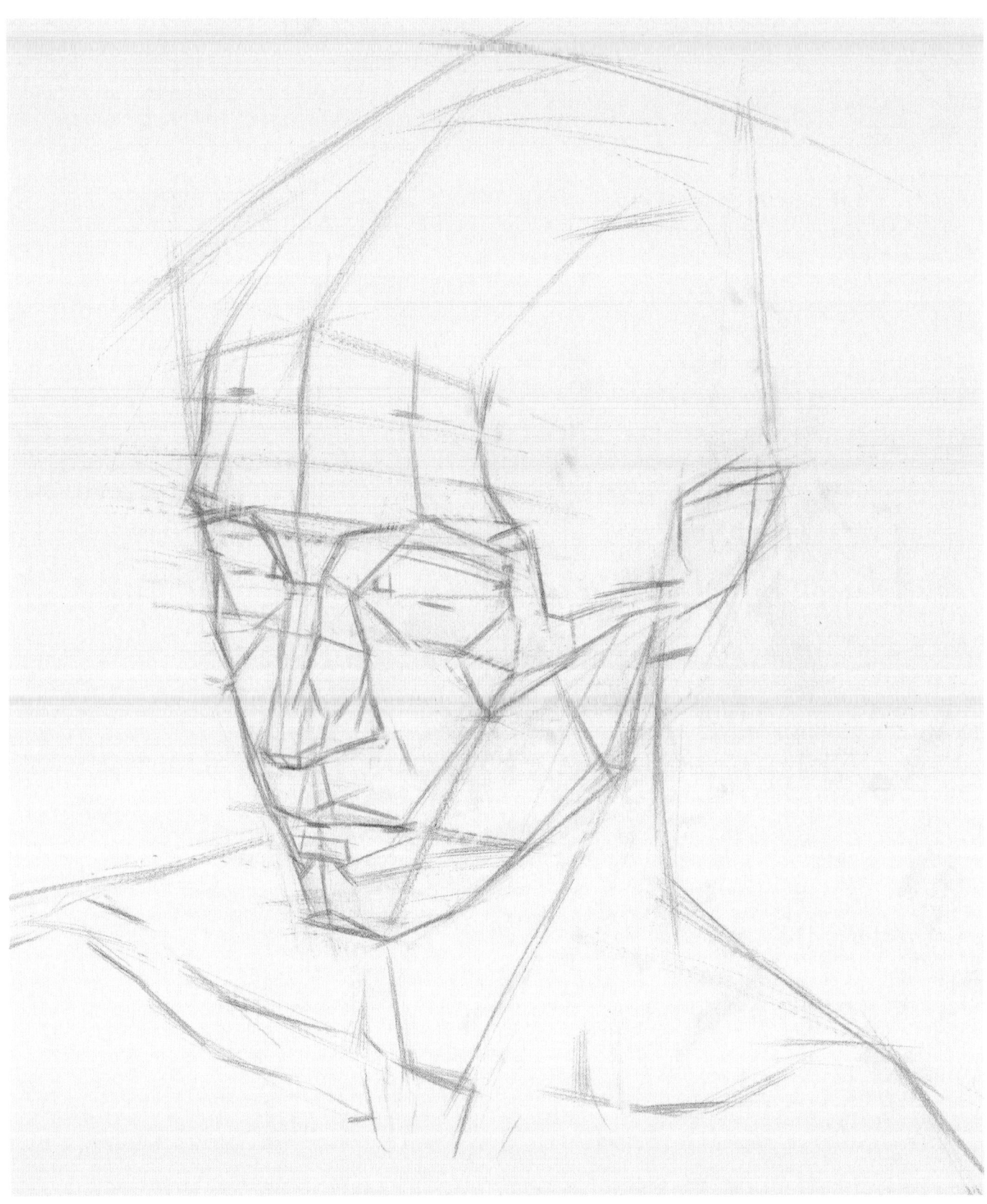

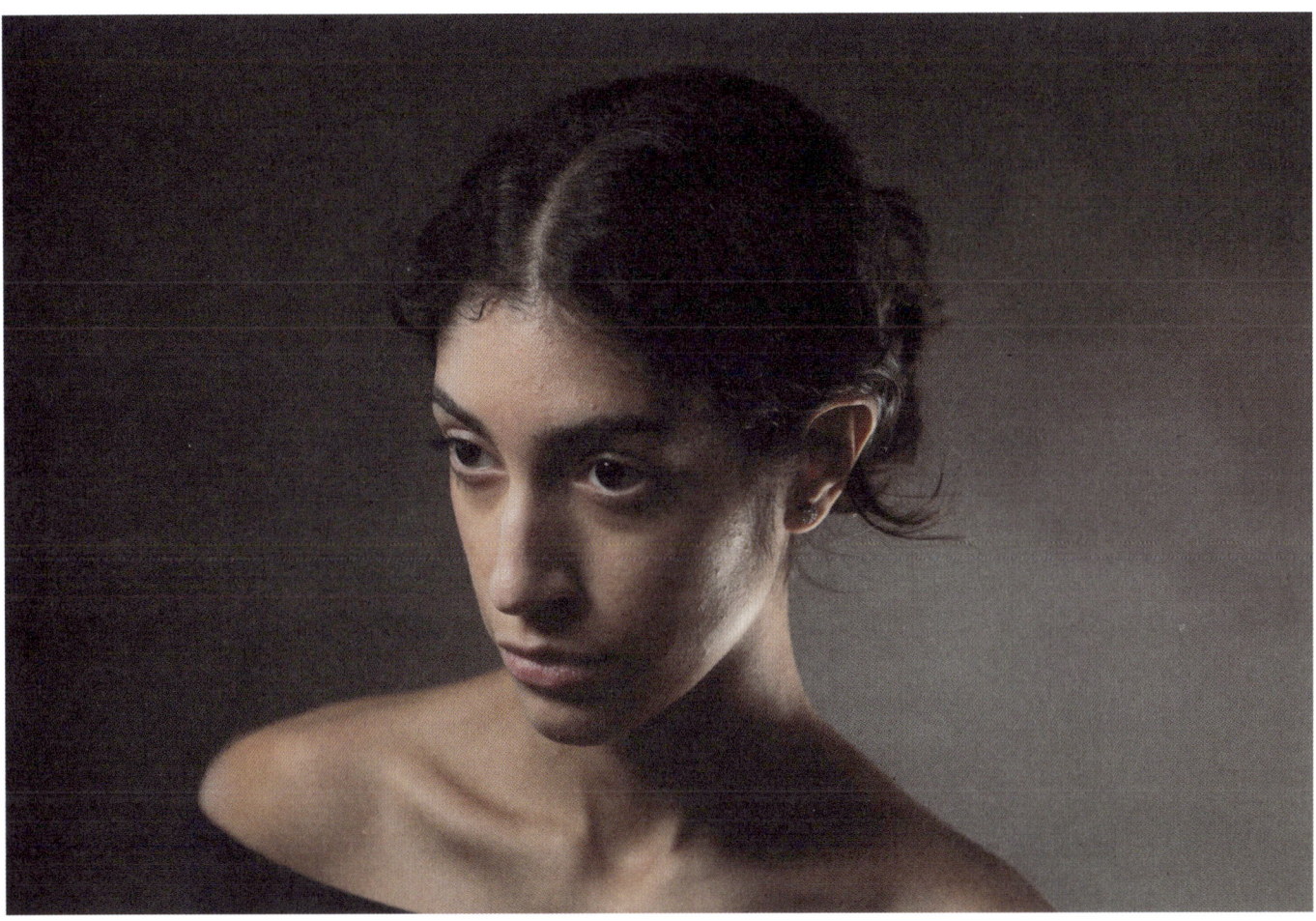

STRUCTURAL BLOCK-IN: STAGE THREE

The search for structure in drawing the human head is essentially a pursuit to understand its various roundnesses. This is primarily achieved through the observation of how light interacts with its forms. As you build your structural block-in, some planes will reveal themselves effortlessly through the play of light across the form, while others with be derived through your knowledge of the structure and anatomy of the human body. It's important to emphasize that there is no single way to observe and study structure that is sufficiently categorical to be used in the absence of all others. Instead, a versatile approach is necessary – accessing and cross-referencing multiple resources simultaneously.

Advancing anatomical information

At this stage, the depth of anatomical information becomes more integrated. The nose, for example, has advanced from being a simple four-planed block into a feature that includes conceptualizations of the major cartilage pairings, as well as indications of the finer undulations in the form of the side planes. The zygomatic bones now contain a plane break along both the horizontal axis and the vertical axis, creating a clearer visualization of their true form. All of this is added while continuing to track and mark the structural symmetry of the features.

Finding plane breaks

Consider that anywhere a roundness can be observed, there can be a plane break assigned to it. This mentality will ensure that your analysis of form can be applied to your subject, regardless of your experience. It also ensures that as you grow in practice, your designs will become more keen and discerning. As it is with all learned behaviours, repetition will ensure a growing familiarity and comfort that will, in turn, translate into better performance.

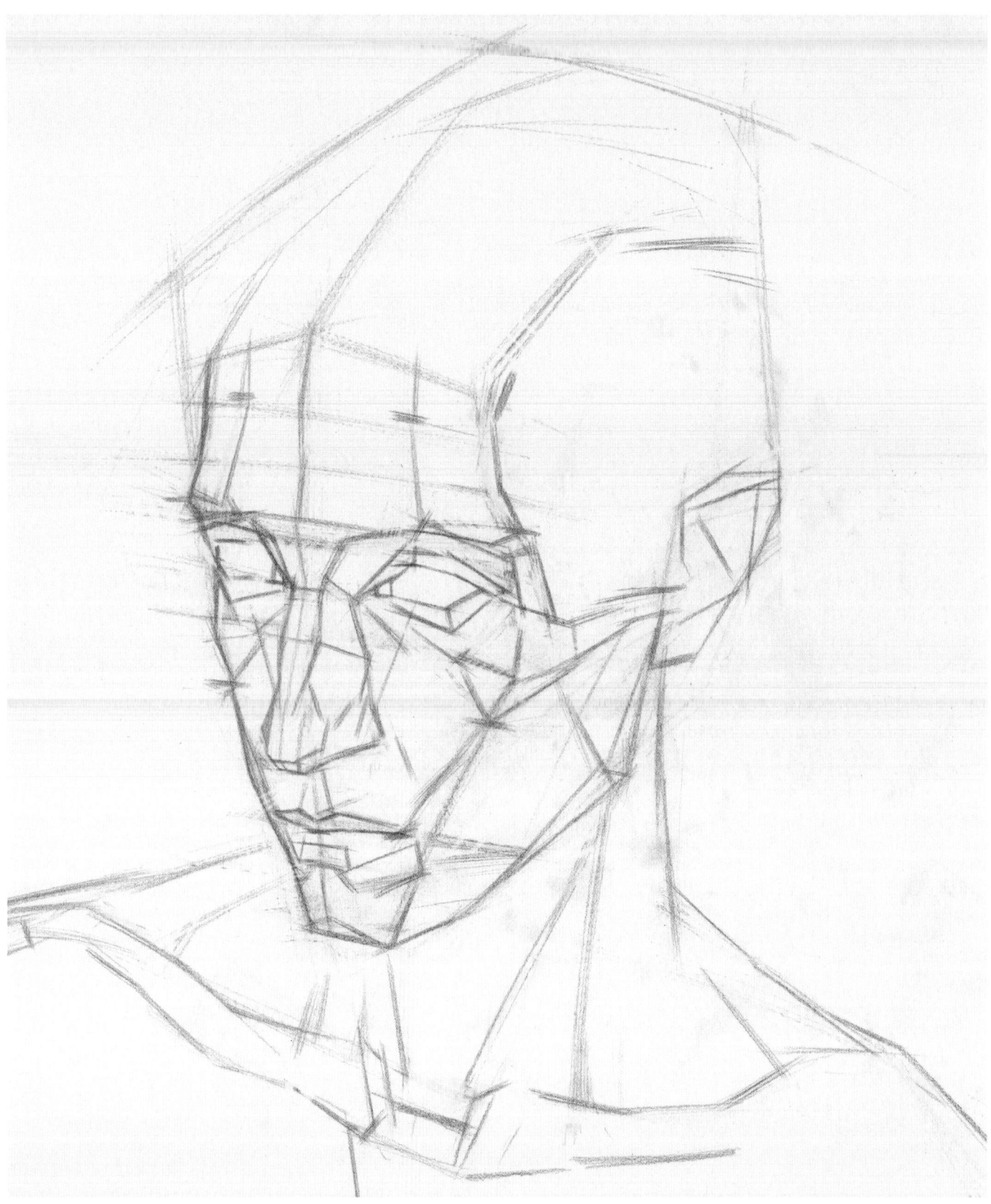

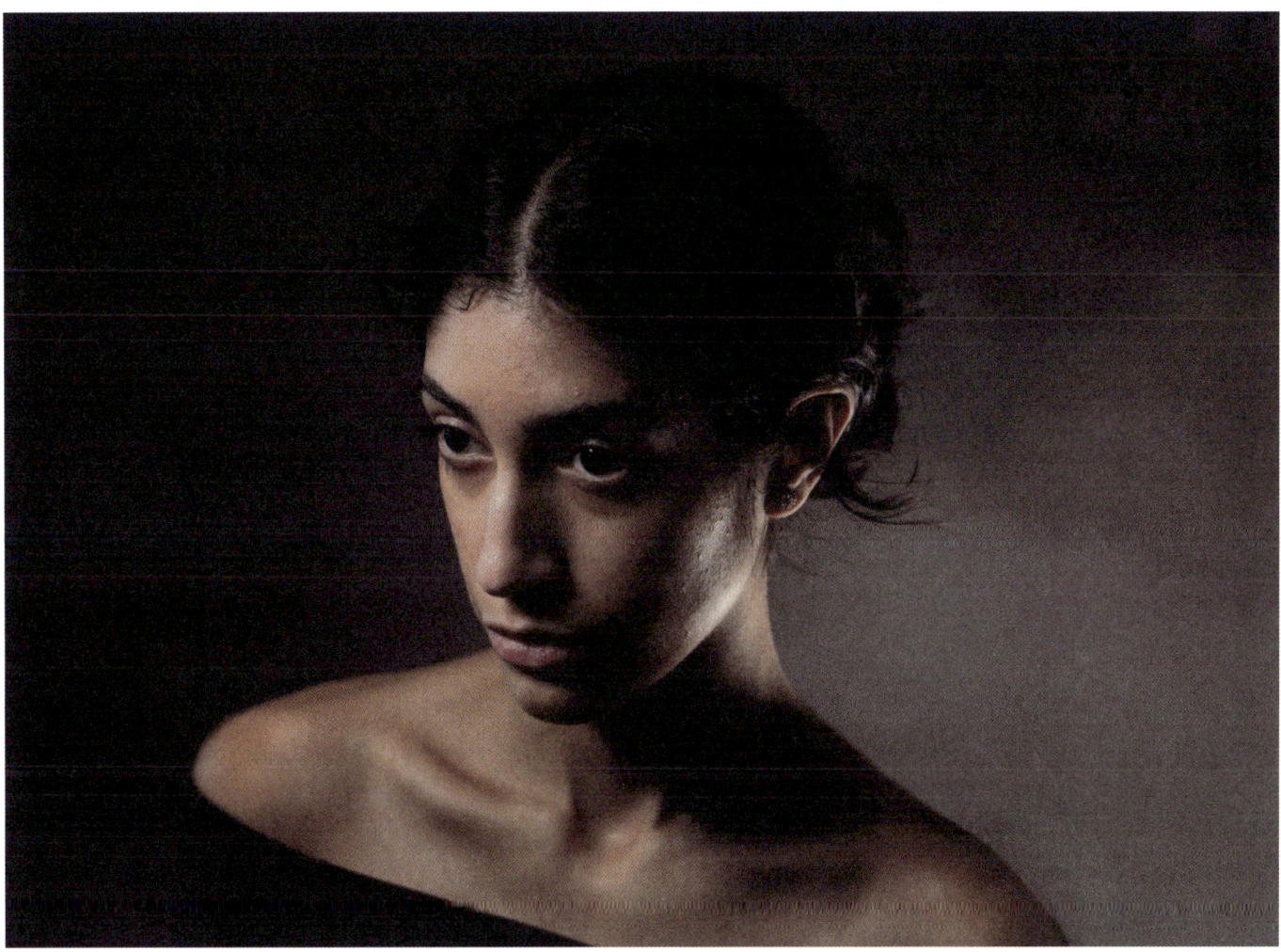

STRUCTURAL BLOCK-IN: STAGE FOUR

Measure twice, draw once

We have now broken out of the minimalist design of the first stages and into a more complex and specific design. These advances have been made with an increased confidence in the accuracy of the proportions in the drawing. It cannot be stated often enough that measuring and observing the relative likeness of your drawing to your subject will ensure that you are able to work as efficiently as possible. What seems to take the longest when drawing is taking two steps back for corrections in order to make one step forward in complexity. So, measure twice, draw once.

A comparable likeness

This stage is characterized by a closer likeness to the reference image than is attained at any point previously. The features of the face are 'complete' in the sense that they contain all of the plane breaks necessary to indicate their composition. What is also true, in most cases, is that they must now be shifted into more accurate positional relationships to each other. As simple as this advice seems, I ask that you stay in this stage and observe longer than you believe is necessary. It has been said countless times in the history of drawing, let alone in this very book, that there is no easy formulae for accurate drawing. There is only the deliberate and time-consuming work of measurement and attention to simplicity. In great and fully realized works of portraiture, this is how accuracy and likeness are achieved.

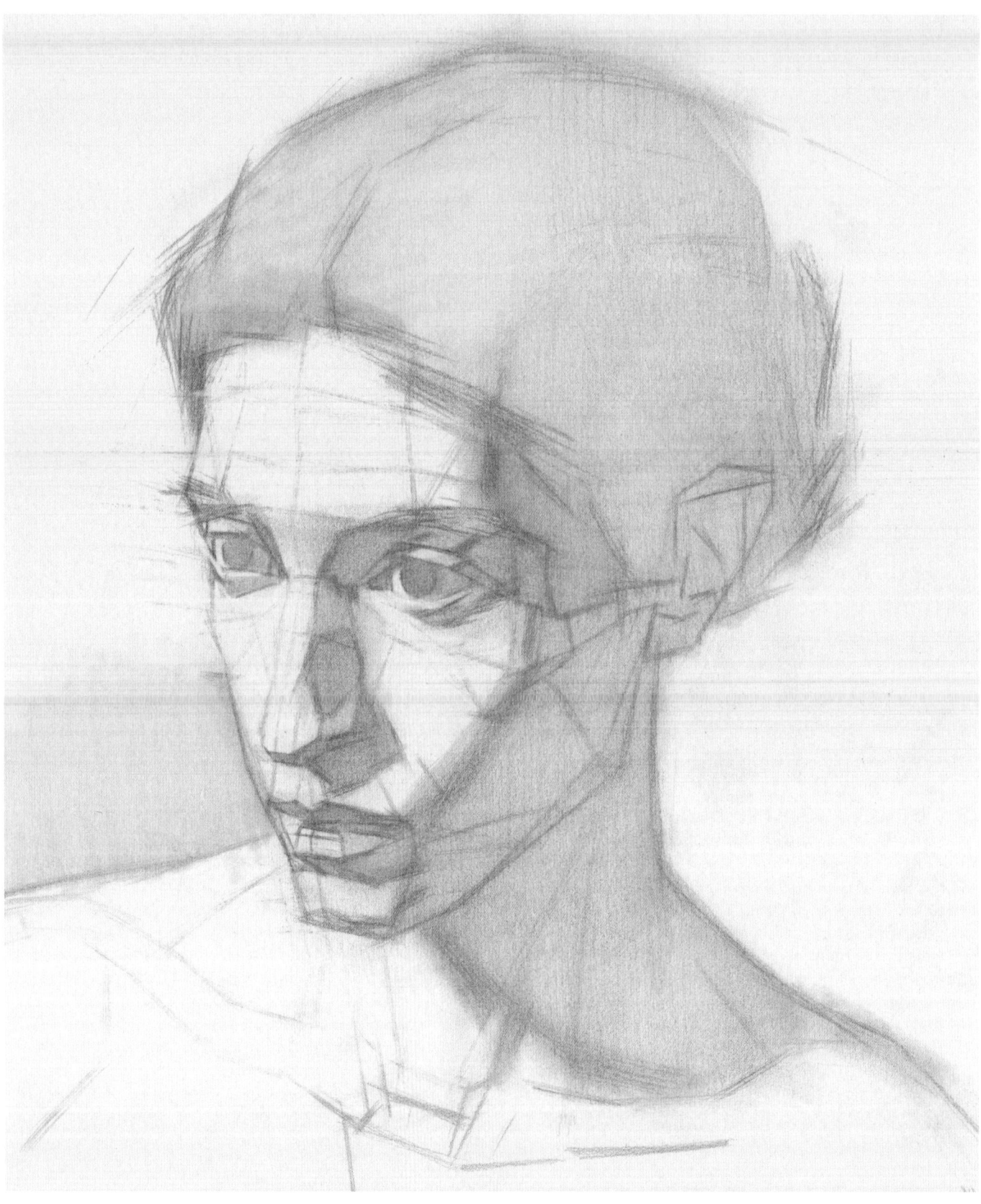

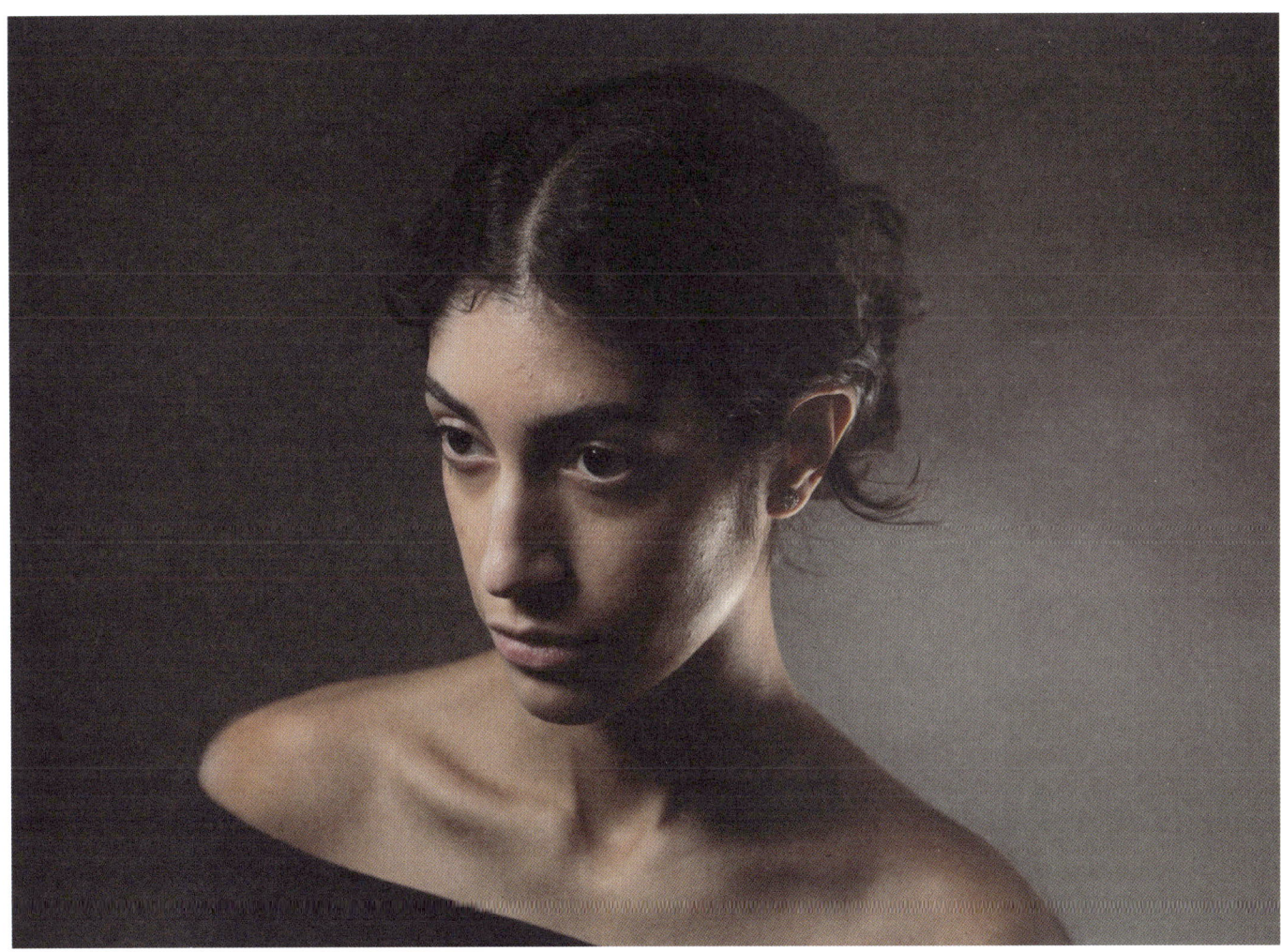

STRUCTURAL BLOCK-IN: STAGE FIVE

Structural drawing could reasonably be described as an exercise in abstraction. Certainly it is made with a clear reference to the visual world, but it is more like a blueprint for a building, rather than a drawing of a building from the outside. This brings us to the final stage of this study: applying light and shadow to our structural block-in. It's time to consider what we see and recognize as part of everyday life, as after all, that is what defines representational work.

A lighting concept

If we have proceeded well through our analysis in this drawing, the application of a lighting concept should proceed with relative ease. Think back to the sphere exercise (page 158) – once the sphere itself was defined, the application of light and shadow was implicit in the design. This is not so different, only

more complex. In addition, the pattern of light and shadow should reveal a series of shapes that roughly coincide with those that you can find in the source image.

The first time is the worst time

This particular kind of study is likely the furthest outside the norms of what the uninitiated will think of when prompted by the phrase 'portrait drawing'. Because of this, it is also likely to be a great growth opportunity, as you will be observing the model and searching for information in this way for the first time. There is a saying that follows experiences like this: 'the first time is the worst time'. Briefly, it is a reminder that your first attempt at something is unlikely to reveal its true value. Persist with these structural studies, even if only for a few repetitions, and the progress and insight should be clear.

Mass drawing

Target of the exercise: To practise reducing the subject into flat tonal shapes that reflect its optical appearance.

The term 'mass drawing' is often associated with the teachings and writings of Harold Speed, a noted twentieth-century British painter and art instructor. Speed's approach to drawing focused on the representation of objects as masses, a technique that emphasizes tonal values over lines. This perspective on drawing is a departure from traditional line-centric methods, advocating for a holistic view of the subject, where light, shadow, and form play pivotal roles. In this exercise we'll explore Speed's principles of mass drawing, shedding light on how they revolutionize the way artists approach the canvas and perceive the world around them.

In the simplest terms, mass drawing is a reduction of the subject or scene into flat value shapes. At the heart of the theory is the science of how light impacts the retina, the light-sensitive layer at the back of the eye. When light hits an object, it is reflected in varying intensities and wavelengths, which are then perceived as different tonal values and colours by the retina. The brain processes these signals, enabling us to discern shapes, depths, and textures. Understanding this process is crucial for artists, as it allows them to recreate these visual experiences on a two-dimensional surface.

Contrast, defined as the difference in luminance or colour that makes an object distinguishable, plays a crucial role in how we perceive images. In mass drawing, artists manipulate contrast to guide the viewer's focus and to create a sense of depth. Higher contrast areas tend to draw the eye more and can appear closer, while lower contrast areas recede into the background. This understanding of contrast is critical for creating a sense of spatial hierarchy in a drawing.

The retina can perceive a wide range of tonal variations, from deep shadows to bright highlights. Artists must be adept at translating these tonal variations into their medium. This skill involves not just replicating the light and dark values, but also understanding how they interact to form the impression of the subject. We'll explore this in detail in the exercise on the next few pages.

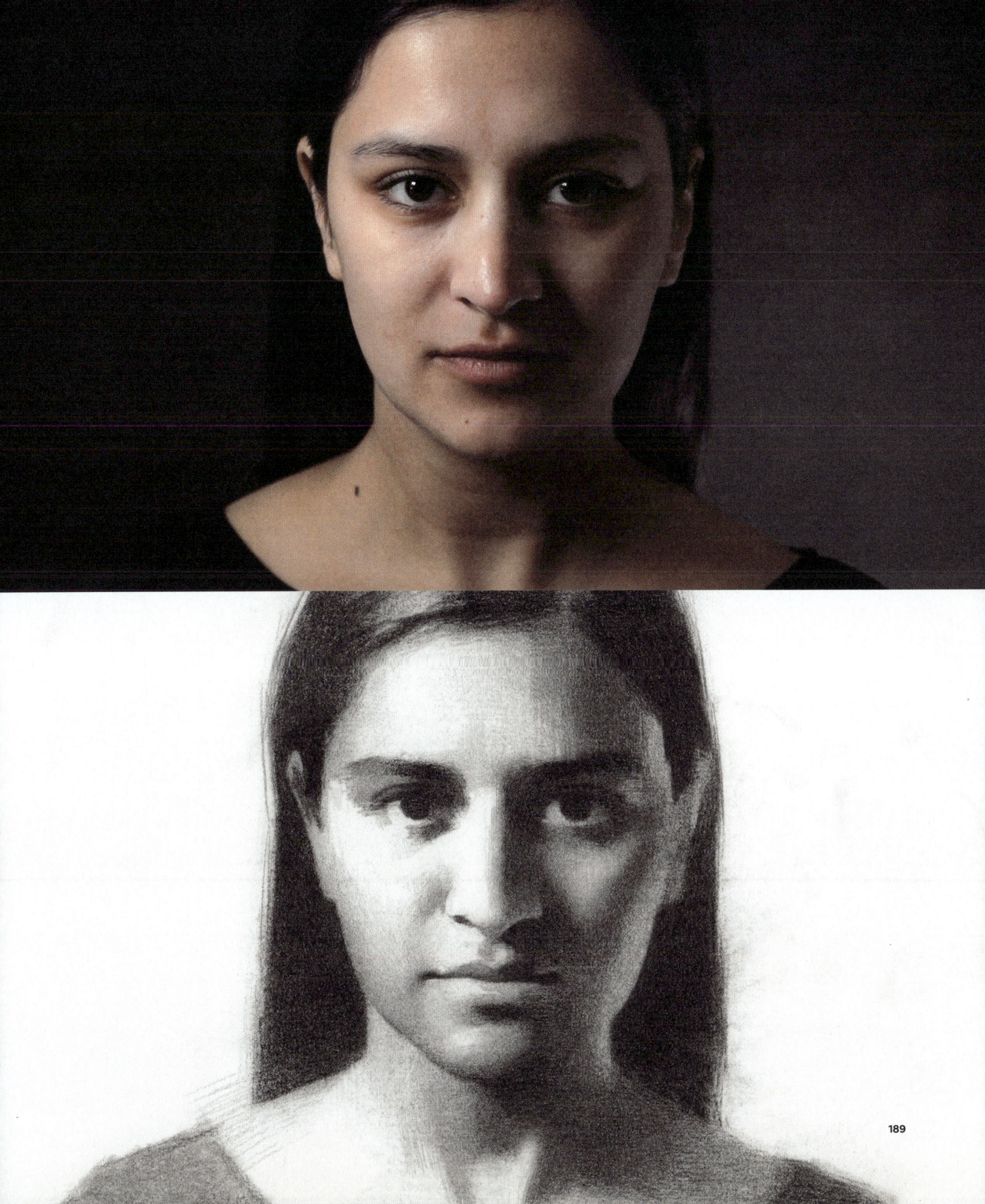

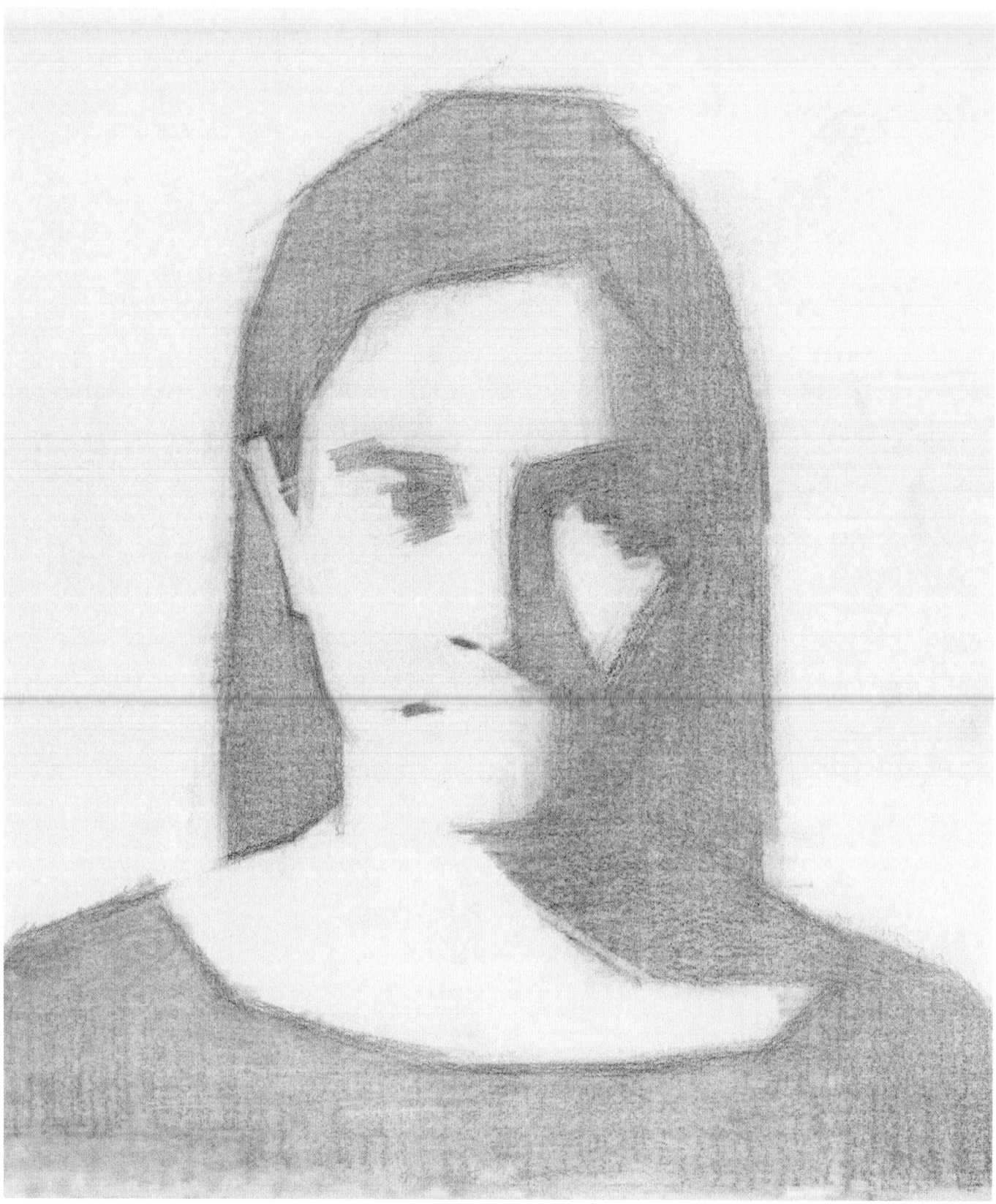

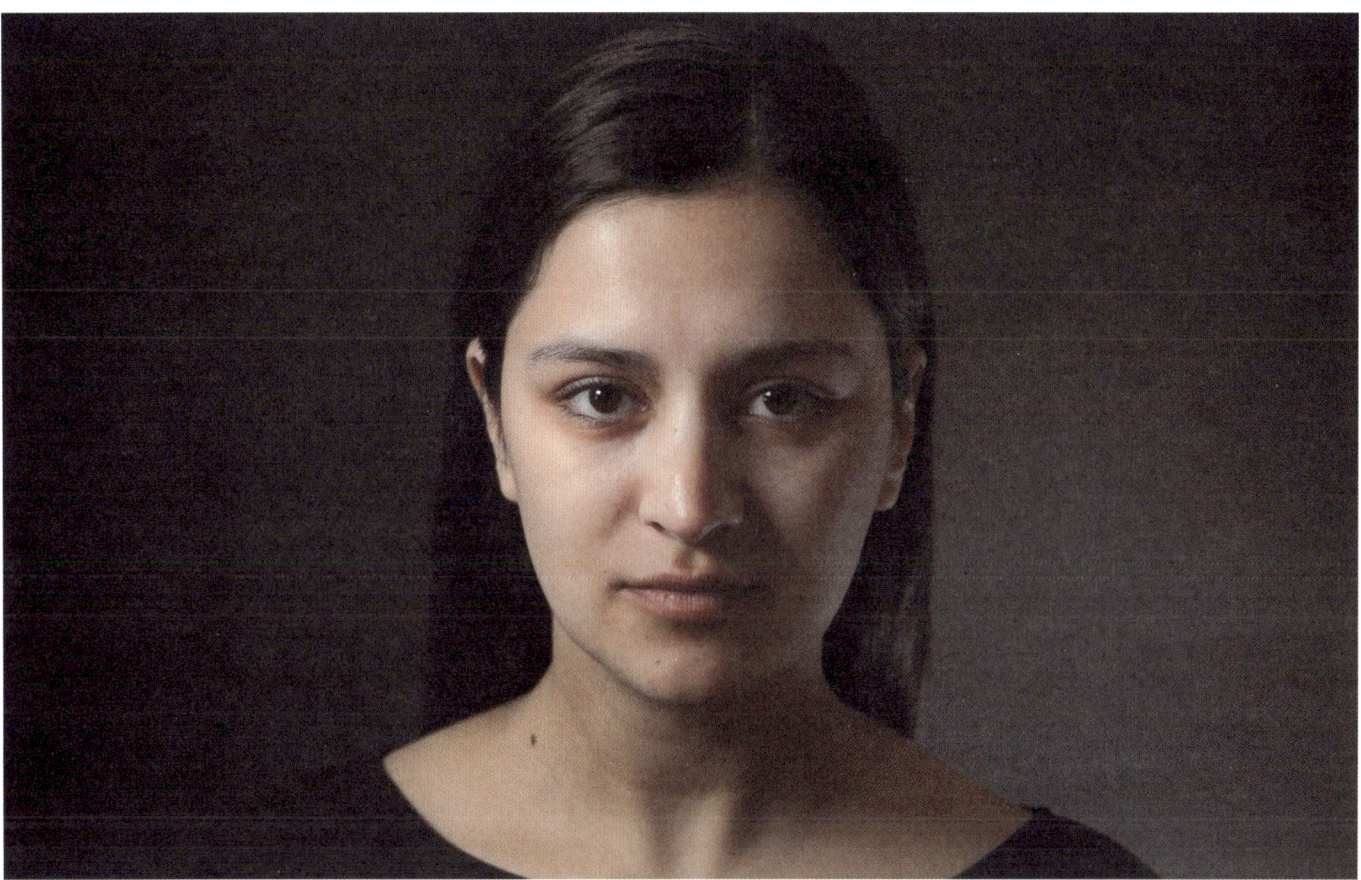

MASS DRAWING: STAGE ONE

Simplest possible expression

Mass drawing begins with the establishment of the largest, most generic value shapes possible. This initial stage is concerned with observing and laying down the broadest areas of shadow, disregarding details to concentrate solely on the large masses that make up the 'simplest possible expression of the subject'. Here, you will work to capture the essence of the subject's structure through generic, bold shapes, setting the stage for subsequent refinement. Begin with a light, structural sketch to lay down the basic proportions and composition, before delving into tonal work. This underdrawing serves as a guide and can be refined as you progress. Keep these initial lines light and easy to adjust.

Though important in all stages, the nature of information selection here is key. Observing the illustration on this page, there are several notable omissions. While there is not a hard and fast rule dictating what to let go of and what to select for inclusion, I can offer several guidelines.

Indicative shapes

In a portrait, the most indicative shapes are the forehead, cheeks, chin, ears (wherever most visible), eye sockets, and nose. The mouth needs the merest of indications, here represented by only its lateral boundary. The hair, conveniently being dark, becomes a frame around the light shape of the face and continues, via the cast shadow of the head across the neck, into the dark shape of the model's blouse.

Likeness over simplicity

Some areas will offer more challenges than others; in this case, the eye on the left. Reducing this down to a flat shape any simpler than this would risk creating a design that bares insufficient comparability to the subject, inhibiting our ability to make an adequate naive comparison to the model. The lesson here is that sometimes your subject will force your hand into selecting slightly more visual information than you would otherwise select. In these cases, prioritize likeness over simplicity.

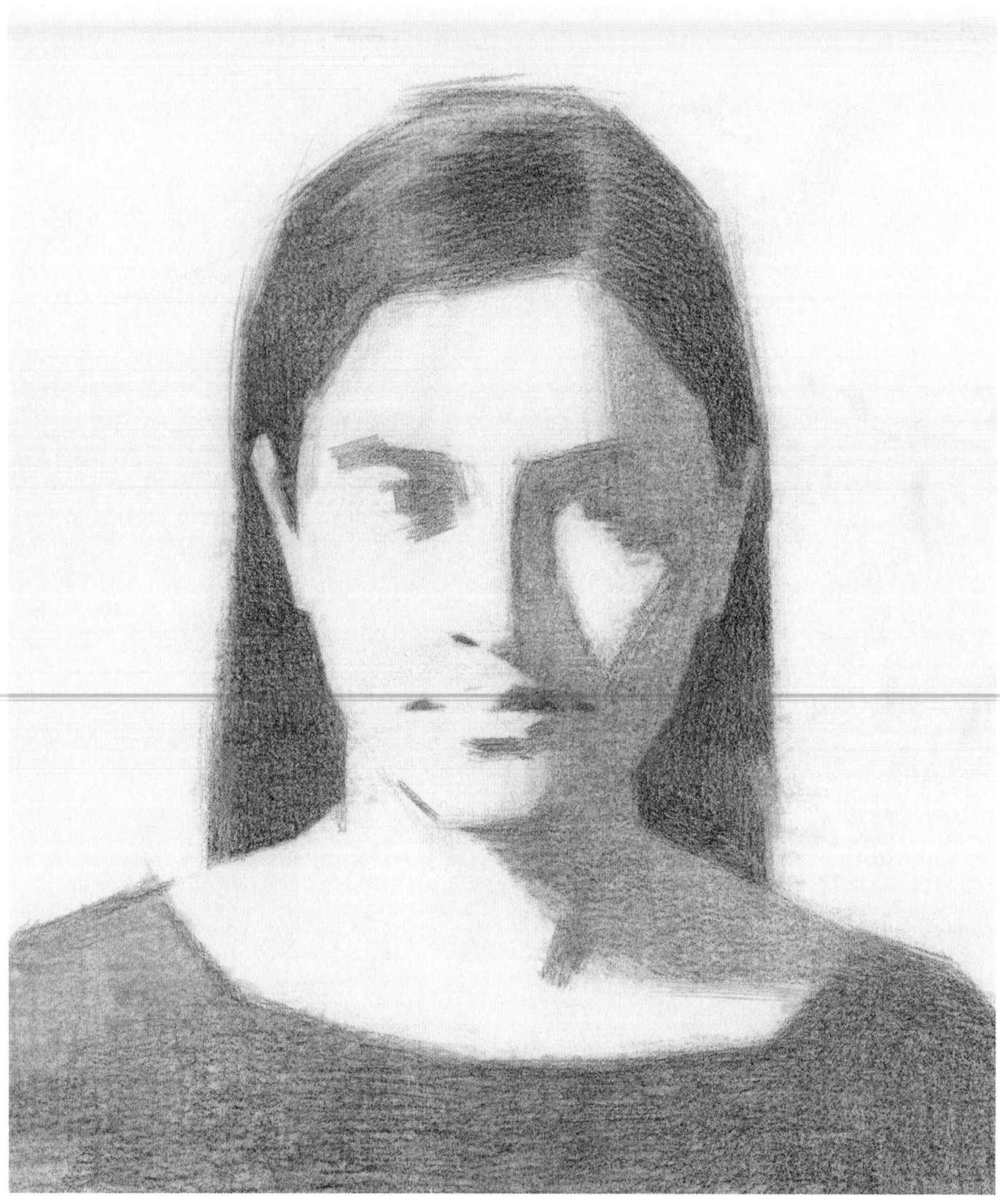

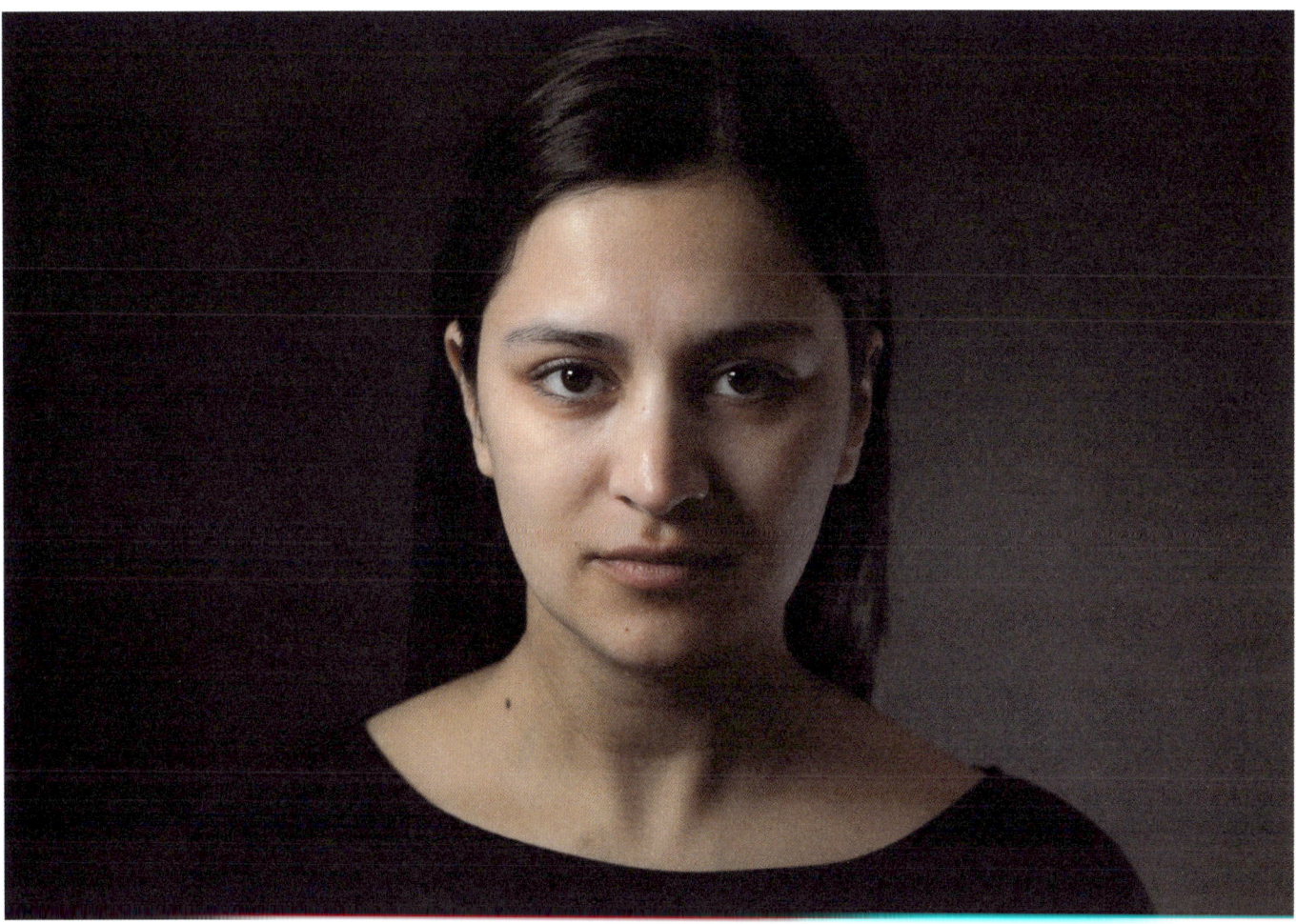

MASS DRAWING: STAGE TWO

The three-value scale

Now you will start to refine these dark value shapes and introduce variations in value. It is a balance between maintaining the simplicity of the initial shapes and beginning to suggest the duo-tone nature of the dark masses. This phase begins the process of recreating the actual 'in the room' impression of the model. By adding this extra value into the dark zones, we are also fulfilling the basic three-value scale that is appropriate for most studio lighting situations: the white of the paper, the initial dark tone, and now an accented darker value. These three groups of value shapes should be sufficient to establish an accurate enough drawing for what this study requires.

Keep it generic

From a conceptual perspective, the shapes that you design here, and the edges in particular, should be generic. For the shapes, this means that they should be composed of as few angle breaks as possible. The edges should be kept in a generic state between sharpness and softness. The discipline to maintain this quality will come more easily with practice. The most important and immediate concern is to avoid overly sharp edges. They will tend to oversimplify and give an impression of permanence, which is out of place at this stage.

Even value application

There is a technical skill required here. The ability to produce an even value application at the desired degree of darkness does not always come naturally. It requires some level of manual dexterity, but more than that, it takes time to hone the surface of the drawing until the result is achieved. There are several pieces of advice to aid this process (see page 175), but with practice the skill can be realized without too much instruction.

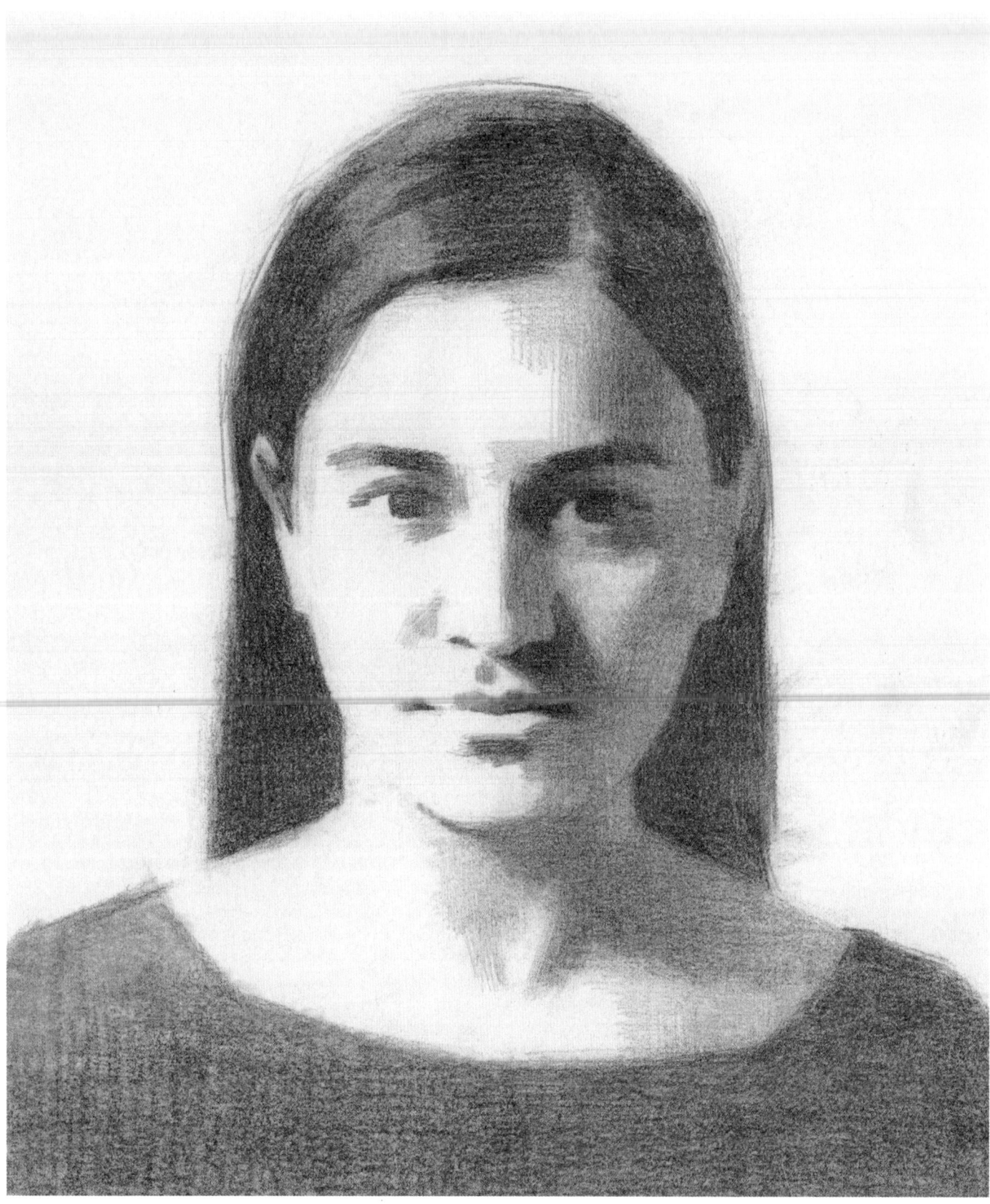

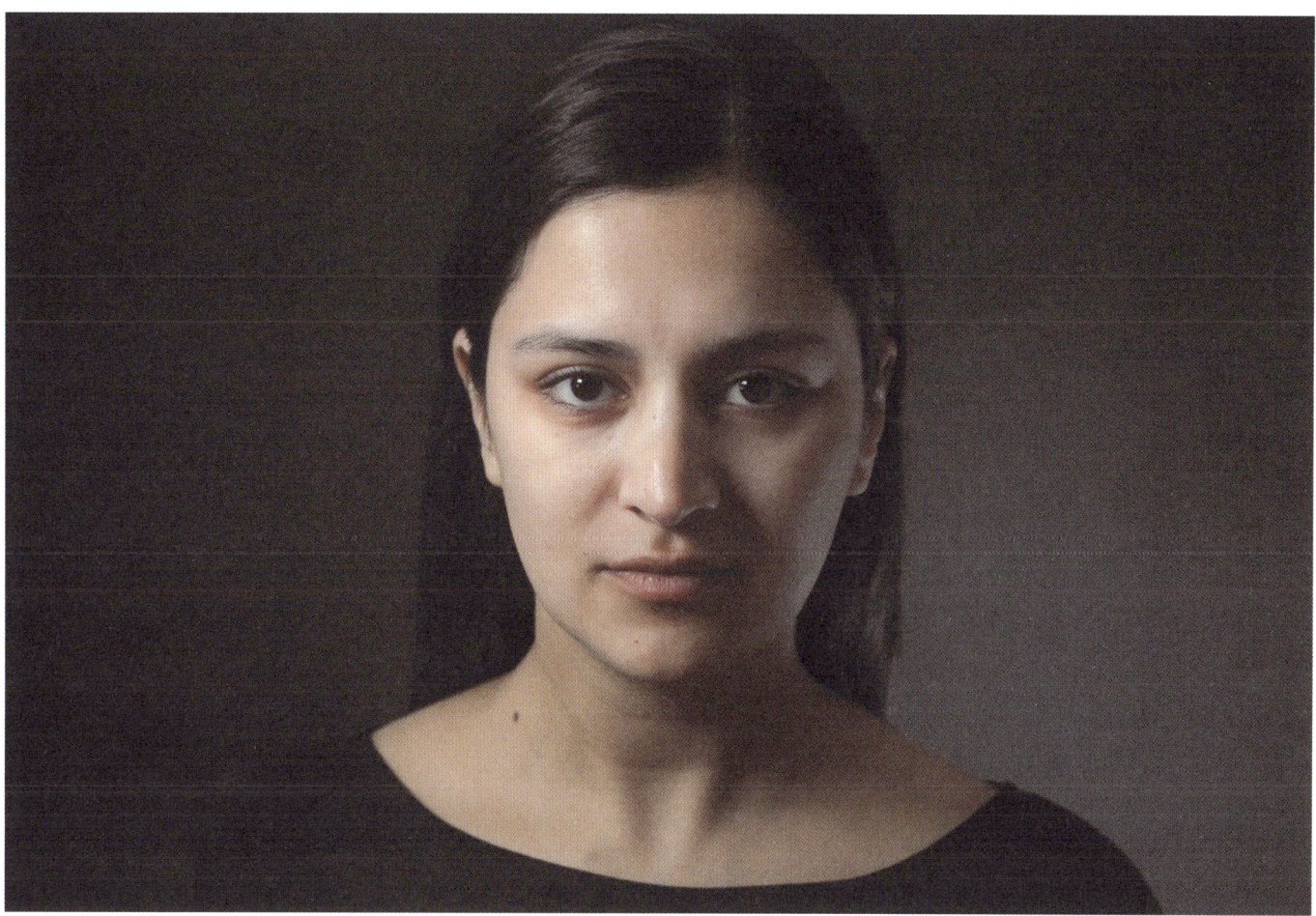

MASS DRAWING: STAGE THREE

Finding the midtones

At this stage, midtones come into play. You will begin to craft the portrait more precisely, using a range of values to build the shapes that help to indicate volume and depth. This stage is critical in conveying not only the roundness of the planes of the cheeks, the curvature of the muzzle form, and other more subtle transitions that are not defined by the darkest tones, but also of the entire head itself.

In this instance, it is useful to consider a midtone as a bridge between two contrasting values. As such, at this moment it's not important that you achieve a soft transition, but rather that you search for the appropriate value that will optically join the two divided values. Think of it as a mosaic of value tiles. The impression of roundness is produced not by the softness of the gradient between values, but rather by the values alone.

The optimum evenness

There is a specific evenness of value application that is most useful at this stage. The target to aim for is when you squint and observe your drawing, the values form a cohesive shape that is distinct from the value shapes next to it. At the same time, it should avoid being so even that the subtle 'static' effect of the paper texture is no longer visible. This respects the fact that the drawing is only at its midpoint. The ultimate level of refinement and smoothness should be saved for the last step of the process.

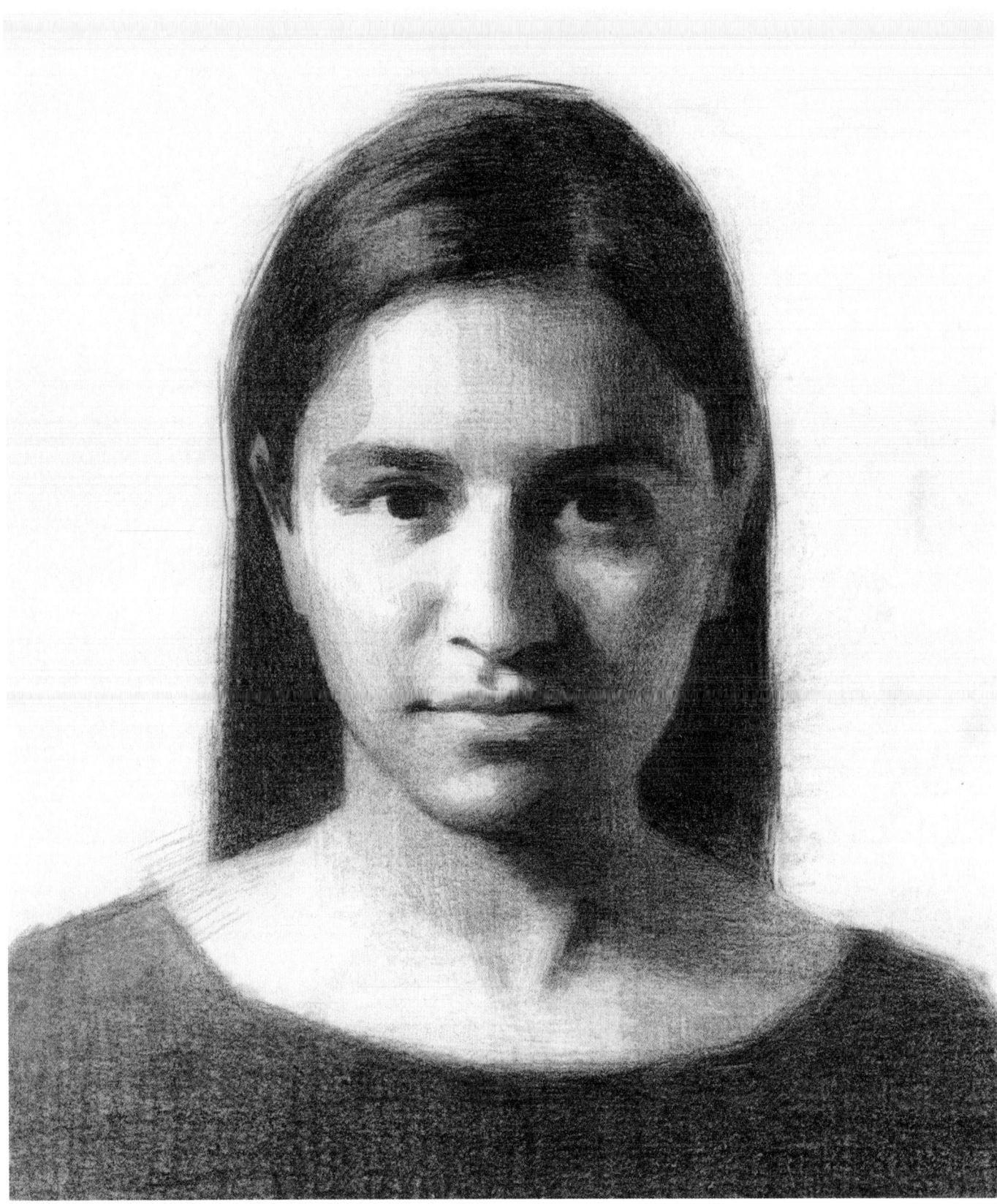

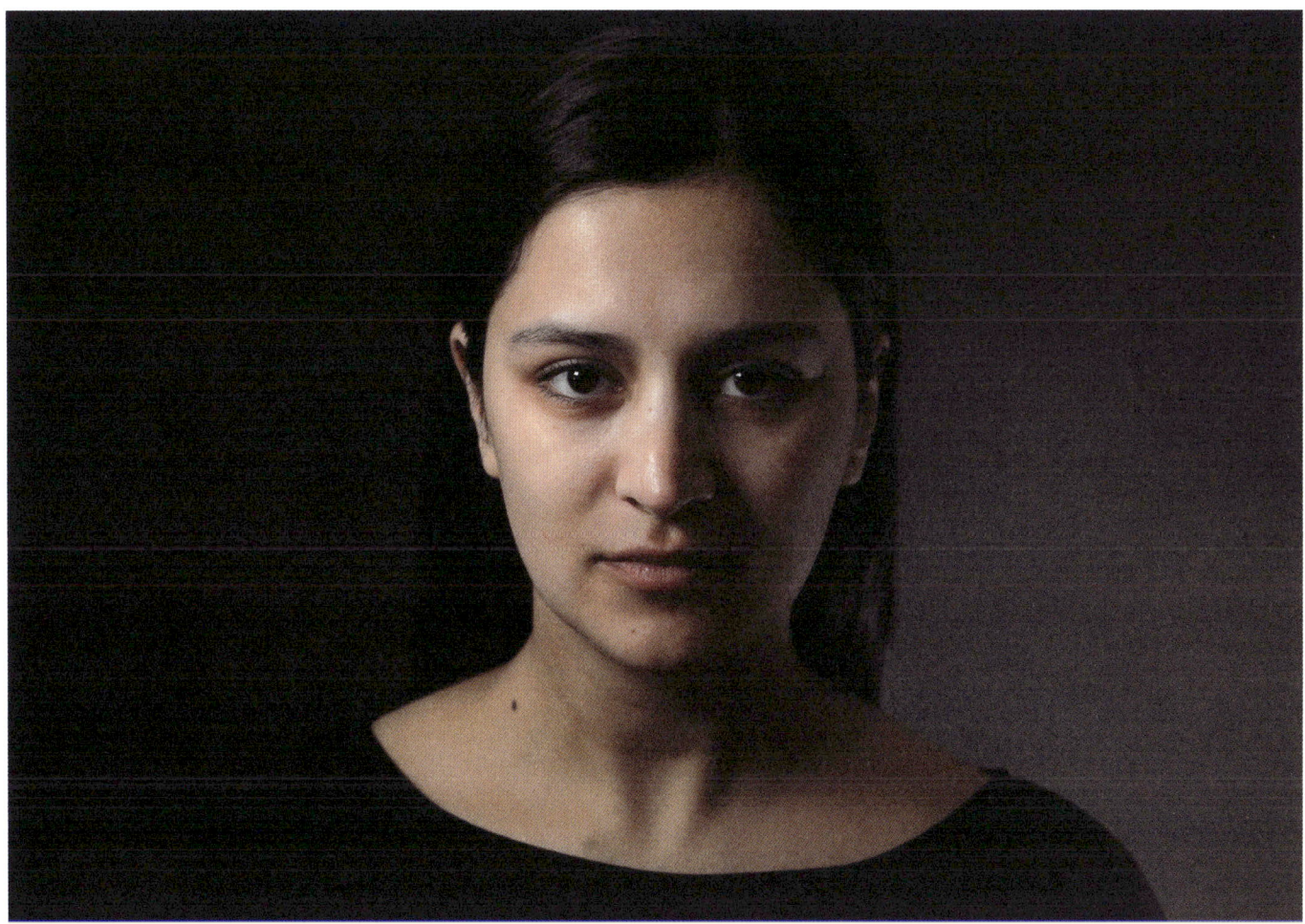

MASS DRAWING:
STAGE FOUR

A shift to subtle

Now you will hone in on the subtler values and features. The eyes, nose, and mouth receive attention. You will also carefully observe and design the specific characteristics that contribute to the subject's likeness. This involves a subtle shift in approach, from broad, sweeping strokes to more careful, considered value applications. It is also where the information set is more or less complete, meaning that everything that will be in the drawing has arrived on the paper. It's a time for deeper consideration, which often results in less apparent action. This is because less action is required, as the bulk of the labour involved – establishing major value groups and making sure to maintain a harmonious value application – has been well established.

Muddy values

A pitfall we might find at this stage is what can be referred to as 'muddy' values. These can be observed when the overall value relationships between value groups are not correctly maintained. Simply put, there are too many dark values in the lightest planes and too many light values in the darkest planes. While it's common for this to occur when expanding the value scale in the drawing, it should also be cleaned up before working to resolve the study.

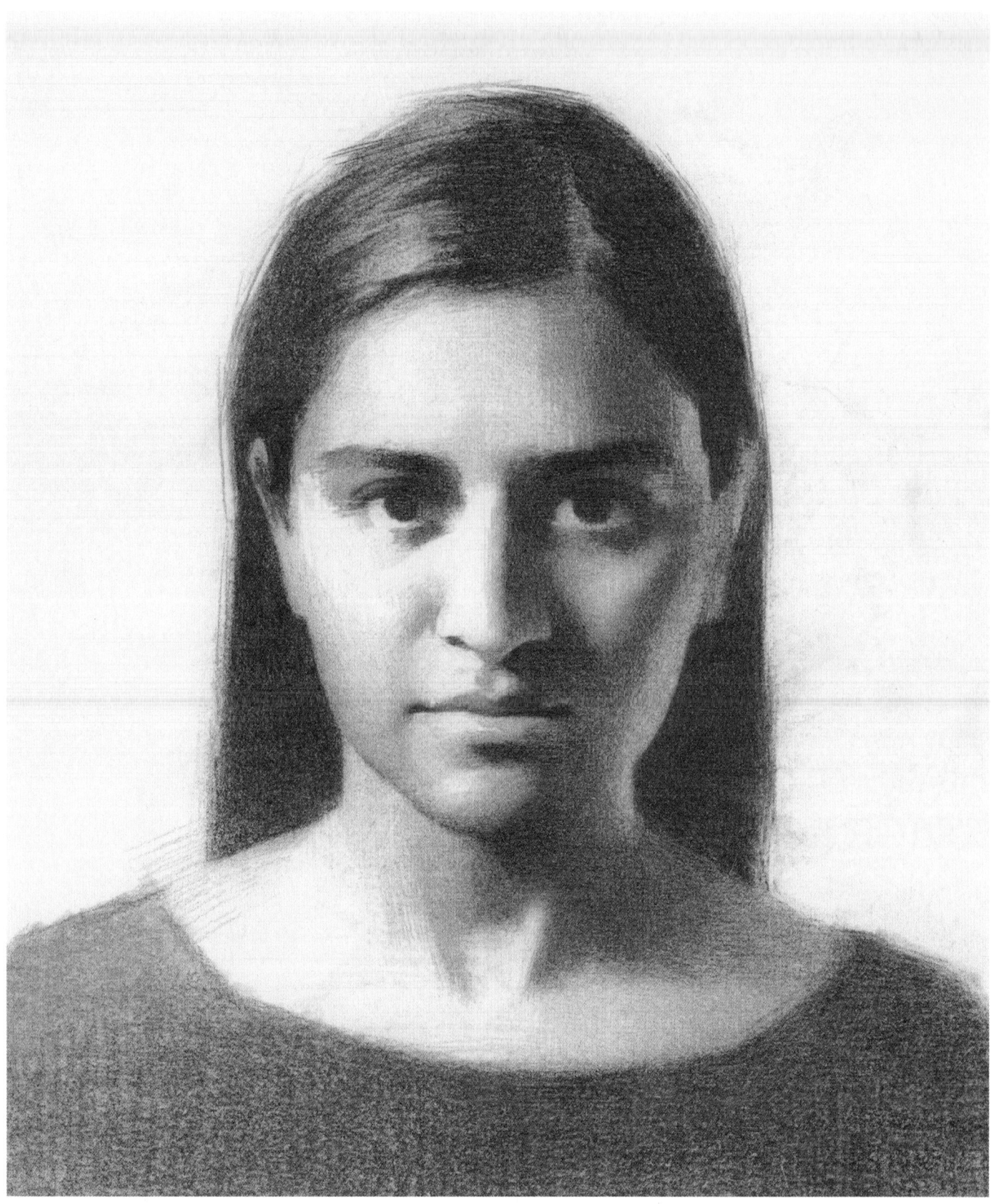

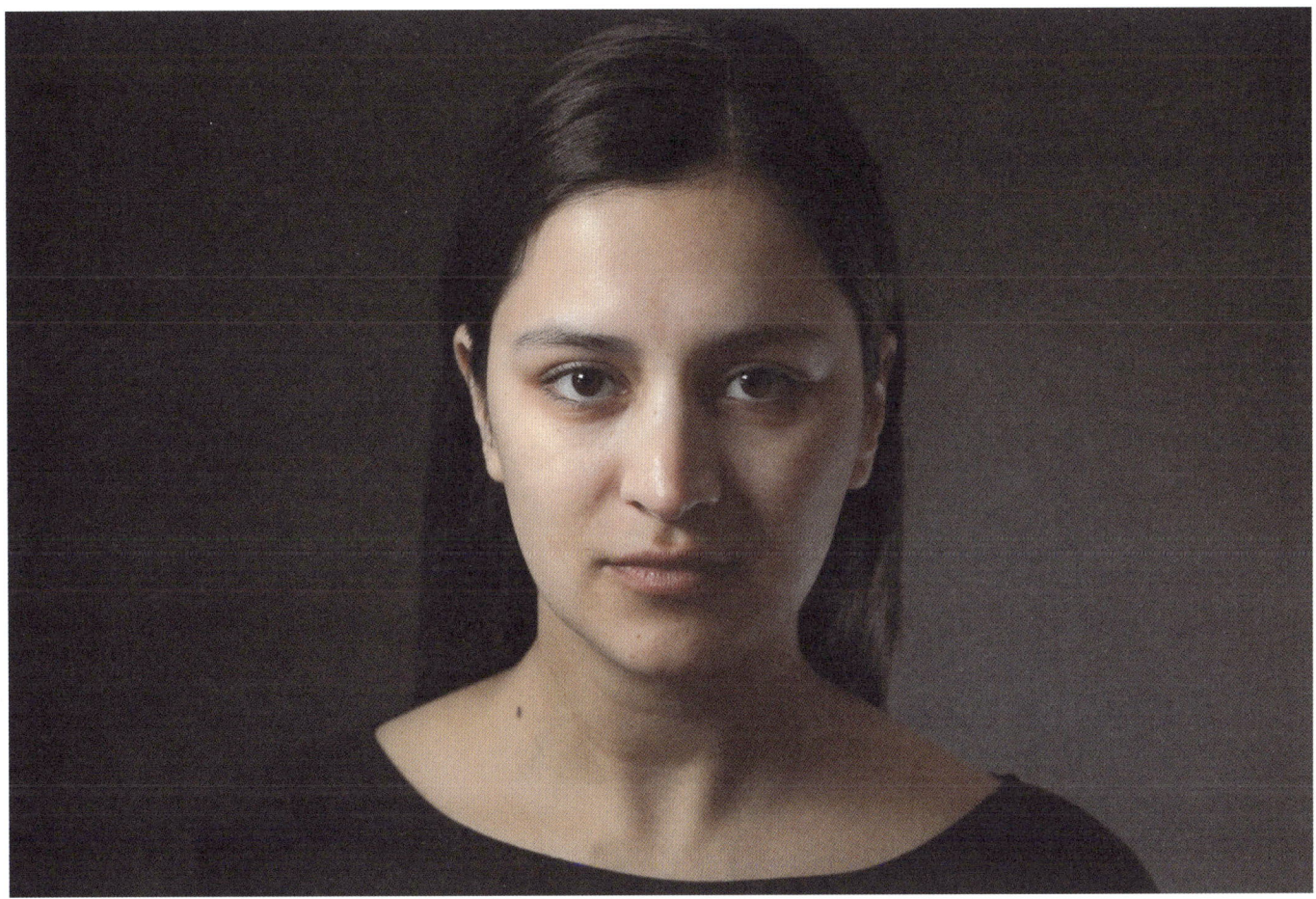

MASS DRAWING: STAGE FIVE

A visual symphony

In the final stage of this mass drawing, the focus shifts towards the finer rendering of edges, the enhancement of the sense of shape design, and the addition of those critical finishing touches that round off the study. This phase is characterized not only by its technical demands, but also by the depth of observation and sensitivity it requires. An intense focus on the value relationships present in the picture is paramount. Mastering the observation of these relationships is akin to a musician understanding harmonies; it's not about the individual notes, but how they resonate with each other to create a symphony. In portraiture, this symphony is visual, where every value plays a role in defining form and space.

Transitions

This stage also involves refining the transitions, which is a delicate balance between defining the form and maintaining a sense of integrity in the nature of the study. The balance here is between sticking to the relative flatness of the value shapes while allowing them to take on a gradient quality. Transitions in a portrait can convey a wealth of information about the character of the light, texture, and spatial relationships.

In conclusion

Mass drawing, as an exercise, will showcase and enhance your ability to see your subject not as it is, but how you need it to be. As with any approach to drawing, it is the point of view of the artist that dictates the result of the endeavour. In this case, the artist's perspective moulds and interprets the subject through a lens of selective perception and intent. This process requires a distillation of the complex visual world into simpler, more powerful value shapes. It is an exercise in reduction and refinement, where the superfluous is stripped away, leaving only what is essential for conveying the subject.

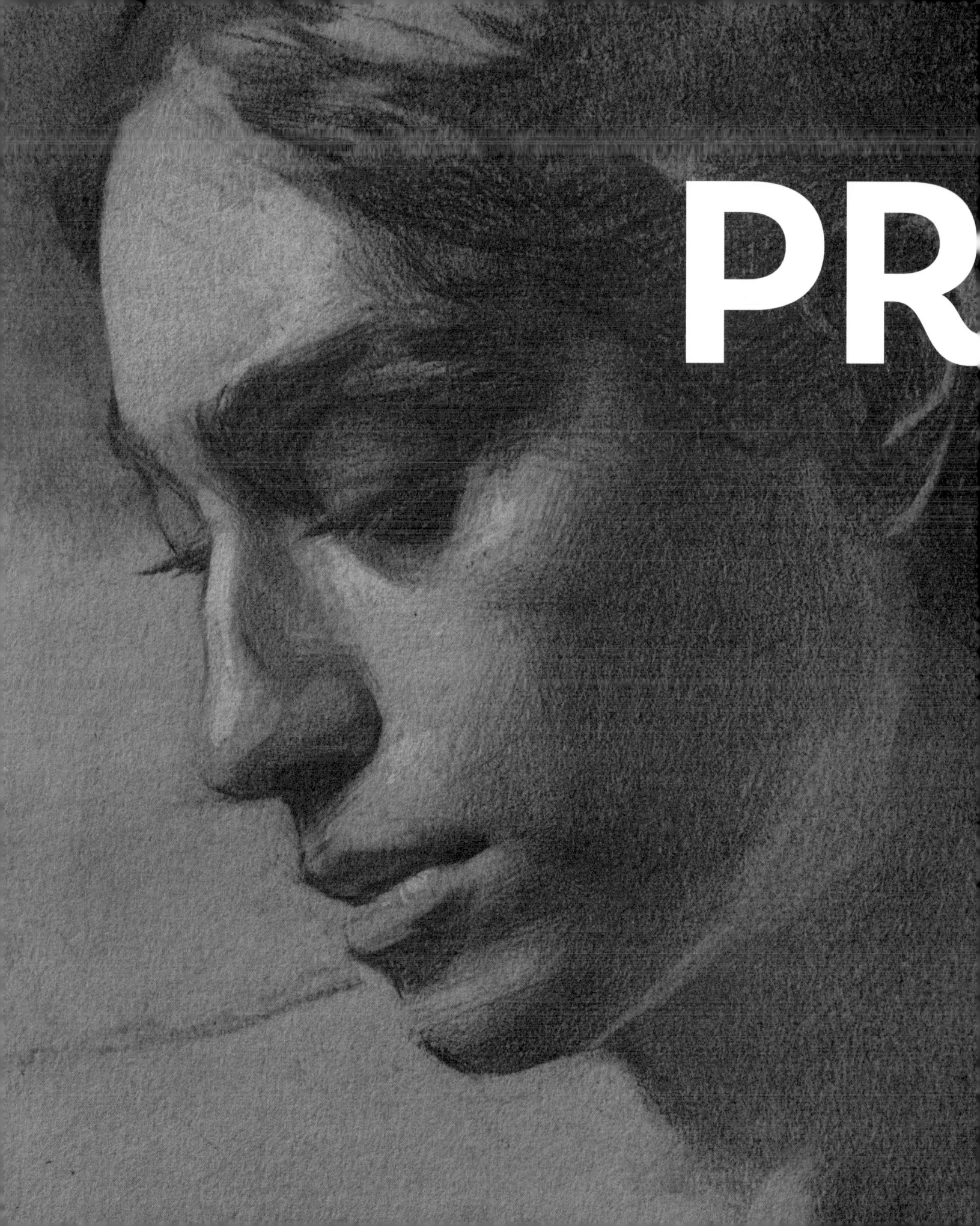

PR

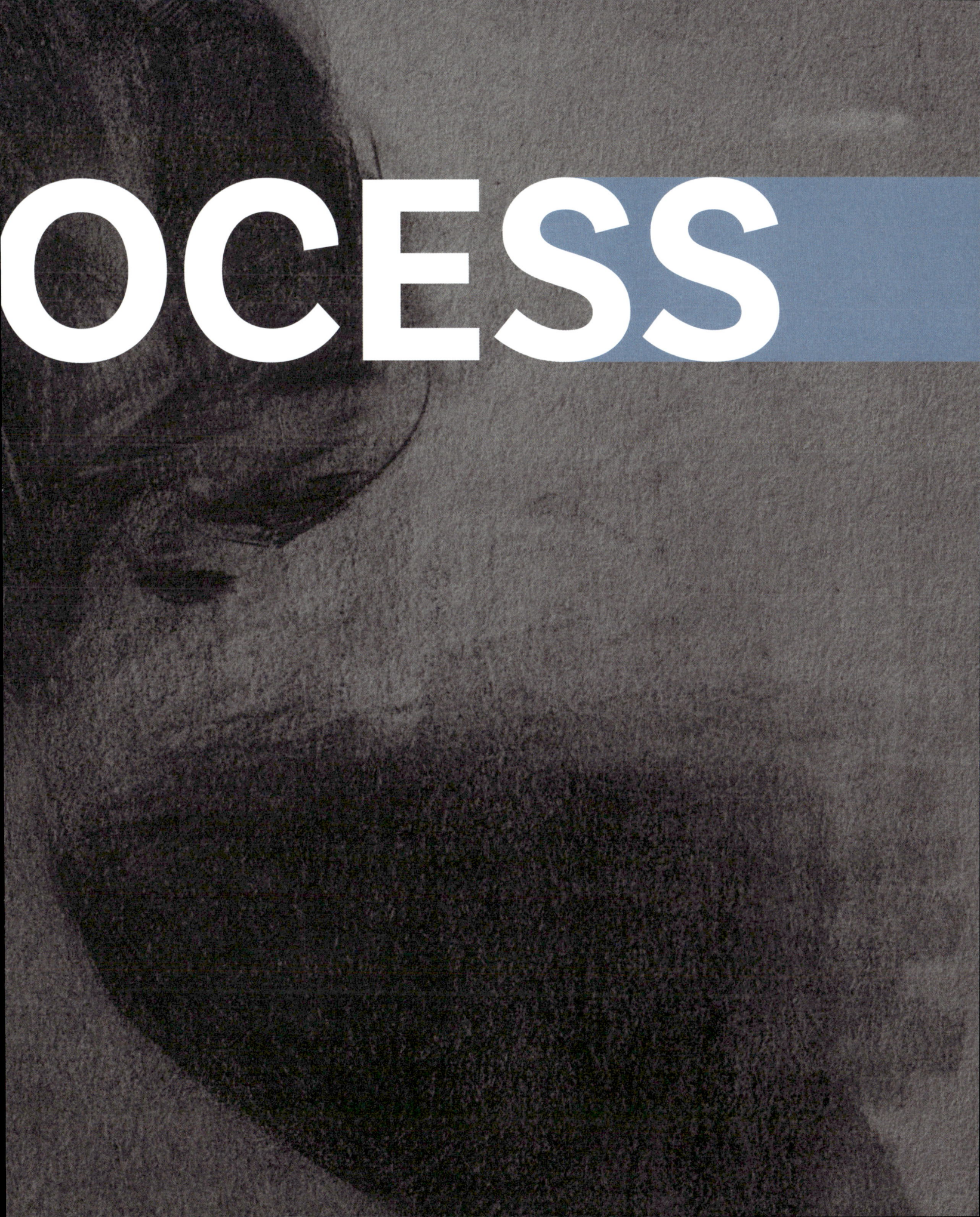

OCESS

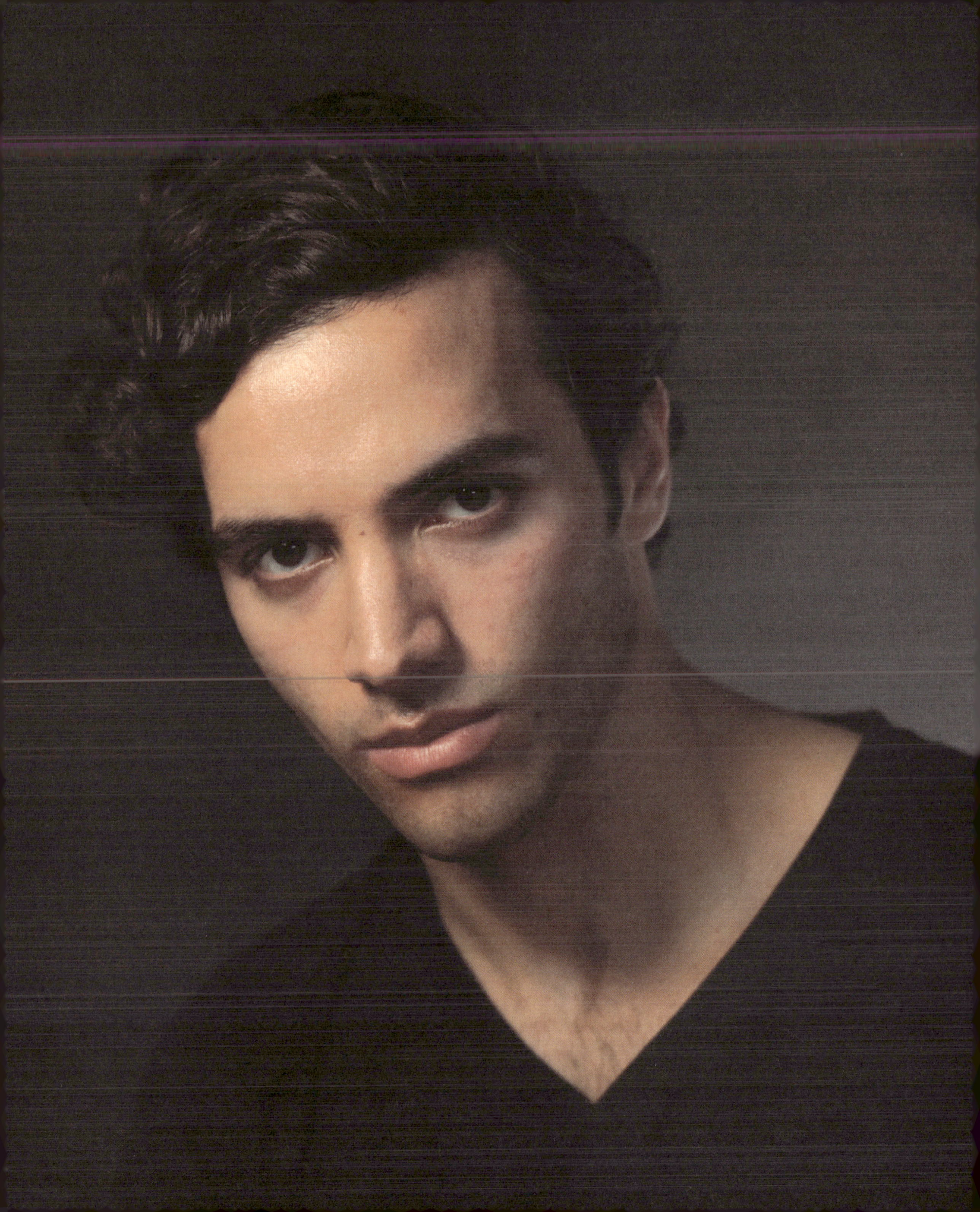

A PORTRAIT IS A STORY

'A film is never really good unless the camera is an eye in the head of a poet.'

Orson Welles

When I set out to write this book, there was one thing above all that I wanted to convey: that drawing is a journey of discovery, not a procedure. With that in mind, there are several things to understand as we set out to create an artfully rendered portrait.

Belief is the single most important ingredient in your artistic life. Where others see an obstacle, you will need to see an opportunity. Rather than thinking mistakes are to be avoided, you must consider what you can learn from them, and store that hard-won knowledge away to refer back to when you need it. This, and all of the other friction you will encounter, can be more than enough to grind your progress to a halt if you lack belief in what you are doing.

Belief comes from recognition of an intrinsic value, something real. But in an art form that exists as a mirror or a proxy for reality, what can we say is real? Even more than that, what *is* real, and universal? The answer to this question is simple, short, and irrefutable. It's *you*.

You, the artist, are the constant in the equation that manifests your work. Reality then is not only the external world that is rendered on paper; it is also the internal reality of the artist. This internal reality comprises your perceptions, emotions, experiences, and thoughts – the entirety of your being that interacts with the external world and interprets it. This interaction between the internal and external realities is where meaningful work is made. Moreover, the universality in art comes from this very personal approach. While the external realities might differ vastly from one person to the next, the internal realities often share common emotional and experiential threads. Fear, joy, sorrow, love … these are universal emotions that every human being understands. When you infuse your art with your personal truth, you tap into these universal emotions, creating a bridge between your internal reality and the external reality of the viewer.

With that in mind, the differences between applying your efforts towards a *study* and later an *artwork* should be noted.

They can be distinguished from each other in several ways. While a study aims to search out and define, an artwork seeks to express or reveal something through the subject; something that alone it may not even possess. A study is a gathering of information, selectively at times, while an artwork involves the purposeful selection and deployment, or even enhancement, of that information in the service of a theme.

The metaphor that seems most apt to me is that of a film director to the film they will make. That film will likely last around 130 minutes, give or take. 130 precious minutes to capture the viewer's attention and sustain it until the final frame. Sometimes hundreds of hours of footage are shot to make a single film. A dozen takes of an actor delivering the same monologue, establishing shots for every location, B-roll filled with extras and atmosphere, action sequences shot over and over just to pull it off, and so much more. The intent of each scene is never forgotten. If the scene playing out is a sad one, the lighting, set design, camera angles, and pace should all confirm and enhance this purpose. One of the most famous films of all time, *Citizen Kane*, is renowned for its use of camera perspective for storytelling. Holes were dug into the ground of the set so that the cameras could view the actors from an even lower point of view, making them appear as titans. Everything that goes into those 130 minutes has to work together towards the same story if the film is to reach its expressive peak.

An artwork is not so different. A portrait is a story and the plot is the theme that you will choose to convey. Whether it be tenderness, vulnerability, strength, intensity, or a combination of these, your sense of light, structure, composition, shape language, degree of refinement, and even mark-making will have to 'rhyme' if you are to engage the viewer from the first moment they spend with your work until the last.

In this final chapter, I will take you through each stage of the process I take to create a fully rendered portrait in graphite.

THUMBNAIL DEVELOPMENT

The aim of this first stage in the process is to develop at least two viable options for the composition. You can then make a comparison between them to determine the design that best represents your chosen theme.

There is a saying: when it's only in your head, every painting is the best painting ever. The process of thumbnail development can be seen as a way to externalize your vision and vet your ideas for quality. Sometimes this will be a very straightforward process. You will set out a sketch and feel that it confirms what you suspected – this composition is fit for the picture you want to make. Other times less so. What is important to remember, and act upon, is that making thumbnail sketches is a way to elevate your vision. To make your composition better, and to choose the pose that is perfect, rather than simply the one that you thought of first.

How should you think about thumbnail development? There are technical evaluations to be made, such as balance, shape design, harmony/discord, placement, and scale. There is also the question of what the pose conveys: the emotion. A more nebulous quality to evaluate, it involves empathy and consideration for the subject. Is the chin raised and the head tilted back? This can communicate a kind of pride and defiance. Is the model's gaze cast downward, the body almost hunched over? This will convey a weight and sadness. These are qualities that are recognizable in everyday life, in the people you spend time with. Getting in touch with your emotions, empathizing with the people in your life and in your environment through sketching, is the most useful way to develop a catalogue of these poses and expressions. The translation of that knowledge into your work will then be seamless.

Beyond the technical aspects of the thumbnailing process, there is the development of the theme. In portraiture, as in much of art-making, the themes are simple ones. Archetypes and symbols play a significant role in this regard. Archetypes, as defined by Carl Jung, are universal, archaic symbols and images that derive from the collective unconscious. They are the psychic counterpart of instinct. In the realm of portraiture, these archetypes can be harnessed to imbue your work with a deeper, more universal resonance. A pose, the scale of the model, an expression in the eyes or lips, or even the value key in a portrait can align with archetypal themes such as the hero, martyr, or sage, thereby communicating a richer narrative.

In developing the composition for this final project, I tried two different poses. The first of the two, with the model's chin raised, shoulders back, and his eyeline directed upward and out of the frame (**fig. 01**), seemed initially quite convincing.

fig. **01**

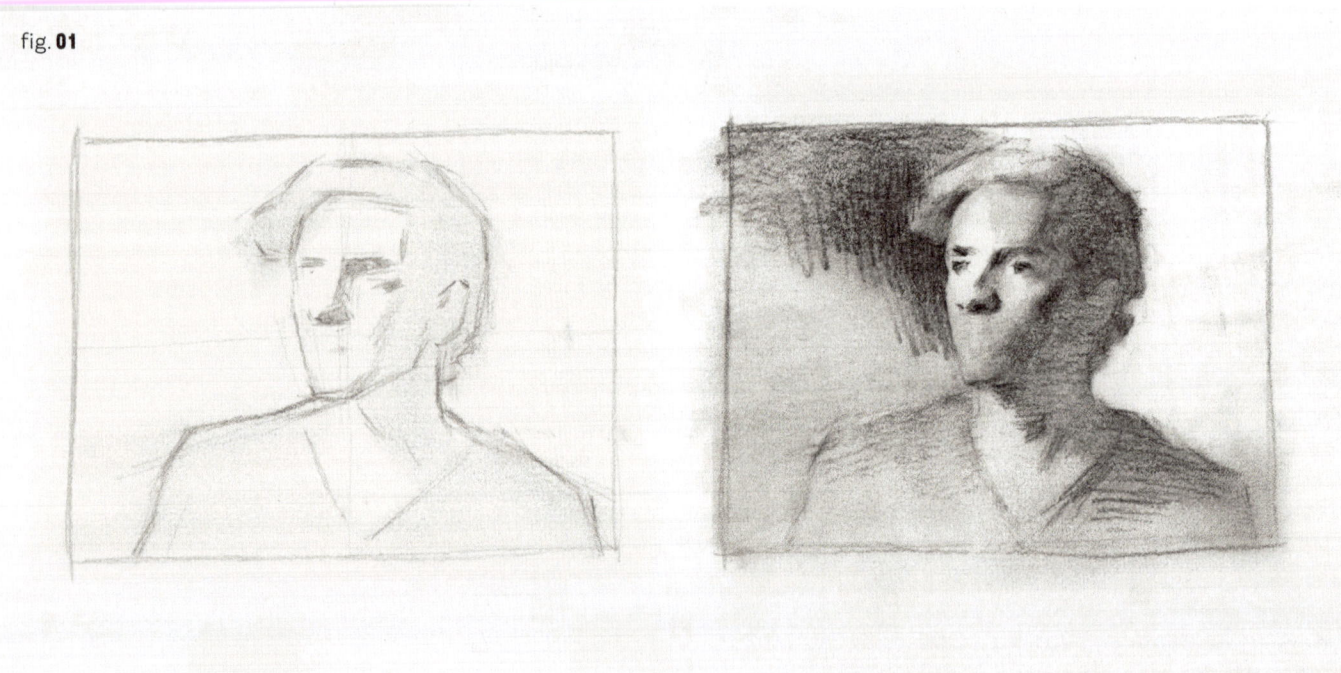

fig. **02**

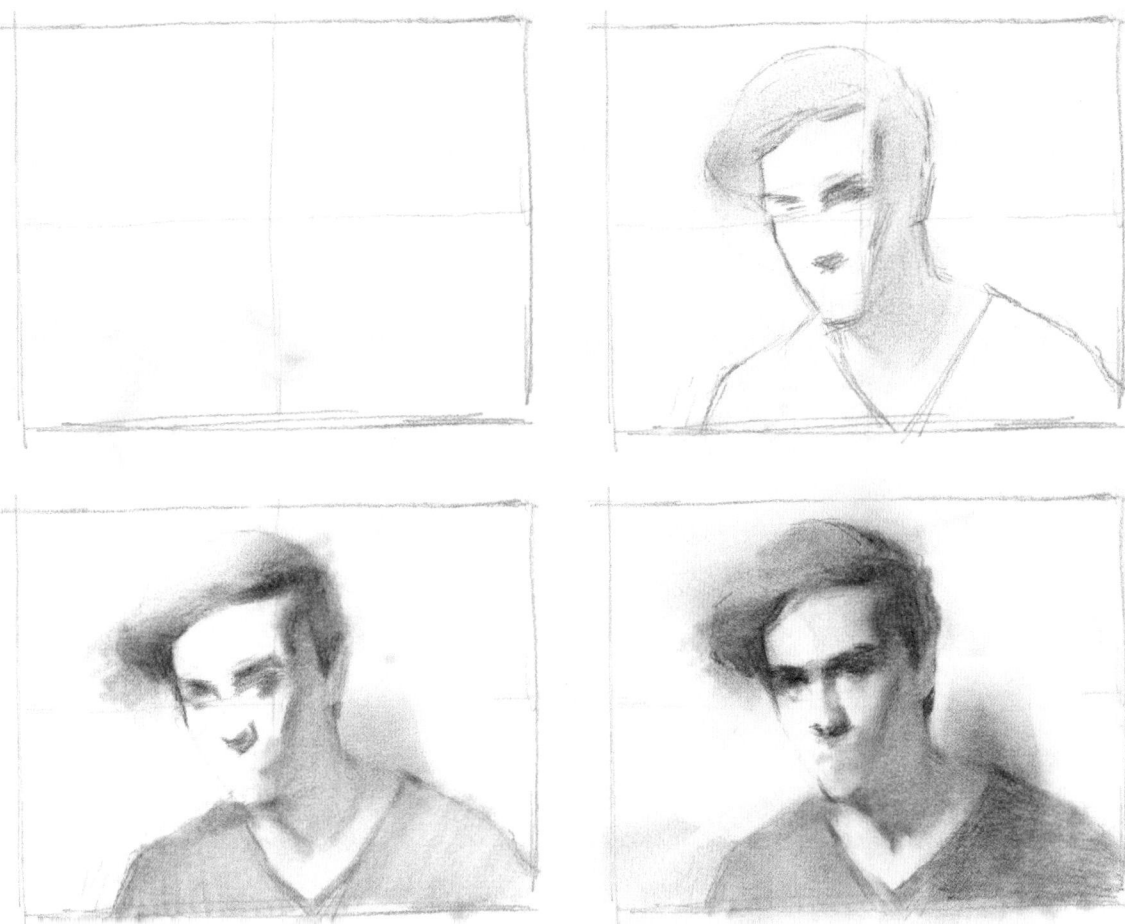

The pose seemed to speak of pride and confidence. For its application, however, it was more detached than what I wanted to convey. After all, this drawing is meant to represent a standard for portrait drawing. As such, I wanted the pose to embody more of a connection to the viewer (**fig. 02**). The reason is a simple one: eye contact engages the viewer. Eyes directed elsewhere are never 'wrong', they simply convey something different.

Initial ideas, which might seem flawless in the mind, undergo a crucial reality check when sketched out. Thumbnail sketches serve not only to materialize the vision for the project, but also to refine it, ensuring that the chosen composition and pose truly reflect the intended message and quality. This process involves both technical evaluations – like balance, harmony, and scale – and emotional considerations: simple and direct messages conveyed to the viewer through body language and facial expression.

'You compose because you want to somehow summarise in some permanent form your most basic feelings about being alive, to set down ... some sort of permanent statement about the way it feels to live now, today.'

Aaron Copland

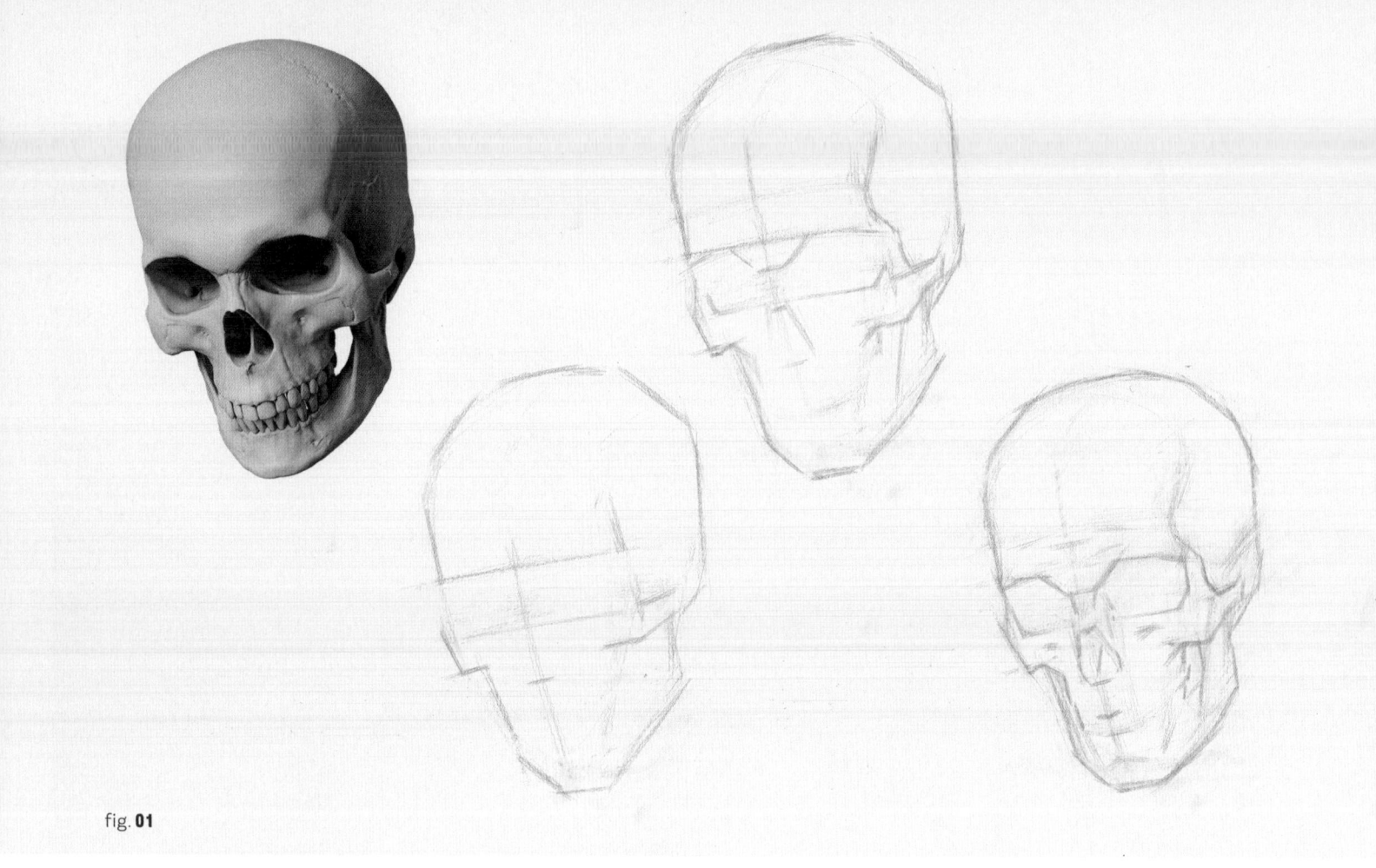

fig. **01**

ANATOMICAL STUDIES

It is easy to believe that we know something well; drawing it is how we make certain that this belief is real. Anatomical studies are probably most important for those who are still learning, but they will benefit any artist engaged in representing the human form. Think of a portrait as a mask composed of layer after layer of blended information. To the uninitiated, these layers are nearly impossible to disambiguate. What is the substance and structure of the nose? All of the subtle forms of the forehead – what is the logic of their formation? These questions, and others, are answered through anatomical study.

Striking a balance

Whenever possible, it's best to study anatomy in a context as close as possible to the artwork you intend to make, rather than a theoretical understanding of the pose. This will ensure the most literal application of insight possible. At the same time, a balance must be struck. A great artwork in the genre of portraiture is not simply the one with the highest degree of anatomical insight. If this were the case, all of the best portrait artists would be medical doctors. Instead, consider this knowledge as a way to raise the believability of your portrait drawing to the threshold required for proper realism. When it is combined with a strong sense of shape design and compositional vision, the results can be extraordinary.

A technological tool

I spent many years frustrated by this process as a student, so much so that as a drawing instructor I developed the HeadStudy app for students. The app facilitates the posing, lighting, and depth of anatomy and structure to be virtually reproduced. It allows users to adjust and control the turn and tilt of the head, as well as the position, intensity, and hue of two separate light sources on any of the four models available in the app. Why is this useful for artists? For the same reason that it is useful to make anatomical studies: the more knowledge about your subject you have internalized, the more you can see. The more you can see, the more you have to choose from when you are composing your picture.

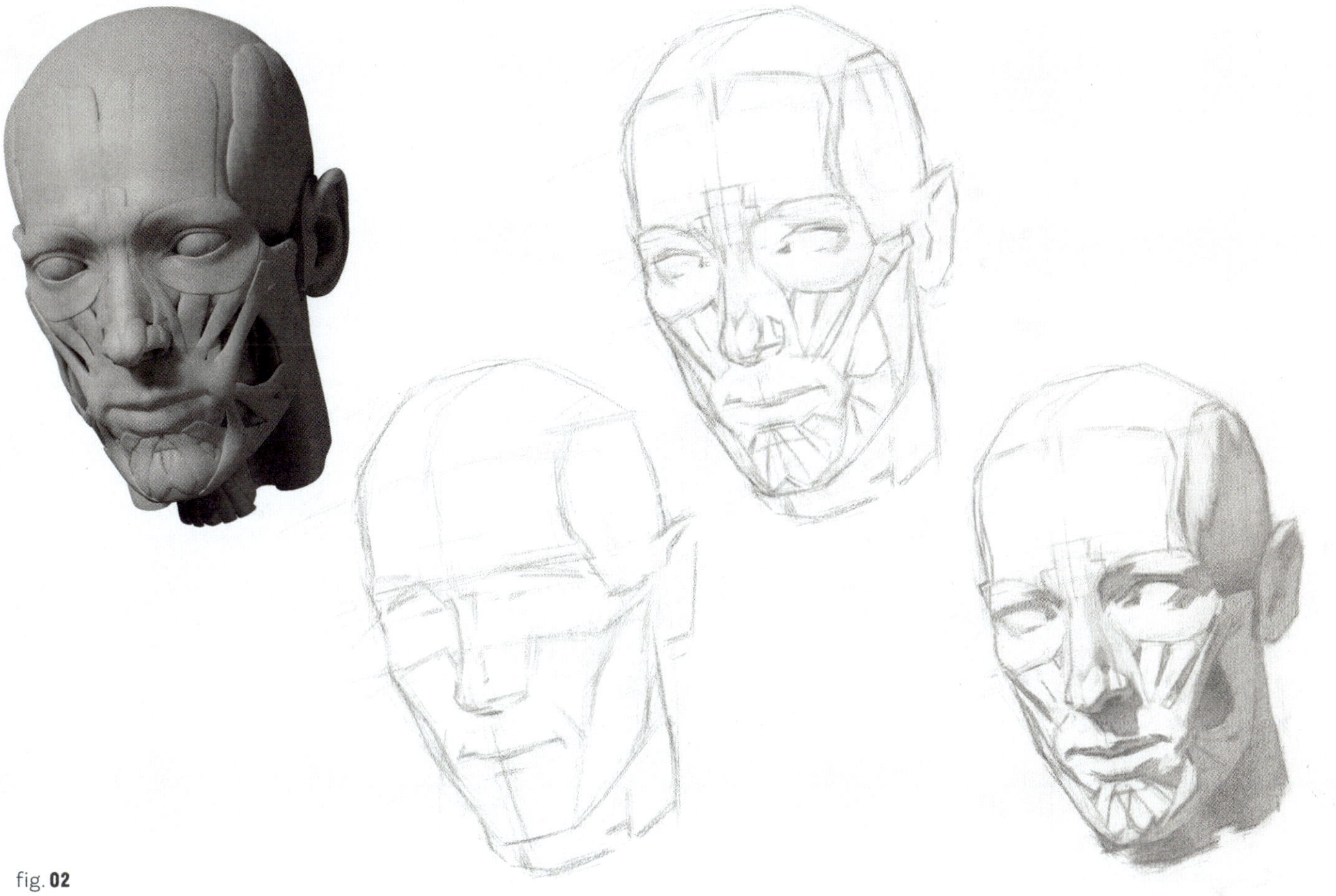

fig. **02**

Skull and ecorché studies

In the two studies above, the models have been matched to the pose of the model in my final composition (page 216). The light and shadow have been arranged to reflect the lighting situation as closely as possible, too. In the study of the skull (**fig. 01**), we can clearly see the forms of the frontal bone expressed more or less exactly as they will be in the final drawing. The exact turn of form along the temporal line and zygomatic bone are laid bare for close observation, and the full extent of the proportion of the head itself is also easily seen. The ecorché (muscle) study (**fig. 02**) assists the understanding of areas of soft tissue, such as the lips and nose; intricate areas where numerous small forms come together for a very complex expression. It also clarifies the position of the major turning edge of the cheek. These points of emphasis are just the beginning of the insights that can be gained through the application of these studies to your art-making process.

While both of these studies serve as practice for the eventual block-in, there is also a particular emphasis on the shadow and light's relationship to the underlying structure of the head. Understanding the form that manifests the pattern of shadow, light, and midtone on the head is critical to your design process. These studies can be conducted with several different targets: visual, mass, and structure, or any combination of these.

Scan this QR code to download the Head Study app.

It provides quick and easy references to help artists understand the anatomy and forms of their portrait models.

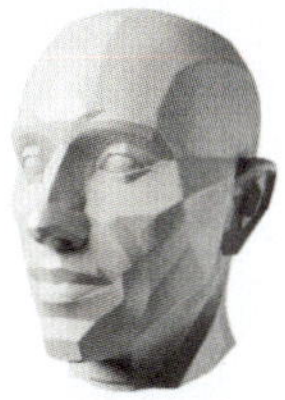

A HYBRID BLOCK-IN APPROACH

The manifestation of an idea

These first two stages in building the actual portrait help to indicate an important aspect of drawing that is likely to be intuitively understood, but nonetheless bears repeating. The stages of a drawing, as they are represented in every drawing book since the dawn of drawing books, are largely symbolic. They are chosen by drawing instructors to illustrate one point or another; to indicate something important that must be understood before progressing. As such they can be incredibly helpful, provided it is understood that they are the manifestation of an idea, rather than a literal waypoint on the path to completion. Represented in these two stages is what can be referred to as a 'hybrid approach' block-in stage. Almost all practising artists will work in some kind of hybrid approach given the varying nature of their education.

fig. **01**

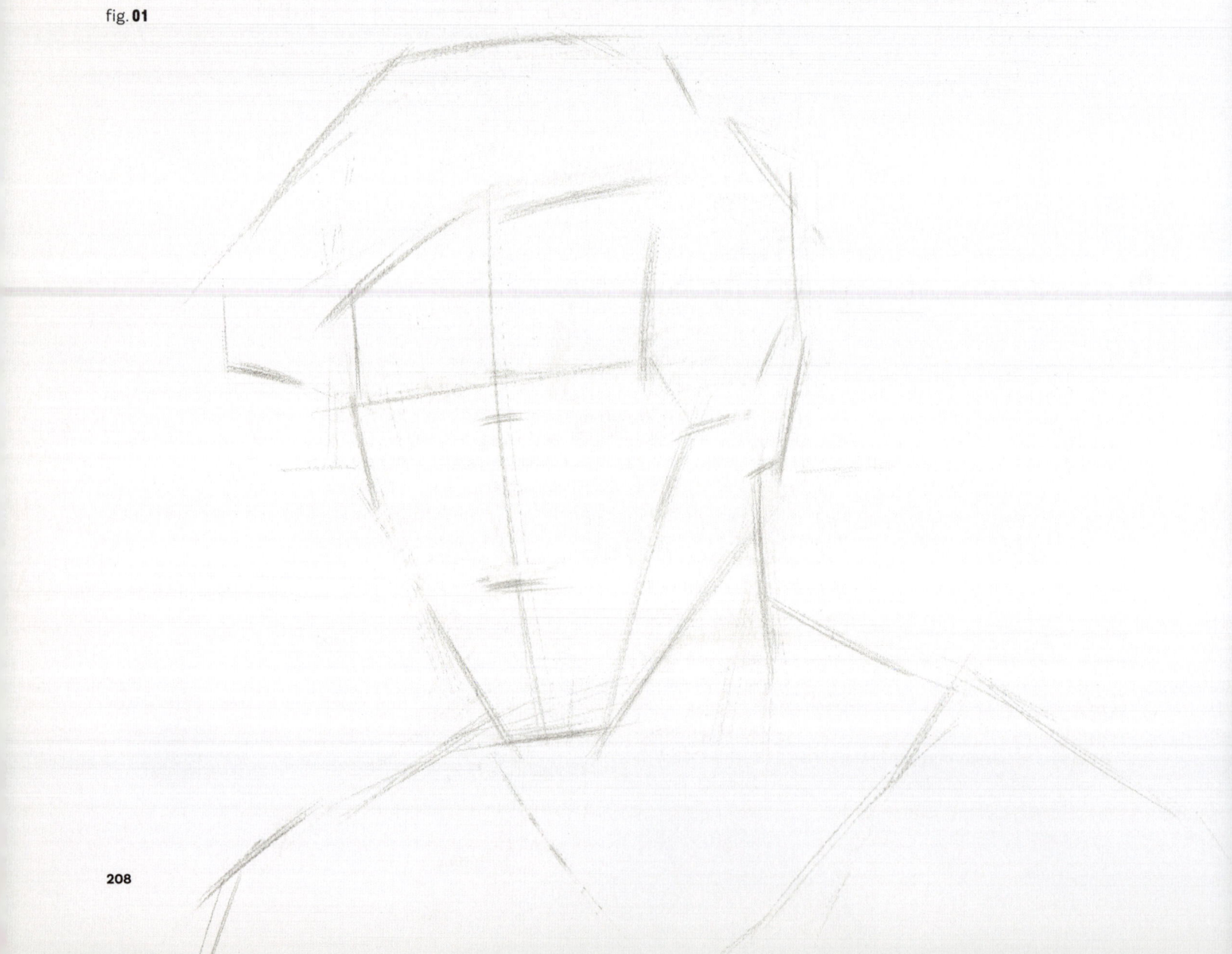

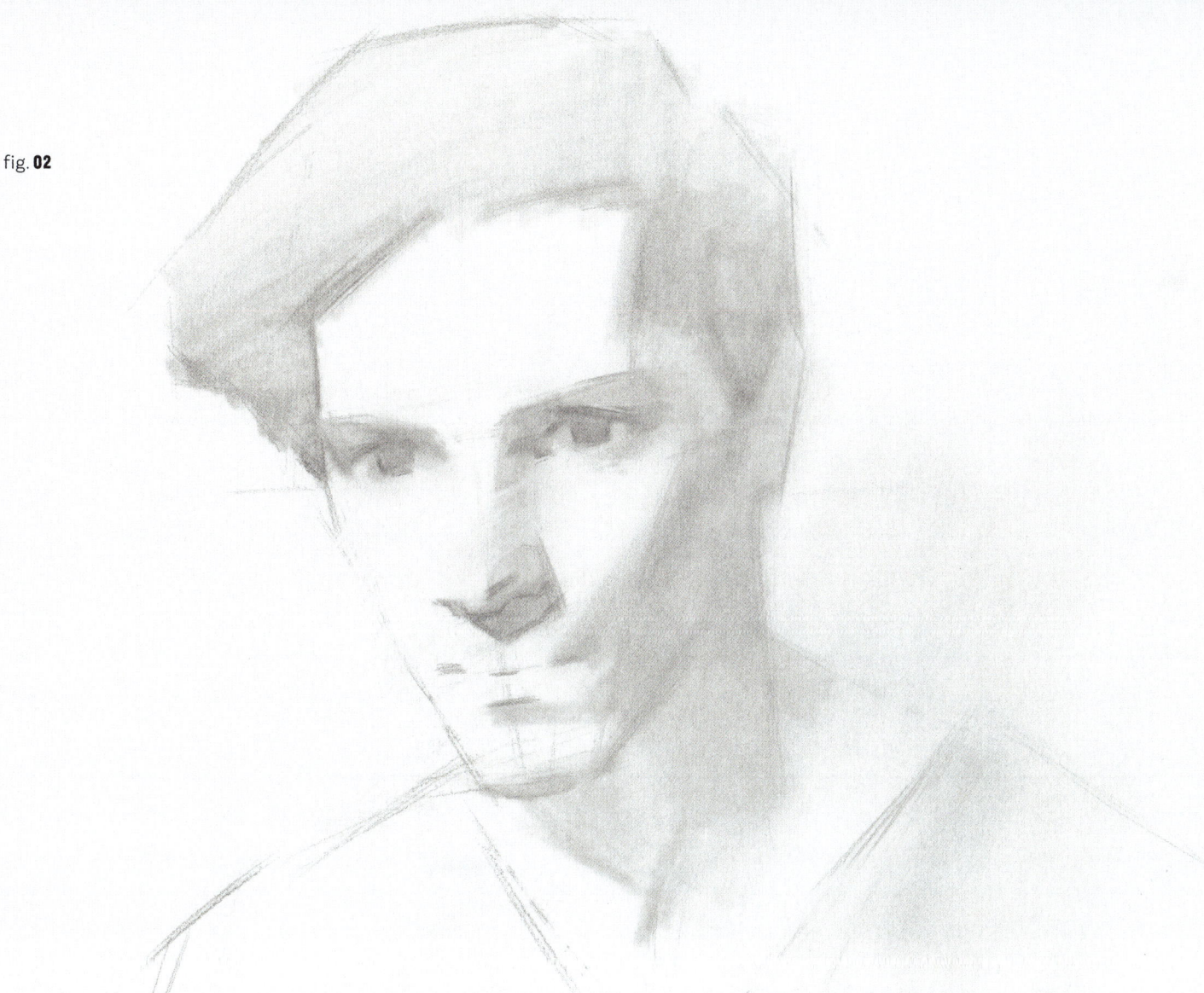

fig. **02**

A practical choice

While the block-in showing the first lines of the face and head (**fig. 01**) can be interpreted as structural, this drawing also contains some concepts that are more akin to a *visual* approach. The outline of the hair, lines of the shoulders, and indications of the neckline of the model's shirt are essentially visual silhouettes. In the second stage (**fig. 02**), these lines have been swiftly enveloped by a soft cloud of value. The features have been developed with a higher degree of acuity, in line with their importance to the composition. There are several reasons why this is a practical choice.

For one thing, the development of a drawing is not a uniform process, like a print of a photograph might be, for example. To achieve a good print, the printer will apply an even application from the top left of the photo paper to the bottom right. Every inch receives the exact same application.

When creating a drawing, however, there will be varying applications of time, attention, and rendering, depending on the desired focus of the composition. In this case the eyes, nose, and mouth will be rendered to the highest degree, whereas the shoulders, chest, and hair will be less detailed. By implementing this dynamic early on in the process, we are simply starting the drawing in the same way we intend to finish it. Not only does this save time, it also saves your most engaged energy for the moments when you will need it most.

Furthermore, this method mirrors the natural way in which we perceive the world. Human vision tends to focus on certain elements, while relegating others to the periphery. By mimicking this selective focus in your work, you can create drawings that feel more lifelike and relatable, resonating with the viewer's innate visual tendencies.

fig. 01

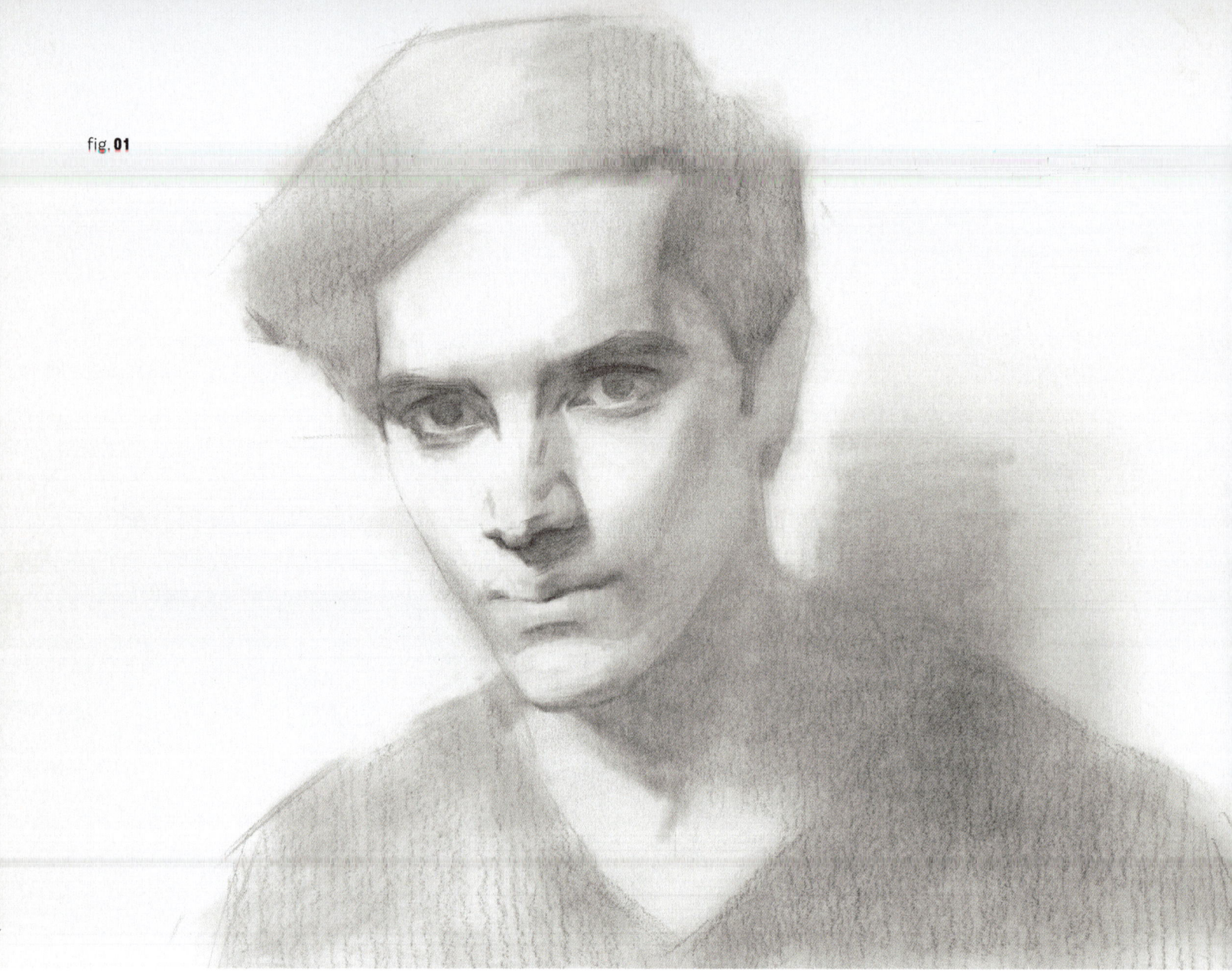

KEEPING YOUR OPTIONS OPEN

The build-up

Building up values in graphite, as has been well documented in this book, is best achieved in layers. To do this efficiently, it's a good idea to start that build up when the drawing is in its simplest and roughest state. The two stages above (**figs. 01** and **02**) represent the beginning of that process in earnest. It is important, if not necessary, to be confident in the proportions of the model in order to initiate this build up, as it will become more difficult to adjust the proportion and location of the value shapes as their density increases. This requires the patience to delay commitment to decisions.

Avoiding hasty decisions

The tendency to make decisions hastily can be attributed to a phenomenon known as the 'availability heuristic'. This cognitive shortcut can influence you to make judgements based on readily available or easily recalled information, rather than considering all relevant data. It operates under the principle that if something can be observed quickly, it must be important – or at least more relevant than other information that is not as easily observed. This idea runs contrary to what we know about drawing, which is that our first set of observations tend to be the least accurate. This inaccuracy then decreases incrementally as the drawing progresses.

fig. **02**

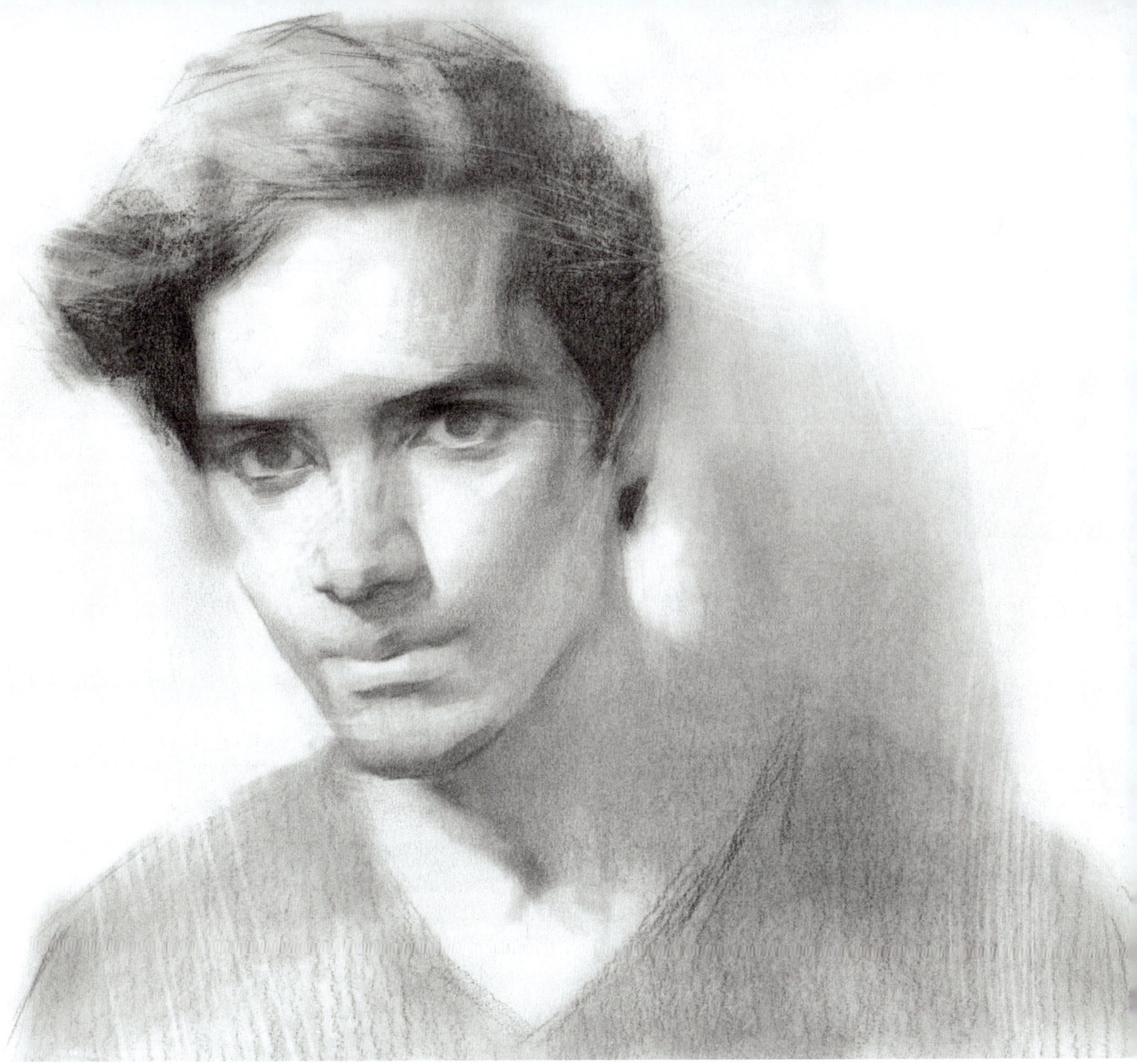

Controlling edges

When seeking to keep your drawing flexible, you should indicate the head and features with a moderately soft edge. The alternative – sharp and contrasting edges – contribute to a feeling of certainty or permanence in a drawing. So, if the target we're working towards is to achieve the highest potential accuracy in the drawing at the very end – rather than at the start – the sharpest and most contrasting edges should be reserved for later in the process. The journey towards the conclusion for any drawing you make should be a predictable one, starting with the maximum possible outcomes and moving towards the final and singular outcome, with every choice you make leading you there. The reality of this progressively narrowing cone of possibility should be reflected in the kinds of edges and density of value application that you use at each stage of the drawing. Inevitably, there will be edges that are harder than others, but this should not lead you to spend too much time refining every edge segment. In order for the benefits to be reaped, it is imperative that this concept is only applied in general terms.

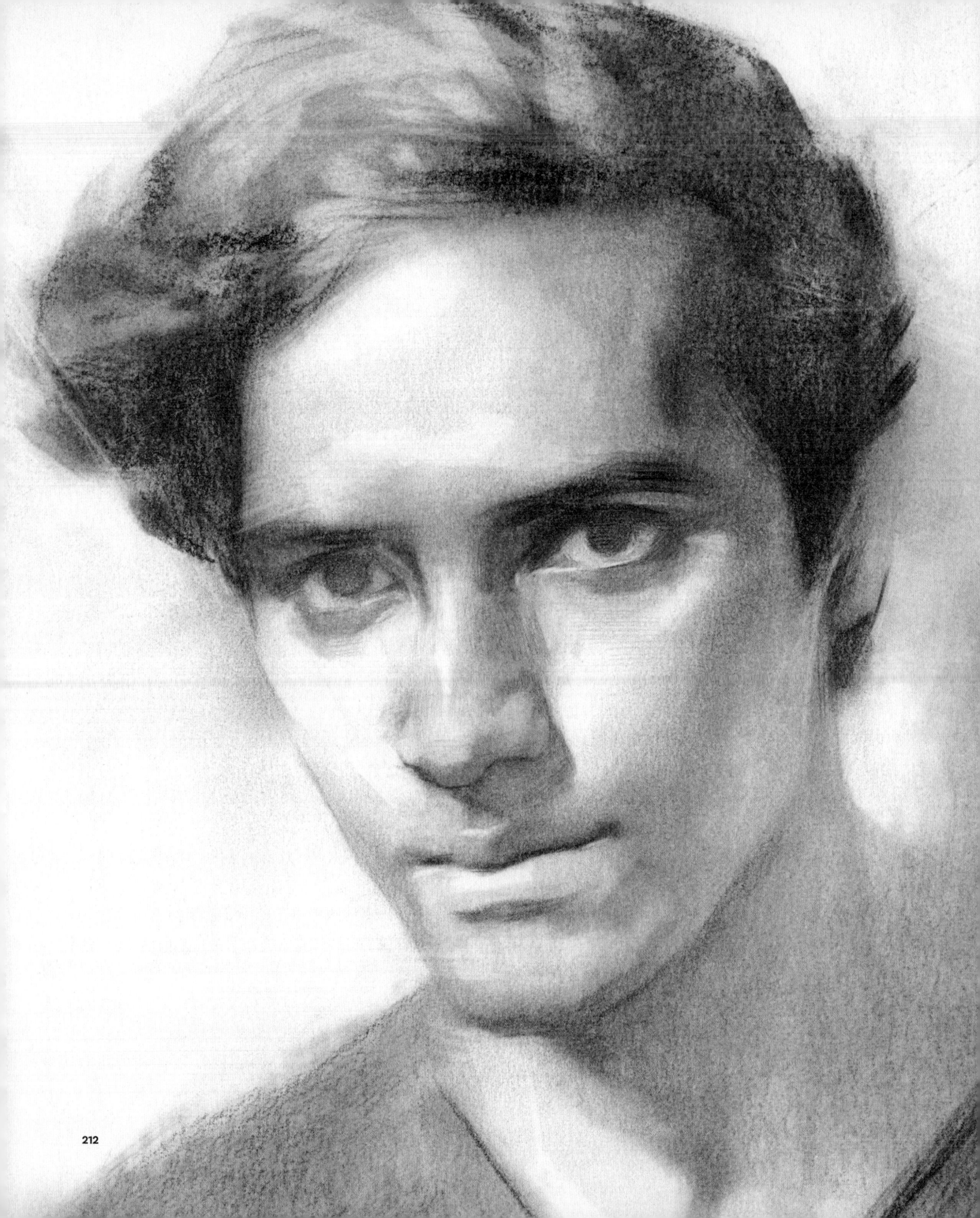

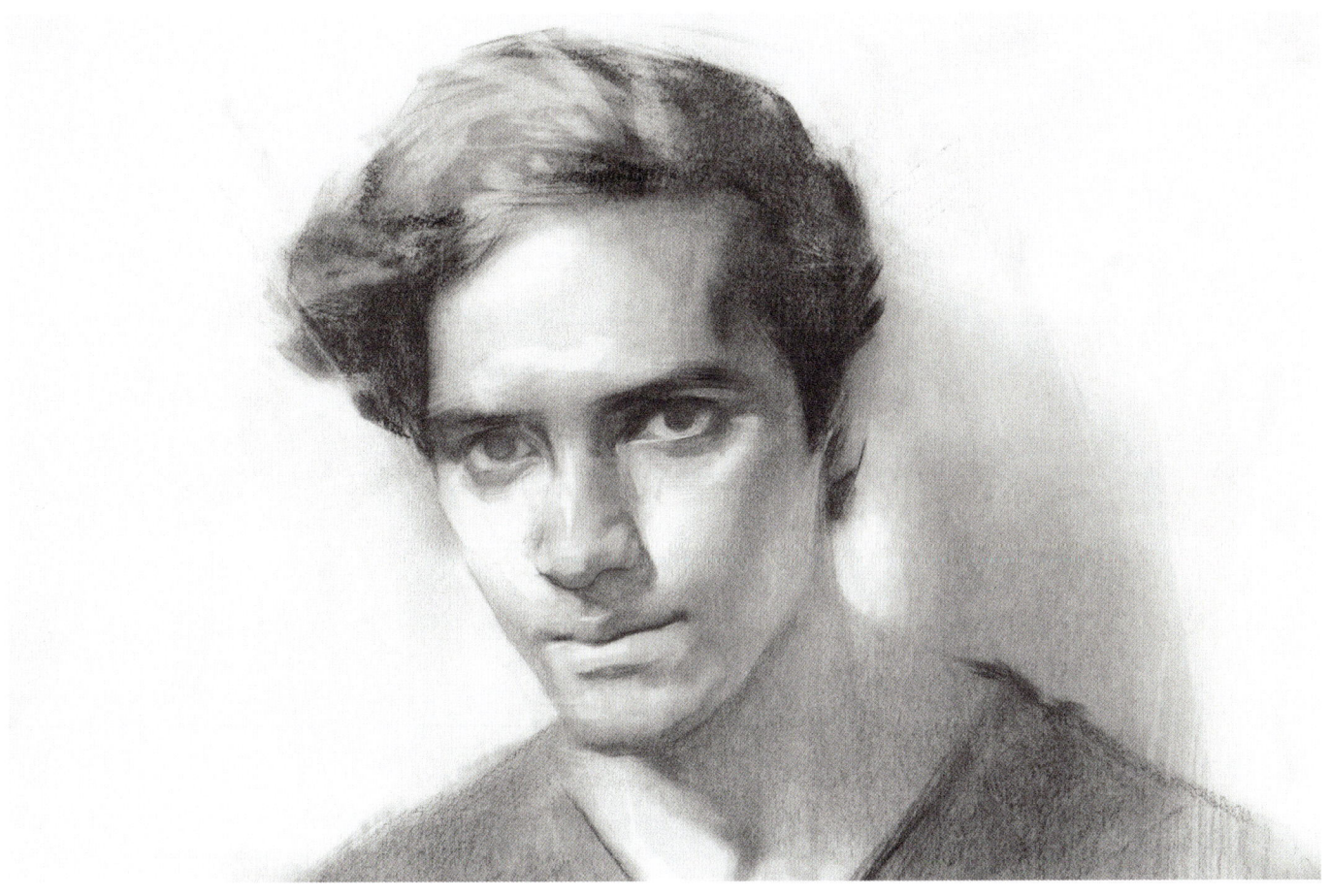

VALUE AND TEXTURE

Scaling up

There is a time in every drawing when the artist has to confront the inevitable issues that arise in the process of scaling up the design from the exploratory thumbnail to the final size. A plain and simple flat value shape in a 2 × 3 inch thumbnail sketch, when scaled up to a 12 × 18 inch drawing, can seem dull and flat if executed without some creative invention. This phenomenon can be partly attributed to the way our visual perception interprets details and textures. In a small thumbnail, the limited space naturally condenses and abstracts details, allowing the viewer to fill in gaps with their imagination. However, when these simplified forms are enlarged, the absence of detail or texture can become glaringly apparent, resulting in a lack of visual interest. The challenge for the artist, then, is to inject vitality into these expanded value shapes without compromising the original vision and composition of the thumbnail sketch.

Maintaining visual interest

As previously noted, it's a good rule to keep your applications even and unified when building up the value. I don't intend to contradict this advice, but I will add an amendment to it. While keeping your value application relatively even, remember that it doesn't need to be one-hundred per cent even. In fact, it should stop well short of total unity. Complete evenness and unity would mean the total removal of visual texture and variation. Put bluntly, this can look quite boring.

The introduction or maintenance of textural elements can greatly enhance the larger drawing. Textures provide visual interest and can break up monotonous areas, adding a layer of complexity that keeps the viewer's eye engaged. It is one of the elements that keeps the drawing looking fresh when it is viewed up close, as long as it harmoniously blends together when viewed from across the room.

fig. **01**

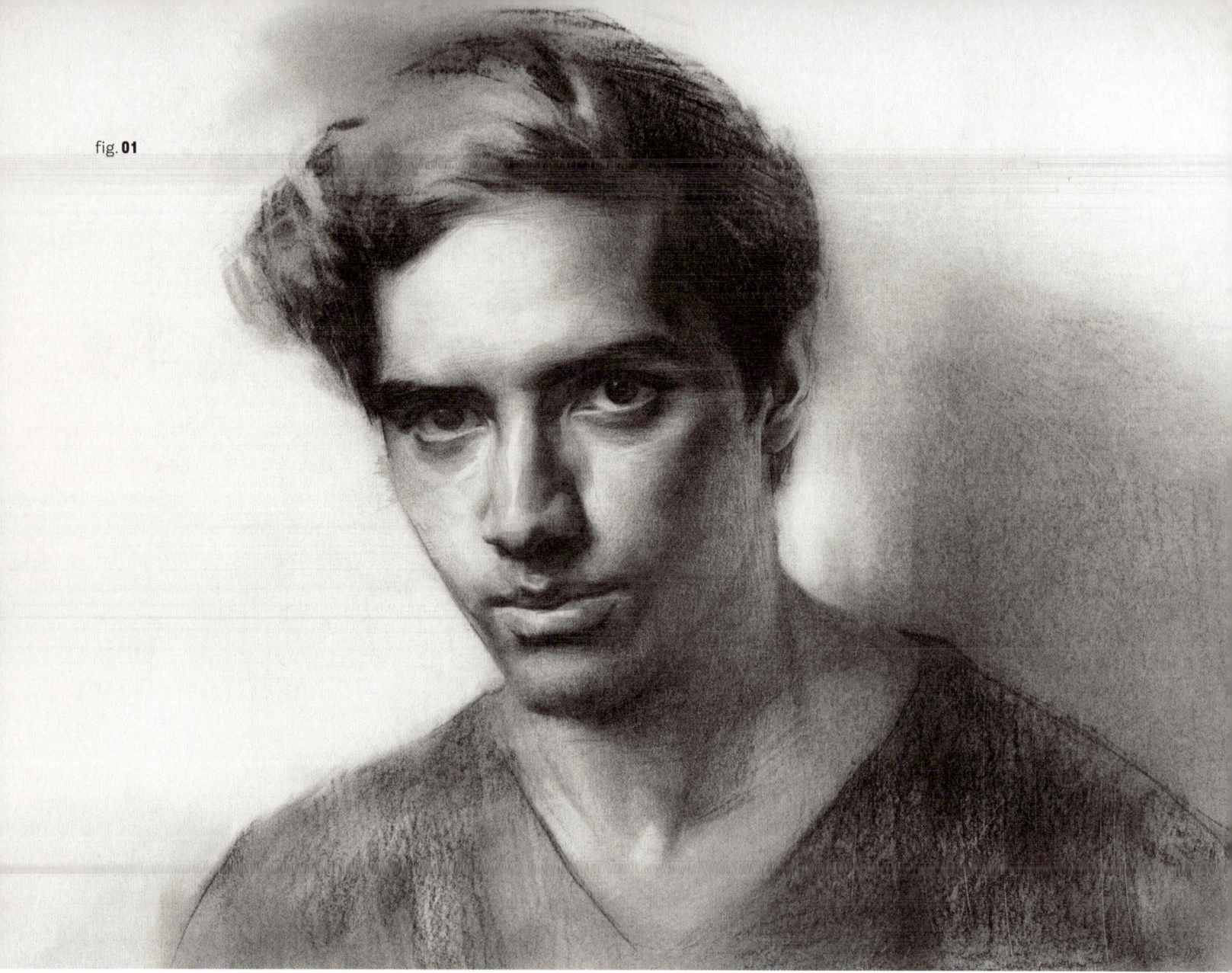

BALANCING VALUES
AND DEALING WITH DOUBT

A balancing act

There comes a time in almost every drawing when the push for a higher degree of detail is confronted by the need to maintain a strict code of value assignment. This is due to the simple reality that adding detail, or information, requires contrast. If added to a light plane, it will lower the overall brightness of that plane. If additional value information is added to a dark plane, it will mitigate the sense of it being a true shadow. Either of these things done in the appropriate balance, however, will result in a sense of form and light that will carry the drawing to its conclusion.

Finding that balance can be a messy process, as good – or 'accurate' – values are about the interrelationship between all of the values in the drawing, not just a series of accurately chosen pixels. When one value changes, a series of other values will change too. This may sound like a roundabout way to arrive at the perfect key (the range of values), but the reality is a little different. Considering that the key of the drawing is made of many variable parts, it's possible to arrive at a close approximation, which will then require only smaller adjustments.

fig. **02**

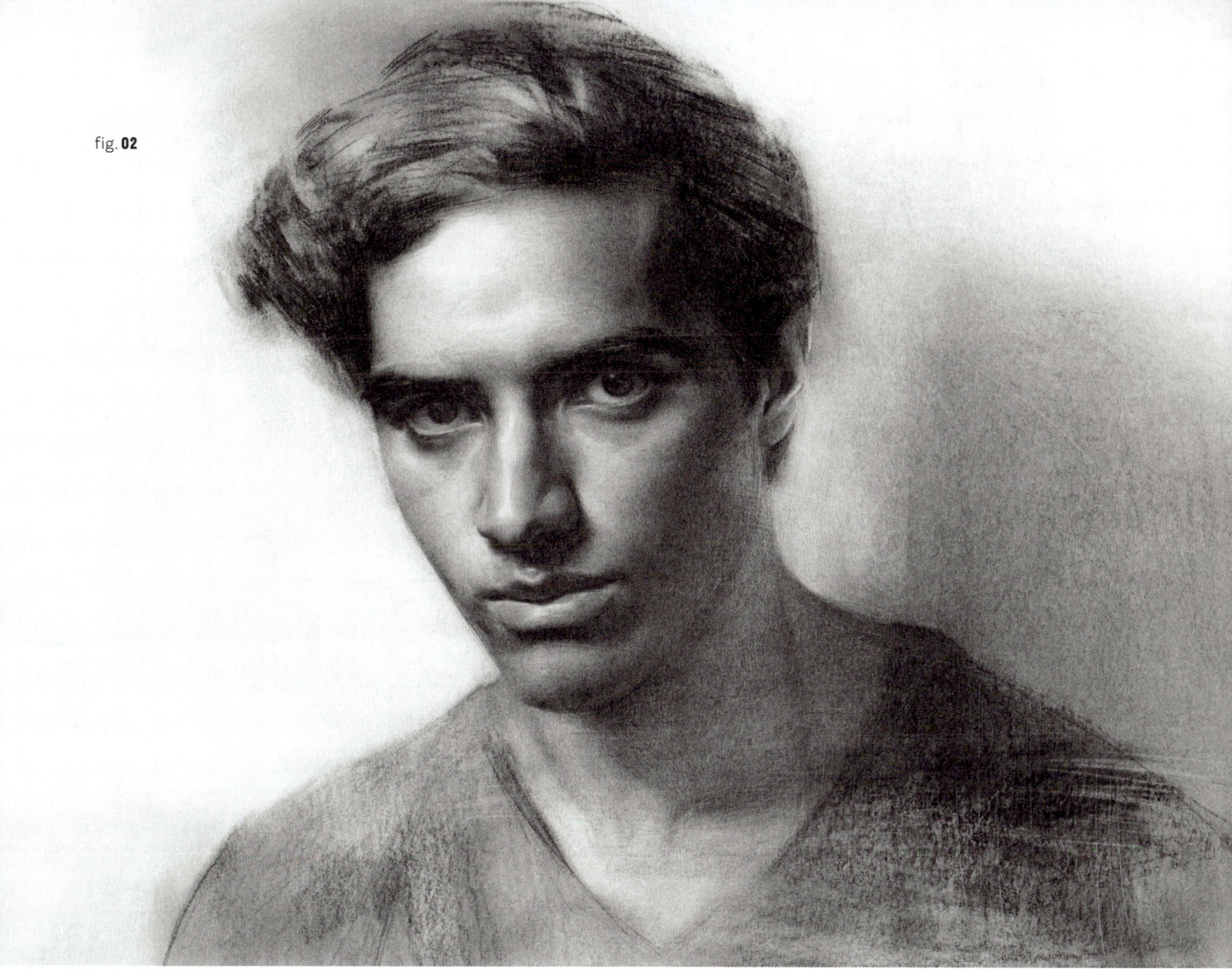

Navigating the dip

Often this moment of the drawing will correspond with a dip in the artist's confidence or momentum. I have experienced this myself and observed many students over the years hit this apparent incline on the journey to a finished drawing. It parallels experiences in various domains where individuals face obstacles that disrupt their progress towards a goal. A pertinent example from behavioural psychology is the concept of the 'valley of despair' in the Change Curve Model. This model, used to understand reactions to big changes or challenging endeavours, illustrates how individuals initially experience a high level of enthusiasm and commitment, followed by a significant dip in confidence and motivation as they encounter difficulties. To navigate this phase, there are strategies you can learn and employ.

Break it down

Where large, overwhelming problems are presented, it is useful to break them down into smaller, more manageable parts by focusing on one area of the drawing at a time. Considering that the focal areas of the drawing, like the features of the face, should be more refined than other areas, this becomes an opportunity to manifest that difference. Approaching the drawing this way reduces the cognitive load and can make the task seem less daunting.

In the drawing stages shown above, values have been built up in the light and dark planes of the drawing. This build-up can take a very rough and planar appearance (**fig. 01**), but over time they should resolve into the more soft and subtle indications of form (**fig. 02**).

fig. **01**

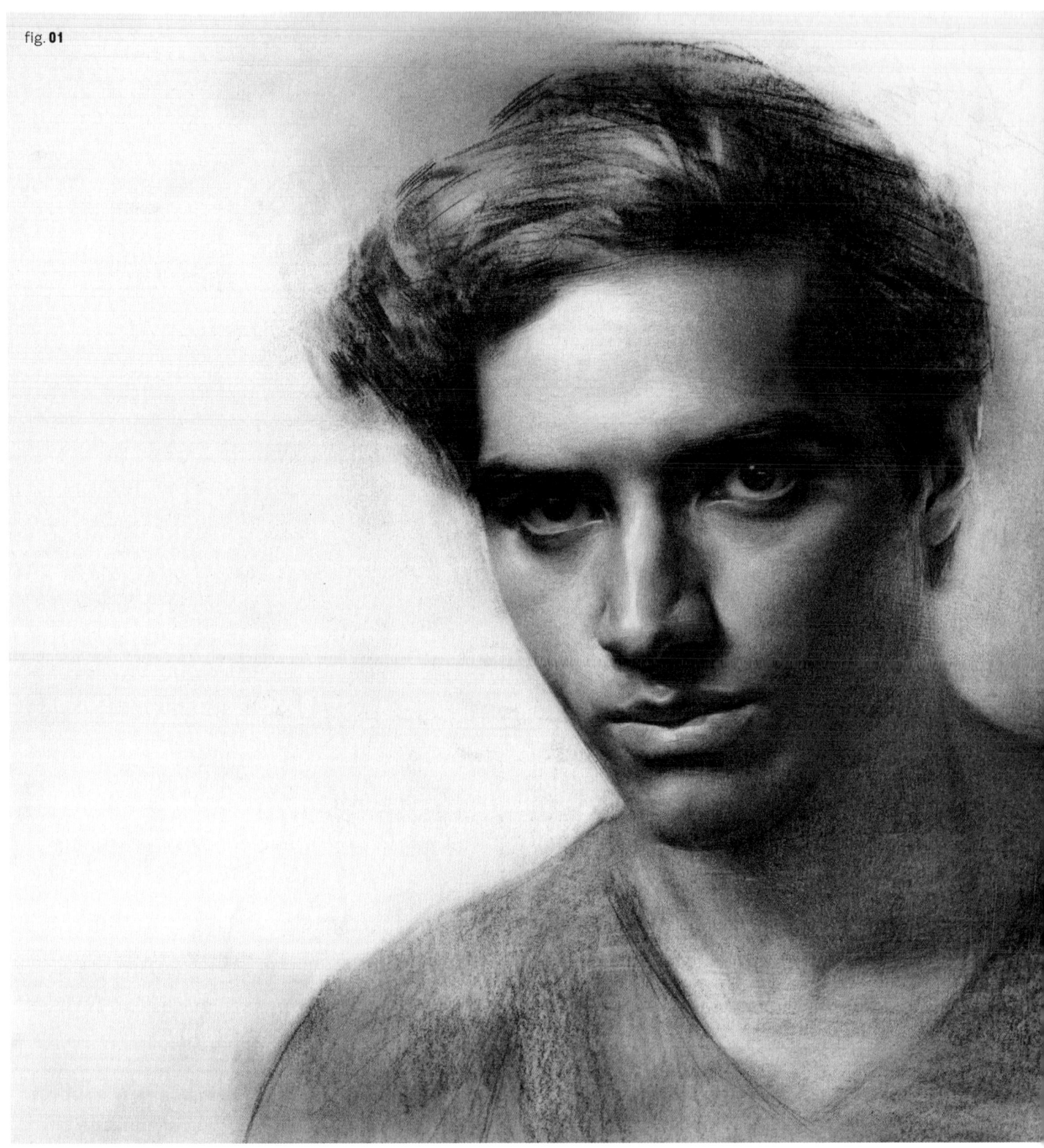

THE FINAL STAGE

Allowing for reassessment

A perfect plan for a drawing is often not as perfect as it first seems. As you grow into a project, perspectives will be revealed to you that were not available during the ideation phase. Flexibility is the optimal approach to finishing a portrait drawing, providing the opportunity for you to adapt and evolve your work in response to these new insights and discoveries. This flexibility is not a sign of a flawed initial plan, but rather a testament to the dynamic and fluid nature of the process. As the drawing progresses, subtle nuances of the subject's character, expression, and even the interplay of light and shadow on their features become more apparent. These nuances might prompt a reassessment or adjustment of the initial concept. For instance, a value arrangement that seemed fitting at the outset may evolve as you get closer to realizing the fully rendered composition. Experiences like this represent a pivotal opportunity for growth.

Aiming for thoughtful agility

This echoes the idea of adaptive expertise in educational psychology, where the ability to apply knowledge flexibly and creatively is considered a higher level of expertise than merely being able to apply written procedures. In artistic terms, this translates to the ability to deviate from the original plan when the evolving work suggests a more compelling direction. Also, a flexible approach allows for the incorporation of technical discoveries. During the drawing process, you may find a new way to render texture or shadow that better captures the desired effect. Rigidity in 'sticking to the plan' could prevent the integration of these insights, potentially stifling progress. It is, however, essential to balance this flexibility with a certain degree of direction. Constantly changing the plan without a clear rationale can lead to a disjointed drawing. The key is thoughtful agility; being open to change while maintaining a clear vision of the drawing's overall goal and integrity.

In finishing this portrait drawing (**fig. 01**) I found the need for a last-minute pivot in the design. There was not enough depth between the model and the background, almost as if they were in different lighting situations. Before making a change in the final drawing, I went back to the thumbnail (**fig. 02**) and made the changes I thought were suitable (**fig. 03**). When making professional work, it is always advisable to separate creative (thumbnailing, ideation) from production.

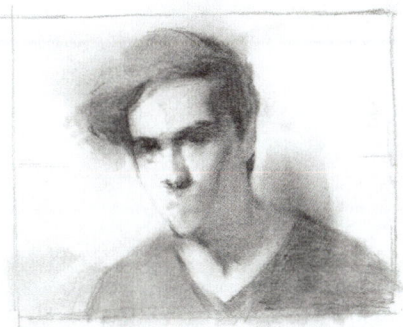
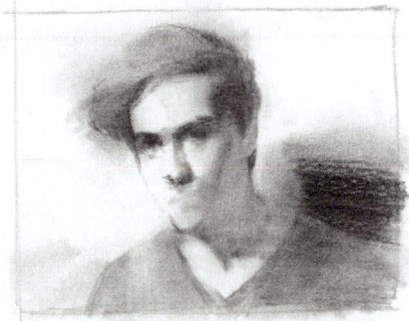

fig. **02**

fig. **03**

A NOTE ON SELF-ASSESSMENT

The process of self-assessment is critical in understanding your growth and preparing for the work that lies ahead. Its particular challenge lies in its biased source: you. From my own experience, and from years of observing students embrace this challenge, there are both positive and negative tendencies that influence this practice.

B.F. Skinner, a noted behavioural psychologist, pointed out that rewarding an action increases the likelihood of it being repeated. In the simplest of terms, we are talking about positive reinforcement. As you assess your work, reward yourself by focusing on the strides you've made in technique, the hard work you put into developing the theme, and even the simple fact that you are one drawing closer to proficiency. These are your positive reinforcements; the tangible outcomes of your dedication and effort. Celebrating these achievements not only bolsters your confidence, but also solidifies the positive behaviours that led to these successes.

It's also crucial to be aware of the negative tendencies that can emerge during self-assessment. Negativity bias – the phenomenon wherein negative experiences have a more significant impact on a person's psychological state than neutral or positive experiences – is one such pitfall. This bias can lead you to focus disproportionately on any perceived flaws or areas of struggle in your work, overshadowing any of your accomplishments. Recognizing this bias is the first step in mitigating its effects, allowing you to maintain a balanced perspective on your work.

Above all, the goal is to arrive at an accurate self-assessment that acknowledges your strengths and areas for improvement without falling into the trap of overconfidence or undue self-criticism. Celebrate your achievements, acknowledge your challenges, and set your sights on the self that you imagined at the start of your journey. Embrace this artistic life with an open heart and a reflective mind, ready to take on whatever comes next with confidence and curiosity.

'Every now and then go away, have a little relaxation, for when you come back to your work your judgement will be surer, since to remain constantly at work will cause you to lose power of judgement. Go some distance away, because then the work appears smaller and more of it can be taken in at a glance, and a lack of harmony or proportion is more readily seen.'

Leonardo da Vinci

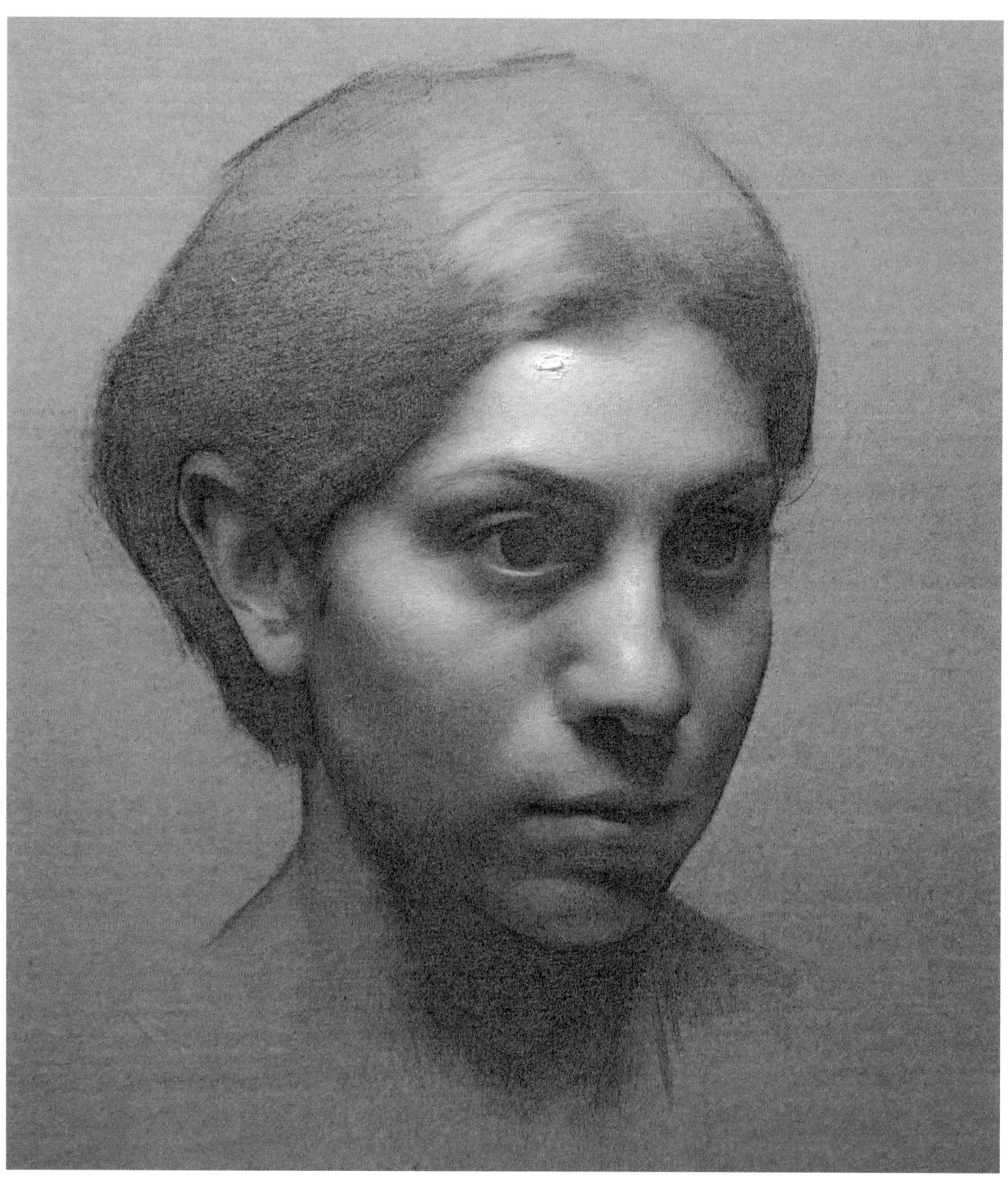

Sasha | graphite, chalk, and gouache on paper

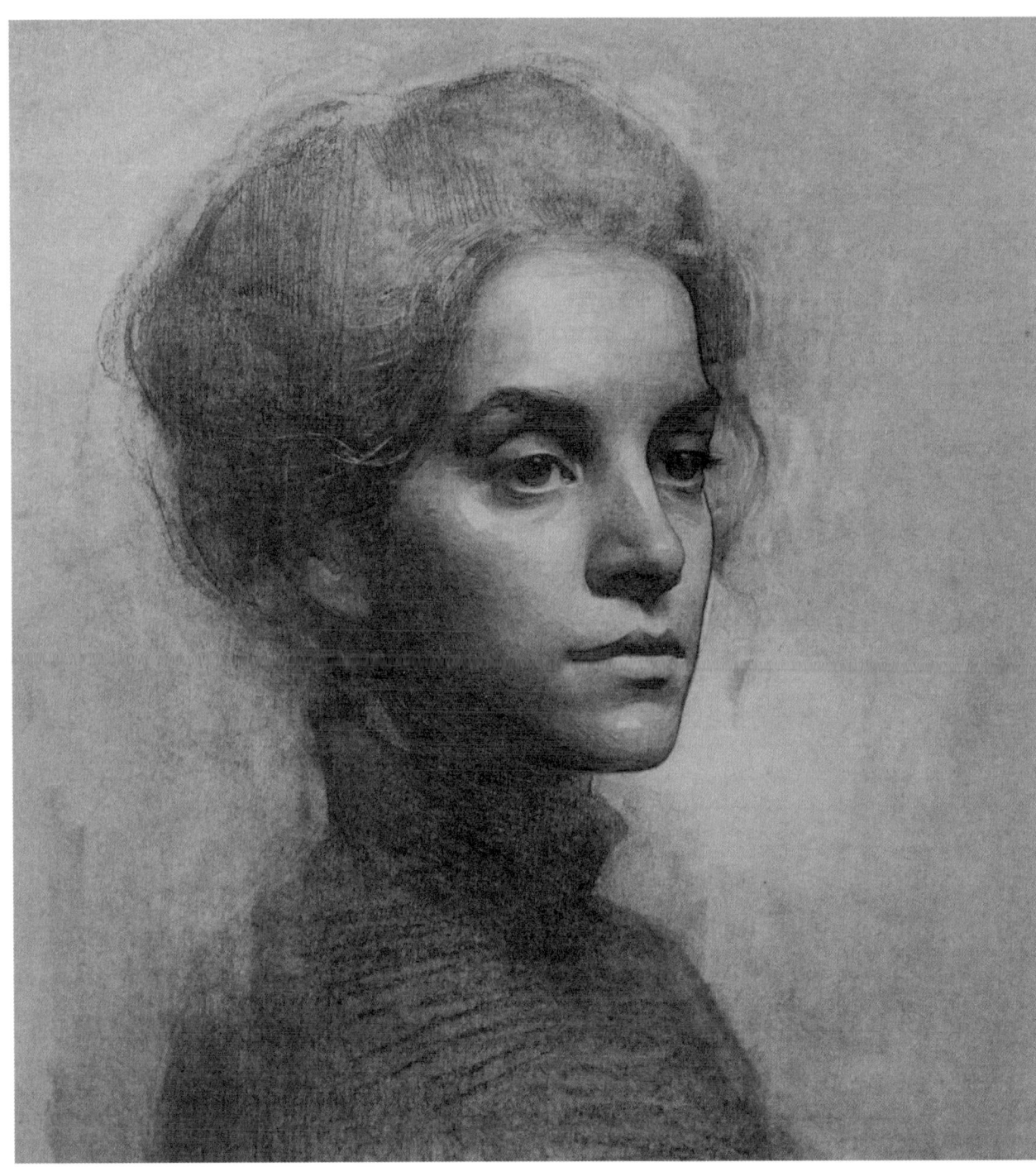

Alena | graphite and charcoal on paper

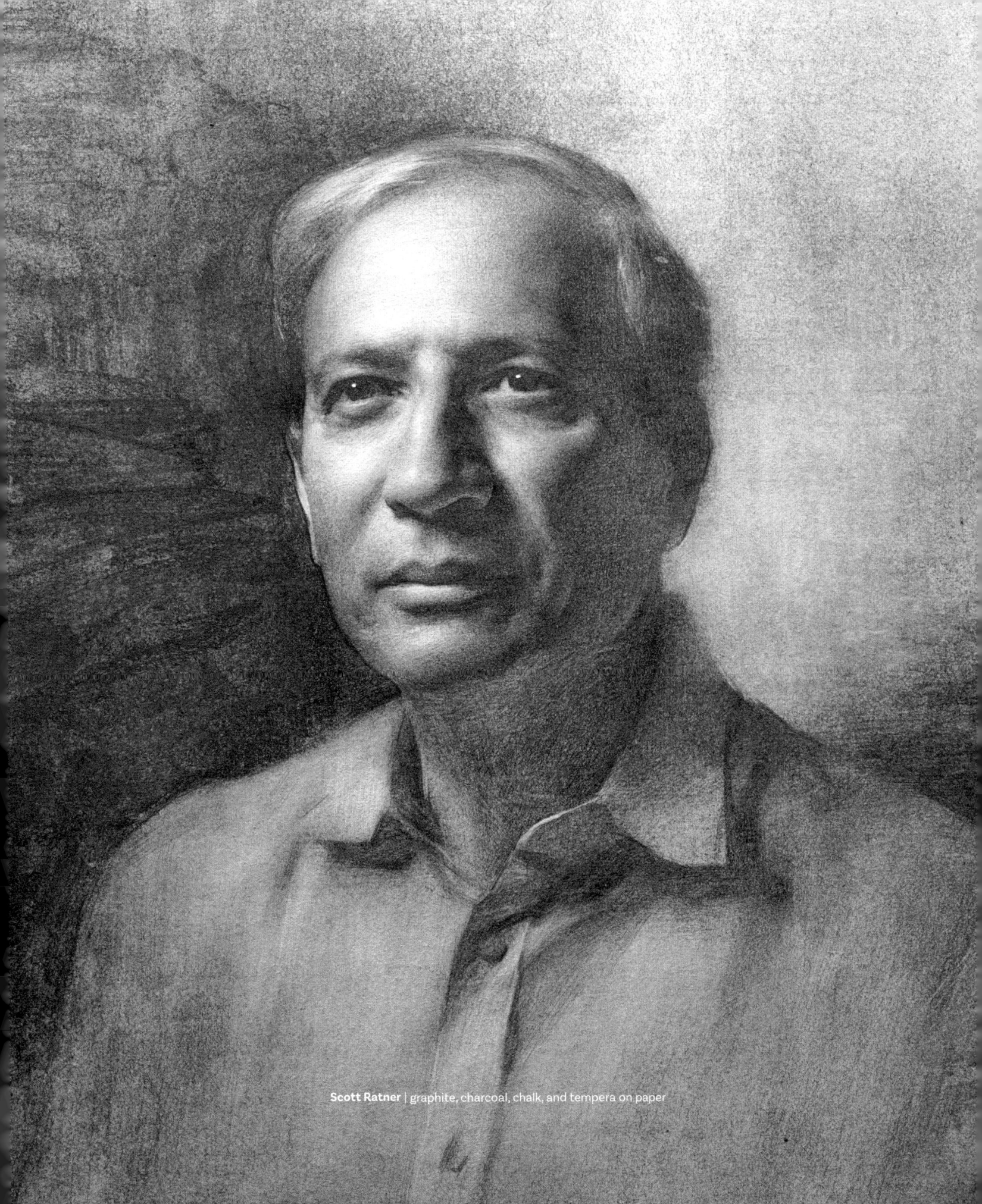

Scott Ratner | graphite, charcoal, chalk, and tempera on paper

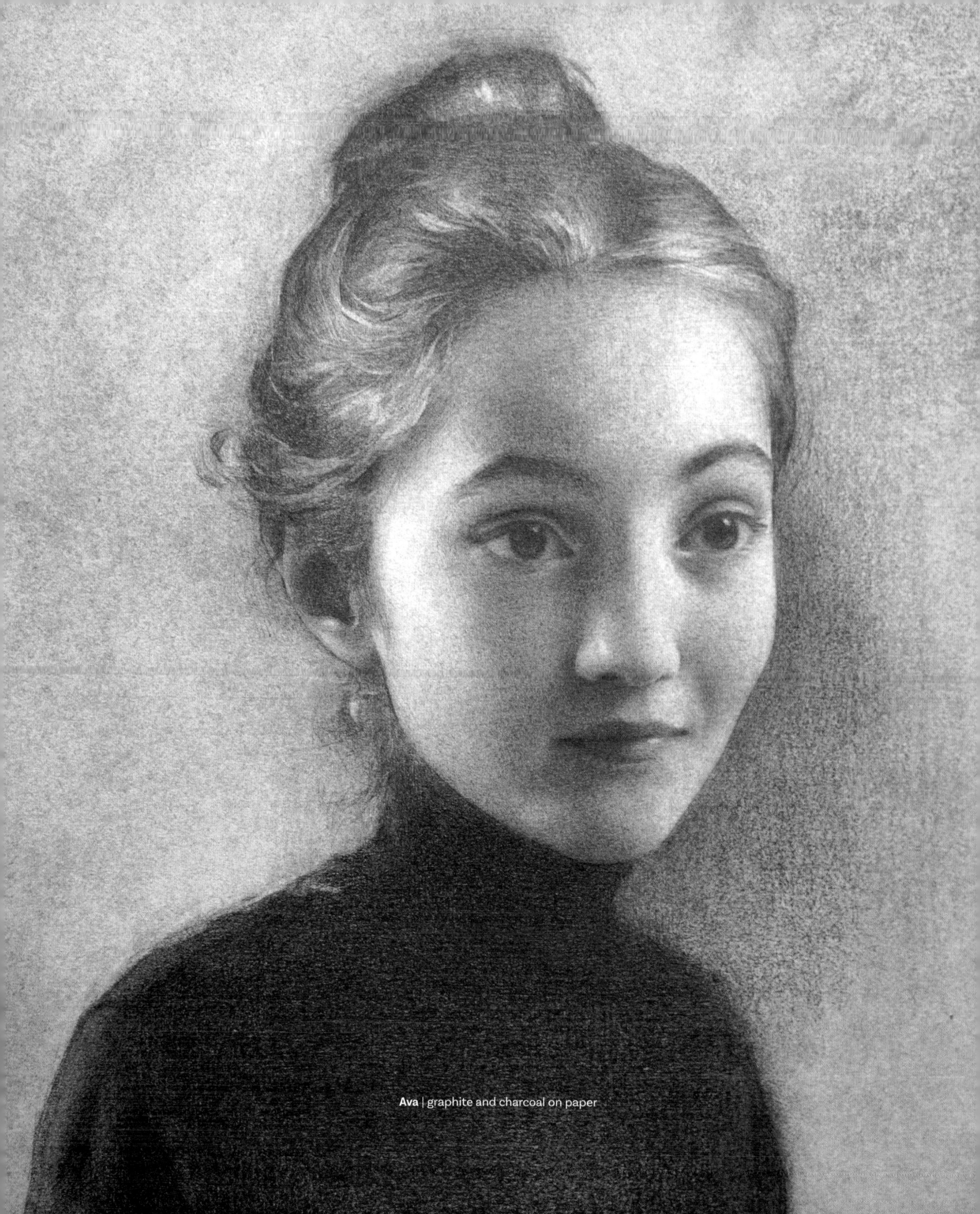

Ava | graphite and charcoal on paper

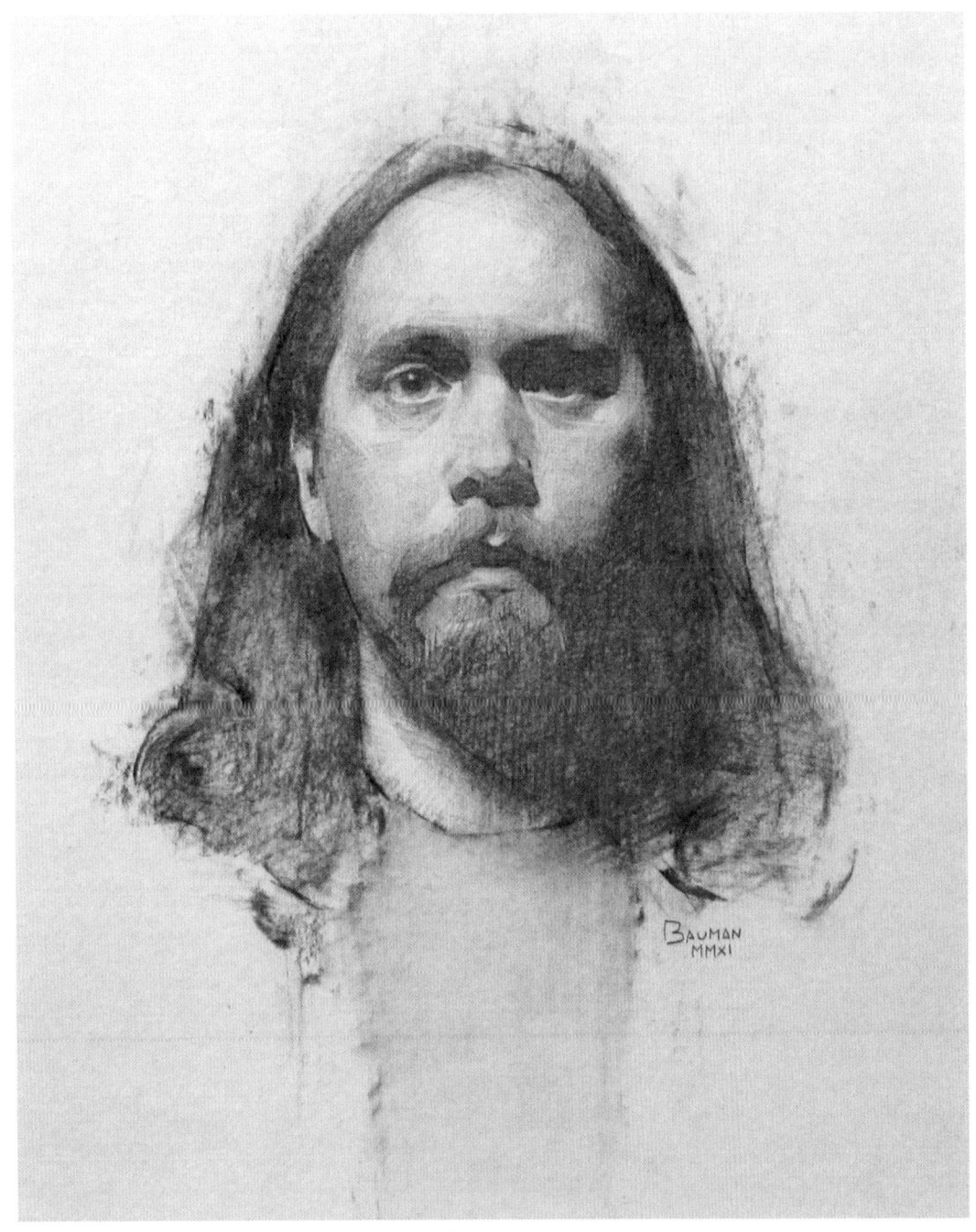

Joakim | charcoal on paper

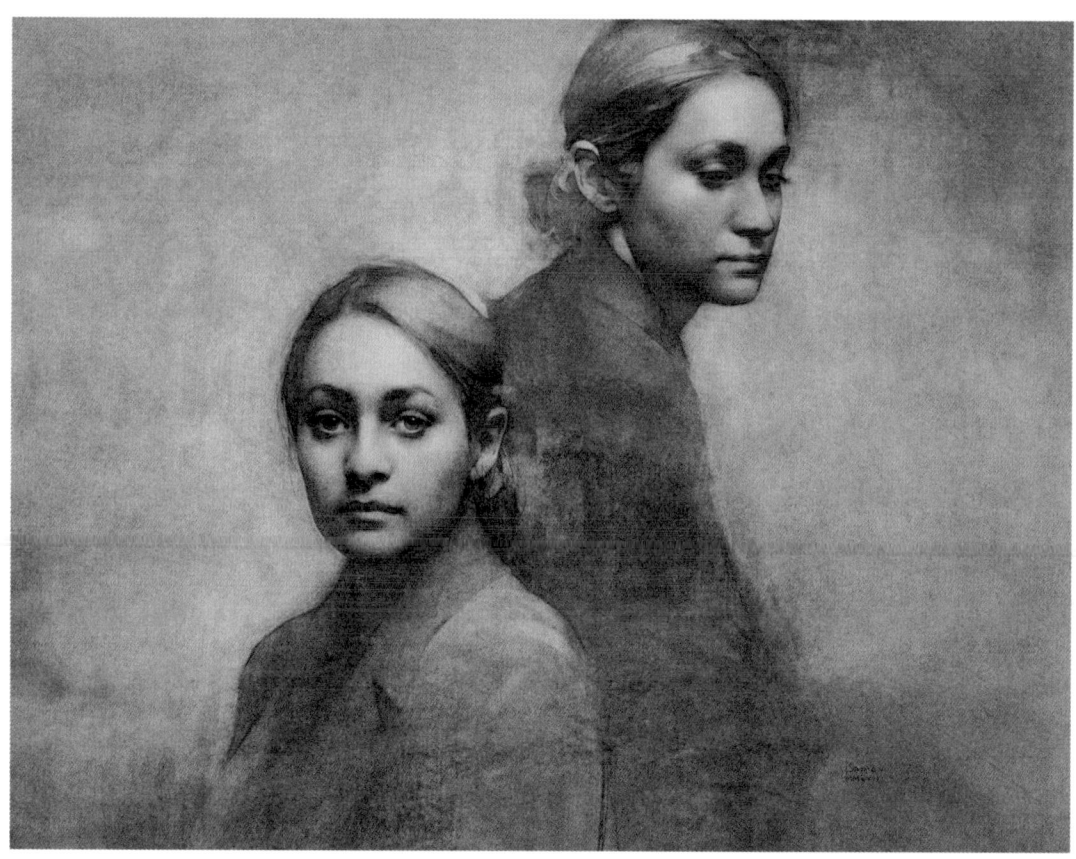

Maids of Bond Street | graphite, charcoal, and chalk on paper

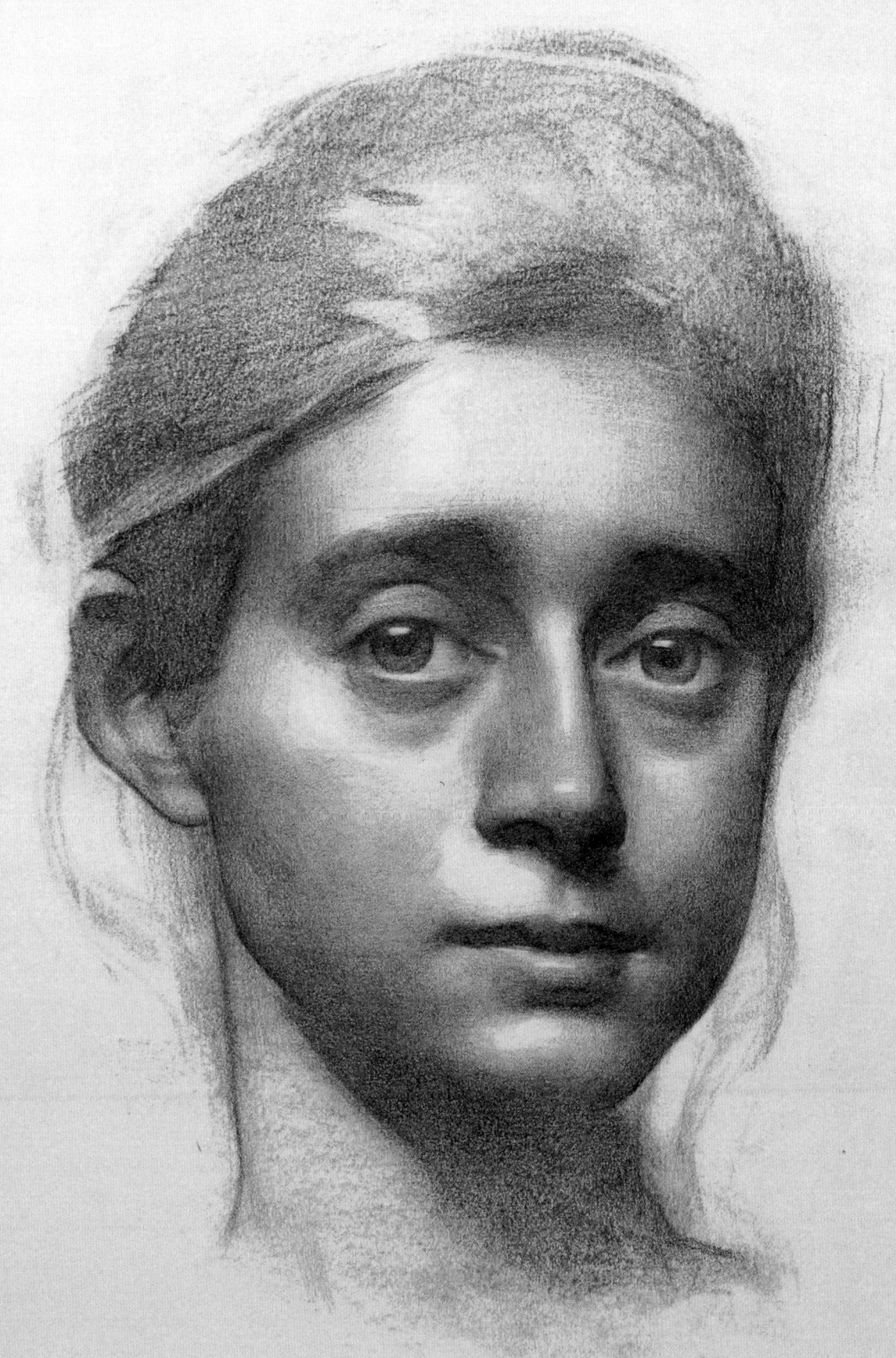

Isabel | graphite on paper

Glossary

Atmosphere
Referring to atmospheric perspective, the unity or compression of value in a zone.

Blocking-in (block-in)
The first stage in a drawing.

Cast shadow
An occlusion where one form blocks the light from reaching the surface of another form.

Chiaroscuro
In Italian, literally light and dark.

Comparative measurement
A technique used to accurately capture proportions and relationships in a drawing by comparing the size and position of one element to another.

Composition
The arrangement of elements within a drawing – including subjects, objects, and negative space – to create a harmonious and visually appealing whole.

Compression (value)
The technique of narrowing the range of values in a drawing to enhance readability and focus.

Contour
The outline that defines the edge of a form or shape in a drawing. Contour lines can vary in thickness and darkness to suggest depth and form.

Contrast
The difference in tone, colour, or texture that makes an object or its representation in drawing distinguishable. High contrast draws attention and can create a focal point, while low contrast blends more subtly into the background.

Contrast ratio
The ratio of the brightness of the brightest white to the darkest black within a drawing. A higher contrast ratio signifies a greater range of tones, enhancing depth and dimensionality.

Core shadow
The darkest part of a shadow on a form, representing the area where light from the light source does not reach directly, found at the shadow's edge.

Cross-contour drawing
A technique that uses lines to describe the surface and form of a subject by moving across it, suggesting three-dimensionality. These lines follow the object's contours in multiple directions, enhancing the sense of volume.

Cross-hatching
A shading technique that involves drawing intersecting sets of parallel lines to create a range of values. The density and orientation of the lines control the darkness and texture of the shaded area.

Dry media
Materials used for drawing that do not involve the application of water or solvents, such as pencil, charcoal, crayon, and pastel.

Edges
The boundaries between shapes or tones in a drawing.

Edge quality
The characteristic of an edge in a drawing – which can be sharp, soft, blurred, or lost – affecting how forms and spaces interact and are perceived.

Fall of light
The inverse square law states that the intensity of light is inversely proportional to the square of the distance from the source, resulting in a rapid decrease of light's brightness as distance increases.

Focal point
The area in a drawing that most attracts the viewer's attention, often due to contrast or detail. Artists use focal points to direct the viewer's gaze to the most important parts of the work.

Foreshortening
A technique used to represent an object or figure in perspective, making it appear to recede in space by shortening the depth dimension.

Form shadow
The less intense area of shadow on the form itself, as opposed to cast shadows, which are projected onto other surfaces.

Geometric drawing
A drawing that employs straight lines and angle breaks to construct more complex forms and structures.

Hatching

A shading technique using parallel lines to build up value and texture. The closeness and angle of the lines determine the darkness and density of the shaded area.

Highlights

The brightest areas on a subject where the light source directly hits, used to indicate the lightest values in a drawing. Highlights help to define the texture and form of the subject.

Light source

The origin of light that illuminates the subject in a drawing, determining the placement of highlights and shadows. The direction and intensity of the light source affect the overall mood and three-dimensionality of the drawing.

Line weight/quality

The thickness or thinness of a line, used to convey depth, importance to the composition, and focus.

Naive recognition

A term referring to the immediate, unanalysed perception of the subject in comparison to the drawing.

Negative space

The empty or open space around and between the subjects, which helps to define the boundaries of positive space. Negative space is crucial for balancing compositions and enhancing the readability of the drawing.

Occlusion

A phenomenon where an object blocks light from reaching another, creating a shadow. All shadows are a form of occlusion.

Positive space

The area in a drawing occupied by the main subjects or forms, as opposed to the background or negative space. Positive space is the focus of the artwork, containing the primary visual information.

Proportion

The relationship in size and placement between different parts of a drawing, ensuring that each part is correctly sized in relation to the others. Accurate proportions are essential for creating realistic and harmonious compositions.

Reflected light

Light that bounces off surrounding surfaces and illuminates the shadowed areas of an object, often softening the contrast between light and dark. Reflected light adds subtlety to the modelling of forms and enhances the sense of volume.

Shading

The technique of varying tones to represent light and shadow, creating the illusion of depth and form.

Shadow

The dark area produced when an object blocks light, helping to define the shape and position of objects within a drawing. Shadows contribute to the perception of light direction, form, and distance.

Simplification

The process of reducing complex forms into more basic shapes or tones, making it easier to capture the essence of the subject in a drawing.

Structural drawing

A drawing that focuses on the construction and framework of objects, emphasizing their three-dimensional form and geometry. It serves as a foundation for more detailed and finished work by establishing a linear wireframe.

Structural symmetry

When a face is divided down the middle, both halves mirror each other in terms of shape, size, and placement of features. This is an inherent property in human facial anatomy.

Study

A drawing or painting created to practise or understand specific aspects of a subject, such as composition, colour, or lighting, often used as preparation for a larger work.

Subcutaneous

Pertaining to under the skin, often referenced in drawing to describe the layer just below the surface that affects how forms appear, especially in portraiture and figure drawing.

Thumbnail sketch

A small, quick sketch that captures the essence of a subject or composition idea, used for planning the layout, values, and proportions of a larger, more detailed work.

Tone

Synonymous with value.

Unity (of value)

Evenness of tone across an area, plane, or shape.

Value

The degree of lightness or darkness of a colour, independent of its hue.

Value scale

A range of shades from white to black, including all the grey tones in between, used as a reference to understand and replicate different levels of lightness or darkness in a drawing.

Visual drawing

A method of drawing based on direct observation of the subject, focusing on capturing what the eye sees rather than what the artist knows or imagines. It emphasizes the interaction of light and shadow.

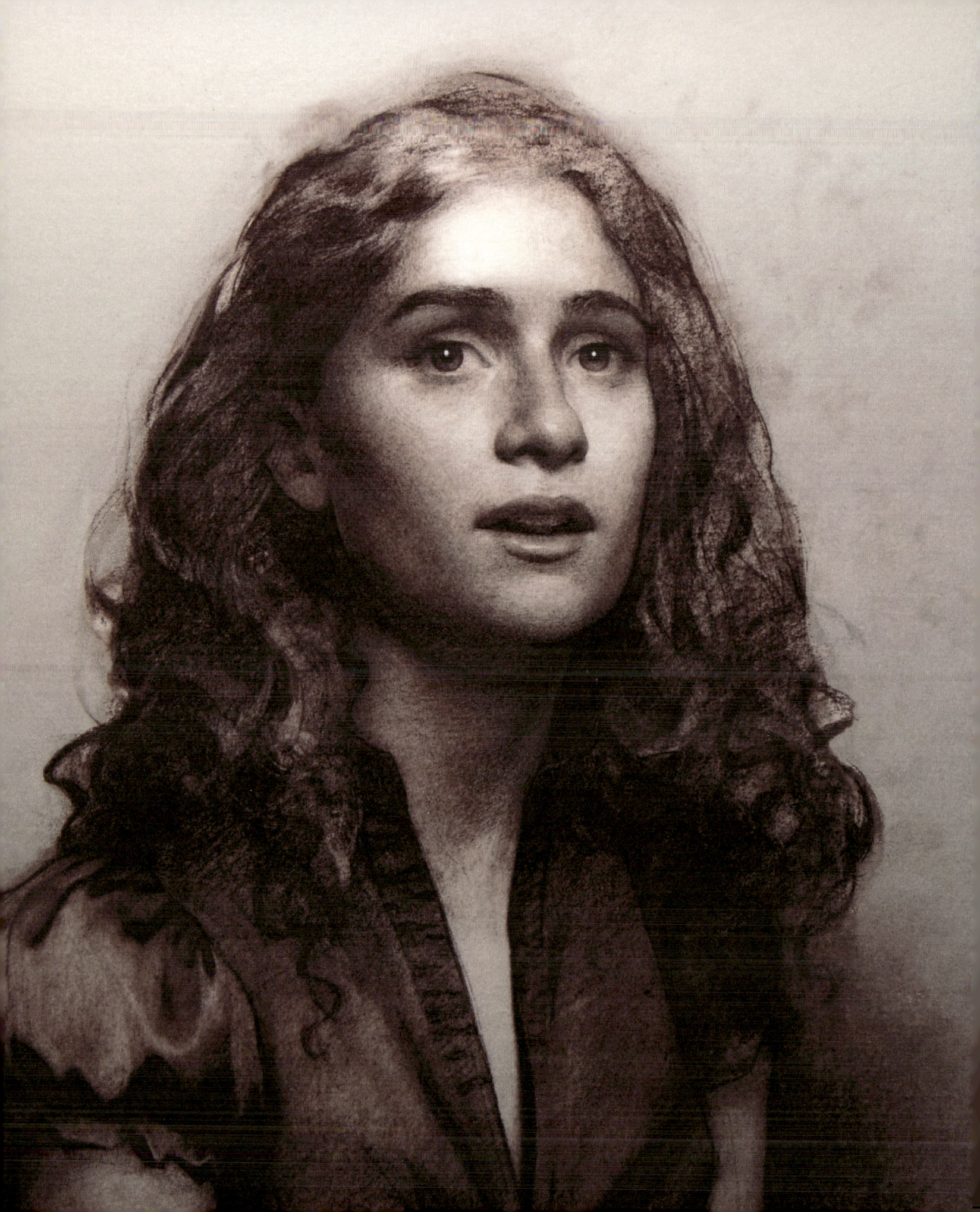

Acknowledgements

As a young man it was easy to consider that I simply worked hard at a difficult task and thereby improved in my craft, eventually arriving at where I am today. The benefit of my age at the time of writing this is that I am now able to see, with virtually perfect clarity, the support I have received along the way to becoming a proficient artist. To make a complete list would take the entire length of this book all over again, so I will do my best to keep this as brief as possible. I'd like to express my gratitude ...

To my wife, Cornelia, for everything that we've been through and everything that we are looking forward to. You are my centre of gravity.

To my sister, Stephanie. You have always been there for me, especially when I have needed you the most.

To my closest friend, Steven Forster. My life is so much richer with you and your family in it. Rebecca, Elijah, Evie, and William, I appreciate you all more than I can say.

To Daniel Graves, for giving me my first opportunity to teach. You didn't have to take the chance on me but you did, and for that I will always be grateful.

To Simona Dolci and Maureen Hyde, there are too many instances in which your generosity helped me on my journey to mention them all here. Thank you for your patience.

To David Foster and Alexander Kafoussias, for applying all of your vast expertise to this project.

To Stan Prokopenko for being the most helpful professional artist I have ever worked with. Artists like you inspire artists like me to do better.

To Rian Fike, you know exactly why you are here. Enough said.

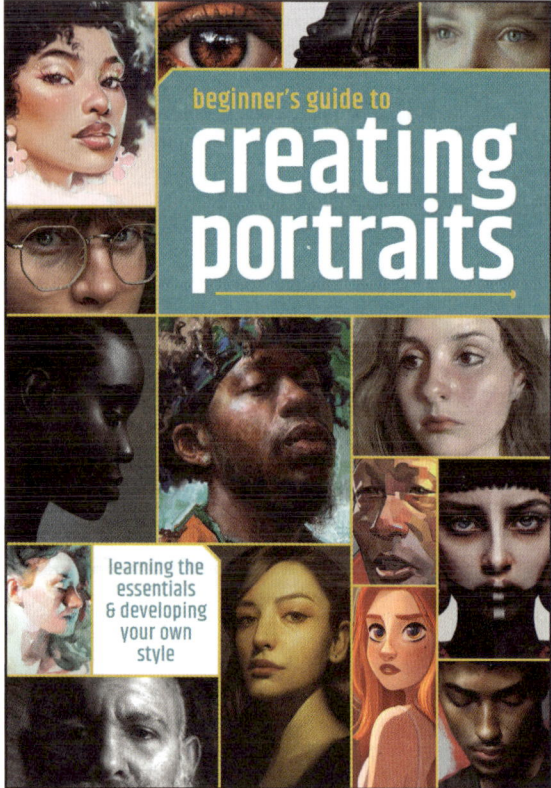

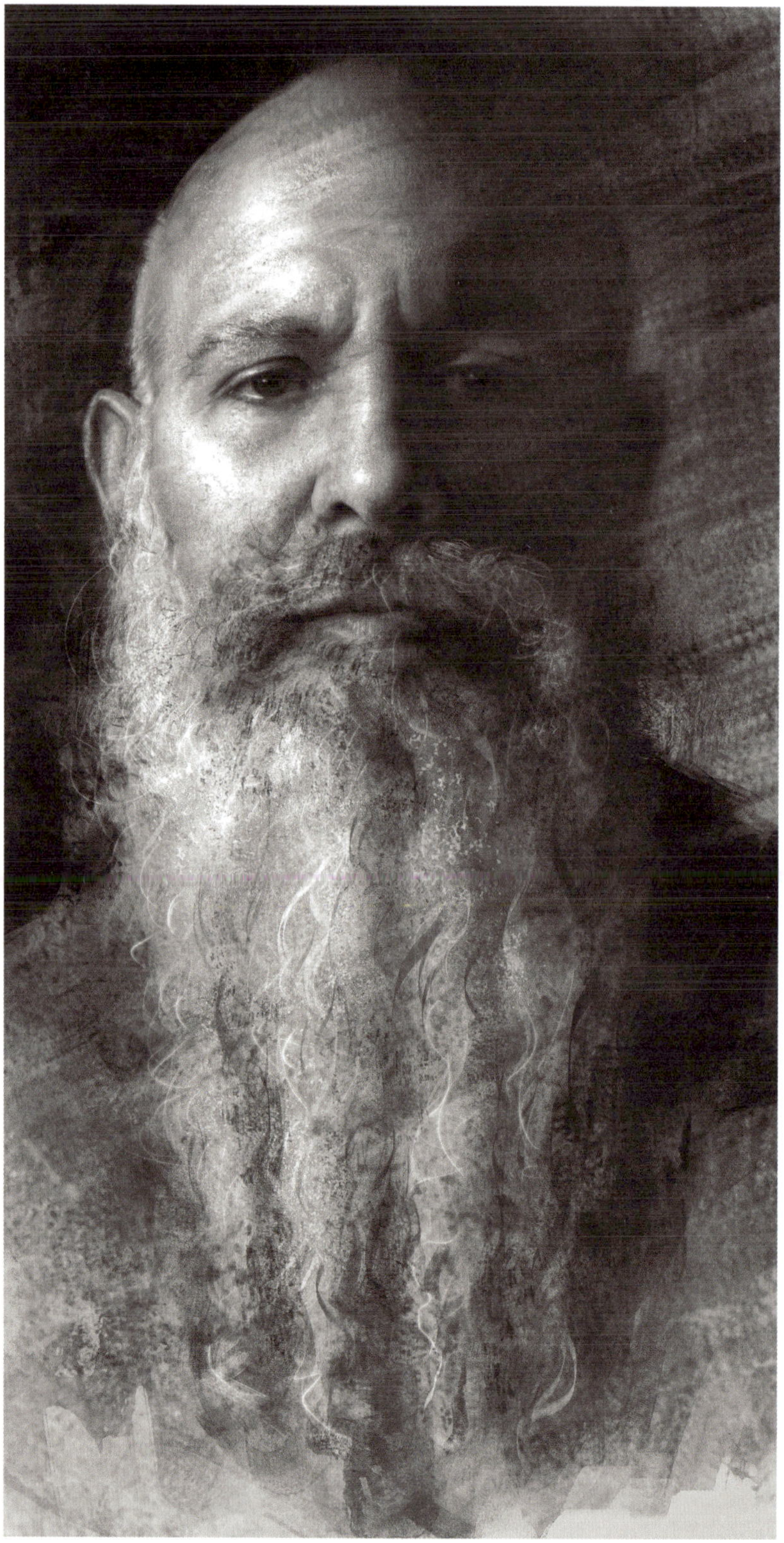

ARTISTS' MASTER SERIES

Elevate your art skills with definitive advice, tutorials, and inspiration from the world's most talented art masters. Each title focuses in-depth on one fascinating fundamental of art.

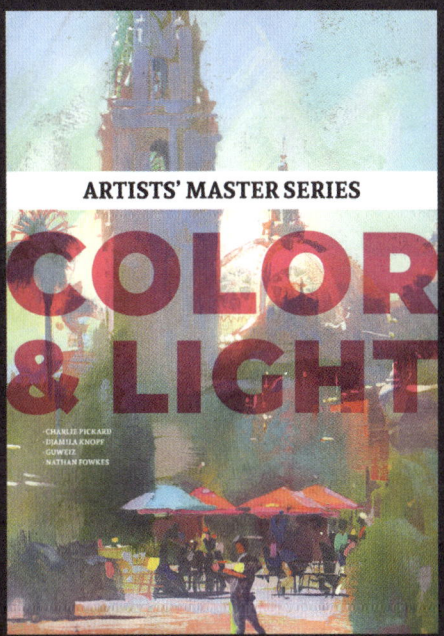
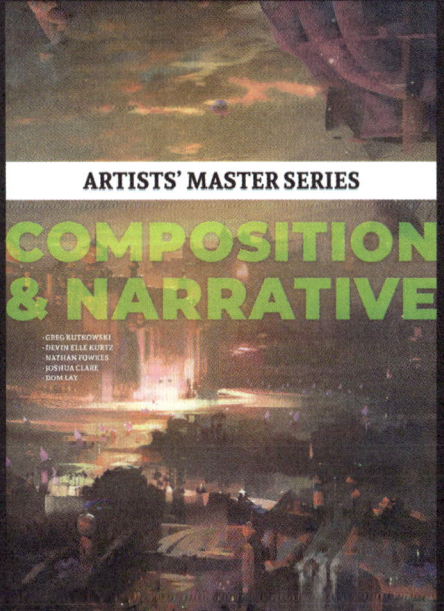
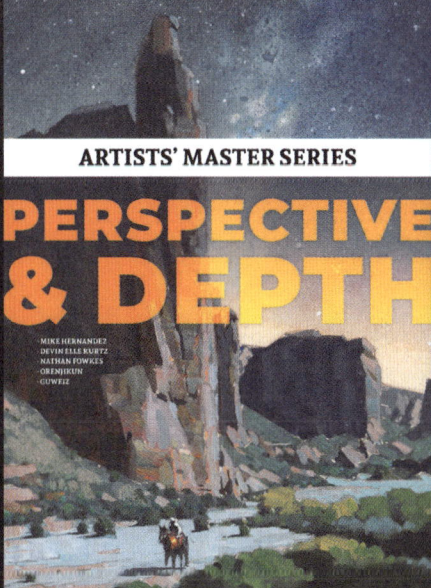

COLOR & LIGHT

COMPOSITION & NARRATIVE

PERSPECTIVE & DEPTH

If you're an artist who takes their work seriously, whether as an enthusiast, student, or budding professional, then you're ready to step up to our best-selling series, *Artists' Master Series*. This comprehensive first volume explores the use of color and light in both digital and traditional media, with theory, tutorials, techniques, and tips written and illustrated by the world's best known and most talented artists.

The second volume of our innovative and definitive *Artists' Master Series* explores composition and narrative in a fresh, contemporary context. Both the principles and their execution are shown through techniques and tutorials written and illustrated by world-renowned experts in the field, including introductory chapters by master of his craft, Greg Rutkowski.

Aimed at enthusiasts and professionals alike, *Artists' Master Series: Perspective & Depth* unpacks the theory and practice of using perspective and depth to advance your art. Artists from across the digital and traditional worlds share a deeper mastery of the subjects through theory chapters, extensive tutorials, inspirational gallery artwork, and expert tips, providing a single, in-depth reference at your fingertips.

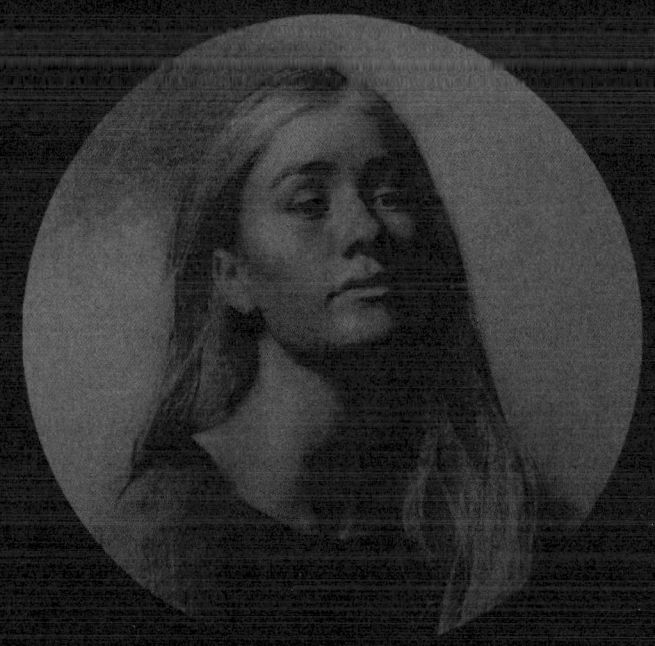

3dtotalPublishing

3dtotal Publishing is a trailblazing, creative publisher specializing in inspirational and educational resources for artists.

Our titles feature top industry professionals from around the globe who share their experience in skilfully written step-by-step tutorials and fascinating, detailed guides. Illustrated throughout with stunning artwork, these bestselling publications offer creative insight, expert advice, and essential motivation. Fans of digital art will enjoy our comprehensive volumes covering Adobe Photoshop, Procreate, and Blender, as well as our superb titles based around character design, including *Fundamentals of Character Design* and *Creating Characters for the Entertainment Industry*. The dedicated, high-quality blend of instruction and inspiration also extends to traditional art. Titles covering a range of techniques, genres, and abilities allow your creativity to flourish while building essential skills.

Well-established within the industry, we now offer over 100 titles and counting, many of which have been translated into multiple languages around the world. With something for every artist, we are proud to say that our books offer the 3dtotal package:

LEARN • CREATE • SHARE

Visit us at store.3dtotal.com

3dtotal Publishing is part of 3dtotal.com, a leading website for CG artists founded by Tom Greenway in 1999.